"Here is an abundantly wise and carefully crafted survival guide for the wild soul currently dozing (or dying) at the heart of your civilized life. Plotkin has wandered again and again into the nourishing darkness, and has returned with this earthly bundle of insights and images — talismanic tools for awakening to the outrageous depths both within us and all around us. He has bound them into a book that is immensely practical, alive with ritual intelligence, thick with useful tools from a host of courageous comrades."

— David Abram, author of *The Spell of the Sensuous*

"The fundamental worldview of industrial society is that Earth is like a gravel pit or a lumberyard — just a resource for human use. We live disconnected from the evolving earth community, but our deepest allurement is a rich, intimate participation in nature and the ongoing adventure of the Universe. In this stunningly original and inspiring guidebook, Bill Plotkin shows us how to reconnect with the sacred powers of life, of nature, of soul, and the ways that each one of us can reinvent ourselves and discover our unique way to flower forth."

— Brian Swimme, author of *The Hidden Heart of the Cosmos*
and *The Universe Is a Green Dragon*

"Those who allow Bill Plotkin's musings to pass have allowed a diamond to fall from their pockets. Those who value the mystical secrets, the magic and mysterious in nature and the human soul, had better check their pockets, for there are priceless items here, far rarer than diamonds. There are huge questions here, and wisdom worthy of the twenty-first century. For in *Soulcraft* we find a new language, a new therapy, and a burning passion to get to the very heart of the universe. *The answer* to our difficulties? If not, a very important part of the answer. Check your pockets!"

— Steven Foster, Ph.D., and Meredith Little,
directors emeritus, School of Lost Borders

"Every now and then a book is birthed into the world that is destined to irrevocably alter the spiritual face of modern culture. Bill Plotkin's *Soulcraft* is just such a book. This book provides a fresh heart-opening soul language, a new mythos for fathoming the depths of change, and time-tested practical methods for navigating the landscape of authentic transformation. In essence, *Soulcraft* is Plotkin's 'soul gift,' a user's manual for the journey of the human soul, as well as a guide to the futurescape of why we are all really here. It is the book I wish I could have had at my fingertips when I began to feel the ancient call for rites of passage in my early youth. It is required reading for anyone guiding other people in soulwork, or delving deep into their own. As philosopher Parker Palmer has said, 'The way to God is down.' Plotkin shows the way."

— Frank MacEowen, author of *The Mist-Filled Path*

"A poetic and yet intellectually rigorous exploration of the essential relationshop between the human soul and wild nature, *Soulcraft* guides the reader on a journey of descent, to return with gifts for a hungry world."

— Molly Young Brown, author of *Growing Whole* and co-author with Joanna Macy of *Coming Back to Life*

"Radical, embodied, and mature, *Soulcraft* lays a map for those seeking to launch beyond the psychic and social limitations assumed in modern society. Please read this book. Please live it."

— Chellis Glendinning, Ph.D., author of *Off the Map* and *My Name Is Chellis and I'm in Recovery from Western Civilization*

"Within the concepts, principles, and practices embodied in *Soulcraft* rests the foundation for a possible future that is worthy of humanity's coming of age. *Soulcraft* is a culmination of a quest for understanding that goes back 6,000 years. This book will permeate the collective consciousness of the future in the same manner as Erik Erikson's *Childhood and Society* shaped the 1950s and the work of Abraham Maslow shaped the 1960s."

— Dan Popov, Ph.D., author of *The Family Virtues Guide*

"How can we begin our life's deeper conversation within the greater world of Nature? Bill Plotkin shows us the path."

— Dolores LaChapelle, author of *Sacred Land, Sacred Sex*

SOULCRAFT

SOULCRAFT

Crossing into the Mysteries of Nature and Psyche

BILL PLOTKIN

NEW WORLD LIBRARY
NOVATO, CALIFORNIA

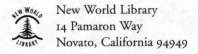

New World Library
14 Pamaron Way
Novato, California 94949

Front cover design by Cathey Flickinger
Text design and typography by Tona Pearce Myers

Library of Congress Cataloging-in-Publication Data
Plotkin, Bill
  Soulcraft : crossing into the mysteries of nature and psyche / Bill Plotkin.
     p.   cm.
Includes bibliographical references and index.
  ISBN 978-1-57731-422-6
  1. Self-actualization (Psychology) 2. Soul—Psychological aspects.3. Vision quests. I. Title.
BF637.S4P58 2003
158.1—dc21   2003010036

First Printing, September 2003
ISBN 978-1-57731-422-6
Printed in Canada

New World Library is committed to protecting our natural environment. This book is made of material from well-managed FSC®-certified forests and other controlled sources.

30   29   28   27   26   25

Dedicated to the soul of the Earth
and all its wild inhabitants and habitats;
to the men and women
brave enough to descend into the mysteries
to retrieve the gifts of vision
that might engender a livable future for all beings;
and to the growing council of true elders.

And
in gratitude to
Steven Foster and Meredith Little
for showing us how to cross beyond the borders.

The breeze at dawn has secrets to tell you.
          Don't go back to sleep.
You must ask for what you really want.
          Don't go back to sleep.
People are going back and forth across the doorsill
          where the two worlds touch.
The door is round and open.
          Don't go back to sleep.

— Jelaluddin Rumi

CONTENTS

SOULCRAFT PRACTICES

CULTIVATING A SOULFUL RELATIONSHIP TO LIFE

FOREWORD

Soul is fundamentally a biological concept, defined as the primary organizing, sustaining, and guiding principle of a living being. Soulcraft is the skill needed in shaping the human soul toward its fulfillment in its unity with the entire universe. The universe and the human soul find their fulfillment in each other. Soul gives to the multitude of living forms wondrous powers of movement and reproduction, but even more wondrous powers of sensation and emotion. Soul, in all its diversity of expression, enables the flowers to bloom in the meadows. It enables all manner of living forms, the birds, the fish, and other living beings to find their way through thousands of miles on their migration journeys back and forth across the continents and in the dark depths of the sea. The entire universe is shaped and sustained in all its vast interwoven patterns by the mysterious powers of soul. Such was the understanding of soul in our western world until the sixteenth century when René Descartes (1596–1650) taught that the natural world was simply a mechanistic process to be known simply by scientific measurement.

Humans differ from other living beings in having a soul capable of reflecting on itself, thereby providing it with intellectual and moral capacities associated with spiritual beings. Once the existence of soul in the other-than-human world was rejected, it was difficult to sustain any acceptance of soul in the human world. Such was the situation throughout the nineteenth century and throughout the industrial civilization in the twentieth century. Then, in our psychological studies, we began to realize that nothing made much sense without the presence of soul. Acceptance of the soul dimension of the natural world was begun in the studies of C. G. Jung. He saw the need for restoring the human soul in its integral presence with the vital powers of the earth.

Further, in our association with indigenous peoples, we began to appreciate the profound sense of realism they manifested in their ritual communion of the human soul with the deeper powers of the universe. In these earlier cultures, the universe was experienced primarily as a presence *to be communed with and instructed by,* not a collection of natural resources *to be used* for utilitarian purposes. The winds, the mountains, the soaring birds, the wildlife roaming the forests, the stars splashed across the heavens in the dark of night: these were all communicating the deepest experiences that humans would ever know. The inner life of humans, the joy and exaltation we experience in celebrating our place in the great community of existence, these depended on our experience of a universe that provides us with both our physical and our spiritual nourishment. All this was recognized as the world of soul.

Above all, this larger context of human existence was a caring world. It provided food and shelter, and healing in time of sickness. Beyond economic needs, the natural world in all its wonder provided inspiration for song and dance and poetry. Such we find with the Australian aborigines, who saw the visible world as the creation of a more profound reality known as the Dreamtime. Each aspect of the landscape was identified as related to its songlines.

Throughout this earlier world, not only in its indigenous phase but also in the earlier classical civilizations, this manner of relating human affairs to the larger universe was dominant. Life was liveable. As Henri Frankfort tells us in his study, *Before Philosophy*, the entire world was addressed as "Thou," not as "It." Life in its comprehensive extent was a meaningful and a fulfilling experience. The tragic dimension of existence could be dealt with by the assistance we received from this other world. The integrity of our psychic world was preserved.

Indigenous peoples attained the inner strength needed to deal with the challenges they confronted in the wild through their ritual communion with these powers present throughout the natural world. The Plains Indians of North America identified and sacralized their human presence at any moment by offering the sacred pipe to the four directions, then to heaven above and the earth below. In this manner they knew where they were. They knew also that they were not alone. They were at the center of the universe. The powers present throughout the natural world were there to guide and support them in the hunt, in their endurance of the heat and cold of the seasons, in their confrontation with enemies.

Civilizations also found their validation in their ritual integration with the great cosmic liturgy of the seasons as well as with the celebration of the dawn and sunset. These transition moments were sacred. To know how to insert our human affairs into the larger functioning of the universe was the primary context of existence in all its forms. The integral functioning of the entire human order depended on this relationship. Government found its authority and the efficacy of its functioning in its alliance with this larger design of the universe. Education was based on initiation into this process. The whole of life was thought of as a celebration of existence. There were the anxieties concerning food and shelter, there was sickness and death. Yet so long as there was assistance from the powers of the universe, these could be accepted and dealt with creatively. Suffering and death could be endured without fear because they occurred in a meaningful context of interpretation.

In those days the Plains Indians of this continent were already practicing soulcraft in their Vision Quest with its days-long fasting and praying on some mountain top. The initiate was taken far beyond the visible realm, into the abiding world beyond sight and sound, into the world of soul. This inner psychic world in its relation to the outer world was already familiar to the person facing the later challenges of life. These peoples also established rituals for the dangerous transition moments of individual lives. Especially at the moment of birth it was important for the Omaha Indians to present the infant to the universe with the invocation that both heaven and earth would care for the child with all their powers.

In our modern world of scientific insight and technological skills, we have thought that we could do without these spirit powers of the universe. Although we know more about the universe, we have less intimate presence to the universe than any people ever had. The indigenous peoples of Australia, with fewer life possessions and less life security than any other people we have ever known, are more profoundly in communion with the world about them than we, in the industrial world, are in communion with the North American continent.

In losing our sense of soul, we have trivialized our existence. Our industrial accomplishments are simply leading us deeper into a meaningless world, a meaningless, but not an innocent or a harmless world. Nor can all our inventions or our medicinal formulas keep at bay the deep anxieties to which we are subject. Nor can our massive military expenditures keep us secure. We are frightened, both personally and in our communities, by the least threat to life or security. We seek protection through ever greater control over other humans and over the natural world that we inhabit. Yet adequate security ever eludes us. We are threatened, as never before, by natural elements such as the atmosphere, the water, the soil, and various living forms that we have abused. We are threatened by the enemies we have made with the very efforts that we have made toward national security. Not knowing how to relate to the natural world, we are uncertain in our relations with the human world.

We are now finding that without the assistance of the invisible world we become confused and even frightened in times of crisis. We do not know how to call for assistance in these moments of difficulty or how to ask for healing beyond the ordinary medical procedures. We are lacking in people who are sufficiently skilled in guiding us through our individual or community crises. We have never spent days and nights fasting on a mountaintop crying for a vision to guide, strengthen, and protect us throughout our lives.

I propose these observations as a basis for appreciating the teaching of Bill Plotkin in his book *Soulcraft*. The word itself, *soulcraft,* a newly minted word to most of us, has a startling precision and a stunning power in saying exactly what his teaching is all about. For his teaching is about teaching in its most meaningful form. The term *soul* sounds mightily throughout his writings. The term *craft* also indicates the need of a skill that has been weakened considerably in this industrial age but is now revived in its full grandeur. Each of us, throughout our lives, is involved in crafting our souls into some meaningful reality that we become for the unending future. We are also involved in assisting others in the self-shaping work of their lives. Those who guide us, from our parents to our schoolteachers and our university professors, are assisting us in crafting our own souls even while we are learning to assist others in shaping their deepest reality.

But then we have the situation beyond our individual souls. The industrial world seeks to exploit this lovely planet with its flowering meadows, its sky-reaching forests, its flowing streams, the wildlife of its forests and fields, until only remnants will exist. Yet now, as we begin the twenty-first century, we start to realize that the industrial world has had its day. Those of us who have lived through its twentieth-century dominance believe, as I do, that a new age is dawning. The industrial-commercial world can go no further. It has achieved its goal. It dominates the planet. Everything opposed has withered in its presence. Yet such high moments in history seem to last only about a century. Such was the high moment of the Augustan Age of Rome and that of medieval Europe. Within a century, the gothic cathedrals, the universities, the great intellectual syntheses came into being. Then in the opening years of the thirteenth century, with the culminating moment of Dante's *Comedia,* the creative genius of the period came to an end.

Now as the twenty-first century opens we have begun our renewal of the Earth. The industrial age will continue its destructive path, but new creative forces are already presenting a future where humans and the natural world are more intimate with each other. The alienation of these past four centuries has already ended. We need no longer spend our energy critiquing the past.

As we enter this new age, we will surely be powerfully influenced by this new guide to the mysteries of nature and psyche. In *Soulcraft,* Bill Plotkin gives us an authentic masterwork. In the substance of what he has written, in the clarity of his presentation, and in the historical urgency of the subject, he has guided us far into the new world that is opening up before us. We will not soon again receive a work of this significance. Plotkin understands fully that the mentality of the future will be closer to the insight of the indigenous peoples of the world than to any patterns of our more recent thinking. Above all, we will begin to find the deeper meaning of our lives, and the psychic support that we need in our participation in the great cosmic liturgy; in the exhilaration of the dawn, the healing quiet of evening, in the springtime singing of the birds, the summertime showers, the autumn ripening, and the winter quiescence.

These are the forces that will craft our souls into the realities for which these same forces brought them into being.

Thomas Berry
June 14, 2003

ACKNOWLEDGMENTS

Many people contributed generously to this book's conception, birth, and growth, a process of at least four years — perhaps, more accurately, a lifetime. Often it has felt as if these pages have emerged from the collective longing of a whole community, or even from the earth itself, rather than from the efforts of a single person. I bear the blessing and burden of gratitude to many.

For the final form of the book, I am most indebted to five people. Donna Medeiros, steadfast friend and colleague, gently encouraged me throughout the process, offered thoughtful editing, and asked penetrating questions that awakened me again and again and kept me diving deeper. Geneen Marie Haugen, gifted writer, masterful generator of perception-expanding images, outlaw, and woman of the wild, edited every page with care, taught me how to love sentence crafting, and tenaciously urged me to bring my heart and the heart of the book — the stories — to the forefront. Anne Depue, my courageous and persevering literary agent, had the initial vision for this book's form and offered keen editorial insights along the way. Georgia Hughes, New World Library's editorial director, is a rare phenomenon in today's publishing world: a highly engaged, hands-on editor, both visionary and practical. She offered discerning suggestions, guidance, encouragement, and inspiring challenges throughout the book and its birthing process. Annie Bloom, my dear friend, underworld partner, and heart teacher, lent her gifted and gifting hands in many ways, including the contribution of her own extraordinary stories, her editorial insight, and her spiritual guidance.

Many other generous friends and colleagues reviewed one or more chapters, contributed invaluable recommendations, and helped the book find a home. These include Sabina Wyss, Kerry Brady, Jamie Reaser, Peggy McCauley, Peter Scanlan, Michael Thunder, Len Fleischer, Patti Rieser, Trebbe Johnson, Ann Debaldo, Christina Hardy, Laura Sewall, Julia Dengel, Lynn Goodwin, Michael DeMaria, Tony Putman, Mary Lou Murray, Mary Gomes, Steffi Lahar, Deborah Bradford, Megan McFeely, Liz Brensinger, Tom Lane, Molly Young Brown, and Mike Ashby.

I am indebted to the thousands of people with whom I have been privileged to wander into the wilds of nature and soul, and for their stories that have been food for my soul — and for this book. In addition to those named elsewhere, I wish to thank Lauren Chambliss, Bettina Seidl, Nancy McGahey, Jerry Derstine, Miguel

Grunstein, Dorothy Mason, Mary Janet Fowler, Rowen Hurley, Christi Strickland, Tree Andrew, Nora Wood, Mark Norman, Liz Faller, Anna Anderson, and Kate Errett. Thanks to all of you and to the many others unnamed.

I offer my most heartfelt thanks to the gifted teachers whose work enriched and made possible my own: Steven Foster and Meredith Little, Dorothy Wergin, Roger Strachan, Eligio Stephen Gallegos, Dolores LaChapelle, Elizabeth Cogburn, Peter Ossorio, Steven and Jessica Zeller, and Mel Bucholtz.

Special thanks go to teachers I've not studied with personally but whose work and lives have greatly nurtured my own: Robert A. Johnson, James Hillman, Joseph Campbell, Thomas Berry, Brian Swimme, Jean Houston, Martín Prechtel, Malidoma Somé, James Hollis, and Carol Pearson.

My gratitude goes to Derrick Jensen for telling the uncensored truth and breaking open our hearts in all the right ways, and for his phrase "a language older than words" in his vital book of that title.

Through the years, my wilderness work and writing have been deepened by the work of the great soul poets, many of whom are quoted in these pages. Chief among them are David Whyte and Rainer Maria Rilke whose radiant verses bookend the twentieth century. Their poetry has immeasurably deepened my understanding of the descent to soul and added fathoms to the stories and ideas in this book. David Whyte's eloquent work is unmatched in providing a contemporary voice to the desires of the human soul; in the end, it became impossible for me to complete a single chapter without his poetic counsel. Other poets to whom I am indebted include Mary Oliver, William Butler Yeats, Jelaluddin Rumi (and his inspired contemporary translator Coleman Barks), Morgan Farley, and David Wagoner.

I want to thank the staff, board members, guides, and consultants, past and present, of Animas Valley Institute for their loyal and loving support and encouragement in creating a dynamic form and home for soulcraft. Those not already named include: Rachel Posner, who brightly and brilliantly kept Animas thriving while its director retreated to the writer's desk; Mado Reid and Steven Hart who lit the initiating fires; Kerry Brady for her wholehearted enthusiasm and glistening brilliance; Rob Meltzer for cocreating the institute's structure and shining his visionary light; and Malti Karpfen, Chris Moulton, Betsy Fields, Bill Ball, Ron Margolis, Paul Lemon, Martin Goldberg, Steve and Jessica Zeller, Dianne Timberlake, Louden Kiracofe, Jadé Sherer, Ron Pevny, Ann Roberts, Wes Burwell, Jeffrey Allen, Esther Olney, Michael Barndollar, Anita Sholiton, Deborah Kenn, Kimberly Werner, Ann G. T. Young, David Montgomery, Joe Woolley, Cathy Edgerly, Jan Garrett, Peter Lert, Wendy Elliott and, of course, Fred Schwartz, the soulcraft cabby.

Special gratitude goes to Hermes for his underworld lessons.

Neither this book nor its author would have been possible without the love, faith, sense of humor, encouragement, and lifelong support of Bernard and Betty

Plotkin, who introduced me to this world and constantly insisted I go my own way. My loving gratitude to them is beyond words.

All those named above, and many others, contributed heart and soul to whatever commendable qualities this book may possess. Its flaws are all my own.

Finally, I owe the greatest debt to wild nature as she appears in the astonishing forms and living forces of Earth as well as in the tenacious desires and creativity of the human soul.

PROLOGUE

WEAVING A COCOON

One spring morning, as the land awoke from its long slumber of cold shadows and dark dreams and filled again with wild blossom, butterfly wanderings, and birdsong, I vacated my house, parted with friends, abandoned my brilliant career, and steered my old Toyota west.

I was in my late twenties, a university-based psychologist in New York, a professor and research scientist. I taught personality theory and ran a research lab studying dreams, hypnosis, and non-ordinary states achieved through meditation and biofeedback. My research reports appeared in the best professional journals. People said I had a great future as a scientist.

My soul, however, had something different in mind.

Three months earlier, in January 1979, I stood alone and transfixed on the summit of a snow-shrouded mountain in the Adirondack range. The sky was cloudless, the air perfectly still, and the light both fierce and bewitching. I had come for the simple joys of a solo winter mountaineering experience, but when I reached the top, without warning a staggering mix of grief and hope shot up through my belly and into my throat, and I knew in the next instant I was not meant for academia. Miles below, in the vastness of the white land, I spotted something glimmering on the edge of a shadow. Inexplicably, it felt as if that bright thing held the answer to a true way of belonging to the world and that I must go off wandering until I uncovered its secret. Everything depended on this.

For a year and a half, I wandered — outwardly on foot through wilderness lands of the Pacific Northwest and inwardly through emotional and spiritual self-discovery practices. Landing in Oregon, I studied the art of psychotherapy as an intern at a mental health center.

As my internship ended, I knew I would not retreat to the confining safety of the university, but what I would do was anything but certain. I ended up leaving Oregon in the summer of 1980 with two friends. We were nearly broke but had plenty of inspiration, including plans to create a center for "personal and social transformation." We headed south and searched for home in the enchanting expanses of the American Southwest, a wild land of multicolored deserts and canyons, rugged mountains, whitewater rivers, and pungent sage plains.

Although I had managed to pry myself loose from Mother Academia, I suffered a good deal of anxiety for having done so. Academia was the only community in which I felt like a true member. Now, in addition to the university, I had left my homes in New York and Oregon. Living out of my car and a backpack, I began to suspect I had embarked on a harebrained scheme with a couple of lunatics — and that I, too, was probably crazy. A harsh voice chided that I had given up a promising and secure career in science for a chimerical dream. Another softly counseled me to trust my intuition and the image of something bright on the edge of shadow.

As we traveled through the towns and wilderness lands of Colorado, New Mexico, Arizona, and Utah — looking for a place to be from — my entire life boiled itself down to a single question, variously articulated as: Where is my community? What is my true place in the world? Who am I in my depths? Slowly I came to understand that my identity could not be separated from place and membership.

In August, I heard the soul's call again, this time as an urgency for wilderness solitude, to look inwardly as far and as innocently as possible, and to wait until some truth rang out.

I had been corresponding with Steven Foster and Meredith Little of California, who were creatively reintroducing wilderness fasting rites to the modern West, and I convinced myself I knew enough about vision quests to give it a try. I would go out on the land, alone, to a wild place, dwell there for several days without food, look into the mirror of nature, and cry for a vision.[1]

I chose a vast wilderness arena without human trails, one of the most rugged alpine reaches of the Colorado Front Range, a place I had backpacked years earlier.

Although I knew the route in would be difficult, its physical dangers didn't seem as daunting as the inevitable confrontation with my own darkness. I feared that when the moment finally arrived to peer into the center of my self, I would find a monstrosity — or even worse, nothing. At other, less jittery moments, I found myself split between two predictions of what would happen on my quest — one anemic and the other inflated. On the one hand, I didn't expect much; I suspected I would simply confirm the rightness of leaving academia and feel reassured I'd find a way to survive outside the university community. Perhaps I'd receive support for a career as a psychotherapist, or something else reasonably manageable and imaginable. On the other, I expected something grandiose — that spirit would bestow upon me a magic wand, an instrument of great power, capable of transforming others by the simple wave of my wizardly arm.

Late one August afternoon, I drove into the brooding mountains. Night fell when I was still many miles from the trailhead. Tired and unconfident, I stopped early for the night, pulling off the highway onto a lonely dirt road. I unfolded my sleeping bag onto tall grass beneath a forest canopy. Sleep came with great difficulty as I faced my fears of getting lost, breaking a leg, dying of hypothermia, getting sick alone ten miles from nowhere — and my belief that I did not possess the psychological, spiritual, or ceremonial tools needed to successfully undertake this journey.

That night, I dreamed I was in a foreign language class and having great difficulty. The other students were quite able — dancers of language and artists of words. I felt awkward, a fraud or interloper. The tools I'd brought to class (something incongruous like silverware) seemed useless and ridiculous.

In my waking life, meanwhile, I held precisely the opposite fear: that academia might be my only community and that I might not survive anywhere else.

In both cases, I feared I had the wrong tools.

Waking at dawn, I felt tormented by this sense of being unprepared, incapable, ineligible. I sat up in my bag, groggy, propping myself up with my arms behind me. Ready to abandon my quest, I became aware of something cold and metallic in the grass beneath my right hand — a couple of somethings, actually. I folded my hand around them and brought them in front of my face: a hammer and a pair of pliers.

I laughed out loud. I had long owned the standard set of hand tools, but sometime during my year in Oregon, someone had borrowed my hammer and pliers and never returned them. Materially, at least, these were the sorts of tools I needed!

I took this synchrony as a comic omen, a sign that I did possess at least the basic tools I needed for this wilderness journey of self-discovery and that I should just get on with it. And lighten up.

I tossed my sleeping bag into the car and drove deeper into the mountains.

Two hours later, I reached the trailhead at a mountain pass 10,758 feet above sea level. I was encircled by snow-capped peaks, timberline only a few hundred feet above. Stretching away from my boots on a carpet of browning grasses, the tiny color banners of late summer wildflowers waved in the cold morning breeze.

At the edge of the small parking lot, a sign announced Old Fall River Road, the words carved into dark, stained wood. This was the trail on which I would begin. Its name sounded like a place in New England where I was born and raised. The name was comforting because I didn't want to think of my journey as "Indian"; I was here to become more like myself, not less.

As I took my first step toward the dark boreal forest on Old Fall River Road, two women drove up in a truck. They asked if this was Ute Pass Trail — *Ute* referring to the predominant pre-Columbian people in these mountains.

I told them no, I didn't think so. But, just to be sure, I pulled out my topographic map. "Old Fall River Road" is how it named the trail at its start, but about a mile in it was indeed labeled "Ute Pass Trail." Then one of the women, pointing to the sign, said quite emphatically that it was too bad names like that were changed by white people, that it should still be called "Ute Pass Trail."

As I hiked off, I imagined these two women as outer representatives of my anima, the feminine presence within a man's psyche that serves as his guide on the inward journey to the Mysteries. Perhaps they had come as a reminder that the path

I traveled was an ancient one, the way taken by a people who lived in much closer reciprocity with the land. I decided I needn't let my wariness of imitating Native Americans interfere with the deeper opportunity to learn how to truly belong to this American land and its more-than-human community. Perhaps the appearance of these anima women indicated that I had something to learn from native people everywhere who know they belong to the earth.

The trail climbed for a mile through a cold forest of spruce and fir on a north-facing slope. Upon reaching the pass and the sunshine, I stepped off Ute Pass Trail and onto my own pathless path, one that began at my feet and ended in mystery.

I headed south, plodding through boggy alpine tundra beneath craggy peaks. With map and compass, I navigated my way through ancient spruce forests. By mid-afternoon, I reached a spellbinding gorge of silver granite carved by ancient glaciers, the chasm now lush and heavily wooded. A steeply cascading creek surged over boulders and thundered through the gorge.

I set up my simple, spare camp in a meadow by a small tarn, Rock Lake. A vast tumble of boulders reached down to my camp from the vertical mountain wall to the south. On the east end of the lake, the calm waters poured over a lip into a cataract plunging a thousand vertical feet to the impenetrable forest below.

Wanting to travel as light as possible, I had brought only one small, five by seven foot tarp. It would have to serve as a ground cloth as well as a roof if needed. I placed my bag on one side of it so I could fold the other half over me were it to rain. Otherwise I preferred sleeping with a view of the stars. With metal rings and cord anchored to trees, I rigged a system to bring the roof into place by simply pulling a cord at my shoulder and tying a knot. I could do this quite simply, even in the middle of the night, without fully awakening.

It did rain that night, and, remarkably, my roof system worked. Several weeks later, I was astonished to find a similar design illustrated in a backpacker's manual. The author referred to it as "The Cocoon." Unknowingly, I had woven myself a cocoon for my vision quest.

That first evening, I ate my last meal for the next four days.

In the morning, the sky was clear, although patches of mist lingered in the gorge. I pulled on several layers of clothes and observed a moment of silence in the space where breakfast might have been. Cascading waters roared and echoed off the granite walls.

With a small day pack of basic survival gear, I headed into the upper gorge that rose abruptly from Rock Lake. Waterfalls and spray were everywhere, forming mini-rainbows ahead of me as sun broke through mist. Luminescent green moss covered the streamside rocks.

Emerging from a willow thicket, I found myself in a tiny meadow perched pre-cipitously on the mountain slope. I was overtaken by a memory of having been in that precise spot seven years earlier. A tremor moved up my spine and my chest expanded. It felt like I was gazing into the center of my self as I viewed scenes from the years between my two visits to this place: the two love affairs; my successes and failures as a student, teacher, and scientist; my adventures with spiritual practice — Buddhist, Yogic, Sufi, and Taoist. I was flooded by a conviction that my life had been the perfect preparation for something trying now to be born through me. But what exactly?

Then, in the very next moment, I felt utterly alone and afraid. I wept. I felt at the end of my rope. My career as a scientist was over. I despaired of never having a mutually loving, enduring relationship with a woman. My future was an enigma. I tried to reassure myself that this gloom was just a normal and transient reaction to fasting, isolation, and wildness. But somehow I knew my life would not turn out to be anything like I once had imagined and, in that moment, all hope seemed lost.

When I left the meadow, I continued ascending. Kicking steps into soft snow, I climbed a near-vertical snowfield on the north side of a rock wall. Gaining the sloping face of the rock, I scrambled over the top. There, a large sapphire lake lapped against sheer granite walls on three sides. The arrow-shaped lake pointed further up the gorge to what my map showed to be the highest tarn, Love Lake. I wondered if I would ever be able to reach such a place on this journey of life.

After returning to camp, I sat the rest of the day, looking into the mirror of Rock Lake. The twin fears of the underworld journey reappeared and taunted me, more severely this time. I worried that nothing at all would happen on my fast, that despite all my efforts I would go away without answers, forsaken by the gods and goddesses. At the same time, I trembled that something might happen, something requiring a complete shake-up of my life, compelling me to forsake everything I held to be dear or sacred. Be careful what you ask for, a voice chided.

Gradually my awareness shifted to my growing hunger and weakness. I thought about the psychological comforts of meals, how they allow us to break up and define our days with comforting little events.

And then I thought I was thinking too much and decided to sit in meditation. Vipassana.

That evening, thick clouds moved in from the west. The wind began to blow. I was cold. And tired. And incredibly hungry. It began to rain. I crawled into my sleeping bag and, before sleep claimed me, I worried about many things, including how I would find true community.

I awoke on the morning of the third day of my journey from a dream about being a new member of a community:

> I seem to be accepted even though I am a bit klutzy. I show someone a
> brochure announcing a workshop in Durango, Colorado, by a spiritual master,

a Zen roshi. Some of us are planning to attend. Later, my female companion, maybe a girlfriend, goes to an old car to get something. The car hasn't been opened in years. Inside, she finds a dozen dead cats, and I am grossed out. She tells me a story about an old sealed barrel someone once opened and found hundreds of cats inside. I have a queasy feeling, a sense of the seaminess of organic existence.

In my dream life, at least, I was finding community. And although I was opening to the spiritual in the form of the masculine, upperworld, Zen-oriented, contemplative life, my dream self was still keeping some distance from an older "vehicle" of an earthy, feline, feminine underworld — a life sealed off some time ago. I wondered what exactly in me had been sealed off, and why.

There was also a suggestion in the dream that I would find something important in Durango — perhaps spiritual education.

Dawn brought a beautiful, clear sunrise. But by mid-morning it was overcast again. And cold and windy. I moved my camp under a rock overhang, roomier shelter from both the wind and the likely rain.

I spent the day observing a community of chipmunk-sized pikas. One at a time, they would scurry beyond the safety of the rocks to grab a juicy morsel of grass or watercress by the roots. They were busy gathering despite the dangers all about. They were good at it. I aspired to be as good as they at the spiritual gathering I had come to accomplish, to be as courageous, as persistent, as attentive. I also hoped someday to be a member of a community as cooperative and genial.

As I sat there quietly, the pikas, squirrels, gray jays, little finches, butterflies, and magpies resumed their daily rhythms despite my presence. High overhead, a hawk slowly circled Sundance Mountain. I felt I'd become a part of the mountain life, no longer an interloper.

The next morning, I awoke with this dream:

I am staying at a family's home, a mansion. They have many pianos in their house. I am struck by how often the mother and daughter in this family sit down to play duets on the keyboards. They make beautiful, mysterious music. At first, I am puzzled by the fact they almost always sit together and use the same piano, even when there are three or more in the same room.

I awoke with that curious but by now familiar mixture of grief and hope. I envied the beautiful harmony, music, and synergy of the mother and daughter. I longed for that quality of support, partnership, and love in my life. As in my Zen-community dream and in my time with the pikas, I was again a welcomed visitor in another's home. I wondered how I might create such soulful communion in my waking world as well as within my psyche. The key appeared to be the feminine — as embodied in the mother and daughter, the woman with cats, the two women at the trailhead, and the presence of nature all around me. Would the sensual, emotionally vibrant, musically resonant feminine powers within me and in nature help me find my place, my gift, my community?

On this fourth day, I was finally feeling the high energy and perceptual clarity I had been told would eventually result from fasting. I spent the day in the posture and attitude of meditation, gazing out upon the lake, observing the community of pikas, and feeling a warm gratitude for all the living things of the land and sky as they wove their web around and through me. I became vibrantly alert, my senses exceptionally keen and my heart wide open. Letting the wild fill me with its rhythms, I fell in love, outwardly and utterly, with the world.

Through the day, my attention was increasingly drawn by a beautiful large spruce standing alone at the edge of the lake. After some time, I saw that the spruce was more than what I had first recognized — it was a Zen monk dressed in a simple blue-green robe, a hood covering his head. It's not that the tree disappeared and was replaced by a monk. Without astonishment, I was simply able to see that the spruce was a monk, as if this was perfectly ordinary.

Standing very still, his back to me, the monk faced the lake. Occasionally, he hailed the beavers with a subtle movement of his head, the gesture returned by a splash of tails.

Then the monk slowly turned to his left and pointed with his outstretched arm toward a stand of smaller spruce about a hundred feet away. There, frolicking among dark green branches, I could make out the sprightly movements of a large yellow butterfly. She flew toward me in a flutter-by spiral dance. She flew right to me. With her wing, she touched my face — my cheek — and said my name in the same moment: "Cocoon Weaver."

That's all she said. And flew off.

My first thought was, That's interesting. I think I just received a spiritual name. Hmmm. Cocoon Weaver. Not bad. Well, at least it has possibilities. But it doesn't sound quite right, perhaps a bit archaic, but maybe we could change it to Cocoon Spinner or Cocoon Maker or...

Nonplussed, my mind went on with this internal dialogue for several seconds, almost losing the unspeakable preciousness of the moment. Then something broke through my throat — a gasp or a moan. My heart swelled and burst open. I wept tears of gratitude. My mind stopped, and the world began to move again.

Like an embrace, the butterfly's vibrant touch and the monk's sturdy presence began to teach me, in a language older and far deeper than words. They said it was both my opportunity and obligation this lifetime to weave cocoons. "Beautiful contexts for transformation," they said in feeling-images, "sacred spaces in which people can learn again from wild nature as it exists both inside them and outside."

The monk and butterfly made it clear I would not wield a magic wand that transforms people or saves them from the hard work of being born into their soul lives. They explained that magic wands are very rare, and that an agent of change — such as a psychotherapist or a vision quest guide — would rarely want to use them in any case. The greater service is to create opportunities for people to embrace their destinies using their own natural timing and creative impulses, so that they empower and initiate themselves.

I learned that my primary community was the natural world itself and that the key to my fully belonging to that world required me to weave cocoons for members of my *human* community. The monk and butterfly advised that, although I knew little about weaving cocoons with skill, I was to learn by doing — with no excuses or apologies. It was up to me to find my own tools and techniques.

On my final night at Rock Lake, I dreamed:

I have a girlfriend. Her name is Carmen [which means "song" in Latin]. We go to watch a Nordic downhill ski-jumping competition at a huge ramp several hundred feet high. We are standing, in skis, just above the competitors on a vertiginous platform at the top of the ramp. When the starting gate opens and several skiers simultaneously descend down the ramp, we find ourselves, unexpectedly, taking off with them! It is more like flying than skiing — and totally exhilarating! We continue flying with skis on our feet. Since I am new at this, Carmen and a second woman take my hands to help me.

Perhaps a new relationship with my anima had begun. Given her name, Carmen, I became hopeful I might learn the songs of my soul. Perhaps she and I would make beautiful, mysterious music together like the mother and daughter in the earlier dream, and move together in a joyous and fluid way like the ski jumpers. Perhaps here were some secrets to weaving cocoons.

It felt like my soul had been patiently waiting for me to face my fears of her mysteries, shyly hoping that, together, we would once again sing, and trusting I might finally claim my true name. David Whyte writes:

The soul lives contented
by listening,
if it wants to change
into the beauty of
terrifying shapes
it tries to speak.

That's why
you will not sing,
afraid as you are
of who might join with you.

The voice hesitant,
and her hand trembling
in the dark for yours.

She touches your face
and says your name
in the same moment.

The one you refused to say,
over and over,
the one you refused to say.[2]

As is most often the case, my vision quest did not suggest a new career or life direction identifiable by the familiar job categories of contemporary culture, but I was shown something so much more valuable: the essential nature of my soul gift. I was told not what delivery system to use, but what was to be delivered. I learned that my calling is to help people enter the turbulent waters of soul, where their lives might be transformed, and that I was to do this by a process akin to weaving cocoons. And the seed of a vision began to sprout, a vision of a contemporary path to initiation for people of Western cultures, a nature-based way to a soul-rooted adulthood and, eventually, elderhood.

Like all people, I have encountered hardships and suffered losses. But since my time at Rock Lake, I have never doubted the seed image at the center of my calling, the vision that sprang from it, nor the living presence of both within me, a presence that has sustained and empowered me.

The monk and butterfly have faithfully remained with me as complementary teachers. The monk has advocated the Zen-like qualities of centeredness, non-attachment, and patience, while the butterfly has sung the praises of playfulness, alacrity, and spontaneity. And they have insisted I learn to weave together these contrasting qualities.

My encounter with the monk and the butterfly launched me onto my soul path. Yet the moment of first soul encounter is just the beginning.

INTRODUCTION

A TRAIL GUIDE TO SOUL

For over twenty years, I've been guiding people into the wilderness — not just the redrock canyons and snow-crested mountains of the American Southwest but, more essentially, into the wilds of our own souls. I call this work *soulcraft*.

As a psychologist, I've found that my clients' discontents are often rooted in an unmet longing for wildness, mystery, and a meaningful engagement with the world. Psychotherapy's traditional methods, regulated relationships, and confined offices are inadequate to address this craving for the untamed terrain of the soul — its jungles, cataracts, labyrinths, and feral creatures. A radically shifted perspective, an expanded cache of strategies and roles, and much wilder environments are needed to recover the innate treasures, the secrets of destiny, buried beneath the surface of our daily routines. Soulcraft is an approach to the psyche and the world that embraces both wild nature and the depths of our souls; it could be called an eco-depth psychology.

Contemporary society has lost touch with soul and the path to psychological and spiritual maturity, or true adulthood. Instead, we are encouraged to create lives of predictable security, false normality, material comfort, bland entertainment, and the illusion of eternal youth. Most of our leaders — political, cultural, and economic — represent and defend a non-sustainable way of life built upon military aggression, the control and exploitation of nature's "resources," and an entitled sense of national security that ignores the needs of other species, other nations, tribes, and races, and our own future generations. These values do not reflect our deeper human nature.

Successful navigation of this most perilous time in human history requires psychologically and spiritually mature men and women who can engender a mature human species. For nature-based people, initiated adulthood is developed in intimate relationship with the earth, the larger organism who births and sustains us. For contemporary people whose culture discounts or even disdains an intimate relationship with nature and soul, reaching psychological and spiritual maturity is challenging but possible, and never more necessary than now.

Fortunately, many people in the industrialized cultures of Western civilization recognize that a fulfilling life is not about superfluous economic advancement, that modest amounts of security and comfort serve adequately as foundations for a creative and soul-stirring life, and that each of us can bring a unique gift to the world, a world desperately in need of the socially transforming contributions of initiated, actively engaged adults. I hear the world itself calling for a renaissance of the human soul or, as James Hillman says, for a psyche the size of the earth.

This book is a border crossing into mystery. Filled with soulcraft practices, stories, poems, and guidelines, these pages invite you to embark upon a contemporary, Western, nature-based journey into the wilderness of your own soul.

For any journey into the wilderness, it helps to pack a map of the territory. If, before you embarked, you sketched your intended route on your map, you'd be more likely to know where you are at any given point. You could also see what is coming up next — a river crossing, thick vegetation, a swamp, an eagle's-eye view, or a good spot to camp.

This introduction is a map of the book you hold in your hands, something to help you stay oriented while reading.

The book itself is a trail guide for the mystical descent into the underworld of soul: what the descent is, why it is necessary, how to recognize the call to descend, how to prepare for the descent, what the process looks and feels like, and what practices initiate and accelerate the descent and maximize the soul-quickening benefits of the journey.

The first third of the book prepares you to separate from your familiar world. Chapter 1 is a general introduction to the topography of the descent. Chapter 2 familiarizes you with the language that will be used on the journey, what your guide means by soul, spirit, ego, the journey of ascent, the journey of descent, soul encounter, and vision, and how he understands the relationship between soul and nature. Chapter 3 describes how the journey begins, regardless of whether it begins during your young adulthood, later in a midlife crisis, or on your deathbed. We'll look into the call to adventure that signals the opportunity to descend to your depths. You might imagine the first three chapters to be a briefing from your guide on the eve of departure.

Once your descent begins, there are two images that will help keep you focused. The first is the archetype of human nature most resonant with mysterious journeys, the Wanderer. The second is the cocoon, a symbol of the utterly transformative nature of your quest. These images are explored in chapter 4.

Chapter 5 accelerates the descent, offering you several practices for "leaving home" — loosening your attachment to your current persona and the worldview within which you have operated.

The second third of the book, comprising chapters 6 through 10, explores over twenty pathways to soul encounter, specific methods for discovering and investigating your soul's dark mysteries. Although they spring from the traditional waters of nature-based cultures, these pathways are presented here in contemporary Western containers. The methods range from soul-oriented dreamwork to trance rhythms and dance, and include self-designed ceremonies, soul poetry, the way of council, the modern vision quest, and communicating with nature through signs and omens as well as through direct dialogue.

The final third of the book prepares you to return to the everyday world to live your soul path, carrying what was previously hidden as a gift to others. We explore practices for living soulfully, including the art of romance, work with our personal shadows, wandering in nature, befriending the dark, cultivating a personal relationship with spirit, and, most important, joyfully offering your soul gift as a contribution to social and political transformation and the care of the environment.

Throughout the book, you'll find poems that enhance your emotional and imaginal appreciation of the journey. To help you cross into the mysteries of nature and psyche, I encourage you to read each poem out loud, very slowly, and at least twice.

In the back of the book, I've included a section listing numerous resources to extend and deepen your use of each of the soulcraft practices discussed.

My primary intent and greatest hope for this book is to provide support and encouragement as you embark upon the lesser known half of the spiritual quest: the journey to soul.

Best wishes on the descent,

Bill Plotkin
Dark Canyon, Colorado Plateau
April 2003

PART ONE

SEVERANCE

CHAPTER 1

CARRYING WHAT IS HIDDEN AS A GIFT TO OTHERS

... To be human
is to become visible
while carrying
what is hidden
as a gift to others. ...

— David Whyte

There's so much more to who you are than you know right now. You are, indeed, something mysterious and someone magnificent. You hold within you — secreted for safekeeping in your heart — a great gift for this world. Although you might sometimes feel like a cog in a huge machine, that you don't really matter in the great scheme of things, the truth is that you are fully eligible for a meaningful life, a mystical life, a life of the greatest fulfillment and service. To enter that life, you do not need to join a tribal culture or renounce your religious values. You do not necessarily need to quit your job, sell or give away your home, or learn to eat only vegetables. You do, however, need to undertake a journey as joyous and gratifying as it is long and difficult. You will perhaps have to make sacrifices of the greatest sort along the way, but you will not be able to determine what they might be before you start. Nonetheless, to put things in proper perspective, please remember that at no point will you be asked to sacrifice any social roles, material objects, or self-images that you won't lose anyway at the time of your final breath. Something at your core prays you won't reach that moment without having courageously embarked, years earlier, upon the mystical journey of the soul.

There is a great longing within each of us.

We long to discover the secrets and mysteries of our individual lives, to find our unique way of belonging to this world, to recover the never-before-seen treasure we were born to bring to our communities. To carry this treasure to others is half of our spiritual longing. The other half is to experience our oneness with the universe, with all of creation. While embracing and integrating both halves of the spiritual, *Soulcraft* focuses on the first: our yearning for individual personal meaning and a way to contribute to life, a yearning that pulls us toward the heart of the world — down, that is, into wild nature and into the dark earth of our deepest desires.

Alongside our greatest longing lives an equally great terror of finding the very thing we seek. Somehow we know that doing so will irreversibly shake up our lives, our sense of security, change our relationship to everything we hold as familiar and dear. But we also suspect that saying no to our deepest desires will mean self-imprisonment in a life too small. And a far-off voice within insists that the never-before-seen treasure is well worth any sacrifices and difficulty in recovering it.

And so we search. We go to psychotherapists to heal our emotional wounds. To physicians and other health care providers to heal our bodies. To clergy to heal our souls. All of them help — sometimes and somewhat. But the implicit and usually unconscious bargain we make with ourselves is that, yes, we want to be healed, we want to be made whole, we're willing to go some distance, but we're not willing to question the fundamental assumptions upon which our way of life has been built, both personally and societally. We ignore the still, small voice. We're not willing to risk losing what we have. We just want more.

And so our deepest longing is never fulfilled. Most often, it is never even meaningfully addressed.

The nature-based people native to all continents know that to uncover the secrets of our souls, we must journey into the unknown, deep into the darkness of our selves and farther into an outer world of many dangers and uncertainties. They understand that no one would casually or gleefully choose such a thing. Indeed, most people would not begin without considerable social and cultural pressure in addition to the great intrapsychic drive to wholeness. And although the journey is a spiritual one, it is *not* a transcendental movement upward toward the light and an ecstatic union with all of creation. It is a journey downward into the dark mysteries of the individual soul. This is a journey on which, as the great German poet Rainer Maria Rilke put it, we are asked to trust not our lightness but our heaviness:

How surely gravity's law,
strong as an ocean current,
takes hold of even the smallest thing
and pulls it toward the heart of the world.

Each thing—
each stone, blossom, child—
is held in place.

Only we, in our arrogance,
push out beyond what we each belong to
for some empty freedom.

If we surrendered
to earth's intelligence
we could rise up rooted, like trees.

Instead we entangle ourselves
in knots of our own making
and struggle, lonely and confused.

So, like children, we begin again
to learn from the things,
because they are in God's heart;
they have never left him.

This is what the things can teach us:
to fall,
patiently to trust our heaviness.
Even a bird has to do that
before he can fly.[1]

People have felt the downward pull to soul since the beginning of time.

In the mythologies of the world, we find innumerable stories of the hero's or heroine's descent to the underworld. The Greeks told the tale of Orpheus, the fabulously skilled musician who traveled to Hades to find and revive his dead bride, Eurydice. He succeeds at the rescue but then, as he leads her back to the daylight world, loses her again (and this time forever) when he disobeys the gods by turning around to make sure she is still there.

Persephone, the daughter of the fertility goddess, Demeter, is abducted by Hades, the lord of the dark underworld, to be his bride. Eventually, Zeus sends Hermes to rescue Persephone (with only partial success: she must spend one-third of each year below).

The Anglo-Saxon Norsemen told the story of the hero-warrior Beowulf, who descends into a dreadful swamp to do battle with the monster of all monsters, Grendel's mother. Beowulf slays the beast but returns as part monster himself.

From the ancient Sumerian world comes the myth of the goddess of heaven, Inanna, who descends to the netherworld to confront her dark sister, the goddess Ereshkigal, who kills Inanna and hangs her corpse on a peg. Two mourners are sent to Ereshkigal by Enki, the god of waters and wisdom, and secure Inanna's release, but Inanna must send a substitute to take her place in the netherworld.

The Nubian people of Saharan Africa recount the story of a young woman who, because of her beauty, is spurned by the other women of the village. In her despair, she descends to the bottom of a river, a very dangerous place, where she encounters a repulsive old woman covered with horrible sores who asks the young woman to lick her wounds. She does and is thereby saved from the monster of the depths. She returns to the village with great gifts.

Such myths and stories are found in countless cultures. They imply we each must undertake the journey of descent if we are to heal ourselves at the deepest levels and reach a full and authentic adulthood, that there are powerful and dangerous beings in the underworld who are not particularly friendly or attractive, and that we are forever changed by the experience. In contemporary Western cultures, we live as if the spiritual descent is no longer necessary; we live without realizing that the journey is meant for each one of us, not just for the heroes and heroines of mythology.

In his classic text *The Hero with a Thousand Faces,* the great mythologist Joseph Campbell identified in rich detail the universal patterns and themes underlying the journey of descent as found throughout world mythology.[2] These patterns and themes reveal what we can expect on our own underworld journeys.

The hero or heroine of mythology represents you and me, the everyday self (the *I*, or ego). If and when you embark upon the underworld adventure, it begins the same way it does in myth — by leaving home. You leave your commonplace world and roles and your familiar way of understanding yourself. Soon (at the threshold of the underworld, the kingdom of the dark) you encounter a demon — a shadowy element of your own unconscious — that guards the passage. This is the first test. There are two ways you can continue at this point. If you defeat the demon or conciliate it (perhaps by making an offering or using a charm), you enter the underworld "alive" (with some ordinary awareness remaining). If you are slain or dismembered, on the other hand, you descend in "death" (stripped of all normal awareness). But you descend either way, and that's what's most important.

You then journey through what Campbell called "a world of unfamiliar yet strangely intimate forces." This is precisely how the underworld feels — although exotic and uncanny, the beings you encounter there seem to know you because, after all, they embody the previously denied aspects of your larger self.

Your underworld encounters help you in two ways. Some of them further undermine or defeat your former understanding of self and world, while other encounters provide you with helpers or magical aid, supporting your more soul-rooted way of being. At the climax of the journey — it's actually a nadir on an underworld excursion — you undergo a supreme ordeal that puts a decisive end to your old self-image (ego death) and leads to your reward, the recovery of your core soul knowledge.

This recovery may be experienced in a variety of ways: union between your conscious self and soul, perhaps embodied in a sacred marriage or sexual union with a god or goddess; soul knowledge confirmed by a divine being; an experience of self as a carrier of sacred powers; or the discovery of a treasure or boon.

Returning to the middleworld, you are now more consciously aligned with your soul's purpose. Your world is thereby restored both inwardly and outwardly — inwardly in that your image of the world and your place in it has become whole again but in an utterly new and expanded way, and outwardly in that you return with a sacred task to perform in your community, a gift that contributes to the healing and wholing of the world.

The gift you carry for others is not an attempt to save the world but to fully *belong* to it. It's not possible to save the world by trying to save it. You need to find *what is genuinely yours* to offer the world before you can make it a better place. Discovering your unique gift to bring to your community is your greatest opportunity and challenge. The offering of that gift — your true self — is the most you can do to love and serve the world. And it is all the world needs.

We can create contemporary methods to facilitate the underworld journey.

For thousands of years, we have been living in a culture that "protects" us from the hardships and dangers of the descent, a world in which everything is more or less predictable and where most people emulate those getting the greatest socioeconomic rewards. It is a world from which the true elders have largely disappeared, the elders who once possessed intimate knowledge of soul and who waited for us at the underworld threshold to guide us across.

Yet knowledge of the mystical journey remains available. In addition to world mythology, it can be found in the shamanic traditions of nature-based peoples, in the esoteric branches of the great world religions, in the few remaining mystery schools, in the verses of the soul poets, and in modern depth psychology. Most importantly, this knowledge is always and everywhere found within the souls of each of us and in the remaining wild places of the world.

But once we've identified the universal patterns of descent — as articulated by Campbell and others and as found in nature and our own souls — how do we activate those patterns in contemporary Western life?

This question has been at the heart of my work as a psychologist, wilderness guide, and ally to the underworld journey. *Soulcraft* makes the bridge from the recognition of archetypal patterns to the actual *experience* of the descent. It provides practices and pathways to initiate and deepen the journey. Some of these methods are modern adaptations from the cultural wisdom of the ages, and others are what my colleagues and I discovered by simply rolling up our sleeves, along with our participants, and diving into the mysteries.

With the support of nature and an underworld guide, our souls can show us how to re-create a relationship with mystery. We have only to learn how to look and then take our next step upon the journey.

Each of the soulcraft practices presented in these pages is designed to be used hand-in-hand with the others. The introspective practices complement and animate the outer, nature-oriented approaches, and each method deepens and extends the results from every other.

But *Soulcraft* provides more than a grab bag of tools and practices. It encourages a way of life that emphasizes meaning and mystery, celebrates the depths and magnificence of our individuality, and helps reintroduce to Western civilization that other, downward-bearing half of the spiritual journey.

Such an integrated approach to soul discovery and embodiment is what nature-based people have always possessed. Imitating native people of any land or tradition, however, is unnecessary and can be disrespectful to them and to ourselves and, ultimately, of limited value for people who are not born or adopted members of those cultures. It is time for us in the Western world to create our own contemporary and practical path to soul, generated in part by our intimate relationship to land and place.

The most effective paths to soul are nature-based.

Nature — the outer nature we call "the wild" — has always been the essential element and the primary setting of the journey to soul. The soul, after all, is our *inner* wilderness, the intrapsychic terrain we know the least and that holds our individual mysteries. When we truly enter the outer wild — fully opened to its enigmatic and feral powers — the soul responds with its own cries and cravings. These passions might frighten us at first because they threaten to upset the carefully assembled applecart of our conventional lives. Perhaps this is why many people regard their souls in much the same way they view deserts, jungles, oceans, wild mountains, and dark forests — as dangerous and forbidding places.

Our society is forever erecting barriers between its citizens and the inner/outer wilderness. On the outer side, we have our air-conditioned houses and automobiles, gated communities and indoor malls, fences and animal control officers, dams and virtual realities. On the inner side, we're offered prescribed "mood enhancers," alcohol, and street drugs; consumerism and dozens of other soul-numbing addictions; fundamentalisms, transcendentalisms, and other escapisms; rigid belief systems as to what is "good" and what is "bad"; and teachings that God or some other paternal figure will watch over us and protect our delicate lives.

But when we escape beyond these artificial barriers, we discover something astonishing: nature and soul not only depend on each other but *long* for each other and *are,* in the end, of the same substance, like twins or trees sharing the same roots. The individual soul is the core of our human nature, the reason for which we were born, the essence of our specific life purpose, and ours alone. Yet our true nature is at first a mystery to our everyday mind. To recover our inmost secrets, we must venture into the inner/outer wilderness, where we shall find our essential nature waiting for us.

Thomas Berry, the cultural historian and religious scholar, reminds us that the word *nature* comes from the Latin *natus,* "to be born," and that the nature of a thing "has to do with that dynamic principle that holds something together and gives it its identity."[3] The human soul functions in the same way: the soul holds our individuality together and gives us our identity. *Soul* and *nature* are only slightly different ways of talking about the essence of a thing, whether a stone, a blossom, or a person. The soul of a blossom is its essential nature. Our human souls consist of those aspects of self that are most natural, that are most *of nature* — the aspects of self to which nature herself gave birth.

Nature depends on us to embody our souls. The world cannot fully express itself without each of us fully expressing *our* selves; diminished human soul means diminished nature. Just as nature longs for the embodiment of our souls, our souls long for a world in which nature can embody itself fully and diversely.

When, at long last, we gaze into our own depths, we see the same kind of enchantment and resilience we see in undisturbed nature. And when we journey far enough from the routines of our civilized lives — in space or in cultural distance, far enough, that is, into wilderness — we see reflected back to us the essential qualities of our deepest selves.

The underworld journey is not at all the same as psychotherapy, and it is a far cry from a nature walk or an Outward Bound course.

The practices in this book will help you reach the boundary of the world within which you have defined and limited yourself (as we all do), and, when you are sufficiently prepared, help you cross that threshold and dive toward the beautiful and terrifying shapes of your own soul. We'll explore practices such as discovering nature as a mirror, confronting your own death, extended periods of solitude and/or fasting, the art of wandering, working with your sacred wound, the way of council, self-designed ceremony, understanding nature's signs and omens, interspecies communication, trance dancing, and the arts of shadow work and of soulful romance.

Although soulcraft methods can be employed in a variety of settings, sometimes in your own home, the reader must be forewarned: the underworld journey is, in most cases, neither easy nor painless, and even the best psychotherapist will be of limited value as you proceed. There is no quick fix for the alienation from soul. Cultivating a relationship to soul and transforming your life take time and hard work.

Although soulcraft practice almost always generates psycho-spiritual benefits, the full encounter with soul requires the surrender of control and predictability. Your ego must be shocked or shifted in a way that extracts you from your surface life. This book helps you prepare for and invoke such major shifts in consciousness.

The pull toward soul feels like an earthquake in the midst of your life.

The journey of descent begins with a *call to adventure,* a stirring declaration from the depths, from the gods and goddesses, that it is time to leave behind everything you thought your life was supposed to be. The call is much more than an urge for an extended vacation, a challenging project, or a new career or social scene. You may *think* you are simply going to leave home for a while, learn something new, and return to what you always thought was yours, but you will not in fact be in control. You might one day return to the place where home existed and find only ashes.

In the industrialized Western world, the call comes without warning, without help from elders, and without a formal rite of passage. Although unexpected, the call is preceded by ominous tremors. For me, those tremors rippled beneath the ground of my early professional career.

The university was the world for which my family, education, and aptitude — my entire life — had prepared me. By my mid-twenties, I was successful enough to be in danger of becoming entrenched and inflated. I imagined I would one day hold an endowed chair at an Ivy League university; all I had to do was collect data, publish papers, and receive one promotion after another.

Academia was such a good fit for my personality, I could easily have dissipated my life there. Yet, beneath the veneer of outward success, I was an insincere stranger in a strange land of crowded classrooms and deadly committee meetings. I had little passion for the academic life — intellectual interest and ambition, yes, but no true devotion or enthusiasm. But I never thought of leaving — what else *was* there?

Still, I could not deny that my deepest motivations were social and financial security, professional status, and self-aggrandizement. Unbeknownst to me at the time, my university life arrested me in an immature identity. The sprouting tree of my career did not have its roots dug into the deeper desires of soul.

In lieu of a genuine initiation in my teens or twenties, I simply transferred my dependencies from my human parents onto an institutional, academic "parent." For others in our society, the new parent is a corporation or a church, a government job, a professional society or partnership, a business, or the military. For yet others, there are the deadly havens of gang membership, codependent relationships, or addiction.

I heard the call to adventure a few times in my early twenties, but I didn't know who or what was calling. Finally, on that winter day in the Adirondacks, I got rattled in a way I couldn't ignore. As I ascended Cascade Mountain on snowshoes, climbing toward a gold and blue dome, I felt emotionally torn: on the one hand, I exulted in the freedom and wildness of the mountains — untamed nature, where I felt most at home. On the other, I dragged my professorial life behind me like an anchor. I wondered why I didn't find my career more fulfilling and hoped I only needed a little more time to get settled.

But, upon reaching the summit, my understanding of life changed and my adolescent trance ended. Lost in a sea of white peaks, I was pierced by an unfathomable sadness for a loss that was at once mine and not mine, and a hope for something bigger than I knew to hope for. Sadness and hope coursed through my veins and gathered in my belly. I stood perfectly still, hardly risking a breath. Half-crazed, I scanned every facet of the vast snowscape below as if something precious and essential to me was hidden there, in a concealed valley or the shadow of a river bend.

Then, the truth exploded into my awareness. I heard myself gasp. There was no denying it: my university tenure track was a spiritual dead end and I simply had to leave, despite my promising career, despite the inevitable incomprehension from family and colleagues, despite my not knowing where I would go, how I would survive, or who I would be. I would have to abandon my students and all those boxes of painstakingly gathered and unanalyzed data.

Campbell referred to such earthquakes as moments in which we are summoned by destiny, our "spiritual center of gravity" shifting "from within the pale of society to a zone unknown."[4]

Responding to a call on the summit of a New York peak was the central turning point of my life. My journey of descent began, mythically and literally, at the moment I drew my eyes away from the promise glimmering far below and turned to take my first step off that snow-shrouded mountain.

In the Western world, many are called but few respond. Entry into the life of the soul demands a steep price.

Perhaps you remember a time when *you* heard the call to adventure. Often it comes near the end of formal education. As a senior in high school or college, you may have felt an overwhelming desire to chuck it all, to leave everything behind and wander into the world. Alarmed, you wondered if this would mean saying good-bye to everyone you loved and everything you had worked so hard to create.

But this is precisely how it works: We don't enter soulful adulthood merely by reaching a certain age, birthing or raising children, or accepting certain "adult" responsibilities. We must undergo an initiation process that does require letting go of the familiar and comfortable. Through ordeals and ecstasies, we come to know what we were born to do, what gift we were meant to bring to the world, what vision is ours to embody.

Entry into the life of the soul — a life of passion, enchantment, and service — demands a steep price, a psychological form of dying. We do not easily give up our claim on the good life of extended adolescence, what Jungian analyst James Hollis refers to as our "first adulthood."[5] Nature-based societies, understanding this, provide their youth with extensive preparation for the encounter with soul followed by an arduous initiation rite. These rites, now beginning to reappear in our own society, facilitate the radical shift in consciousness required to turn our focus from familiar egocentric concerns to those of the soul, from our first adulthood to our second.

In contemporary Western society, the underworld journey is neither understood nor encouraged by the majority of parents, teachers, health professionals, or cultural leaders, to say nothing of mainstream business, science, or politics. Yet a genuine soulful adulthood is possible for everyone. We need to restore the ways of soul initiation — but not by adoption of other cultures' traditions or rites; rather, through the creation of our own contemporary and diverse models that better fit our postindustrial selves.

It's not too late.

One of the saddest yet strangely hopeful discoveries of recent years is that many profound soul encounters occur for the first and only time on a person's deathbed. The fact of one's imminent death is obviously an ego crisis of the greatest magnitude, one that allows soul to break through into consciousness. Any hospice worker can tell you stories that support this. A border is crossed and the familiar falls away to be replaced by something the personality has never before seen. At these moments, the ego recognizes what the soul has always known.

Although it is the greatest blessing to experience such an opening at any time in life, what a shame that for so many this does not occur until the very end, if at all. Imagine the years and depths of fulfillment that might have been enjoyed if it were otherwise, and the creative, life-affirming contributions that might have been offered by so many!

Rilke reminds us that it is never too late to embark upon the mystical descent to soul:

> You are not dead yet. It is not too late
> To open your depths by plunging into them
> And drink in the life
> That reveals itself quietly there.[6]

I have had the privilege of accompanying thousands of people — from age sixteen to eighty — as they enter life-changing thresholds: endings, beginnings, crossroads, upheavals, crises, and periods of emptiness or healing. Crossing these thresholds, they plunge into depth and mystery. You, too, can make such a crossing. In these pages, you will find stories of people like you who have encountered their souls in the wilderness of their lives. It's not too late for you no matter how tired or skeptical you might be. And it's as natural as being born or dying, as natural as a snake shedding its skin, a tree dropping its leaves, a thundercloud releasing rain ... or a caterpillar forming its cocoon.

CHAPTER 2

GROUNDWORK

A Briefing for the Descent to Soul

It doesn't interest me if there is one God
or many gods.
I want to know if you belong or feel
abandoned.
If you know despair or can see it in others.
I want to know
if you are prepared to live in the world
with its harsh need
to change you. If you can look back
with firm eyes
saying this is where I stand. I want to know
if you know
how to melt into that fierce heat of living
falling toward
the center of your longing. I want to know
if you are willing
to live, day by day, with the consequence of love
and the bitter
unwanted passion of your sure defeat.

I have heard, in that fierce embrace, even
the gods speak of God.

— David Whyte

Like many of my contemporaries, I received childhood training in a Western religion but no true spiritual mentorship; nothing in my youth addressed the longing for meaning or sacred mysteries or that helped me understand the nature of human consciousness. Beginning in my college years, my first spiritual openings came through Eastern paths — Zen, Kundalini Yoga, Taoism, Sufism, and Tibetan Buddhism. But something essential seemed missing even then. Although these disciplines opened consciousness to the peace and joy of the eternal present — to God's love, perhaps — they seemed dry and austere, too distant from the full human experience. In addition to peace of mind, I sought something more wild, earthy, and sensual, something spiritually fulfilling in a juicier and more personal way. Like the poet, I wanted to find out, not just about God but about what was uniquely meaningful and essential to me — what I would be willing to die for, and "how to melt into that fierce heat of living."

My conviction grew that an essential distinction was being overlooked by all of the spiritual paths I had studied. After years of wondering and exploring, I began to suspect there were actually *two* realms involved in spirituality, not one. But none of the teachers with whom I had studied nor any books I read spoke about two realms. Gradually, I began to discuss my speculations with friends. This helped. Eventually, I found a few books and articles that referred to two realms, confirming a fundamental distinction virtually unmentioned in contemporary society.

Most religions omit or obscure the underworld half of the spiritual journey. Those of us coming to understand this are in a position similar to women raised in Western religions who have long suspected that half the story — the divine feminine — has been left out. But this similarity is not coincidental. As we shall see, the wild, earthy, sensual half of the spiritual journey is the half that the uninitiated masculine mind experiences as feminine and therefore as nonessential and perhaps undesirable or even harmful.

The differences between the two realms of spirituality — and how they *both* differ from psychotherapy — are the keys to understanding what I call soulcraft.

Spirituality is that sphere of experience that lies beyond the commonplace world of our surface lives and that opens our awareness to the ultimate and core realities of existence. There are two realms of spirituality. They are distinct yet complementary. Together they form a whole. Either alone is incomplete.

One realm of spirituality turns upward toward the light, aids us in transcending our (ego's) insistence that the world be just a certain way and not any other, helps us to disidentify from the commotion of the strategic mind so we can reclaim the inner quiet, peace, and wholeness of our true nature, and assists us in cultivating the blissful experience of being fully present in the moment and one with all of creation.

Soulcraft is an exploration of the *other* realm of spirituality, which leads not upward toward God but downward toward the dark center of our individual selves and into the fruitful mysteries of nature. This journey of descent prepares us to live in the world with its harsh need to change us, as David Whyte says, and shows us where and how to make our stand, firmly and uniquely. On this half of the spiritual journey, we do not rise toward heaven but fall toward the center of our longing. Although equally sacred and perhaps even more ancient than the journey of ascent, this second spiritual realm may be unfamiliar to people of Western cultures.

SPIRIT AND SOUL:
TRANSPERSONAL ASCENT AND DESCENT

Life invites us to grow in many ways — physically, emotionally, interpersonally, and spiritually. Spiritually, we can grow in two directions: toward spirit, on the one hand, and toward soul, on the other.

Now these are loaded terms, *spirit* and *soul,* words used in so many ways within so many traditions that it's difficult to know what we ourselves mean by them. Yet I haven't found better alternatives. The best solution is to tell you exactly how I use these two words. My uses might be different from yours, but don't get hung up on the words; keep in mind that what's most important are the meanings explained below, not the words themselves.

By *soul* I mean the vital, mysterious, and wild core of our individual selves, an essence unique to each person, qualities found in layers of the self much deeper than our personalities. By *spirit* I mean the single, great, and eternal mystery that permeates and animates everything in the universe and yet transcends all. Ultimately, each soul exists as an agent for spirit.

The concept of soul embraces the essence of our *particular* individuality. This individuality reflects our unique and deepest personal characteristics, the core and enduring qualities that define our personhood, the true self, the "real me." Soul is what is most wild and natural within us.

David Whyte's poetry offers several evocative images for soul: "that small, bright and indescribable wedge of freedom in your own heart," "the one line already written inside you," the "one life you can call your own," the "shape [that] waits in the seed of you to grow and spread its branches against a future sky," and "your own truth at the center of the image you were born with."[1]

In contrast to soul, the concept of spirit points to what all people, all things, have in common, our shared membership in a single cosmos, each of us a facet of the One Being that contains all. Spirit both transcends all things and is immanent *in* all things. Spirit, in other words, can be thought of as something majestic "out there," something removed from ordinary life; but spirit is simultaneously that which infuses all and everything — the land, the air, the animals, all peoples, our human creations, our own bodies and selves.

Soul embraces and calls us toward what is most unique in us. Spirit encompasses and draws us toward what is most universal and shared.[2]

Our human souls are embodied (i.e., made visible in the world) through our *core powers,* our deepest and most enduring powers, those central to our character and necessary to manifest our soul-level uniqueness. Our core powers can be divided into our most central values, abilities, and knowledge.[3] Our *core values* are the ideals for which we would be willing to die and for which we in fact live. Our *core abilities* are the natural talents or gifts indispensable for performing our soul work; these abilities are developed effortlessly or are capable of being honed to exceptional levels. Our *core knowledge* consists of those mysterious, soul-level things we know without knowing how we know them and that we acquire without effort; they are the facts essential to performing our soul work. My core powers, for example, allow me to weave cocoons of transformation. These powers include the value — my utter conviction — that what humanity most needs now is a contemporary path of initiation into soulful adulthood; the ability, for example, to weave cocoons or to interweave Zen and alacrity; and the knowledge of what an effective context for transformation looks and feels and sounds like. I am an apprentice to these powers.

Few people begin to consciously recognize their core powers until sometime after their teen years. In the Western world, most people *never* come to know themselves this way. Soul discovery requires a lot of work.

The soul is the sacred realm of our most heartfelt purposes, our unique meanings, and the ultimate significance of our individual lives.[4] Soul holds the keys to our central lessons — and to the gifts that are ours and ours alone to carry to others.

The soul is like an acorn. Just as the acorn gives instructions to the oak about how to grow and what to become, the human soul — a type of spiritual blueprint — carries an image or a vision that shows *us* how to grow, what gift we carry for others, the nature of our true life. Unlike oaks, however, we humans are the one part of creation capable of ignoring or refusing the flowering of our own souls.

Spirit and soul are both sacred; they imbue life with meaning, beauty, and mystery. Spirit and soul are both spiritual or transpersonal — they exist beyond the personal, beyond the conventional mind or personality. They might each be referred to as the "sacred Other."

Soul is that sacred Other whose purposes each person has been uniquely designed to serve. Even though the soul is at our very core, soul appears to the conscious self as mysteriously other. Spirit is the ultimate Other that encompasses all that exists. Nature, as the universe itself, is either synonymous with spirit or is immanent spirit. What all three have in common — soul, spirit, and nature — is their wild Otherness, the fact that they are indisputably beyond what we can create or control or claim as possession. We belong to and serve the Other. We are here to serve the soul. Spirit creates *us*. We don't own the land; the land owns us.

Your soul is transpersonal and other because it is deeper and far more expansive than your conscious mind. Your soul encompasses many qualities of which you are not yet aware and may never become aware, including qualities you may flatly deny. Your soul may desire, for example, that you sing your heart songs, or that you assist others through major life transitions, but maybe you don't have a clue about this. Or, if you do have a clue, you might refuse that desire out of fear, a sense of unworthiness, or any number of other "good" reasons. As you delve into the mysteries of your soul, you discover your core powers and learn to integrate them into your daily choices and actions.

Spirit, of course, is transpersonal, too. It is independent of *any* beliefs or knowledge you have about yourself, no matter how shallow or deep, ridiculous or sublime. Spirit is not so concerned with the particularities of your life direction. Spirit simply invites you to return to spirit (and the universal essence of your self) through surrender to the present moment. You can also come into alignment with spirit by responding to the bidding of your soul. Soul is ultimately an agent for spirit. And a *healthy* ego or personality is an agent for soul and, by extension, for spirit as well.

Although both are transpersonal, spirit takes you in one direction from the conscious mind or personality, and soul takes you in the other. The movement toward spirit is a journey of ascent, a journey of transcendence, while the movement toward your soul is a journey of descent, or what Thomas Berry calls "inscendence," a journey that deepens.[5]

Transcendence is commonly associated with the rising sun (and thus the compass direction of east), an ascension to the boundless emptiness of space, a journey into the upperworld, a union with the light — conversing with angels or the ascended masters.[6]

The soul path is often associated with the *setting* sun (and thus the direction of west), the descent to our earthy roots, into the wildness of the soil and the soul, a journey into the underworld, a voyage into darkness or shadow as in the apparent destination of the sun as it sinks below the western horizon.

People who live excessively upperworld lives take a transcendental view of everything. They tend to see light, love, unity, and peace everywhere. They are attracted to the Course in Miracles or aspire to "enlightenment" via an ungrounded approach to Buddhism. They avoid getting dragged down into the particulars of life or actively addressing the social, political, or environmental deterioration of the world. They want to exist above it all and are encouraged to do so by many approaches to spirituality. But eventually they feel the downward pull of dark events in the world, in their families, or within their own psyches. They resist, perhaps submitting only after a great struggle.

People who live excessively underworld lives see the world darkly. They tend to see hidden meaning, mystery, and the undoing of things everywhere.

They gravitate toward the occult and the paradoxical. They prefer the night or the shadows and may find themselves addicted to the gothic and the arcane. They want to penetrate to the center of everything and to understand it all by standing under. But eventually they feel the upward pull of the light. They resist, but sometimes love brightens and lifts them.

A holistic approach to spirituality interweaves the ascent and the descent, rendering balance to the experience of both the upperworld and underworld.[7]

It is due to its downward and darkward bearing that many people misunderstand or fear the journey of descent. Western religious traditions associate the downward direction with a turn *away* from the sacred, toward evil and wickedness, toward "hell." We have been taught that entering the underworld is sinful, suicidal, or a one-way trip reserved for those who have been particularly bad.

Likewise, nature has been rendered as evil. Pan, the Greek's horned god of the forest, was transformed into the devil of Christian mythology. Most Western cultures have feared wild nature and have thought of it as unruly, a realm whose laws clash with society's.

We have, in short, been led to believe that nature and soul are not merely wild but inherently dangerous, forbidden, tainted, or evil. This portrayal is not likely to be a coincidence. Perhaps our religious and political forefathers were afraid of the influences of nature and soul, steered us away from the wild, and tried to control or destroy wildness wherever it might be found. Fear of nature and soul is a fear of our own essence.

Some of our cultural forefathers also felt threatened by femininity (their own as well as women's) and therefore oppressed women, in part because the feminine (in men) is fully conversant with nature and soul. A man's fear of the feminine is often a fear of his own soul and his own deeper nature.

The uninitiated masculine mind (in both men and women) understands the upperworld as masculine (and thus the preponderance of male gods and male prophets, priests, imams, *roshis,* and yogis) and the underworld as feminine (and thus witches are more common than warlocks). The initiated adult experiences both worlds as equally masculine and feminine, or neither.

The upward and downward journeys support one another. Although distinct — even opposite — they are the two halves of a single path toward fulfillment and wholeness. While either journey alone is better than neither, the two together constitute a more complete spirituality.

Although opposite in one sense, soul and spirit are not in any way *opposed* to one another. They are — to borrow a phrase employed by depth psychologist James Hillman — "two polar forces of one and the same power."[8] We might call that one power the transpersonal, the sacred, or the Great Mystery. Spirit is the mystery of the One, of the Light, of eternal life. Soul is the mystery of the unique and the infinitely diverse, of the underworld and depth, of the dark and of death.

Soul shows us how we, as individuals, are different (in a community-affirming way) from everybody else. Spirit shows us how we are *no* different from *anything* else, how we are one with all that exists.

In relation to spirit, everyone has the same lessons to learn; for example, compassion and loving-kindness toward all beings, as Buddhism teaches. Our relationship to spirit makes possible the experience and expression of such universal transpersonal qualities as unconditional love, perennial wisdom, and healing power.

In relation to soul, we each have lessons and qualities as unique as our fingerprints.

Hillman expresses the distinction between soul and spirit in delightfully and characteristically irreverent terms:

> Soul likes intimacy; spirit is uplifting. Soul gets hairy; spirit is bald. Spirit sees, even in the dark; soul feels its way, step by step, or needs a dog. Spirit shoots arrows; soul takes them in the chest. William James and D. H. Lawrence said it best. Spirit likes wholes; soul likes eaches. But they need each other like sadists need masochists and vice versa.[9]

Where soul is associated with the many earthly mysteries, spirit is associated with the one heavenly bliss. Soul opens the door to the unknown or the not-yet-known, while spirit is the realm beyond knowledge of any kind, consciousness without an object.[10] Soul is encountered in the subconscious (i.e., that which lies *below* awareness), while spirit is apprehended in states of *super-*consciousness. Both are associated with states of ecstasy (i.e., outside the ordinary), but the encounter with soul is characterized by dreams and visions of personal destiny, while spirit realization engenders pure, content-free awareness.

When a person experiences ego transcendence or enlightenment, we often say she has merged with the Light or with God, the Self, Buddha-nature, Christ consciousness, Emptiness, or Being — the ultimate sacred Other. This is the Other who is dreaming the world into manifestation, the Other of which our everyday mind is a tiny part, the Other who is both inside us and in whom we are inside.

When a person encounters her individual soul, on the other hand, we are more likely to say she has uncovered her unique gifts, her destiny, her life purpose, or personal meaning. Through soul encounter, she learns why spirit and nature gave birth to the exceptional individual she is and about her particular way of belonging to the world.

THE COLLECTIVE HUMAN SOUL AND THE HUMAN ARCHETYPES

It's not just we humans who have souls. Everything — a rock, the wind, a song, a moment, a building, or a marriage, as well as the earth itself — has a soul, an essential and unique quality. Even the universe has a soul, and we call that soul "spirit." So, too, humanity as a collective, as a species, has a soul. Certain essential qualities mark humanness in all times and places — certain enduring themes and patterns called the human archetypes.

Each human archetype consists of an identifiable pattern found in every society and, as a potential, within every human being: the Hero, the Wise and Gentle Queen, the Courageous Warrior, the Virtuous Maiden, the Seductress, the Nurturing Mother, the Holy Child, the Young Redeemer, the Rebel, the Tyrant, the Trickster, the Sacred Fool, the Innocent, the Sage, the Crone, the Magician. A given individual will resonate more with some patterns than others, or at a certain stage more with one archetype than another, but in any human community each archetype will be found embodied in someone. The human archetypes represent the patterns and possibilities of being human. Without each of them embodied in some way, a human community and its soul are incomplete.

When people speak or write about "the human soul," sometimes they mean an individual person's soul and other times the collective human soul. It's an important distinction. The former is what is unique about a person; the latter is what is universal within that unique realm we refer to as humanity. But of course the two are related: an individual's soul is a mosaic of themes from the universal archetypes. One person might embody the Hero and the Monk, while another resonates more with the Wise Old Man, the

Fool, and the Trickster. Each individual is a unique collection of archetypes expressing a gestalt as individual as a snow crystal.

THREE REALMS OF HUMAN DEVELOPMENT: EGO GROWTH, SOUL EMBODIMENT, AND SPIRIT REALIZATION

Most cultures, traditions, and philosophies emphasize one pole of spiritual development or the other; few embrace both equally. The shamanistic traditions of indigenous, oral cultures emphasize the discovery and embodiment of our unique soul, as do the twentieth-century depth psychologists Carl Jung, Marie-Louise von Franz, James Hillman, Marion Woodman, Robert Johnson, James Hollis, and others. In contrast, the major world religions of Hinduism, Buddhism, Judaism, Christianity, and Islam focus upon the realization of — or union with — spirit, as do the theories of some transpersonal psychologists such as Ken Wilber, or the lessons of contemporary spiritual teachers such as Eckhart Tolle.

Spirit realization and soul embodiment, together as spiritual pursuits, contrast with a third realm of human development, the healing and growth of the everyday personality — the ego — and its relationship to the human body and to other people.

In many traditions, these three realms correspond to three different worlds. The upperworld is the home of spirit, the underworld the home of souls, and the middleworld the home of our human personalities and bodies. The middleworld represents the personal and interpersonal (including the social and political) and the upper and lower worlds represent the two poles of the transpersonal, or spiritual.

Different sets of practices are employed to facilitate development in the three realms, although some individual practices support progress in more than one of the three worlds.

The middle realm of ego growth includes the healing of emotional wounds, the development of personal bonds, the cultivation of physical grace and emotional expression, and the blossoming of empathy, intimacy, and personality-level authenticity. A healthy ego is skilled in imagination, feeling, intuition, and sensing, in addition to thinking. Adequate ego growth is essential to personal well-being and cannot be bypassed through the other two realms. Meditation practice by itself is not going to facilitate growth in this realm; nor is the journey of descent.

Ego growth takes time and effort, and indeed it is never finished no matter how much we may also be developing transpersonally. There is always more to heal, more to express, and deeper levels of intimacy. In contemporary society, when ego growth has faltered or stalled, we seek help from psychotherapy and related disciplines such as social work, personal coaching, art and movement therapies, and bodywork.

The second realm of development, the underworld of soul embodiment, deepens individuality through the discovery of our particular place in the world and the embodiment of our unique form of service. Soul embodiment is facilitated by practices that I refer to collectively as soulcraft and that include underworld dreamwork and deep imagery journeys, self-designed ceremonies and traditional rituals, wandering in nature, and conversing with birds and trees, the winds, and the land itself. Soulcraft practices evoke non-ordinary states of consciousness that reveal aspects of ourselves hidden from everyday awareness. Many of these practices are found in the ancient (and continuing) traditions of nature-based peoples. Currently soulcraft is finding its way back into contemporary Western life through modern mystery schools, through individual disciplines (such as trance dancing and drumming, council work, story-telling, symbolic artwork, soul-oriented poetry, and shadow work), and through the work of depth-oriented psychologists such as Carl Jung and James Hillman.

The third realm of development, spirit realization (sometimes referred to as Self-realization), supports the upperworld journey. On the path of ascent, we *surrender* attachment to individuality and learn to transcend *both* ego identification and soul identification, ultimately seeing through the illusion of a separate self. We ascend toward an ecstatic merging with the Infinite, the Eternal, the Absolute. Development in this realm is brought about by meditative and yogic disciplines, by many religious traditions (especially their mystical branches), and by transcendental paths and schools. Most often, the core practice is meditation, prayer, or contemplation, disciplines that quiet the mind and cultivate peace, stillness, and centeredness in the present.

The descent — and the darkness into which it leads — have their own value; the journey to soul is not a misfortune or a necessary evil. In Western cultures, we rarely enter the underworld except when abducted, like Eurydice or Persephone, by a great loss or depression. Then the descent can be harrowing indeed as we enter a blackness we fear we won't escape. With no guides or allies, no preparation or relevant skills, and few inner resources to call upon, we're not likely to enjoy the journey. But we may yet benefit from the experience. Better to be carried off than not go at all. Abduction is the soul's way of pulling us down toward it if we will not voluntarily step through the gates and over the edge. When the descent *is* chosen, it is likely to offer exhilaration and ecstasy as well as frights and ordeals. Initiation has its hardships; yet the descent can be joyous even when it begins with calamity.

Jungian analyst Marion Woodman says the descent need not be about meaningless suffering endured only for the hope that it might end someday. When we descend with resistance, we suffer, perhaps getting yanked back by therapeutic interventions or psychiatric medications: no lasting contact with the soul is made. The unprepared person wants to get out of that hellhole as soon as possible and return to the daylight world. The opportunity is thus wasted.

People fear the descent when they are taught to expect either meaningless suffering or suffering with the possibility of a benefit that perhaps they don't even want. But when entered purposefully, with courage, humility, and humor, the downward journey becomes a time of what Woodman refers to as "soul-making."[11]

Many ascent-oriented spiritual paths see the descent as simply unnecessary and avoidable, or perhaps as necessary but only a temporary diversion from the ascent, or, at best, an experience from which we can learn something that will help us return to the light. I have heard Buddhist teachers say that paying heed to a vision — even of personal destiny — is a distraction from the spiritual path. The light is seen as the only goal.

Consider, in contrast, that the descent has its own rewards both independent of the ascent and in conjunction *with* it. As Rilke wrote:

If we surrendered
to earth's intelligence
we could rise up rooted, like trees.[12]

The rooting (of trees, of our selves) is as important and as necessary as the rising. We have the opportunity to sink roots into soul and rise up with branches in heaven. I like to imagine Rilke would have found the following an equally pleasing verse:

> If we surrendered
> to earth's intelligence
> we could root down ascendant, like trees.

Our spiritual growth is meant to go in both directions, toward the fertile darkness and the glorious light, each of us having the opportunity to bridge earth and heaven — the underworld and the upperworld — through the trunks of our middleworld lives. Rilke saw the intrinsic value of darkness:

> You darkness from which I come,
> I love you more than all the fires
> that fence out the world,
> for the fire makes a circle
> for everyone
> so that no one sees you anymore....[13]

Although different, the goals and processes of soul embodiment and spirit realization are fully compatible and complementary. We can deepen our individuality and its expression while at the same time transcending our *identification* with that individuality; each process facilitates the other.

Spirit-oriented practices such as meditation help us surrender attachment to a limited understanding of self, a restricted ego identification. The ability to disidentify from a smaller, safer self-concept helps us move downward toward transpersonal soul as well as upward toward transpersonal spirit. Touching soul is easier when our minds are quiet.

Likewise, as we deepen our understanding of our souls, we discover our unique place and value in our communities; we recognize our gifts that will make the world a better place. This reassurance helps us surrender our more limited roles and ego identifications and thereby eases our opening into the realm of spirit.

The descent and ascent are opposite and complementary poles of spiritual development. They share the intention of becoming more present in our lives — present to soul and to spirit and thereby more present to the world. Since the ascent and descent are paired opposites, one cannot exist without the other. The world and the psyche seek balance. Upper and lower. Male and female. Light and dark. Spirit and soul. Right and left. Universality and uniqueness. The ascent and the descent.

There's no conflict between spirit-centered being and soulful doing, between transcendence and inscendence. Each supports and enhances the other. Like Rilke, we discover we can have both:

> You see, I want a lot
> Maybe I want it all;
> The darkness of each endless fall,
> The shimmering light of each ascent.[14]

Ego growth, soul embodiment, and spirit realization are equally vital to growing whole. Although all three components can be engaged concurrently, there is a natural sequence to their unfolding: ego growth is the foundation upon which soul embodiment rests, and the latter, I believe, most effectively galvanizes spirit realization.

Yet some self-development paths omit one or two of the components, or try to make one substitute for another. American Buddhism, for example, has recently endorsed ego growth through psychotherapy, but Buddhists rarely discuss soul-oriented depth work or do not distinguish it from ego growth.

Having practiced psychotherapy for many years, I have found much to be gained by recognizing that true soul work is not therapy, and vice versa. The goals differ fundamentally. Even with some overlap in methods (e.g., both may employ dreamwork, deep imagery, art, or solitude and fasting in nature), soulcraft has an initial underworld goal while psychotherapy functions entirely in the middleworld.[15]

Unlike psychotherapy, soulcraft's aim is neither for or against saving our marriages or facilitating our divorces, cultivating our social skills or friendships, enhancing performance or enjoyment in our current careers, raising economic standing, ending our depressions, helping us understand or express our feelings, gaining insight into our personalities or personal histories, or even making us what we would normally call "happier." These outcomes might result from soulcraft, but they are not its goal. The initial goal of the descent is to cultivate the relationship between the ego and the soul, and that is underworld business, business that might, at first, make our surface lives more difficult or lonely, or less comfortable, secure, or happy. Soulcraft practices prepare the ego to abandon its social stability and psychological composure and to be reassigned as an active, adult agent for soul, as opposed to its former role as an adolescent agent for itself. Psychotherapy aims for enhanced coping and social adjustment, and soulcraft for initiation and cultural change.

Soulcraft can be counter-therapeutic. It often involves — even requires — a dissolution of normal ego states, which can traumatize people with fragile or poorly developed egos, thereby further delaying, impeding, or reversing basic ego development and social adjustment. A good foundation of ego growth — through psychotherapy or otherwise — is required if soulcraft practice is going to realize its ultimate promise of cultural evolution and soulful service to community. A well-balanced ego is the necessary carrier of the gift of soul. Soulcraft at the wrong time can undermine the ego's viability. Shadow work, for example, which helps us recover rejected parts of our selves, may not be the best idea for people in the early stages of recovery from substance addictions, sexual abuse, or other emotional traumas. A vision quest or fast would not be advisable for a clinically depressed person. The soulcraft use of hallucinogens, even if they were legal, would not be wisely recommended to children, most teenagers, or adults with poor ego boundaries.

At the same time, psychotherapy can interfere with soulcraft. To move closer to soul, a person might need to leave a relationship, job, home, or role. Some therapists might discourage such changes, fearing an abdication of "adult responsibilities," a lost opportunity for deepened intimacy, or economic self-destruction. Or the client ready for a soul-uncovering exploration of her deepest wound might be counseled that such a journey is unnecessary. Some soulcraft practices — wandering alone in wilderness, practicing the art of being lost, or a solo vision fast — may be deemed nontherapeutic, too dangerous, or even suicidal. Or a therapist might discourage efforts toward soul-rooted cultural change, thinking his client is merely projecting personal problems onto the outer world. Although sometimes therapists would be wise to counsel against soulcraft work, at other times, if the individual is ready for the descent or if a sacrifice, psychological dying, or social-cultural risk is necessary to encounter or embody the soul, then such counsel would impede the soul journey. Without an appreciation of the soul's radical desires, psychotherapy can interfere with psychological and spiritual maturation and promote a non-imaginative normality that merely supports people to be better-adapted cogs in a toxic industrial culture.

Malidoma Somé, an African shaman of the Dagara people, gives us an extreme example of how therapy and soulcraft goals can diverge.[16] When Dagara boys undergo their initiation ordeals, the people of the village realize that a few boys will never return; they will literally not survive. Why would the Dagara be willing to make such an ultimate sacrifice? For the boys who die, this is certainly not a therapeutic experience. Although the Dagara love their children no less than we do, they understand, as the elders of many cultures emphasize, that without vision — without soul embodied in the culturally creative lives of their men and women — the people shall perish. And, to the boys, the small risk of death is preferable to the living death of an uninitiated life. Besides, when we compare Dagara society with our own, we find that an even greater percentage of our teenagers die — through suicide, substance abuse, auto accidents, and gang warfare — in their unsuccessful attempts to initiate themselves.

In ascent-oriented spiritual disciplines and in some psychotherapies, soul too often ends up as the abandoned stepchild. Sometimes *soul* is used as just another word for *ego.* Transpersonal theorist Ken Wilber, for example, writes of the distinction between "a person's immortal-eternal spirit and a person's individual-mortal soul (meaning ego)." At other times, oddly, Wilber uses "soul" as a synonym for spirit.[17] The actual *subject matter* of soul is completely absent from Wilber's theories.

Buddhist teacher and author John Tarrant has enriched American Buddhism by including *soul* in the conversation. He writes about the importance of emotional healing work and developing the capacity for genuine intimacy — ego growth — but refers to this as "soul" work (to distinguish it from what happens through meditation practice). Jack Kornfield, a popular meditation teacher and psychologist, has written several exceptional books that address the upperworld (the "life of the spirit: the blossoming of inner peace, wholeness, and understanding, and the achievement of a happiness that is not dependent on external conditions") in addition to the challenges of the middleworld ("from compassion, addiction, and psychological and emotional healing, to dealing with problems involving relationships and sexuality"), but offers little or no attention to the underworld.[18]

THE EGO

Enormous historical baggage accompanies the word *ego,* which simply means "I" in Latin. Beginning with Freud's pioneer usage, myriad connotations of the word have accumulated from religious, psychological, and philosophical traditions. There are now so many meanings of ego, it would be best to toss the word if it wasn't so embedded in everyday conversation. But reader beware: I may not be using ego in a way familiar to you.

Throughout this book, when I write *ego,* I refer to *a person's everyday conscious self.* The word *everyday* is key: I mean *the conscious self while in its normal, everyday state of consciousness.*[19] Our state of consciousness — our way of being conscious — can and does change, sometimes becoming deepened, heightened, or otherwise shifted. The conscious self in a significantly altered state lies outside what I mean by ego. For example, upon emerging from a period of expanded consciousness, we might say, "I was not myself then; that wasn't the ordinary me, wish as I might it was." We mean, in essence, that we were conscious but not in our ordinary ego state. The observer or witness aspect of consciousness is distinct from ego.

Examples of significantly altered states include dreaming or sleepwalking; trance; delusional, amnesic, or fugue states; revelation, vision, or other encounters with soul; and emotions so overwhelming they change self-understanding. At such times, we are not acting or experiencing from ego.

As a hypothetical example, imagine a poet named Walt, who writes in his normal state of ego consciousness. But the *source* of his poetry is not his ego. His inspiration, his muse, arises from the dreamworld, from nonordinary states of love or nature-inspired rapture, or from states of heightened perception during illness, grief, or fasting. Later, Walt, in his normal state, writes, reworks, and polishes his verse.

The ego is only one aspect of the larger self. In most forms of dreamwork, for example, we treat the *me* in the dream as representing the ego, and the other dream persons as aspects of our psyche with which we are not so consciously identified, such as our inner child, our soul, or our shadow. Dreams unmask intrapsychic characters and expose the relationships among them.

At the time of initiation, the ego transforms as a result of the encounter with soul: the ego becomes an agent for soul, but it is still an ego, still *me.*

Even in the highest stages of human development, an enlightened person chooses and acts from ego — from an everyday conscious self — but hers is an expanded ego, *so* expanded that it is quite different from what the rest of us experience as ego.

As you see, I am not using *ego* in a disparaging way — as in "he's got a big ego" or "she's on an ego trip"; I don't imply selfishness, self-importance, fixation, vanity, or conceit. Although people with immature egos may be selfish, those with mature egos are genuinely loving and altruistic.

Ego refers to a normal and necessary feature of being human. The existence of the ego is what makes us human, for better and worse. If all goes well in our early development, a healthy ego appears around age four, and then shape-shifts, time and again, as it matures and sees us through a lifetime of adventures. At its inception, the ego is naturally narcissistic, but if it develops wholesomely, guided by both soul and nature, it identifies with an increasingly wider slice of life.

A mature ego understands the occasional necessity of surrendering to — or being defeated by — a force greater than itself, sometimes during the death-rebirth of soul encounter (when ego surrenders to soul) and other times during ego transcendence (when ego surrenders to spirit). Ego obstructs personal development when it gets stuck, lost, or entrenched at any life stage — when it resists change, loss, grief, or radical transformation at the hands of the gods and goddesses.

A VISION WITH A TASK

Each of us is born with a treasure, an essence, a seed of quiescent potential, secreted for safekeeping in the center of our being. This treasure, this personal quality, power, talent, or gift (or set of such qualities), is ours to develop, embody, and offer to our communities through acts of service — our contributions to a more diverse, vital, and evolved world. Our personal destiny is to *become* that treasure through our actions.

Wisdomways throughout the world agree that life's greatest fulfillment sprouts from our sacred work, deeds embodying our soul treasures. Our sacred work is what nature-based traditions call our *giveaway* to our people and place.

The giveaway bridges the opposition between selfishness and altruism. We cannot experience soul fulfillment without performing true service, and vice versa. The theologian Frederick Buechner said this in an elegant way: "our calling is where our deepest gladness and the world's hunger meet."[20]

Psychologist Abraham Maslow makes the same point in describing people who are psychologically and spiritually healthiest:

> Self-actualizing people are, without one single exception, involved in a cause outside their own skins, in something outside themselves. They are devoted, working at something, something which is very precious to them—some calling or vocation in the old sense, the priestly sense. They are working at something which fate has called them to somehow and which they work at and which they love, so that the work-joy dichotomy in them disappears.[21]

Rabindranath Tagore, the Bengali poet, philosopher, and Nobel laureate, put it this way:

> I slept and dreamt that life was joy,
> I awoke and saw that life was service,
> I acted and behold, service was joy.[22]

Ruth Benedict, the eminent anthropologist, found this concordance between work and joy in all "good cultures" throughout the world. Benedict defined good cultures as those that exhibited *synergy*. In synergistic societies, "the individual by the same act and at the same time serves his own advantage and that of the group.... Nonaggression occurs not because people are unselfish and put social obligations above personal desires, but when social arrangements make these two identical."[23] What I must do merges with what I want to do; work and play become indistinguishable.

Even in Western society, our deepest yearnings go far beyond a vacation or retirement. We long for a vision of our destiny, and, equally, for a way to carry that vision as a gift to others. The following lines, attributed to sources as diverse as Chief Seattle, Winston Churchill, and Anonymous, say it quite neatly:

> A task without a vision is just a job.
> A vision without a task is just a dream.
> A vision with a task can change the world.

It is this sacred work, this "vision with a task," that we seek, individually and collectively. The rarity of finding sacred work is at the root of our Western despair and sorrow. When not acknowledged and embraced, our grief is acted out through violence, against ourselves (e.g., addictions, suicide, masochism), each other (e.g., sadism, racism, sexism, war, child abuse, ethnic cleansing), and the environment (e.g., toxic waste, resource depletion, species extinction, forest destruction, environmental degradation). Unacknowledged grief also manifests as depression, anxiety, and a growing sense of meaninglessness.

By consciously honoring our grief — the absence of vision and sacred work — we take our first steps toward soul discovery and personal fulfillment. We begin the return to our true nature.

SOUL: YOUR PLACE IN THE MORE-THAN-HUMAN WORLD OF NATURE

Your soul is your true nature. Your soul can also be thought of as your true place *in* nature. You were born to occupy a particular place within the community that ecophilosopher David Abram calls the more-than-human world. You have a unique *ecological role,* the way you are meant to serve and nurture the web of life, directly or through your role in society. At the level of soul, you have a specific way of belonging to the biosphere, as unique as any maple, moose, or mountain.

"A particular place" also means a specific *physical location.* The Australian aborigines, for example, say that for each person there is one place in the natural world where he most belongs, a place that's part of him and where he is part of that place. In finding that place, he also finds his true self.

You, too, can reclaim your membership as a natural being in a natural world. The easiest and most direct way to begin is to simply spend time outdoors, quietly, observantly, and gratefully. By innocently immersing yourself in nature, you will discover, in time, that nature reflects your soul, revealing your particular place in the more-than-human world. Throughout this book, you'll find stories of contemporary people who have discovered their place in just this way.

You can count on wild nature to reflect your soul because soul is your most wild and natural dimension. Nature gives birth to your soul — and that of all other animals and plants on the planet. Your ego, on the other hand, is not born directly from nature, but rather from the matrix of culture-language-family. Soul initiation is often described as a death and a second birth. Like entering a cocoon, your first ego dies and later a soul-rooted ego is birthed, not from culture this time but from the womb of nature.

Wild nature contains all the terrestrial patterns of belonging. Every niche of the world is filled with a life-form that perfectly fits there because it was born to do just that. The wilder the environment (the more complex and diverse it is), and the more likely it contains patterns of belonging that resonate with your destiny. No matter who you are, no matter what possibilities you contain, there are forms and forces in wild nature that will reflect the nuances of your soul.

The poets understand this. Mary Oliver, for example, writes:

> Whoever you are, no matter how lonely,
> the world offers itself to your imagination,
> calls to you like the wild geese, harsh and exciting—
> over and over announcing your place
> in the family of things.[24]

Your soul is both of *you* and *of the world.* The world cannot be full until you become fully yourself. Your soul corresponds to a niche, a distinctive place in nature, like a vibrant space of shimmering potential waiting to be discovered, claimed, . . . occupied. Your soul is *in* and *of* the world, like a whirlpool in a river, a wave in the ocean, or a branch of flame in a fire. As the anthropologist-biologist-ecologist Gregory Bateson shows in his work, psyche is not separate from nature, it is *part* of nature.[25]

Brian Swimme and Thomas Berry (the mathematical cosmologist and the cultural historian, respectively) propose in their book *The Universe Story* that everybody and everything not only has a unique place in the world but is a unique place:

> Walt Whitman did not invent his sentience, nor was he wholly responsible
> for the form of feelings he experienced. Rather, his sentience is an intricate
> creation of the Milky Way, and his feelings are an evocation of being, an evo-
> cation involving thunderstorms, sunlight, grass, history, and death. Walt
> Whitman is a space the Milky Way fashioned to feel its own grandeur.[26]

The essence of the human soul cannot be separated from the wildness of nature. This is why an adequate psychology must be an eco-depth psychology. It's no surprise, even in the contemporary world, that profound encounters with soul often occur during solitary wilderness sojourns, just as they did for the founders of the major religions: Moses on Mount Sinai, Jesus in the desert for forty days, Muhammad in a cave outside Mecca, Buddha under the bodhi tree. For inspiration and vision, we, too, must learn to search outside the customary world of the village, to wander again in the inner and outer wilderness.

THE EXPERIENCE OF SOUL LOSS

When we confine ourselves to the village, we lose touch with our true natures. No wonder soul alienation is suffered by most people in the industrialized cultures of the Western world. The repercussions are seen in every corner of life, on every socioeconomic level, and in every organization. At one time in our lives — or chronically — we've experienced an emptiness at our core, a sense that our lives don't make sense, that something essential is missing.

The full experience of soul loss can be terrifying and disorienting. Not knowing how to make contact with soul, we might deny its very existence in order to lessen the grief. But this sorrow is difficult to fully suppress.

Even in our synthetic, egocentric society, the soul stirs in our subterranean depths, endlessly calling, pushing up like a flower through the cracks in the concrete pavement of our lives. We catch glimpses in our dreams and in fragments of poetry and song, in the distant howl of a coyote or in a bird's sudden flight, in sunsets and the rapture of romance.

Many are beginning again to hear the soul's call and want to follow it into the unknown. But there are fears. What will happen to me? What will others think? There are few societal practices or values to support us on the journey. When the soul is heard but not engaged, we fall into a type of sorrow, a soul depression.

We yearn to connect with soul and to live the life that awaits us there. We want to make the world a better place. But it often seems we are drifting further from these goals. It breaks our hearts to see the widespread human misery and environmental degradation. Our fear and despair sometimes erupt as guilt and anger.

Many people fill their days with a thousand and one distractions in an attempt to muffle the cry of their souls. Often these distractions become our addictions — consumerism, eating disorders, substance abuse, compulsive sex, pornography, workaholism, religious fundamentalism, obsessive thrill-seeking or gambling, and excessive TV watching — all of which contribute further to the deterioration of the world.

As a psychotherapist, I see symptoms of soul loss every day: emotional and relationship problems, anxieties and depressions, addictions and other dependencies. Yet the alienation from soul is more than a mental-health crisis. It is, quite possibly, the most fundamental problem on the planet, the knot at the very center of our dilemmas.

For it's not just our inner afflictions that arise from soul loss; the crises of our outer world can be traced there as well. When we become alienated from soul — our inner nature — we lose respect for outer nature, resulting in pollution and degradation of the environment. The violence and depravity in our cities and among our youth are a direct consequence of soul loss and the absence of soul-oriented initiation rites. When we lose touch with our souls, we don't know what we are good for, and this absence of a sense of purpose and self-worth can lead to increased unemployment, welfare dependence, and economic crises. Shallow politics, impotent government institutions, and our interracial and international conflicts are public embodiments of soul alienation. The instructional failings, absence of meaningful initiations, and moral inadequacies within many of our religious institutions are a spiritual reflection of this loss as well as a generator of it.

We must face the brutal fact that neither religion nor science is going to save us from our self-inflicted tragedies. Our technologies, psychotherapies, politics, and religious organizations have been leading us further every day from wholeness and soul, and from harmony within ourselves, between each other, and between us and the more-than-human world. It is time for a radical change that can only begin within the wild reaches of our individual lives, each of us asking whether our souls may know something that will help.

CHAPTER 3

SINKING BACK INTO
THE SOURCE OF EVERYTHING

The Call to Adventure

You are not surprised at the force of the storm—
you have seen it growing.
The trees flee. Their flight
sets the boulevards streaming. And you know:
he whom they flee is the one
you move toward. All your senses
sing him, as you stand at the window.

The weeks stood still in summer.
The trees' blood rose. Now you feel
it wants to sink back
into the source of everything. You thought
you could trust that power
when you plucked the fruit;
now it becomes a riddle again,
and you again a stranger.

Summer was like your house: you knew
where each thing stood.
Now you must go out into your heart
as onto a vast plain. Now
the immense loneliness begins.
The days go numb, the wind
sucks the world from your senses like withered leaves.

Through the empty branches the sky remains.
It is what you have.
Be earth now, and evensong.
Be the ground lying under that sky.
Be modest now, like a thing
ripened until it is real,
so that he who began it all
can feel you when he reaches for you.

— Rainer Maria Rilke

At some point in your life, you began to wonder if perhaps there is more to life than another round of success (or failure) at the Standard Game of Security Building — the pursuit of your personal selection of career, material possessions, physical safety, comfort, social and sexual relationships, and economic position. Perhaps you have explored the ascent-oriented spiritual life through a meditation practice; you've learned to be more present in the moment and you don't take conventional life — the Standard Game — quite so seriously as you once did. This helps, maybe even makes a huge difference, but it's not quite enough either.

Perhaps now you feel a call, like the trees' blood of which Rilke writes, to "sink back into the source of everything," to "go out into your heart as onto a vast plain." You've recognized the descent as a necessary complement to the ascent as well as to the further fluffing of the pillows of everyday life.

You're no longer willing or able to continue your life the way you have. You will have to loosen your beliefs about the world and the way you exist in it. Second, you will have to open yourself to those mysterious possibilities — your destiny — that the soul has in store for you. Finally, you will gather up those soulful intentions and powers and learn to manifest them in the world. Not coincidentally, these three stages of the journey — severance, initiation, and incorporation — correspond to the three stages of any rite of passage:

- *Severance* (temporary or permanent) from your current role in the community or at work, but most especially from your way of understanding your self.
- *Initiation* into the life of your soul (or, for those who have already experienced a first initiation, into deeper levels of your soul path).
- *Incorporation* into a new role, a new place in your community.

In this chapter, I focus on what happens just before you embark on the journey, just before the beginning of the severance stage. We'll look at why the call to adventure happens when it does and what it's like to hear the call, to feel the approaching storm, to know the time is drawing near to go out into the wilderness — your heart — "as onto a vast plain." We'll explore how to listen to the call, how to know it's genuine, how to test it, and what to do with your inevitable fear and resistance.

PROLOGUE TO THE DESCENT

The call to adventure is the prologue to the journey of descent. The call comes when it's time to inherit a greater life, to plunge yourself into the limitless expanse and depth the world affords. This is both a crisis and an unsurpassed opportunity. The old way of life has been outgrown. The familiar goals, attitudes, and patterns of relationships no longer fit your developing sense of who you truly are. The time has arrived to step over a threshold into a whole new way of being.

In the soul-suppressing environments of Western society, the call may never be heard — or answered — in an entire lifetime, or perhaps not until midlife or the deathbed. The vast majority of midlife crises might be better understood as overdue calls to adventure, as spiritual opportunities triggered by a personal crisis — an affair, severe job dissatisfaction, or an empty nest. Perhaps we so often hear a belated call in midlife because we have reached that age at which we can no longer pretend we'll live forever. After years of raising a family and/or building a career, we begin to ask again what is most essential.

Midlife crises often begin like this: your life has been humming along for some time, fairly secure in its basic socioeconomic qualities, and then *wham!* Suddenly the roof caves in and everything about your life seems wrong. Your job has become a dull cage, your social scene an unremitting replay of the same characters and conversations, and your family a lifeless mockery of intimacy — sometimes polite, sometimes seething with hostility. Or at least so it seems at the outset of the crisis. This is the soul appearing on the scene with an attitude and with a comment about the course of your life, shouting, "Hey, look, I've come a long way to deliver a gift to the world and I'm tired of this damn foot-dragging, so excuse me while I tilt the floor a bit!"

Some arrive at this point *before* the advent of a midlife crisis. Maybe you had the great good fortune of finding a teacher or guide who understood the necessity and joy of the soulful descent. Perhaps as a young adult you encountered a true elder and were spiritually adopted. Or maybe you suffered a terrible calamity: a terminal diagnosis, a near-death experience, a physical accident that left you disabled, the loss of a loved one, a divorce, the destruction of your home or homeland, a suicidal depression, or the utter loss of your religious faith.

Whatever allows you to hear the call, you find your nose suddenly pressed up against the existential questions you had been successfully avoiding: What is my life about, anyway? For what do I live?

Joseph Campbell writes:

That which has to be faced, and is somehow profoundly familiar to the unconscious—though unknown, surprising, and even frightening to the conscious personality—makes itself known; and what formerly was meaningful may become strangely emptied of value.... This first stage of the mythological journey—which we have designated the "call to adventure"—signifies that destiny has summoned the hero and transferred his spiritual center of gravity from within the pale of his society to a zone unknown.[1]

It is always possible, however, to refuse the call entirely and to turn the ear back to the egocentric interests of unrewarding work, relationships, and "culture." The refusal of the call turns our flowering world into a wasteland of open-pit mines and clear-cuts, strip malls and billboards.

LEAVING YOUR SUMMER HOUSE

If you say yes to the call, you'll feel, like Rilke, that you are standing at the window watching a great storm arrive. And you'll know there's no way to flee *this* storm; this one has your name written on it. You know you must open the door and walk straight into the tempest. In doing so, you fall increasingly under the influence of the soul, like the inexorable tug of the full moon upon the tides, like an autumn wind tearing leaves from tree limbs. Your soul has been waiting for this moment, the moment your ego was ripe for the descent, developed well enough to withstand the experience of dissolution, yet still vulnerable enough to be dissolvable.

Opportunities like this are not commonplace. During childhood and the early teen years, the ego is not sufficiently developed to survive a descent. The soul waits for an opening. Meanwhile, the ego is creating ways to avoid the underworld journey. (Resisting self-change is the way the ego understands its job before initiation.) All too often, the soul finds one day that the ego has become too hardened, too entrenched in its routines, so that almost nothing can budge it. In contemporary Western culture, our egos often develop in such a way that we are *both* underdeveloped and overly hardened. If, in our youth, there had been elders about, they would have provided initiatory experiences to soften us up or crack us open. Without elders, the soul waits for — or creates — a trauma, something extreme that will loosen the ego's grip on its old way of belonging to the world.

If and when your grip loosens, you will feel a strong downward pull. Unable to resist the bewitching call from the depths, you'll turn your back on conventional society for a while, and, perhaps for the first time, fully face the enchanting and dangerous portal to soul — though the fright of that turning is as great as its allure. You will turn away from the appetites and fruits of your first adulthood as you prepare for soul initiation sometime in the uncertain future.

Once you have been called, you will have to separate — psychologically if not physically — from the ordinary life of your community. During your young adulthood, you had some confidence in your personality and you felt you could trust the powers of nature. Now, as Rilke writes, your life becomes "a riddle again, and you again a stranger" — to yourself and others. You will have to relinquish your temptation to conform or to seek acceptance from others. You will have to go out on your own.

You will have to move beyond any requirement to be "good," any obligation to be held back by shame about who you are. As the American poet Mary Oliver says in "Wild Geese":

> You do not have to be good.
> You do not have to walk on your knees
> for a hundred miles through the desert, repenting.
> You only have to let the soft animal of your body
>   love what it loves.[2]

The task of severance is not repentance for the sins of your past but a surrender to the desires of your deeper human nature, that which the soft animal of your body loves. Mary Oliver says this is *the only thing* you have to do, but she doesn't say it's easy. This is a surrender that takes some time and work.

What's involved is both a surrender *of* and a surrender *to;* first a surrender *of* your beliefs about how you were supposed to be and how the world was supposed to work, and then a surrender *to* your deepest and wildest passions.

What you must surrender is nothing less than the summer house of your first personality, the worldview you began forming in the expansive growing season of adolescence and that carried you through your first adulthood. This is the house you have been carefully building, furnishing, and accessorizing at least since puberty. Now, just as you are getting ready to enjoy the completed house, you hear a knock and the front door swings open. There stand three strange angels, as D. H. Lawrence called them, motioning to you, informing you it's time to leave — forever. You begin to protest but you know it's useless; it's time to go.

This knock on the door, the call to adventure, comes as soon as you have done enough work on your first personality that it is fully inhabitable. The greatest value to be derived from building that first house comes from the building of it — not from the living in it.

The angels have arrived to summon you to the adventure for which you have longed. They are your guides to soul. But the opportunity does not arrive in the form you had imagined. It arrives in the middle of an enormous storm: now the immense loneliness begins.

Why an immense loneliness? In surrendering the mainstays of your former worldview and separating yourself from everyday community life, your old anchors and familiar reference points disappear. You will have to rely on yourself more deeply and fully than ever before. You will have to surrender the cherished belief that someone is going to protect you, save you, do the work of growing for you, or show you the way. The descent necessarily begins with an immense loneliness, and only someone who possesses the skills required to complete a first house of personality — only *that* person is going to be ready to handle that degree of loneliness. Although the knock on the door does not require you to be alone per se, it does require you to go your own way.

Leaving your summer house, however, does not mean you must betray your preexisting responsibilities. It doesn't necessarily require you to quit your job, sell your house, leave your marriage, or end friendships. It can be done without abandoning your children. Most parents recognize their commitment to their children as sacred as their commitment to their own souls. Although the descent for a parent may be logistically different, perhaps more challenging, than it is for others, it can still be accomplished. What leaving your summer house does require is that you surrender what no longer supports your exploration of your deepest nature. You will discover soon enough which roles, relationships, activities, and possessions get in the way of that exploration: you are being asked to radically simplify your life.

Nature-based people understand that the more complete the separation from former routines, the more effective the descent. This is in part why their rites of initiation into adulthood occur *before* the individual is burdened with adult responsibilities — children, spouse, and community obligations.

THE KNOCK ON THE DOOR

When the knock on the door arrives, you are being asked to descend into psycho-spiritual darkness, the nightworld of mysteries, the womb of true character. David Whyte describes this moment in the intimate voice with which a wise and caring elder might speak to a frightened initiate:

> ...Time to go into the dark
> where the night has eyes
> to recognize its own.
>
> There you can be sure
> you are not beyond love.
>
> The dark will be your womb
> tonight.
>
> The night will give you a horizon
> further than you can see.
>
> You must learn one thing.
> The world was made to be free in.
>
> Give up all the other worlds
> except the one to which you belong.
>
> Sometimes it takes darkness and the sweet
> confinement of your aloneness
> to learn

anything or anyone
that does not bring you alive

is too small for you.[3]

The world was made to be free in: this we know in our bones, and this definitive and fearful knowledge is what both supports us and requires us to turn away from our secure but less-than-joyful lives.

As is common in Western societies, the knock on the door came for me during my first adulthood after I had achieved an adequate adjustment to my social world and was in the midst of a career that, although successful, did not provide sufficient meaning. It was as if my soul had been waiting in the wings for the moment I could be opened and softened by a significant shift in consciousness, that moment on a bright snowy summit when untamed nature and wild emotion acted together to change my life forever.

The knock, however, can come earlier or later than midlife. You may remember, for example, a call you received in your teens but perhaps did not recognize at the time. Annie Bloom, a massage therapist and wilderness guide in her forties, recalls the day in the winter of her sixteenth year when she sat in the locked bathroom of her family's home in a Chicago suburb, a razor blade poised over her wrist. For two years she had been engulfed in blackness and despair. As hard as she tried, she could not find a valid reason for continuing her life.

As I clenched the blade, an image suddenly flooded my head. I saw a boy walking with his books in the hallway of our high school. Being a grade ahead of me, he was someone with whom I had no contact. I knew his name and face but little else. He was a mysterious presence to me, his hair long and disheveled, someone who didn't gather in any of the social cliques but seemed at peace in his self-containment. The image of him wrenched me from my desperate reverie and I decided I would call him. I found his name in the school directory and dialed the number. He answered. I mumbled some garbled words and he took them in, immediately understanding. He did not address my hopelessness, but instead began to talk in poetic phrases, asking me if I had ever been to the edge of Lake Michigan in winter and watched the great chiasmic breathing of the ice floes. This mysterious phrase—the great chiasmic breathing—entered my being like a waterfall of fire, beginning to thaw the rigid numbness inside.

Annie seized on this image like a lifeline and resolved to see the breathing ice floes for herself. A week later, she stood on a lakeshore jetty, the thrumming city of Chicago at her back.

The day was bleak and gray as is typical in a Midwestern winter. As I looked down, my breath caught in my throat and my stomach did flip-flops. Stretched out before me lay an endless landscape of ice chunks. As the lake's swell came up under them, they arose, fitting perfectly together to form a continuous sheet, and as the swell receded, the ice sheet dropped down and separated into thousands of fragments. Then the lake rose again and the ice came together, and then it sank and the ice fell apart. I stood there watching and breathing with the lake for a very long time, and knew forever in my body the great chiasmic breathing of the ice floes of Lake Michigan. I felt bathed in a beauty that was breath-taking. My in-spiration, that is, was full, and at the apex of that fullness lived wonder and hope.

Chiasmic is an enchanting term from the field of anatomy that refers to those patterns in which things become crossed in the form of an X, as, for example, the way the optic nerve, at the base of the brain, crosses from one side of the central nervous system to the other. Cell biologists also employ the word: a chiasma is the point at which the exchange of genetic material takes place between paired chromosomal strands.

The winter breathing of Lake Michigan was chiasmic for Annie in at least two ways: First, she witnessed the crossing, uncrossing, and recrossing of an immense being's form, somehow catalyzing *her* capacity to change form, to cross over, as it were, from "the pale of society to a zone unknown." Second, as young Annie stood at the edge of that lake in such an extraordinary and tender moment of openness and vulnerability, an energetic transmission took place from the body of the lake to her body, like the exchange of genetic materials between two paired beings. The frozen expanse, breathing and separating, was a message to *her* body to allow the numbness inside to break apart. She understood in her cells that she needed to breathe and move, breathe and move.

Standing there spellbound at the edge of deep water, Annie knew in that moment, as surely as she had ever known anything in her life, that it was time to cross over; for her, this meant leaving Chicago and all it represented to her. The city was big and impersonal, her family life was miserable for her, school offered no rewards, and she had no true friends. "What I experienced on that shore was the poetry of the natural world, and my whole being resounded."

Before these events, Annie had been making plans for college even though the prospect depressed her. In contrast, her shoreline encounter with nature enthralled her. Eventually she settled on the idea of working on a dude ranch in the West. She packed her bags and left home, heading for the Two Bar Seven Ranch in Tie Siding, Wyoming.

> I was leaving behind all I had known and heading smack into the Big Unknown. I knew nothing about the western landscape and didn't have a clue what one did on a dude ranch. I was terrified and exhilarated. Once at the ranch and in my daily routine, I alternated between sobbing in my room (huddled under my covers) and having an ecstatic love affair with the land. On my two-hour afternoon breaks, I would go for solitary walks. My body was so enraptured with those wide open and magnificent spaces, I would cast off my clothes and dance, sensuously rolling around on the ground and pressing up against rocks and trees, wanting to drink in texture and shape and color through my pores.

Annie's time at the ranch — the commencement of her journey of descent — had a profound effect on her life path. She has become a remarkable healer of extraordinary skill and sensitivity. Her great love for people and for nature have been the twin passions, the primary motivators that have led to her becoming what she calls "a naturalist for humanity." In later chapters, we'll learn what happened for Annie after she left the ranch in Wyoming and how she discovered the nature of her soul work. But, for now, just note that her soul path, like so many others, began with a single ray of hope in the midst of ruin, in a locked bathroom of despair at the moment she said yes to the image of a mysterious young man.

Everyone who hears the call to adventure and responds to it does so in their own way. There are as many stories as there are spiritual adventurers.

Buddhist author Natalie Goldberg tells her story in *Long Quiet Highway:*

Waking Up in America. "By accident," she writes, "not intended, not even wanted, I had a deep awakening experience in front of a sixth-grade class I was teaching in the Northwest Valley in Albuquerque, New Mexico."[4] She was twenty-six, doing her best at her first teaching job with a classroom of uncontrollable pubescent kids. Then, suddenly,

> I turned and looked out the window. I looked at the smoky appearance of the spring cottonwoods near the parking lot. Any day now they would break into leaf. There was a spindly Russian olive near our window. Suddenly it looked beautiful. Then I had one simple vision: I saw myself wandering in autumn fields and I felt that nothing, nothing else was important. This was a profound feeling, a big feeling. It wasn't a passing momentary flash. I knew I had to stay true to that one vision.
>
> Understand, I had no idea what was happening. . . . I was frightened. I didn't want it. I just wanted to be a writer and to earn a living keeping this class in front of me quiet. I didn't understand what was going on, and I had no clue about those autumn fields.[5]

Goldberg quit her job, knowing she had to go out into something vast and wander there. Like all of us who long to grow into our deepest destiny, she had to leave the home of her first adulthood and separate herself from conventional life.

> This is what I had wanted to do for a long time, to sit in the raw nakedness of myself, with nothing else but myself. No parents, no culture, no New York background, no workshop, teacher, school. Just who was I? Where did I come from? How was I becoming a writer, given my family? What part of us is born apart from family? How was I heading in a whole different direction from my upbringing. . . ?[6]

She stopped reading books and referring to authorities outside herself. She went wandering and wondering alone in the mountains, opening and cleansing her senses, cultivating a relationship with the more-than-human world. She said Yes! to the call to adventure.

GOING THROUGH THE DOOR: IDENTIFYING AND RESPONDING TO THE CALL

How do you know when a call is truly a call to spiritual adventure and not, for example, a momentary disorientation, a mood, a rogue feeling, or an excuse for fleeing responsibilities that have become too much or too fearful? How do you know it's not just a sudden encounter with unsown wild oats or the need for a long overdue vacation?

Good question. There are, fortunately, ways to tell. There are several experiential qualities that accompany the call. Joseph Campbell, as quoted earlier, notes four of them. First, if it is a true call, you will know that responding to it is, in fact, *not* an avoidance of responsibility, but rather a facing of something difficult, something unknown and frightening that summons you. Far from looking to you like an opportunity for escape, a call feels more like a compelling need to walk into the mouth of a whale, or out into the night and into a storm. You have a profound sense that something essential is waiting for you in the midst of a wilderness and your one true life depends on your being willing and able to find it.

Second, Campbell reminds us of a paradox at the heart of the call: this strange thing that calls to you somehow feels "profoundly familiar to the unconscious—though unknown, surprising, and even frightening to the conscious personality." It has the character of déjà vu but it is even more disorienting; you know you belong to it even though you have never before encountered it and can't really explain anything about it.

Third, you have an astonishing and inexplicable sense that the chapter of life you had been living is suddenly over, whether you wanted that ending or not, and usually you have not. What formerly was meaningful becomes "strangely emptied of value."

Fourth, the call is almost always unexpected, and unwanted. Yet you feel summoned by destiny, as if your own future has grabbed you by the collar and is tugging you forward, as if you have been volunteered by life to a task you hadn't sought. You feel as if your "spiritual center of gravity" has been transferred "from within the pale of society to a zone unknown."

Also, like most encounters with the Great Mystery, a call to adventure is typically experienced as uncanny or numinous, suffused with the sacred or holy. More often than not it is accompanied by enormously powerful emotion — as either cause, effect, or a coincident event. Non-ordinary states of consciousness are also common, states in which you may apprehend something astonishing about the world for the first time, like Natalie Goldberg *really* seeing the cottonwoods and Russian olive outside her classroom window, or Annie penetrated by the chiasmic rising and falling of the lake.

Another way to know if a call is genuine, a way to test it, is to imagine not acting on it and then notice how you feel. Imagine you are going to ignore the call, or even laugh it off. How does that feel? Do you detect a building dread, a huge sadness, a guilt that comes from refusing a sacred invitation?

The other obvious way to test it is to begin to act on it, to move your life toward the call and see if a feeling of rightness grows stronger, above and beyond the background noise of fear, which may also grow. If it is a true call, you'll feel like you are drawing near a promised land or your true home for the first time. The fear will be the sort a child feels when lost or too far from home.

It is natural to experience fear and resistance. It is important to acknowledge your fear, first to yourself and then to at least one person close to you, someone who will not be threatened by your experience and who will not hold you back from your destiny. Describe how the fear feels in your body, what images arise with it, what memories it evokes. As deeply as you can, tell the truth about your fear. Simply acknowledging it out loud to another or in writing goes a long way to summoning the resources you need to meet that fear and to enable you to proceed *despite* it.

Then, to your confidant or journal, describe the call itself in great detail, including where you were, what happened, how your body felt, what emotions you experienced, what symbols you noticed, and the connections you see with other significant life experiences or with myths and archetypes. Telling someone will relieve some of the burden of carrying the experience by yourself. And it will begin to get the experience of the call outside yourself and into the world, where it belongs. It's very difficult to face a storm alone, even if it is your own storm.

There is no need to have an immediate plan as to how you will act on the call, but by sharing it with a trusted confidant, it will help keep the call alive within you. A friend who will not let you betray yourself is a friend indeed.

It is also good to draw or sculpt the images involved in the call, or dance the experience, play it on a musical instrument, give it voice in poetry, or sing, drum, shout, or cry it.

Should you find yourself resisting the call, ask yourself what part of you is creating the resistance. (Of course, it may be more than one part, in which case you have a little extra work to do.) Lie down, get yourself as relaxed as you can, and ask the resisting part to reveal itself in your imagination. Let yourself be surprised by what form it takes. Ask that part what it *really* needs. Tell it you will not take anything away from it, but rather hope to offer it new options.

Through imagery sessions of this kind, develop a relationship with your resistant part. As you learn what it needs and as *it* learns what *you* want (i.e., to get on with your underworld journey), you will find ways of proceeding that allow its deeper needs to be met. Then it will be able to support your journey or even help facilitate it. The resisting part, for example, may need some assurance of safety or protection, in which case you will need to find some other part of you (it is always there) capable of protecting that first part. (If you do not know how to access your deep imagery, find a friend or professional who can help you, or consider the deep imagery resources listed at the end of this book.)

When you are ready to proceed toward your one true life, consult the rest of this book for guidance; you might also seek out a teacher, guide, or elder who understands the spiritual descent and can help you prepare for the journey. Also mobilize your *inner* resources and allies, whether they be angels, archetypes, gods, goddesses, spirits, ancestors, imagery-based animals, or other teachers and guides.

It is essential that you act on the call as soon as you are ready, even in the most general way. The window of opportunity may not remain open long. Look hard at yourself in the mirror and decide whether you will cross the threshold. You are a prospective immigrant, as Adrienne Rich tells us, and you must make a choice between safety and a dangerous passage:

Either you will
go through this door
or you will not go through.

If you go through
there is always the risk
of remembering your name.

Things look at you doubly
and you must look back
and let them happen.

If you do not go through
it is possible
to live worthily

to maintain your attitudes
to hold your position
to die bravely

but much will blind you,
much will evade you,
at what cost who knows?

The door itself
makes no promises.
It is only a door.[7]

Crossing that threshold into your uncharted future is an act of great courage and self-compassion, and it changes your relationship to life in a fundamental way. It embodies your willingness to employ a new form of risk-taking, to consciously choose growth-stimulating, soul-nourishing conflicts, to live through the accompanying anxiety, and to accept your life as open-ended and unpredictable. Passing through that door commits you to living in the present in a way you never before have. Your personal, cultural, or religious past no longer provides you with a map to your future.

Nan, a teacher and homemaker, found herself poised at such a threshold when she was in her mid-forties. She had been an exemplar of her social and religious worlds, doing almost everything as close to perfect as anyone could. She grew up within an insular religious community in the American West that provided opportunities as well as rules for all the approved domains of life. There was no need to question or doubt anything because all the answers were laid out in plain sight for anyone who had been born or adopted into that particular world. As a child and teenager, Nan made excellent grades, attended church, and observed the religious rites and practices of her community. She accepted her place among what was considered the less potent, less spiritual gender. She married a good man and they brought six children into the world — their church called for large families — and taught them the ways of membership. She was active in all the expected church activities. She taught part-time at the local college. She tried to be everything for everybody — and nearly was. She and her family thought of her as "Mother Bear." Her life was full and satisfying.

Except for the fact that it wasn't hers. Although she tried hard to keep all the rules, she couldn't do it perfectly, and this filled her with guilt. From time to time she would "slip" and sneak a prohibited cup of coffee or iced tea. When things got really bad, she would even retrieve the hidden bottle of alcohol from the closet. Painfully aware she was hiding something from her husband, children, and others, she felt like a liar, a fraud, and a failure. She felt more and more like a mere role, less and less like a real person.

When Nan was forty, her father passed away. A good man by most anyone's standards, he had had a hard time keeping all the rules, too. On his deathbed, he was consumed with guilt and shame — and fear of what would become of his soul after death. Watching her beloved father suffer in this way became Nan's knock on the door, the personal crisis that called her to spiritual adventure. She found herself face-to-face with the fact that if the teachings of their church were true, her father was going to be stuck for eternity in a realm a good deal lower than heaven's highest kingdom. Refusing to believe this was just, she began to research their church history. She discovered many doctrines she could not accept. She spoke obliquely about her concerns with her husband and friends, but they told her this was a common element of religious life, a test of her faith in God. The isolation she felt was sometimes overwhelming.

Nan's underworld journey began in earnest a couple years later when her husband, Richard, lost his job and was stripped of his status in the church because of problems that occurred within the church-owned business he managed. It was painfully clear to Nan and her family that Richard had been framed and hung out to dry by senior church officials trying to avoid public recognition of their own culpability.

These events propelled Nan into a dark night of the soul that led to her first wholehearted response to the call to adventure. She confided in a new friend outside the church, a woman she trusted and with whom she felt safe to share her fear, anger, grief, and despair. Going for help outside her religious community was an act of the greatest courage for Nan. Although finally expressing her emotional truth was a huge relief, it felt like walking into the mouth of a whale. Crossing that threshold initiated her underworld journey. (We'll revisit Nan's story in chapter 5.)

THE HERALD

In the mythology of countless cultures, the call — the opening of a destiny — is signaled by the appearance of a herald: a frog, serpent, dragon, or other beast, or an attractive but mysterious man or woman. The herald is often dark, strange, and frightening but also irresistibly fascinating. Such fantastical beings are mythology's way of capturing the enigma and power of the call to adventure.

In our actual lives, the herald takes the form of any number of otherworldly and emotionally profound experiences. We may not encounter a serpent or mysterious individual, but the call is always an experience full of portent.

The herald's appearance is accompanied by enormous feeling. An overpowering mixture of sadness and hope is what awakened me on that Adirondack summit. Nan was ushered across the threshold by grief, fear, and anger provoked by her sense of spiritual betrayal. Annie's awakening, as she stood on the shore of Lake Michigan, was galvanized by wonder and hope. For a man I know, the herald came in the form of a face-to-face encounter with death and with sunlight breaking through cloud.

Tom was a college student in New England in the early eighties. He had been suffering from a yearlong depression that began when his first love broke his heart and continued as he lost all interest in academic education. He could barely get himself up in the morning to go to classes. He began to lose hope.

> I decided I really did not care if I lived or died. As far as I could tell, it was simply the momentum and inertia of my family's expectations that had brought me this far. Being a student was not my life. It was a wish or demand that others had for me. I felt trapped.

One summer day, out of despair, Tom consumed a potentially lethal amount of drugs and alcohol and soon reached the point at which he knew he could simply let go and die. Looking back many years later, he writes:

> *This was the most definitive moment in my life.*
> I had a choice: live or die. What astonished me then was that there was something to actually hold on to, a something that was almost tangible. I

realized in that moment that there was an essence of *me* beyond the compilation of my nerves and tissue. There was a *me* I could hold on to. I could feel my *will*, my *self*, my *soul*. It was as if I was experiencing the essential force at the center of life itself. I knew holding on would be tough—I had taken a lot of drugs and could feel how badly I had abused my body. But I knew I had to hold on.

Tom eventually passed out and slept for nearly two days. He was awakened by a phone call informing him that a close childhood friend had died suddenly in a terrible accident. Tom was devastated.

How could I be so arrogant as to consider ending my life? How could I take life for granted so easily? I still have a deep sense that, somehow, Richard died that night so I could live, *really live*.

These events completely shifted Tom's life. Classes started a few weeks later, but he had no interest in them. One morning in September, he walked out of his apartment and, rather than turn right toward campus, he turned left and ended up at a lake, where he sat and stared off at the mountains across the waters to the west.

I fell into a trance. I became keenly aware of the beauty — the reflection of the mountains in the calm, glassy water; the birds circling and calling; the dramatic gray clouds. I noticed that in one spot the sun was shining through a blue hole. Rays of splintered sunlight struck the high peaks across the lake. I had a sense of being beckoned by that hole. I knew without a doubt I was being called to go through that hole and over the mountains.

Within a few days, Tom was driving west. He had begun his time of wandering. He lived for a time in the Colorado mountains, toured with the Grateful Dead, traveled to Africa. After two years he returned to college. With the benefit of his wandering time, his education became a true adventure that blossomed into a highly creative career as an educator.

Trebbe Johnson's first call from soul was a simple yet life-transforming event that occurred in her mid-twenties. For her, the herald was a flower.

After college, Trebbe, an aspiring writer, worked for a best-selling author in New York City. But having always dreamed of traveling, she quit her job after three years and flew to Europe. Following three months of wandering, she decided she would live for a while in England. She would spend her days writing poetry, reading, and walking the land. Like most young adults, Trebbe didn't know where her life would lead even though she knew she wanted to be a writer. Soon after arriving in England, she, like Tom, had an unexpected vision of nature and light.

> My earliest revelation was in August 1973, the night I moved into an old stone cottage in the Berkshire Downs. In the rampant, overgrown garden outside my window I saw a lily at twilight, still holding the light of the sun, and then, as I watched, I saw the sun drain out of it as night fell over the garden. This vision astonished and shook me in a way that changed my life: I realized that if I had looked out at the garden a moment earlier, I might not have seen the vision of a lily holding sun against the fading light, a moment later and I would have missed seeing that light extinguished. I realized that if only I looked for the miracles in nature, they would appear to me. I haven't stopped looking since.

This singular moment in the life of a young woman was the commencement of her journey of descent that led to her soul work as a successful writer and an inspired guide of wilderness rites.

PATTERNS

Perhaps you have seen the patterns in this chapter's stories. The call to adventure occurs at a moment of major life change: a social or psychological turning point, a move to a different landscape or country, a dark night of the soul, a divorce, the death of a loved one, in the middle of an immense struggle, or at our wits' end. At moments like these the soul recognizes an opportunity to break through our usually well-defended personalities; we are more vulnerable to aggressive acts from inside our psyches and from outside, and — fortunately for us — the soul takes advantage of us. If we can stay awake long enough, we can turn such moments of apparent adversity or uncertainty into the most soulful of advantages, often wresting personal transformation from the brink of disaster.

Another pattern involves nature. The call to adventure arrives by way of a being of outer nature (such as a winter lake, a shaft of sunlight, or a lily illuminated at twilight) and/or a being of inner nature (such as an encounter with death or a vision of autumn fields). There is no requirement that we be in wilderness, or even outside the city or outdoors. Nature is everywhere, and nature and soul are paired twins.

A third pattern is simply this: the call to adventure occurs as if by accident, without warning, at moments when we do not intend it and least expect it.

CHAPTER 4

THE WANDERER AND THE
SECOND COCOON

Not all those who wander are lost.

— J. R. R. Tolkien

Twenty years from now you will be more disappointed by the things that you didn't do than by the ones you did do. So throw off the bowlines. Sail away from the safe harbor. Catch the trade winds in your sails. Explore. Dream. Discover.

— Mark Twain

A good traveler has no fixed plans
and is not intent on arriving.

— Lao Tzu

The call to adventure is the first omen that your life won't work in the way it has before. Now you have a choice: will you descend purposely to the underworld like Inanna or Beowulf, or will you wait to be abducted like Persephone? Or find a way to avoid the journey altogether?

If and when you descend, you could use some assistance. The value of teachers, mentors, and elders cannot be overstated. But inner, spiritual help is available and invaluable as well. An archetype waiting inside you — the Wanderer — can be of the greatest support, comfort, and inspiration.

THE WANDERER

The journeyer in the underworld might be known — in a soul-oriented community — as a candidate for initiation, a seeker, an aspirant, an exile, a pilgrim, a solitary... a Wanderer. This is the time in life when a person is most intensely in search of her deepest self, a self she knows she will not find reflected back to her from within the familiar arenas of her merely human culture. She searches for the seeds of her destiny in the more diverse, wild, and mysterious world of nature. She no longer conforms to nor rebels against society. She chooses a third way. She wanders, beyond the confines of her previous identity.

The Wanderer crosses and recrosses borders in order to find something whose location is unknown and unknowable. She will conclude she has found it not by its location in a certain place or by its matching a prior image, but by how it feels, how it resonates within her upon discovery. She doesn't know where or when or how clues will appear, so she wanders incessantly, both inwardly and outwardly, always looking, imagining, feeling. In her wandering, she makes her own path.

The Wanderer discovers her unique path by perceiving the world with imagination and feeling. She senses what is possible as well as actual. She sees *into* people and places and possibilities, and she cultivates a relationship with the invisible realms as much as with the visible. She is in conversation with the mysteries of the world, on the lookout for signs and omens. She attends especially to the edges, those places where one thing merges with another, where consciousness shifts and opens, where the world becomes something different from what it initially appeared to be.

Of the four windows of knowing (thinking, feeling, imagining, and sensing), imagination is the Wanderer's most potent tool, her way of seeing into the dark, of illuminating the shadows, of digging deeper into soul.[1]

The Wanderer cultivates this ability to see into the dark. She learns to access and retrieve the images waiting for her in her soul, the images she was born to make manifest in the world, that identify her gift to the world.

The Wanderer creatively ventures into the dark depths, like Orpheus looking for Eurydice, to bring back to the dayworld what is yet unknown. The rules and conventions of society are not going to help the Wanderer do her work; new possibilities and patterns must be tapped. She allows her inner vision to take precedence over tradition.

The task that lies before the Wanderer — retrieving her soul — is truly daunting. Although it lies at the very center of herself, her soul is, at the outset of her wandering, something about which she has little or no conscious knowledge. The elders have explained to her that this is an unavoidable feature of being human, that it is in fact part of the rich drama that makes us human, a kind of hide-and-seek with the soul that prepares us for the challenges inherent in our individual destinies. By the time her ego had formed, at age four or five, she, like everyone else, had misplaced the image with which she was born. During childhood, after all, she needed to learn how to become a part of her human community and family with their needs to define her in a more or less limited way. But now, years later, having secured a good place in the village world, she strikes out on her own in search of her lost soul.

My experiences during my teens and twenties are representative of what we — American youth — do in our unconscious attempts, sometimes successful, to wander. In my final two years of high school, I attempted to differentiate my life from mainstream norms by adopting the dress, art, and manner of the sixties' hippie counterculture. I let my hair grow long and wore tie-dye. I bought an electric organ, joined a rock-and-roll band, and traveled to gigs in an old hearse. I papered the walls of my bedroom with black-light posters. My parents, of course, were puzzled and, sometimes, terrified. Each American generation of the twentieth century, in the absence of genuine societal support for wandering, has found one way or another to be different: from flappers and beatniks to punk, grunge, and goth.

But wandering is both different from and more than mere rebellion. I didn't commence to wander in earnest until my first year in college. I experimented with psychedelics, studied Buddhist literature and practiced daily Zen meditation, read and listened to Taoists like Alan Watts and to psychedelic luminaries like Timothy Leary, and studied Tai Chi and martial arts. I bought a motorcycle and roamed with my friends increasingly further from campus.

One college summer, my friend, Mark, and I motorcycled from North Carolina to California and back, encountering exotic places — and even stranger people and social scenes — along the way. We knew we weren't on the road just to see the country, but we could not have told you more at the time about our deeper goals. Experiencing so many unusual people and places, however, was surely instrumental in loosening our attachment to our adolescent identities.

The next fall at college, I took up the daily predawn practice of Kundalini Yoga, exploring both a novel lifestyle and non-ordinary states induced by lengthy sessions of yogic breathing techniques *(pranayama)* and postures *(asanas)*.

Graduate school in Boulder, Colorado, afforded the opportunity to study other realities: sleep and dreams, hypnosis, biofeedback, Tantric Yoga, and the divinatory tools of astrology and the I Ching. I spent my summers either at Naropa Institute (now University) studying Tibetan Buddhism and other spiritual traditions and practices or at Esalen's summer Institute of Consciousness Studies.

There are so many ways to wander, each individual finding ways that personally resonate. For me, technical rock climbing and mountaineering expanded the possibilities of belonging to the world, a sometimes crash course in developing a relationship to the vertical, the seemingly insurmountable questions of balance and rhythm, the limits of strength and finesse, the need to surrender to what is, and the inevitability of crisis and failure.

My early wanderings held intrinsic value, but I can see now they were, in addition, my diverse and wild explorations of outer realms with the hope of uncovering some clues for the inward journey. But, as I have said, in the absence of mature guides, there were only occasional results of any lasting significance.

THE SECOND COCOON

Upon embarking on the downward journey, the Wanderer enters a peculiar and demanding stage of social and spiritual existence. I imagine this stage as a cocoon because during it the individual undergoes a radical metamorphosis — from a life centered in society to a life centered in soul.

Previous to this one, the only transformation so extensive occurs in early childhood. I think of those first four or five years of human life as the first cocoon, or the family cocoon, the time when we make that great sea crossing from the pre-birth realm of spirit to the realm of culture and human consciousness within which we play out our lives. No one *really* knows how a drooling, babbling infant can morph into a storytelling, trick-playing preschooler.

In the second cocoon of life, the transformation we seek is as mysterious and as momentous — from an individual whose goal is to improve his social and/or economic standing to one whose primary motivation is to turn his soul's vision into reality.

In the first cocoon, the family serves as the protective environment for the work of transformation. In the second, the Wanderer requires a much larger space, as big as the world. There can be no predetermined limits to his wandering. The whole world — the wild earth, in particular — forms the boundaries of his cocoon. When he finally emerges, it will be the earth herself who gives birth to him this second time.

But the wild earth is not the only substance with which the Wanderer weaves his cocoon. Other strands might include his solitude, his deepest wounds from childhood, karma from previous lifetimes, his dreams, his mortality, ceremonies, the dark, and his own shadow — all woven together to form an alchemical cauldron of change.

When the caterpillar weaves his silk cocoon, he dies to his previous life and enters a liminal time of being neither earth-crawling worm nor winged flier. Likewise, the Wanderer is neither adolescent nor mature adult; he is betwixt and between. Within their respective cocoons, the caterpillar pupa

(the chrysalis) does not feed and the Wanderer does not draw further susten-
ance from society. Upon emerging from his cocoon, the Wanderer is
reborn — as butterfly, as initiated adult.

This is such a difficult and often lengthy life passage that the second
cocoon can be viewed as a long middle phase of an extended rite of passage
with a separation at the beginning (at the time of the call) and a return at the
end (at the time of soul initiation). For some people or in some cultures,
the second cocoon might be divided into two stages: first, a period of preparation in which the individual continues to live in the general community;
then a period in which he withdraws from all regular contact with everyday
society. In nature-based cultures, the period of exile might last anywhere
from a month to several years and may include components of both solitude and periods of instruction from elders. In our contemporary Western
cultures, in which the journey of descent is not well understood, this exile
may be experienced as a psychosocial banishment, an inability to fit in anywhere, and may last decades or have no definitive ending.

Dorothy Mason, a psychotherapist, was in her second cocoon for fifteen
years. Dorothy was the sixth of seven children in an upper-middle-class,
conservative, Christian family in which girls and women came second. She
married at twenty-three, moving from one dependent situation to another,
family to marriage. She first began to feel "the strength and miracle" of
her own personhood when, at age twenty-seven, she gave natural birth to her
first child. But, living in the shadow of her husband as a housewife and part-
time Head Start teacher, she felt confined by her social and family-based
identity. Within two years,

> my descent began in earnest. Dragged into the underworld, I thrashed
> through the shadow lands, attempting to individuate from the expecta-
> tions of family, society, and other people's visions. It was dangerous terri-
> tory, fraught with an intense fear of death and catastrophe and a terrible
> loneliness. I remember putting our daughter in a stroller and walking
> down the street in the middle of town, saying a silent good-bye to life, not
> knowing at the time this was a metaphor for the transformative work hap-
> pening deep within me, attempting to bring new life.

In the midst of this period of inner dying, Dorothy's signal to enter the second cocoon came in the form of a meeting with a remarkable person who served as her herald and guide.

> Sharon was a quiet, kind, wise woman, deeply connected to spiritual life, and an excellent psychotherapist with a Jungian-based practice in dreamwork. Hearing about her through a chance conversation, I called her and enrolled in a dream group. At the first meeting, sitting on the floor of the living room, I had this deep realization I was going to live. I could breathe again. I entered into therapy with Sharon and plunged headlong into the mystery and wisdom of the unconscious and the guidance of my dreams. I began to teach weaving at home and read extensively in the areas of metaphysics and mystical literature. This led me — in my mid-thirties, when my children were still small — to go back to school for a master's in counseling psychology. It was a choice that came from my soul — urgent, clear, and undeniable. So, when I arrived in the desert at age forty-four for my first vision quest, having traversed my own inner desert for years, I felt courageous and terrified...once again, open and resistant...prepared in my mind and yet utterly unprepared for the full impact the experience would have on my life and world.

Dorothy, now in her mid-fifties, is a highly skilled psychotherapist, ceremonialist, dreamworker, weaver, vision quest guide, and trainer of guides. We will come back to her soul story in a later chapter.

As her time in the second cocoon gets underway, the Wanderer must move beyond her psychological dependence upon others and upon her social roles. She will no longer adopt, in whole or part, other people's identities or ways of belonging to the world. She will no longer sacrifice her one true life in order to make herself and others comfortable. She knows what she has to do. She must leave her old home and step out into the wild night of her life.

STRIDING DEEPER INTO THE WORLD

One day you finally knew
what you had to do, and began,
though the voices around you
kept shouting

their bad advice—
though the whole house
began to tremble
and you felt the old tug
at your ankles.
"Mend my life!"
each voice cried.
But you didn't stop.
You knew what you had to do,
though the wind pried
with its stiff fingers
at the very foundations,
though their melancholy
was terrible.
It was already late
enough, and a wild night,
and the road full of fallen
branches and stones.
But little by little,
as you left their voices behind,
the stars began to burn
through the sheets of clouds,
and there was a new voice
which you slowly
recognized as your own,
that kept you company
as you strode deeper and deeper
into the world,
determined to do
the only thing you could do—
determined to save
the only life you could save.

— Mary Oliver[2]

The Wanderer seeks to discover her unique and authentic place in life. Not just any place will do. Her authentic place is not simply one that some- one will pay her to occupy (like a job), nor a task she happens to have the talent to perform (like an art or a craft), nor a career a vocational counselor rec- ommends for her (like banking or social work), nor a social role (like caregiver, student, parent, servant, leader, whore, or rebel) in which other people will accept her. It's got to be *her* place, one in keeping with her vital core. It is a place defined not by the deeds she performs, but by the qualities of soul she embodies; not by her physical, social, or economic achievements, but by the true character she manifests; neither by her capacity to conform to the masses nor by her ability to creatively rebel against the mainstream, but by the unique way she performs her giveaway for her community.

The Wanderer must go off in search of the one life she can call her own. Joseph Campbell reminds us:

> The differentiations of sex, age, and occupation are not essential to our character, but mere costumes which we wear for a time on the stage of the world. The image of man within is not to be confounded with the garments. We think of ourselves as Americans, children of the twentieth century, Occidentals, civilized Christians. We are virtuous or sinful. Yet such designations do not tell what it is to be a man, they denote only the accidents of geography, birth-date, and income. What is the core of us? What is the basic character of our being?[3]

Mary Oliver suggests that, in Western society at least, when a person finally goes off in search of her core, it is, psychologically, "already late" in her life and it does not happen in a quiet, sunlit, or easy moment, but rather in the middle of a "wild night," when there is darkness and chaos all about. At times like these, her greatest need is for the company of her own true voice, yet she is not likely to hear that voice until she has progressed some distance down the road. She must leap into the night with blind faith or not at all.

In Oliver's poem, the journeyer is "determined to save/the only life [she] could save." This is not a recommendation for selfishness. The journeyer identifies this savable life only by "[striding] deeper and deeper into the world," and in so doing, she finds the place in which her life and the life of the world are one; she finds the place where, as Frederick Buechner says, "our deepest gladness and the world's hunger meet." The life she saves is what Campbell calls "the core of us... the basic character of our being," which leads to a life of joyful service to the world. This salvation is an act of love, love of both self and world.

As terrifying as it is to leave home, as much as the old wounded and wounding voices of childhood keep pleading with us not to go, there comes the time when we hear the call, open the door, and step out.

WHAT THE BUTTERFLY KNOWS

Soul-oriented and nature-based societies do not leave the commencement of the wandering time to accident. They provide carefully designed ceremonial opportunities — cocoons — for those who are properly prepared. The Australian aborigines, for example, embark on a walkabout as a component of their preparation for adulthood. During his walkabout, the aboriginal youth wanders into the bush alone for several weeks or months, avoiding the company and conversation of other humans. He goes in search of the one place where he belongs, a place that's part of him and where he is part of that place. In finding that place, he finds himself.

Contemporary author and anthropologist Angeles Arriens grew up in the Basque culture of the Pyrenees Mountains along the French-Spanish border. For Basque children raised in the traditional way, there are several stages of cultural and spiritual training in childhood and early adolescence. At age sixteen, some Basque youth undertake a yearlong solo "earth walk," an extended period of wandering. From age fourteen to sixteen, the initiates undergo intensive preparation in all aspects of survival, from the physical to the emotional and spiritual, culminating in the earth walk for those who choose this ordeal of solitude and wandering. If a youth elects to go, as Angeles did, she carries with her a blanket or shawl, woven by her mother, containing 365 warp threads. The Wanderer pulls out one warp thread each day, thereby keeping track of the temporal expanse of her journey as she walks a remote trail from one end of the Pyrenees to the other.

The wandering time is neither easy nor painless. It tests what you are made of. It reveals you to yourself, down to your very marrow. The second cocoon will result in the disintegration of almost everything you know about yourself and the world. The butterfly, of course, understands this.

There are three phases to the butterfly's life cycle: the larva (caterpillar), the pupa or chrysalis (in the cocoon), and the imago (a mature adult, a butterfly). The transformational chrysalis phase is one of the great mysteries of biology. No one knows exactly how the caterpillar changes form in such a dramatic way. But this much is known: inside the caterpillar's body are clusters of cells called, of all things, imaginal buds. *Imaginal* refers to the imago, the adult phase, but it also means "to imagine," and psychologists use the word *imago* to mean an idealized image of a loved one, including the self. The imaginal buds contain the idealized image, the blueprint, for growing a butterfly. While the caterpillar goes about its earth-crawling business, these cells, deep inside, are imagining flight.

The caterpillar's immune system believes these imaginal cells are foreign and tries to destroy them, not unlike the way uninitiated human egos and their egocentric cultures often try to destroy the soul, nature, and the feminine. It's as if the caterpillar doesn't realize its destiny is to become a butterfly. Likewise, the uninitiated ego doesn't realize its destiny is to become an agent for soul. (It's no coincidence the Greek word for butterfly means "soul.") Once in the cocoon, the buds link up, the caterpillar's immune system breaks down, and its body literally disintegrates. The buds then build a butterfly from the fluid contents of the cocoon.

The caterpillar and butterfly are not really opposed to each other; the butterfly is not an alien organism within the caterpillar. They are, in fact, one and the same organism with the same genetic code. The caterpillar is to the butterfly as an uninitiated ego is to an initiated one. The imaginal buds are to the caterpillar as the soul is to the uninitiated ego.

Inside the second cocoon, you come to understand what the butterfly knows: upon forming your cocoon, you prepare to die in order for something new to be born — and to take flight.

Once wrapped inside the cocoon, you have abandoned your previous life. Only empty branches and sky remain, as in winter when the creative life of the land has gone underground. Relative to the busy surface life of society, this is a fallow time, a time of waiting for spring. It is a time to be modest, as Rilke writes, "like a thing ripened until it is real," until you are prepared to directly encounter your soul at that moment when the Other reaches for you.

CHAPTER 5

THE DARKNESS SHALL
BE THE LIGHT

Practices for Leaving Home

I said to my soul, be still, and wait without hope
For hope would be hope for the wrong thing; wait without love
For love would be love of the wrong thing; there is yet faith
But the faith and the love and the hope are all in the waiting.
Wait without thought, for you are not ready for thought:
So the darkness shall be the light, and the stillness the dancing.
Whisper of running streams, and winter lightning.
The wild thyme unseen and the wild strawberry,
The laughter in the garden, echoed ecstasy
Not lost, but requiring, pointing to the agony
Of death and birth.

— T. S. Eliot

As a Wanderer, an apprentice to the unknown, you long to be initiated into the fully embodied life of your soul. You will have to wait. The fallow time of the second cocoon, the time between death and rebirth, cannot be dodged. To catch up to your soul, you will have to learn, as T. S. Eliot did, to place your faith and love and hope in the waiting.

But you will be anything but idle. Two essential tasks must be addressed: saying good-bye to the old and making yourself ready for the new. More specifically, you must first leave the home of your former identity, and then prepare yourself for soul initiation. This chapter explores several soulcraft practices that support the first of these tasks, leaving home. As you leave your old way of belonging to the world, you enter a rich spiritual darkness that will serve, for the time being, as your "light" as you move forward by way of descent.

There are two subtasks involved in truly leaving home: honing your skills of self-reliance, and relinquishing attachment to your former identity.

HONING THE SKILLS OF SELF-RELIANCE

As with the doorways of death and birth, you journey alone through strange and unfamiliar realms on your way to a soulful or second adulthood. You must learn to conduct yourself boldly and to make difficult and critical choices without the comforting presence of a life partner, guide, or teacher at your side. You must sharpen your skills of physical, social, psychological, and spiritual self-reliance. There are some skills you are undoubtedly lacking and that you'll soon need if you are going to truly wander, skills that may never have been necessary if you had planned on "staying home" your whole life.

For example, if your wandering will take you into wilderness lands or foreign cultures, you will need certain practical skills. You will need the ability to get around safely and efficiently in exotic terrain and extreme weather, to locate yourself when you get lost (or learn to relax and *enjoy* being lost), to acquire necessary goods and services, and to negotiate the language and customs of different peoples.

But even more important are psychological and spiritual skills. You must be proficient at making friends and allies, defending yourself against enemies, and resolving conflicts. You will need to know what to do when you lose heart, when you feel more deeply than you thought possible, when you want to run, when you need to let go of what is dear to you but holds you back, when you get stuck, when you suddenly break through. You must become conversant with the paradoxes and mysteries of your gender and sexuality. You might need to know how to pray and to whom or what to pray, how to obtain help from spiritual allies, and how to access strength and courage during times of danger or difficulty or in the absence of faith.

How will you acquire these skills? You will learn from mentors and peers, from books and courses, but mostly you will learn through experience, through trial and error. You will learn by courageously choosing new experiences with unfamiliar places, people, activities, and relationships. When you run into trouble, you will seek counsel and instruction from friends, teachers, and your own inner guides and resources.

I first met Liz Faller when, with bright scarves and blonde hair flowing, she literally danced into the room where I sat, her intense blue eyes laughing. An accomplished dance teacher, ceremonialist, and healer, Liz has been called many times into the underworld, this being an element of her particular destiny.

One day in her late thirties, while sitting in meditation, her inner guide, Laughing Man, appeared, telling Liz that now was the time for her long-awaited journey to Africa. A half hour later, her African dance instructor phoned to say a master teacher of their acquaintance was taking a dance group to study in West Africa — would she like to go? (Sometimes the call comes by phone.) She put her everyday life on hold, including her busy hypnotherapy practice, and left for three months. Some of that time she traveled alone through outlying regions of the African continent, relying on inner guidance. Laughing Man — an African trickster, Liz notes — was always with her and always laughing.

One day I was on a ferry to the Casamance region of Senegal, which is known for its outback world of magic, spirit, and voodoo. It can be a dangerous place for foreigners. When the ferry landed, I had no idea where I would go. I prayed for a guide to appear. I went out on the deck and started stretching. A friendly young man appeared and inquired about my stretching. He spoke to me in English, a rare language in this area. I immediately knew I could trust him. I told him I wanted to go to a village where I would be safe and could dance. He offered to take me to his village, where dancing was frequent and there were many festivals. When I arrived in his compound, a small woman came running toward me with open arms, crying, "My baby, my baby!" and scooped me in her arms. Over the next few weeks, she cradled me on several occasions. Instinctively she seemed to know I had not received all the cradling I longed for and she was going to make up for it. She did. She became my African mama. We communicated mostly through nonlinguistic sounds. Our favorite was "yoo hoo." Mama Sira seemed to know only two English words — "baby" and "eat." Her eldest son, Keita, appeared one day, laughing. He never quit laughing. Here was my Laughing Man! Keita, a medicine man in the village, gave me cowrie-shell readings, made me protective pouches, and did rituals outside my door every morning and evening to protect me. My young guide, Sam, became my interpreter. When I left for Ghana, Keita sent me off with a protective pouch and said, "You are not leaving us, for you live in our hearts and will always be with us." These parting words have offered me great solace. This tribe was the Djole people.

This is a fine example of what can happen when we say yes to the call to adventure and wander into unfamiliar domains. Liz's account also enriches our understanding of the range of skills involved in self-reliance. Her journey may have turned out quite differently had she not known how to use and trust her intuition about people and places. She also had the ability to pray, to play, to ask for help from inner guides, and to access inner sources of courage.

We may or may not travel outwardly as Liz did, or as grandly, but we will always be traveling inwardly when we wander into the unknown precincts of our lives. At such times, we must rely on our own resources, no matter how foreign or unprecedented the circumstances.

Greg, a successful health care professional, had a satisfying life but knew he could offer himself more imaginatively to the world. Writing fiction had been his primary creative outlet, but for several years he had rarely been inspired to write. In his desk drawer sat a stack of mostly unfinished short stories and the beginnings of a novel. He began to doubt he had anything original to say.

One day Greg had a sudden recognition of what he needed to do. Waves of grief and fear shook his body like a fever. He went to his study and pulled every page from his desk, lit a fire in his woodstove, and burned them all. Then he deleted every associated computer file. As if appeasing a god, he made a sacrifice of all his creations, somehow recognizing this to be a necessary step toward authentic expression.

Then he opened the door of his house and went for a run, leaving behind his dreams of being a writer. An odd mixture of feelings overtook him — grief, blithe disbelief in what he had done... and relief. He ran.

Three miles down the road, without warning or desire, out of nowhere, the first line of a story came to him, descended upon him in a voice he had never before heard — or read. Just the first line, in a voice so clear and fresh it stopped him alive in his tracks, mouth agape, arms hanging at his sides, eyes staring into the distance where the road disappeared over a rise.

In the midst of emptiness, a new freedom found him, a radical opportunity to reenter his life. He stood at the threshold of a creative self-reliance opening into unexplored terrain. The next day, he began to write with his own voice, relying upon his own depths.

This is precisely the sort of courage and action required of the Wanderer: to sacrifice his dependence upon old forms and routines derived from other hearts and minds, to learn to rely on a deeper identity.

THE SURVIVAL DANCE AND THE SACRED DANCE

Harley Swift Deer, a Native American teacher, says that each of us has a *survival dance* and a *sacred dance*, but the survival dance must come first. Our survival dance, a foundational component of self-reliance, is what we do for a living — our way of supporting ourselves physically and economically. For most people, this means a paid job. For members of a religious community like a monastery, it means social or spiritual labors that contribute to the community's well-being. For others, it means creating a home and raising children, finding a patron for one's art, or living as a hunter or gatherer. Everybody has to have a survival dance. Finding or creating one is our first task upon leaving our parents' or guardians' home.

Once you have your survival dance established, you can wander, inwardly and outwardly, searching for clues to your *sacred* dance, the work you were born to do. This work may have no relation to your job. Your sacred dance sparks your greatest fulfillment and extends your truest service to others. You know you've found it when there's little else you'd rather be doing. Getting paid for it is superfluous. You would gladly pay others, if necessary, for the opportunity.

Hence, the importance of self-reliance, not merely of the economic kind implied by a survival dance but also of the social, psychological, and spiritual kinds. To find your sacred dance, after all, you will need to take significant risks. You might need to move against the grain of your family and friends. By honing psychological self-reliance, you will find it easier to keep focused on your goals in the face of resistance or incomprehension, initial failure or setbacks, or economic or organizational obstacles. And spiritual self-reliance will maintain your connection with deepest truths and what you've learned about how the world works.

Swift Deer says that once you discover your sacred dance and learn effective ways of embodying it, the world will support you in doing just that. What your soul wants is what the world also wants (and needs). Your human community will say yes to your soul work and will, in effect, pay you to do it. Gradually, your sacred dance becomes what you do and your former survival dance is no longer needed. Now you have only one dance as the world supports you to do what is most fulfilling for you. How do you get there? The first step is creating a foundation for self-reliance: a survival dance of integrity that allows you to be in the world in a good way — a way that is psychologically sustaining, economically adequate, socially responsible, and environmentally sound. Cultivating right livelihood, as Buddhists call it, is essential training and foundation for your soul work; it's not a step that can be skipped.

RELINQUISHING ATTACHMENT TO YOUR FORMER IDENTITY

Leaving home means divesting the provisional identity you developed in adolescence and have been refining (or not) ever since. Regardless of your age, if you have not yet embarked upon the underworld journey, you are still operating from that adolescent identity and its social roles, no matter how polished they may have become. An adolescent or first-adulthood identity is *primarily* focused upon social standing, psychological security, interpersonal and physical comfort, wealth, fame, and/or the sort of personal power that is *power over* rather than *power with*. A soul-rooted identity, in contrast, is primarily focused upon the discovery of and joyous offering of the gift of soul to the world.

The Wanderer's separation from her adolescent identity is a gradual and challenging process that will not be complete until the time of her soul initiation. During the second cocoon, the Wanderer adopts several practices that loosen her hold on her current way of belonging to the world. The particular set of these practices varies from one cultural context to another, but there are certain common themes that can be expected. What follows are seven examples of practices that support the Wanderer's separation from her former identity.

COMPLETING UNFINISHED BUSINESS FROM EARLIER LIFE STAGES

There is always some remedial work in the second cocoon. No matter how wholesome your childhood and teen years, no matter how loving were your parents and teachers, no matter how much you avoided the major traumas of this human life, there are going to be some spotty areas in your earlier development. There will be some aspects of ego growth — which is the foundation of your soul path — that were neglected or glossed over. Now, in the second cocoon, there's both time and need for some catch-up.

You are never done, of course, with the tasks of ego growth. It's a lifelong project. Every personality is an unfolding story, never a completed product. Upon reaching a new plateau of development, additional material will appear for you to work on. What is important in the second cocoon, especially at its beginning, is to complete those pieces of old business that otherwise would keep you imprisoned in your former identity.

Unfinished business arises in relation to the developmental tasks of the life stages that precede the second cocoon.[1] For example, the cultivation of emotional skills is an essential task of early adolescence. Your success in later developmental stages depends, in part, upon your emotional foundation. Do you know how to fully experience, understand, express, *and* act on your emotions? In a way that respects both yourself and others? If you have difficulties with any aspects of emotional competence, it would be wise to seek guidance or mentoring through psychotherapy, support groups, relevant workshops, or an emotionally mature friend or family member.

Another example, a task normally completed in a healthy middle childhood, is discovering the enchantment of the natural world and experiencing your full membership in it. Do you need to become more grounded in your relationship to the wild world? If, when you are in nature, you don't experience deep comfort, endless wonder, and an empathic resonance with the natural world, then consider field courses in natural history, guided wilderness journeys, or simply extended time outdoors in undomesticated settings.

Your own body is also, of course, an aspect of nature, and it is essential to be comfortable in your body, appreciative of it, and competent in caring for it. If you need to improve your relationship to your body, consider courses or coaching in yoga, tai chi, sports, dance, herbology, or nutrition; the services of health care practitioners; or sessions of massage, other bodywork disciplines, or body-centered psychotherapy.

The wilderness of your imagination is another essential dimension of your own human nature. If you don't enjoy a robust relationship with the imaginal, especially your deep imagination — your dreams, deep imagery, and visionary capacities — consider courses in dreamwork, imagery journeys, art, dance, music, or creative writing.

Maybe your listening or conflict-resolution skills require some polishing. If so, consider relevant workshops, men's and women's groups, or relationship practices focused upon empathy and communication.

Whatever your weak points are in these areas, this stage of the journey is the best time to fill in the gaps that may otherwise hold you back from — or compromise the quality of — your underworld work.

Cheryl once had almost everything we are supposed to want in mainstream American life. In her thirties, she was married to a good man, lived on a small ranch in the West, had a fulfilling job as a school administrator, enjoyed an active social life, and spent much of her free time in creative pursuits, including her greatest joy since childhood — riding and training horses. Then, in midlife, she saw, over a period of a year or two, that as good as her life was on the outside, it was not fulfilling. She had never really left home; she had never learned to develop a deep relationship with her emotions or dreams, other humans, or nature. To address her unfinished business, Cheryl entered psychotherapy, began reading books on psychological and interpersonal development, and started to spend more time in nature. She learned to use a journal for self-discovery and dream recording.

But more was being asked of Cheryl. She needed to go out into the world in a way she had not before. In order to complete tasks from earlier life stages, she needed to learn to rely more radically on herself, on inner resources she could only hope would appear and be sufficient in times of personal chaos. Over the course of a year, she walked out the door of her old life.

Without a specific plan and taking it one step at a time, she separated from her husband (amicably and compassionately), with whom she had little in common, moved into a small apartment in town, ended several not entirely genuine friendships, and, finally, with the greatest remorse, made a commitment to give away her horses (she could never sell them). As she completed each step, she believed it would be the last one.

But there *was* more. She took a lower paying but more rewarding job as a teacher, made new friends, deepened her work in psychotherapy, and began spending more time alone in nature. She learned to befriend her most frightening feelings and images. She learned to trust her intuition again, to listen to her dreams, and to draw on her inner strength and courage. These changes led to many shifts in Cheryl's experience:

> I now know, without doubt, my life has meaning and is supported by more unseen forces than I can imagine. I have learned to trust a greater wisdom than my own. I am making decisions based on my own values, and willing to face the consequences. I am not afraid to tell people I love them or that they make me happy or that I need them.

GIVING UP ADDICTIONS

Associated with remedial work are those inner places too painful to look into, the places you "successfully" avoided: the losses, the shame, the fears, the guilt, the wounds. You didn't merely overlook those places; the emotions and memories living there had surely been screaming loud enough. Perhaps you avoided those nightmare closets by numbing yourself through addictions.

In the worst cases, these addictions are chemical, creating a primary neurological impairment of your capacity to feel as well as a secondary behavioral impairment — by altering what you attend to (or ignore) and how you spend your time.[2] But there are many other addictions (such as food, impersonal sex, TV, gambling, work) that can effectively cut you off — through distraction and deadening — from your full range of feeling, sensing, remembering, and imagining.

In the second cocoon, as you prepare for the encounter with soul, you will have to leave behind any substances or activities employed to avoid the tender places inside. And you will have to replace them with positive habits of presence and self-encounter. This can be an arduous and formidable task — addictions can be exceedingly difficult to kick. People with substance addictions especially will need help — from friends and family, psychotherapy, twelve-step and other recovery programs, acupuncture, and/or other mainstream and alternative health care approaches.

Television ranks high among the common addictions in our society, along with other "screen" obsessions: the Internet, palm pilots, and videos. We've all read the statistics about how many hours per day the average American watches TV.

Giving up television is an excellent way to start moving beyond addictions (this does not apply to people with *substance* addictions, who *must* start there). To people who watch more than a few hours a week, I recommend they literally remove the TV from their home. The reaction is predictable and, in some cases, extreme. While most people seem a bit embarrassed but agree with me, others declare I must be absolutely out of my mind. They launch into a rehearsed defense of the "quality programming" found amidst all the trash. These are the addicts. Others say their kids or spouse would never allow it. These are the codependents — the enablers of their family members' addictions. I've heard as many "good reasons" for regular TV watching as any alcoholic has ever rationalized to keep drinking. The people who say they'll never go without TV are the same ones who routinely protest there are simply not enough hours in the day to give serious attention to intimate relationships or spiritual practice or soul discovery. During the three to eight hours a day they are sitting in front of a screen, they probably genuinely believe this to be true.

The fact that TV (or compulsive shopping, eating, sex, or gambling) can be so addictive suggests how profoundly difficult it can be to kick the more destructive habits of drug or alcohol abuse. Before enrolling in any soulcraft program, I recommend to substance addicts a minimum of one month of abstinence (along with therapy and/or a twelve-step group). It's simply not possible to open to the mysteries of the inner or outer worlds when you are numbed out and/or craving your next fix.

Many have participated in soulcraft programs within a year of establishing a stable recovery. Their experience in the wilderness often empowers them to take the next step, a very big one: from simple abstinence to the beginnings of a deep emotional healing process and entrance into the second cocoon.

There are many varieties of addiction, but, sooner or later, we each have to address what is the paramount addiction in the Western world: our psychological dependence on the worldview and lifestyle of Western civilization itself. This is the point brilliantly made by eco-psychologist Chellis Glendinning in her book *My Name Is Chellis, and I'm in Recovery from Western Civilization.*[3] The Western worldview says, in essence, that technological progress is the highest value and that we were born to consume, to endlessly use and discard natural resources, other species, technological gadgets, toys, and, often, other people, especially if they are poor or from the Third World. The most highly prized freedom is the right to shop. It's a world of commodities, not entities, and economic expansion is the primary measure of progress. Competition, taking, and hoarding are higher values than cooperation, sharing, and gifting. Profits are valued over people, money over meaning, First-World entitlement over global peace and justice, "us" over "them." This addiction is the most dangerous one in the world, not only because of its impact on most of humanity but because it is rapidly undermining the natural systems that sustain the earth's biosphere.

All other addictions in the West can be seen as components of this larger one. If we are born to consume, then it *is* a dog-eat-dog world, there *is* no deeper meaning, no human soul, and creation is just a huge, dumb joke. That's a conclusion you wouldn't want to live with every day; better to distract and deaden yourself with addictions.

By the time we reach our first adulthood, our ways of thinking about ourselves and the world have been molded and constrained by the predominant values of Western culture. This limits us in ways difficult to see at first; we are like fish in the sea, unconscious of the cultural waters within which we have come of age.[4]

All children and adolescents fashion personalities that fit within their native culture. In the West, that means a society largely materialistic, synthetic, technological, anthropocentric, ethnocentric, and egocentric. Fitting in with such a culture is difficult to accomplish without losing contact with our souls and with nature, the web of life. Western lifestyles that revolve around a constant barrage of anemic distractions may be, in part, ways of self-numbing so as to minimize the pain of that loss. Many people have succumbed to daily routines of soul-starving entertainment, superficial fashion, and mind-numbing jobs.

This way of life becomes an addiction. The more we live this way, the more alienated we become from something deeper and more meaningful, and the more we need this way of life to keep us from *experiencing* that alienation.

How do you address an addiction this pervasive? Begin with the soul-craft practices found in these pages. Relinquishing attachment to the adolescent identity is a primary means of overcoming our dependence on the cultural worldview within which that identity was formed.

WELCOMING HOME THE LOYAL SOLDIER

To loosen your attachment to your less mature identity, you will have to alter your relationship to the sub-personality that is naturally most resistant to such a thing. Sub-personalities are constellations of behavior, feelings, and thought within the psyche that function more or less independently. The sub-personality in question here, the Loyal Soldier, formed when you were very young.[5] Its mission was to develop and deploy whatever strategies were necessary to assure your social, psychological, and physical survival. A Loyal Soldier is a fortunate ally indeed in childhood.

The image of the Loyal Soldier derives from a World War II epilogue. Hundreds of Japanese marines and soldiers who survived shipwrecks or plane crashes in the Pacific found themselves stranded, alone or in small groups, on uninhabited or sparsely settled islands. Some of them managed to endure despite extreme conditions and severe social-cultural isolation.

Several of these soldiers were discovered many years after the war had ended — one of them thirty-five years later! The most astonishing thing is that, when found, these men exhibited an extraordinary, perhaps fanatical, loyalty to their military mission. Unaware the war had ended, each one, upon being found, was ready to immediately return to the war effort. They were told, of course, the war was over (and that Japan had lost). But this was literally unthinkable to them: the war could not be over because their loyalty to the cause was what had kept them alive all those years.

The rescued soldiers were welcomed home in Japan with great honor and celebration despite their stubborn belief in the discredited cause of military empire building. The Japanese people deeply respected the soldiers' capacity to sacrifice their personal agenda for a greater cause. Their sustained welcome as heroes eventually enabled the soldiers to reinvent themselves and to productively rejoin society.

Each of us has a Loyal Soldier sub-personality, a courageous, creative, and stubborn entity formed when we needed somewhat drastic measures to survive the realities (sometimes dysfunctional) of childhood. This subpersonality's primary task was to minimize the occurrence of further injury, whether emotional or physical. The Loyal Soldier's approach to this task was — *and continues to be* — to make us small or invisible, to suppress much of our natural exuberance, emotions, desires, and wildness so we might be sufficiently acceptable to our parents (and/or other guardians, siblings, teachers, and authority figures). The Loyal Soldier learns to restrain another sub-personality we might call the Wild Child, our original sensual, magical, untamed self that has an essential relationship to the soul and is not interested in limiting itself in any way.

Common Loyal Soldier survival strategies include harsh self-criticism (to make us — the ego — feel unworthy and thus ineligible for Wild Child actions that might bring further punishment, abandonment, or criticism); placing our personal agenda last (so as to not displease or arouse anger or envy); other codependent behaviors (e.g., caretaking, rescuing, enabling) to stave off abandonment; pleasing but immature and inauthentic personas; partial or complete social withdrawal (to minimize hurtful contacts); adopting an unpleasant or downtrodden appearance (to protect us from criticism); restricting our range of feeling by encouraging us to always be in charge, busy, angry, ruthless, withdrawn, and/or numb; and suppressing our intelligence, talent, enthusiasm, sensuality, and wildness by locking up these qualities in an inaccessible corner of our psyches. In each case, these strategies keep us safe by splitting off or blocking much of our potential and our magnificence. The Loyal Soldier's adamant and accurate understanding is this: it is better to be suppressed or inauthentic or small than socially isolated or emotionally crushed — or dead.

The Loyal Soldier *did,* in fact, keep us safe (enough) in childhood. The problem is that the Loyal Soldier's strategies become bedrock to our survival and are defended to the death — even after the war is over. A superstitious belief system develops. The Loyal Soldier becomes convinced, outside of our ego's awareness, that these particular strategies are absolutely and eternally necessary to protect a third sub-personality, our Wounded Child, our emotional, sensual, playful, and vulnerable part. The Loyal Soldier's fear of the interpersonal horrors that would result from fully embodying our Wild Child keeps us attached to our former identity. The Loyal Soldier does not and cannot believe the war of childhood survival is over. He may even intentionally provoke new battles just to prove his point.

Meanwhile, our childhood survival strategies prevent us from establishing more mature relationships, finding or expressing our wholeheartedness and our untapped potentials, or loosening our attachment to our adolescent identities. The Loyal Soldier's atavistic methods form the core of our most neurotic patterns, those feeding our low self-esteem and our difficulties with intimacy. And these strategies are deployed on automatic pilot. Launched outside our awareness, they often make us feel victimized.

The strategies the Loyal Soldier uses to protect us from early childhood wounds become, however, more an obstacle to our growth than the original wounds themselves.

The Loyal Soldier's strategies are not just difficult to stop; they're even hard to detect. Keep in mind your Loyal Soldier was born around age two or three, before your ego developed. Having formed outside your conscious awareness, he continues to operate without your consent. His job from the start has been to emotionally and physically protect your Wounded Child, and he has. He doesn't see any reason to stop and you can't convince him otherwise.

So what to do? It's neither possible nor advisable to suppress him or get rid of him! Instead, use the successful approach the Japanese people took with *their* loyal soldiers: They (1) loved them and welcomed them home as heroes; (2) thanked them a thousand times, deeply and sincerely, for their loyalty, courage, and service; (3) told them, gently, over and over again, that the war was over; and (4) when they were ready, helped them find new societal roles for employing their considerable talents.

These are the best steps to take with your own Loyal Soldier. First, determine if in fact the war is over. It's over only when you are no longer an emotionally abandoned child (of any age) in a dysfunctional family, psychologically fending for yourself without the support of loved ones or your own psychospiritual resources. Once the war has ended and you surrender the old protective strategies, then the worst case scenario, should you be criticized or abandoned for being authentic, is emotional hurt, possibly great hurt; but by no means will you be emotionally destroyed or permanently damaged, as you might have been in childhood without your Loyal Soldier. You now have a great variety of resources, both inner and outer. You possess emotional and social skills enabling you to take care of yourself in the face of criticism or rejection. You have healthy friendships to support you in difficult times. When not limited by the old strategies, you know how to generate safety, intimacy, and belonging. (If, on the other hand, you still *do* require the Loyal Soldier's old strategies, then the war is *not* over and you need a different kind of help — psychotherapy, for example, to assist you in cultivating internal and external sources of psychological support.)

When you recognize an occurrence of any one of your old defensive patterns, which you probably employ many times a day, first remember this is a method by which your esteemed Loyal Soldier successfully protected your Wounded Child when you were very young. Instead of berating him or yourself, lovingly thank him for the intention and skill behind that old strategy and the fact that it worked. Welcome him home as the hero he is. Then, employing the powers of your imagination and emotion, gaze inside yourself and tell your Loyal Soldier, on each such occasion, *the war is over*. Gently whisper it in his ear. Again.

By taking these steps, you will be developing a fourth sub-personality — call it the Nurturing Parent — who can help your Loyal Soldier relax and who can encourage both your Wounded Child and your Wild Child to emerge from the protective shadows. The Nurturing Parent is your inner resource, unavailable in childhood but now able to wholeheartedly protect your Wounded Child and allow your Wild Child's expression of emotion, sensuality, and creative chaos — something the Loyal Soldier could never have done.

It helps immensely if your Nurturing Parent can be specific with your Loyal Soldier about the *exact* war conditions of your childhood and why you are no longer subject to them. Patiently describe the specific emotional conditions, your family relationships, and the emotional wounds endured. Then identify for him, specifically and in detail, the resources for loving and for engendering love you now possess. Do these things *each* time your childhood survival strategies show up, as they will for some time. After many months of welcoming home your Loyal Soldier and loving him in this way, you will one day be able to reassign him to a soul-aligned task and thereby preserve his skills in a healthy way, integrating those substantial abilities into your conscious life.

When transforming our relationship to our Loyal Soldier, it helps to have an image of him. For most people, this image is visual, but it can also be aural (his voice), affective (feeling his emotional presence inside you), kinesthetic (how he feels physically embodied within you, or the gestures or movements he makes), or any combination of these. Many people discover their Loyal Soldier image either through self- or other-guided deep imagery work or through dreamwork (both discussed in chapter 7). Once you uncover the way your imagination wants to represent your Loyal Soldier, it's that much easier to develop your relationship with him and bring him home as a hero.

Joseph, a psychotherapy client in his forties, brought the following dream to one of his sessions:

> I am strolling with a companion across the lawns of a college campus. There are other people standing or strolling alone, in pairs, and in small groupings. My companion is George W. Bush and we are there attending some sort of conference. In the dream, George and I are peers. Suddenly a bull elk runs into the area. It seems confused and alarmed. George and several others surround the elk and shoot him. The elk collapses. I look on from a distance, shocked and saddened.

Joseph's unconscious — his dream maker — could not have chosen an image more fitting than George Bush for Joseph's Loyal Soldier. In his waking life, Joseph thinks of Bush as immature, a foe to the natural world and to societal well-being, and dangerously naive. Joseph, like many of us, would have said (at first) exactly these things about his own Loyal Soldier who had been severely limiting Joseph's self-expression since childhood. The dream George, who murders the elk, is clearly an enemy of the wild and of the mature masculine.

Likewise, Joseph's Loyal Soldier had been a lifelong enemy of Joseph's wildness and his mature masculinity. Joseph had grown up with an emotionally distant and ineffectual father. His mother mistrusted men, her husband in particular, and saw her parental job with Joseph to be one of "housebreaking" him. His one sibling, an older sister, also accepted this task of constraining little Joseph's male wildness. Joseph's Wild Child was unwanted by his family from the start. His Loyal Soldier protected little Joseph from even worse emotional trauma and abandonment by limiting his wild or manly behavior. In effect, the Loyal Soldier's job was to kill the bull elk. Given his family dynamics, this was best for Joseph *when he was a child*. The problem was that now, in adulthood, Joseph's Loyal Soldier was still, every day, killing the elk. To continue growing, Joseph needed to revive the elk and integrate its masculine wildness into his conscious personality.

Following this dream, Joseph accepted the therapeutic task of regularly thanking his Loyal Soldier (in the imaginal form of George Bush) for all his years of trustworthy work in keeping him safe. Joseph's goal was to learn to love George (the inner one), as distasteful as that seemed at first, and to welcome him home as a hero. Until George felt loved, he was going to continue to shoot the elk.

As this inner work unfolded, Joseph discovered his Loyal Soldier's many survival strategies. The Loyal Soldier had been regularly counseling Joseph to be structured, restrained, even rigid; to avoid unnecessary risks; to please his mother (and all other women) without getting too close to them; to neither feel nor express his hurt or anger; to accept blame for his mother's unhappiness; and to never embody his wild exuberance. As Joseph learned to recognize when George was enacting, or attempting to enact, any of these strategies, he learned to turn inside, thank George, gently explain the war was over (and why), tell George what he (Joseph) was going to do in place of the old strategies, and remind him of the inner and outer resources available to support the new course of action and to handle any crises that might arise along the way.

HEALING WORK WITH THE SACRED WOUND

When the Wanderer has eliminated all substance addictions and most other psychological dependencies and has begun to welcome home her Loyal Soldier, she finds one inner place in particular that is immensely and uniquely painful. This place harbors an early psychological wound, a trauma so significant she formed her primary survival strategies of childhood in reaction to it, so hurtful that much of her personal style and sensitivities have their roots there. If she grew up in the worst sort of egocentric setting (in which family dysfunction is common), she may have been emotionally abused or neglected in any number of ways. Perhaps an alcoholic father blamed her for his own misery or acted as if she were his girlfriend, or an insecure and jealous mother saw her as a threat to her marriage, or a grandfather treated her as a sex object. Maybe an older stepsister tormented her or a strict and demanding parent told her she was inadequate and would never measure up.

She does not need to be from a dysfunctional family, however, to have such deep childhood wounds. Her wound may stem from birth trauma or a birth defect, or the death of her mother when she was three, or a pattern of innocent but shattering betrayals at the hands of her older brother. Maybe it was her father's absence due to illness, or her guilt at surviving the car wreck that claimed her younger sister, or her own childhood bout with a deadly fever.

The wound does not necessarily stem from a single traumatic incident. Often, the wound consists of a pattern of hurtful events or a disturbing dynamic or theme in one or more important relationships.

Even in the healthiest families each person suffers from at least one significant emotional wound. This might not be an accident, and it might not be unfortunate. Perhaps the soul sees to it, to catalyze a special type of personal development that requires a trauma for its genesis. Think of the birth of a pearl: the tiny grit of sand within the oyster creates an irritation the oyster seeks to eliminate by coating the grain with successive layers of lustrous deposits, ultimately producing the jewel.

It may take a whole lifetime to complete the healing of such a wound, but the point is that we must begin — and there is a treasure inside. The stage of the second cocoon is a propitious time to uncover and recover that trove. The treasure created by the wound may be an extraordinary sensitivity to others' emotions, like a sixth sense, or to the nuances of the natural world; it may manifest as exceptional compassion for others; it may be a phenomenal ability to react adaptively in the heat of a crisis, on one's toes, leaping into skillful action; it may involve an artistic flare, a healing genius, a talent to inspire, or an uncanny knack to see the light side or to extract a shining jewel from the dark. In all cases, to release the full potential of the treasure, the wound must be uncovered, delved into, healed to some degree, as if coated with loving layers of lustrous deposits. Doing so renders that wound sacred.

Doing the healing work with your sacred wound can provoke an encounter with the soul itself. Your wound holds a key to your destiny in this life. As you struggle with the griefs and horrors at the heart of the wound, no longer distancing yourself from what you uncover there, you may find yourself, one day, staring straight into the deepest truths of this lifetime.

The second cocoon stage is by no means the last time in life we will wrestle with a sacred wound. Nor do these wounds occur only in early childhood. Psychologist Jean Houston, reminds us that sacred wounds can occur anytime in life. They can take the form of the loss of a primary relationship, the loss of a job or financial security, or the loss of sanity or self-esteem. Houston says the value of the wound is that it breaches the soul; the psyche is opened so that "new questions begin to be asked about who we are in our depths."[6] These fomenting questions facilitate the death of our old story and the birth of a larger story, a soul story, one revealed by the wounding itself.

Such a wound becomes, Houston says, "an invitation to our renaissance":

> The wounding becomes *sacred* when we are willing to release our old stories and to become the vehicles through which the new story may emerge into time.[7]

By courageously diving into your wounds, patiently allowing the suffering to do its work, neither indulging nor repressing the pain, you reach the deeper levels of the psyche where you encounter your larger (soul) story.

In times of suffering, when you feel abandoned, perhaps even annihilated, there is occurring—at levels deeper than your pain—the entry of the sacred, the possibility of redemption. Wounding opens the doors of our sensibility to a larger reality, which is blocked to our habituated and conditioned point of view.[8]

The risky task with your wounds is to open them so soul can come through. Allow yourself to be worked over until you awake to your greater potential. Avoid making sense of your pain too soon, finding relief too quickly, blaming someone for your anguish, or seeking revenge. Don't cave in and seek refuge in self-blame, self-pity, or playing the role of the victim or martyr; nor through denial, cynicism, abandoning your own dreams and values, or paranoid confidence in a never-ending series of further woundings. Allow the wound to do its work on you even should you descend into a pit of hopelessness. If you remain there long enough, you will be shorn of those personal patterns and attachments that must die so you may be reborn into a greater life. You will learn to forgive and to love again.

Rumi says, "Wherever there is a ruin, there is hope for treasure—why do you not seek the treasure of God in the wasted heart?"[9]

Annie Bloom, a spiritual "heart specialist" and vision quest guide, says that opening to your sacred wound allows you to genuinely fall in love with yourself. You come to see yourself so deeply you form an intimate relationship with the person you most truly are. What's more, you recover a treasure to carry into life, and thereby contribute to the redemption of the world — your family, community, and species.

In the second cocoon, through the experience of heartrending grief, you discover the true nature of your deepest emotional wounds, both their pain and their promise. In this stage of the journey, you will probably find yourself entering at least one such wound.

I recall a woman in her thirties on a summer soulcraft program high in the southern Colorado mountains. Allison was the fourth of five children from a middle class urban family of artists and intellectuals. Her family was, in general, extroverted and animated, while Allison was shy and sensitive. Allison's sacred wound was her feeling of being unseen by her family.

Despite her considerable talents, she felt invisible, overlooked. Her later relationship struggles revolved around this theme of not being seen. She carried the resulting emotional pain like a suit of armor.

One day at our mountain camp, Allison went out for a full day of solo wandering and soulcraft practice. She hiked high up the mountain, above tree line, onto a lonely, rocky ridge and allowed herself, at last, to plummet into her wound. She crashed into the anguish and loneliness of invisibility. She wept for hours and then summoned her animus — her inner man — and asked him to see her, to *really* see her. She shed her clothes and invited him to see her beauty.

In her imagery, her animus appeared and acknowledged the rawness and pain of her wound and her obstructed talents. He told her she must share her beauty nevertheless and that she was not simply a victim of others' refusal to see her. He said she shares the responsibility for being invisible as well as for being seen. Most astonishing, however, was this: he said her true beauty emanates from the fact that she, at her core, is *someone who sees,* someone who sees the world clearly and exquisitely and who has a great talent for interpreting the world through her art. That was the key to the larger soul story waiting to be born through her.

At the end of the day, Allison returned to camp. Standing relaxed and beaming before us, she asked us to witness her, to *see* her. She was so beautifully and vulnerably present we cried tears of wonder. Her usual self-effacing demeanor had been supplanted by a new radiance. With exceptional self-compassion, she told us that it had served her to be the one not seen, to grow up in a family that did not see that she saw. Because she had felt so vulnerable, she had learned to "watch very carefully," as she put it, to decipher the relationship dynamics and thereby avoid most of the conflagrations. If she had grown up in a safer family, she might never have developed her abilities to see so well. By diving into it, her wound became the opening for the recovery of her gift for others.

Self-effacement, shyness, and social vigilance had been part of Allison's Loyal Soldier strategies that made her safe. But they also afforded her the opportunity to develop her skills of seeing, which would be so central to her soul path.

In the contemporary West, the exploration of the sacred wound, when attempted at all, most commonly takes place in those rare psychotherapies that journey deep into the psyche to encounter the demons and monsters of our greatest fears. These wounds can also be approached through exceptional forms of bodywork or through ceremonies that expose our grief and allow its full experience. In a soul-centered setting, the elders, who know we all carry a sacred wound, offer rituals and nature-based practices that help us uncover and assimilate the lessons and opportunities, the treasures, hidden in our wounds. In whatever way we go about it, healing work with our sacred wound loosens our attachment to our former identity and is a vital component of the metamorphosis that occurs within the second cocoon.

LEARNING TO CHOOSE AUTHENTICITY
OVER SOCIAL ACCEPTANCE

As a Wanderer, you must be true to yourself. You cannot continue to follow the crowd.

Prior to the second cocoon, you learned the basics of authenticity. Within the bounds of what your Loyal Soldier would permit, you learned to distinguish what is true about yourself from what is not, gradually becoming clearer about your genuine attitudes, interests, styles, desires, values, and emotions.

You learned you could act in accordance with, or contrary to, your understanding of yourself. Authenticity, you discovered, is a decision and a skill. You learned to distinguish authenticity from deception, and learned about self-deception as well.

When push came to shove, however, you probably treated social acceptance as more essential to your life than authenticity. It was. As you were acquiring social skills, you needed to fit in with your peers and establish a social identity that worked. Social acceptance was the essential foundation for later soulful development.

Even when you weren't afraid of being rejected, you made some choices on the basis of conformity or group consciousness. You went along with the crowd because it was easier and because, often, you didn't know what you really wanted.

Now, in the second cocoon, you must take up the practice of reversing the priority between acceptance and authenticity. Authenticity and integrity become your foundations for asking the deeper questions of soul.

Distinguishing authenticity from deception — at any stage of life — requires the ability to access and understand your emotions, desires, and values. But the more advanced practice of *choosing* authenticity over social acceptance requires something more: you must tell yourself and your intimate others the truth, all of it, as deep as you can, especially when it's difficult. What you express is from the heart and intended to serve both yourself and others. You must adopt the practice of making all your actions align with what you know to be emotionally and spiritually true.

A key authenticity practice is to stop pleasing others at the expense of your own integrity. If the important others in your life — at home, at work, at play, in spiritual community — need you to be someone you are not (e.g., a carefree confidant, a charmer, a rescuer, a victim, a bad boy, a scholar, a hometown hero, a pleaser, a homeboy, a loser, everybody's mother), you will have to surrender your impulse to keep living your life for them. You will have to relinquish your willingness to make major life decisions just to take care of them emotionally or to win their approval.

You will, in essence, have to learn the difference between shallow and deep loyalty — doing what another wants or asks versus doing what your heart tells you is best for all concerned, yourself and others. Shallow loyalty is ultimately selfish if your goal is to increase your acceptance or socioeconomic security through compliance. It is both selfish and destructive if your goal is to give others what they want despite knowing that the "gift" is harmful. If a parent, for example, wants her grown son to live forever at home (physically or psychologically), it would be emotionally harmful to both the son and the mother for the son to comply. Supporting a person's weakness, psychopathology, or addiction is always a case of shallow loyalty, otherwise known as enabling, caretaking, or codependency.

In chapter 3 you met Nan, the college teacher and mother of six who had felt betrayed by her religious tradition. She confided in a friend outside her church who recommended Nan enact a vision quest as a way to inaugurate her journey to soul.

During her quest, alone in the wilderness, Nan grew increasingly angry and sad that her all-powerful church had become so indecently commercialized. She asked herself why and began to understand that true spirituality was largely absent from her religious community — and definitely absent from her own life. A defining moment occurred during her fast when she awoke with the following dream:

> I witness a shackled man (handcuffed behind his back) in prison garb being led up the aisle of a courtroom. He looks frail and disheveled. To my shock, I see it is B [one of the highest ranking officials in the church], a man known for his harshness and meanness, a man who is all black and white, my way or the highway. He is being brought before the judge, who sits much higher. B cries and begs for mercy. The judge responds, "You should have thought about that before you beat your wife. I'll be as merciful to you as you have been to others." I think, "I can't believe B would beat his wife!"

During and after her fast, Nan worked with this dream in a number of ways, deriving some painful but invaluable insights about herself, her church, and her relationship to her religious community. She came to see that the feminine (like the wife in the dream) had been oppressed within her church and also within her own psyche, the feminine that represented the soul of the church as well as her own capacity for deep feeling, compassion, and empathy. She realized there was a harsh and mean masculine part of her ("B") that had "beat down" her own feminine qualities, and another masculine part of her that judged her for this, from on high. She saw that her way of suppressing the feminine had followed the church's model.

Nan's dream haunted her for several years. Her vision quest, more generally, sent immense shock waves through her belief system. Following her quest, she was no longer even certain to whom to pray. She yearned to believe in something again, but something true to her own experience.

Nan's vision quest swept her into her second cocoon. She began the long and difficult process of reclaiming her life from the outer and inner church, extracting herself from conformity. Although she left the home of her adolescent identity and religious affiliation, Nan didn't leave her marriage or children — and didn't need to. She began peeling away layers of social conditioning to ground herself in a more authentic life. She completed her graduate degree and developed friendships outside the church, with friends that supported the person she was discovering herself to be. She asked herself regularly, "Who am I at my core? What is my relationship to God?"

Seven years later, Nan returned to the Utah wilderness for a week of group soulcraft practice. She designed a ceremony of excommunication to formally mark her separation from the church and the less-than-authentic life she had led. In contrast to the patriarchal traditions with which she was raised, this ceremony was led by the feminine. With the creative assistance of the other women, the silent supportive witness of the men, and the evening song of water flowing in the depths of a redrock canyon, Nan severed her ties to the church and reclaimed her wildness.

On that same journey, Nan enacted an all-night vigil under a full moon. In the middle of the night, in a gesture older and more immediate than words, the moon embraced Nan the way a mother embraces a child. In her bones, Nan *experienced* herself as a child of the moon, no longer the property of a man or a church. She reclaimed her primary membership in nature and her embodiment of the sacred feminine. And she recognized and accepted her ability and destiny to help others reclaim *their* original relationships to nature and the feminine.

A few weeks later, Nan took her four daughters on a retreat.

We stayed four nights and three days at a great old ranch in canyon-country. Every evening we sat out on a deck, wrapped in blankets, watching the sky and talking. The girls told secrets I had never heard (like the times they snuck out of the house and took the car to 7-Eleven before they had licenses) and we shared a bond as women we had not felt before. One evening, the subject of the church came up and I knew it was the perfect time to tell them about my ceremony of self-excommunication. As I told the story, I could feel their love and relief. My story of freedom freed them as well. For the first time, they could feel I was not judging them for being less than "perfect" [church members]. My oldest daughter, who was the one most raised within the church and who was then living with her boyfriend, was visibly relieved. It was as if a world of judgment from her mother just vanished. That evening was magical and beautiful. We have not talked about it since — it is sacred talk — but when the subject of the church comes up, I have replied, "I'm not a [church member] anymore," and my daughters make eye contact and smile.

Nan does not, however, minimize the difficulty of her transition, nor should we. Among her losses along the way, Nan had to leave behind her caretaker role of Mother Bear. When her husband, Richard, entered his own dark night of the soul and became depressed, she was sorely tempted to rescue him.

I know Richard must travel into that dark hole and deal with whatever he finds there. I have often protected him from entering that hole. Mother Bear wants to step in and make it better. I need to let him go down into that hole, as far as he needs to go, and wait to see what returns. That prospect is so scary, and yet my soul tells me this is the best path for Richard and for me. It has to be Richard's choice to travel into that darkness. I cannot force him nor can I continue to put bandages on a wound that needs much more serious attention.

The removal of my shackles has freed me not only from a brutal religion but also from long-held beliefs about marriage and motherhood.

MAKING PEACE WITH THE PAST: THE DEATH LODGE

A candidate for soul initiation knows what she has taken on. She's preparing to die in order to be reborn. She must abandon her old home to set out for her new home. She longs for the journey but is understandably terrified by the prospect. To help her approach the edge, the elders might suggest some time in the "death lodge" once she has made progress with the preceding practices.[10]

The death lodge is a symbolic and/or literal place, separate from the ongoing life of the community, to which the Wanderer retires to say good-bye to what her life has been. She may dwell there a full month or more, or, during the course of a year, an hour or two every day, or several long weekends. Some of her death lodge work will take place in the cauldron of her imagination and emotions, while at other times it will occur face-to-face with friends, family, and lovers. She will wrap up unfinished emotional and worldly business to help release herself from her past.

In her death lodge, she will see that the life she is leaving has contained both joy and pain, success and failure, love and the absence of love. Some of the central people in her life have played the roles of villains or victims, others of heroes. No matter. Now all the paths of possibilities within her former life are going to converge at a single inevitable point up ahead: the ending of her old way of belonging to the world.

In the death lodge she will say good-bye to her accustomed ways of loving and hating, to the places that have felt most like home, to the social roles that gave her pleasure and self-definition, to the organizations and institutions that both shaped and limited her growth, and also to her parents or caregivers who birthed her and raised her and who will soon, in a way, be losing a daughter.

She might choose to end her involvement with some people, places, and roles. In other cases, she might only need to shift her relationship to them. Although she must surrender her old way of belonging to the world, she need not violate sacred contracts. Some contracts might have to be renewed at a deeper level. It is essential she does not fool herself: embarking on the underworld journey is not a legitimate justification for abdicating preexisting agreements or responsibilities to others.

Whether ending or shifting relationships, she will feel and express her gratitude, love, forgiveness, her good-byes. She will say the difficult and important things previously unsaid. She may or may not visit with each person in the flesh, but she will certainly have many poignant and emotional encounters.

If her parents were not criminally abusive, she will forgive them for not being who she wanted them to be. If they are still alive, she will attempt this in person. This may be the most important and difficult part of her death lodge. She knows by now no parents are perfect nurturers and all have their own wounds. She knows that surrendering her former identity requires her to heal her own wounds to the point that she no longer harbors the fantasy that her human parents will somehow become perfect (or merely healthy or responsible) or that she will find someone else — a lover or therapist — to be her perfect parent. As in her Loyal Soldier work, she must learn to relate to herself as a healthy parent to a child.

In her death lodge, the Wanderer also mourns. She grieves her personal losses and the collective losses of war, race or gender oppression, environmental destruction, community and family disintegration, or spiritual emptiness. Not only does she cease to push the painful memories away but she invites them into her lodge and looks them in the eye. She allows her body to be seized by those griefs, surrendering to the gestures, postures, and cries of sorrow. She grieves in order to let her heart open fully again. She knows at the bottom of those grief waters lies a treasure, the source of her greater life. David Whyte writes:

Those who will not slip beneath
    the still surface on the well of grief

turning downward through its black water
    to the place we cannot breathe

will never know the source from which we drink,
    the secret water, cold and clear,

nor find in the darkness glimmering
    the small round coins
        thrown by those who wished for something else.[11]

Each of us has been, at times, the one who stood above a dark well and "wished for something else" — namely, that we ourselves wouldn't have to descend into the waters of grief, that our wishes would come true without our having to suffer in the process. In the second cocoon, we surrender our comfortable lives above the waters. We enter depths so dark we fear we will die, and in a way, we will.

Most people come to their vision quests with the intention, or at least the need, to grieve significant losses. The death lodge is an essential preparatory practice.

A man in his mid-twenties came to grieve his father's death that occurred when the young man was eighteen. Thomas, who himself became a father at seventeen, had many questions about what it meant to be a man. He grieved his father's premature death, his uncertainties about his own fatherhood, and his sense of being deprived of the cultural rituals that might have helped him become a man earlier and more completely. Like everyone else's, his time in the death lodge included sorrow for what might have been.

Many people embark on their quests in part to say good-bye to an identity they have outgrown, in a sense to attend their own funeral. Some write a eulogy for themselves, a farewell to the old story. Although the new story stirs inside them, they know the old one must first be laid to rest.

Anita, a professional and mother in her forties, came to formally mark her empty nest as her youngest entered college. She wanted to honor the end of twenty-one years of soul work, the labor of love of raising two fine young men. And then there were the two failed marriages, an alcoholic father, and a mother who died when Anita was four. In the death lodge, she also said good-bye to her way of being a psychotherapist; she knew a more creative and artistic path awaited her.

In the two years before his quest, Steve, a young psychiatrist, lost his mother and brother, his career fell apart, and he at long last severed his abusive relationship with alcohol. He came to formally end his decade or more of what he called "being dead," staggering through a lonely life of despair. In his death lodge, he finally experienced his rage at his dad for the years of brutal criticism and ridicule — and all the grief waiting in line just behind the rage.

Tom, a Harvard M.B.A. in his forties, made millions as a successful (and ruthless) corporate mercenary. He found himself with a trophy home and boat, a second ruined marriage, no idea who he really was, and his only son suicidal at the end of high school. Stunned to find himself bereft of the American dream, he came to his quest recognizing he and his son were facing the same crisis of meaning, one at the threshold of emancipation, the other at midlife, but both with the opportunity for true freedom. Tom, who was beginning to discover the fine human being beneath his former corporate persona, had much to surrender in his death lodge — buckets of tears and everything he once thought life was about.

In the death lodge, you loosen your grip on your former identity and world. You cut the cords, then gingerly step along the narrow ledge above the abyss, your back to the crag. At last, you turn and extend your arms against the half-truths of the old life, your fingers lightly pushing away.

To relinquish your former identity is to sacrifice the story you had been living, the one that defined you, empowered you socially — and limited you. This sacrifice captures the essence of leaving home.

Toward the end of the second cocoon, you begin to live as if in a fugue state. Imagine: after developing an adequate and functional identity, you now have become as if amnesic, dissociated from your prior life. But, unlike the sufferer of amnesia, your goal is not to discover who you *used* to be, but rather who you *really are*.

Your time in the death lodge grants freedom. Untied from the past, you dwell more fully in the present, more able to savor the gifts of the world. You find yourself projecting less and seeing the world more clearly and passionately. You experience a deepened gratitude for the richness of life, for the many opportunities that await you.

LEARNING THE ART OF DISIDENTIFICATION
THROUGH MEDITATION

Meditation practice develops the alertness of a centered mind, the ability to stay focused and calmly present. Meditation also guides you to disidentify from the small self, the self that says, "Not me, I'm not going to die," as Natalie Goldberg puts it. Through meditation practice, you learn to distinguish your personal consciousness — your beliefs about yourself, your ego — from the vast stillness of consciousness, the calm observing witness, at the center of the storm of your life.

During the second cocoon, it is essential to loosen your grip on the small self, the self that is going to die during soul encounters and soul initiation. A meditation discipline will help you open up to your larger self, or what Goldberg calls your "wild mind." As you experience wild mind more regularly, your attachment lessens to any particular way your ego might constellate itself. Your capacity for soulful shape-shifting increases correspondingly. Your ego becomes more fluid, more adaptable to the desires of soul, spirit, and nature.

You might begin with daily meditation periods of twenty minutes, sitting with your spine erect and steadily attending to your breath, both the inspirations and expirations, perhaps counting ten breaths and then repeating. When you notice your attention has drifted away, gently return to your breath.

There are many variations on this theme. Different approaches to meditation employ different foci for attention, whether it be the breath or a candle, a photo of a spiritual teacher, a sound or chant, or simply attending to whatever passes through consciousness without clinging to any momentary awareness. You might choose a mindfulness practice within an Eastern discipline such as Buddhism, Taoism, or Yoga, or you may learn a modern Western approach such as the Relaxation Response, but, in any case, your underworld journey will be greatly facilitated by practicing the art of centering and disidentifying.

These, then, are seven practices for leaving home. None of them are common components of high school or college curricula in the contemporary

Western world (as they ought to be), none of them high on the agendas of our youth themselves nor of most of their parents, none of them staple practices of our mainstream religious communities. We may long for what these practices would prepare us for (a soulful or second adulthood) but might have little idea how to get there. But it *is* possible to get there and, with these seven practices for shedding your former identity, it may not be as difficult as you imagine.

By employing the practices in this chapter, your attachment to your former identity will diminish. Then you must learn to be still, and wait. Learn to put your faith and love and hope in the waiting. Do not cling to unripe answers to questions about destiny. You have now fully entered the cocoon, your previous form has dissolved, and your new form has not yet gelled. The darkness shall be your light. Make peace with your lack of knowing, and trust that place fiercely. As the recording artist Jan Garrett sings:

> The breeze at dawn has secrets to tell you
> The market only wants to buy and sell you
> Fight to stay awake
> Choose the path you take
> Even if you don't know where it's going
> Trust your own unknowing
> (Don't go back to sleep)[12]

PART TWO

PATHWAYS TO SOUL ENCOUNTER

CHAPTER 6

RECOVERING THE IMAGE YOU WERE BORN WITH

. . . Hold to your own truth
at the center of the image
you were born with. . . .

— David Whyte

H aving left the home of his less mature identity, the Wanderer's second task within the cocoon is to prepare for soul initiation: the inauguration of a new, soul-rooted identity. He must ready himself for a birth, a new home. There are two components to this second task: (1) learning and employing techniques for soul encounter, practices that will help him approach the soul and gather what he finds there, and (2) cultivating a soulful relationship to his life, and to *all* life. The first of these two subtasks, acquiring the skills of soul encounter, comprises the subject matter of this and the following four chapters. Chapters 11 and 12 explore the second subtask.

THE WANDERER'S BAG OF TOOLS

Sometimes, without any effort on our part and when we least expect it, the soul shows up, pulls the rug of ordinary life from beneath us, and showers us with its confounding radiance. We hear our true name spoken for the first time, or an angel appears and invites us to wrestle, or we awake in the wilderness at midnight to a deer licking our forehead, or, out of nowhere, God says, "Take off your shoes!" Revelation *can* occur without conscious preparation for the encounter. It "just happens" sometimes, or at least so it seems to the everyday mind.

But more commonly, we must make deliberate and courageous steps in the soul's direction, using pathways that lead to that mysterious and veiled world.

In nature-based cultures, these pathways encompass a great variety of practices, techniques, and ceremonies taught by elders to the youth of their communities. When a young person becomes socially and culturally self-reliant, when her natural curiosity emerges about the mysteries of life, the elders notice. When the time is right, the old ones uproot her from her home and take her to a place where she will prepare for initiation. The elders bring with them a bag of tools, a treasure chest of soulcraft practices.

In nature-based societies, these are the most important things to learn at that time of life, even more important than hunting, horticulture, food preparation, or shelter building.

For contemporary teenagers, too, developing soulcraft competence is more vital to their personal development than math, science, and business know-how. Most teenagers sense this and most would prefer this knowledge. Most of their teachers, however, don't have a clue about pathways to soul. Few of us learned these things as teens or in college. Now, in order to initiate ourselves onto our soul paths, we must acquire these tools later in life. Someday, with good fortune, we may have the opportunity to teach these things to our own children and grandchildren.

A SAMPLING OF PATHWAYS

The Wanderer is not likely to magically transform one shining day from someone who has never encountered her soul to someone who, suddenly, is an initiated adult. Rather, she will meander through a heightened time of self-discovery outfitted with a set of practices for recovering and assimilating soul qualities. Every culture has — or once had — a set of such practices. Some of the most common, explored in the next four chapters, are:

- dreamwork
- deep imagery or active imagination
- the discovery, fashioning, and use of symbols and sacred objects
- self-designed ceremony (a means of conversing with the sacred Other)
- skillful use of hallucinogenic substances within sacred ceremonies
- symbolic artwork
- journal work
- fasting
- breathwork
- extreme physical exertion
- yoga disciplines
- the way of council
- trance drumming and rhythms
- ecstatic trance dancing
- ceremonial sweats and saunas
- the enactment of traditional ceremonies, rituals, and nature festivals

- vision questing
- understanding and responding to signs and omens in nature
- talking across the species boundaries (nature dialogues)
- animal tracking and other methods of sensitive and skillful nature observation
- the telling, retelling, and study of myths and other sacred stories
- personal myth work
- storytelling of one's own personal journeys
- sensitive listening and clear reflection upon others' stories
- sacred speech and ritual silence
- soulful music, poetry, and chanting

Several themes are common to these pathways to soul. Many of these practices, for example, entail the deliberate alteration of consciousness, perhaps explaining why religious historian Mircea Eliade refers to them as "techniques of ecstasy."[1] The ordinary state of ego consciousness must be temporarily dissolved or radically shifted because the uninitiated ego is the primary obstacle to the conscious experience of soul. The encounter with soul will shake up the everyday personality's beliefs about self and world. That's why a conversation with soul is not likely within the defended confines of ordinary consciousness. The conscious self must look at its own psyche from a different perspective, from a unique angle, from a position of altered awareness, like viewing earth from outer space, or returning home after a month in an exotic culture. Most soul-encounter practices induce liminal states of temporary ego dissolution that release us from the usual rules and norms of our personality and culture, opening the way to fresh observations and creative adventures.[2]

Upon entering the second cocoon, the Wanderer has a natural and implacable thirst for these consciousness-altering knowledge and skills. If there are no elders to teach these methods, she will make her own attempts. Most un-eldered teenagers in Western society, for example, end up using mind-altering chemicals — including alcohol — which, outside a ceremonial context and without spiritual guidance, are unlikely to lead to successful encounters with soul, and may be physically, psychologically, and spiritually harmful. Indeed, many of the soulcraft methods discussed in these pages can be dangerous. Mature guidance and adequate preparation are crucial.

In addition to non-ordinary states, the pathways to soul have other common themes. Many are rooted in metaphor and symbol — dreamwork, deep imagery, ceremony, signs and omens, poetry, and art. No surprise: symbol is the currency of imagination, and imagination is the primary window to soul.

Many pathways evoke powerful emotion. When we cross borders into mystery and move beyond our ordinary relationship to the world, we evoke experiences from which we had formerly been "protected." Some terrify us. Others give rise to joys and ecstasies. Sometimes we are flooded with sadness, for losses suffered and unclaimed dreams now irretrievable. Other times we stumble into unhealed wounds and the hurt, anger, guilt, shame, and grief waiting there. In every case, our emotions encountered on the descent provide the opportunity for a deeper alignment with the world and our true selves.

Another common theme is conversation with the sacred Other, that exotic other appearing as a frog or a raven, the wind or silence, a saguaro or a blade of grass, a mysterious dream image, our lover's face in the midst of lovemaking, the voice of God, a dying child, an entranced dancer, or a poem or painting. The conversation may or may not be verbal, but its medium is always the intimate and authentic interaction between the conscious human self and another being from a world quite distant from our surface lives. Deeply encountering that Other changes us as might a profound conversation with a person from a radically different culture. The sacred Other can be found in many terrains, in dreams, deep imagery, ceremony, psychotropic plants, trance dancing, the wilds of nature, sexual ecstasies, and the great mythologies of the world.

Entering the conversation with the Other ushers us to the edge of our world, where we might acquire an astonishing new perspective. The conversation invites us to think outside the box, to enter the unknown, to cross borders, to descend into the dark mysteries.

Another common thread is that pathways to soul stimulate a deep bonding, not just between people but also between humans and the other beings of nature. Bonding across the species boundaries helps us overcome the conflicts and disparities between nature and culture and within human culture itself. By deepening our identification with all life-forms, with ecosystems, and with the planet herself, we begin to discover within us what deep ecologist Arne Naess calls the "ecological self" or what James Hillman calls "a psyche the size of the earth" — the broader and deeper self that is a natural member in the more-than-human community.

Wandering in nature is also a common theme of soul-encounter pathways, nature being a mirror of soul (and vice versa). And finally, story, rhythm, music, and the arts in general are regular features. Indeed, some say all arts originally arose as methods for approaching or celebrating the sacred.

SOUL ENCOUNTER VERSUS SOUL INITIATION

Before exploring the pathways to soul in detail, it's important to appreciate the distinction, only implicit so far in the discussion, that *soul encounter* is an experience of the mysterious image you were born with, while *soul initiation* is the developmental transition from psychological adolescence to true adulthood. An experience of soul encounter does not necessarily result in soul initiation, and soul initiation does not necessarily occur at the moment of a soul encounter.

During a soul encounter, you glimpse one or more features of your soul image. This image can be multifaceted and complex like an elaborate tapestry that has many sub-images. Woven into the fabric of the image is a mysterious symbol that holds within it the secrets of your life purpose. Through one or more soul encounters, you learn about that symbol and how it reflects your unique soul qualities or core powers, the gift you were born to carry to others. The fact you have *your* particular soul qualities, and not others, is the truth at the center of the image you were born with.

Soul encounters are rare before our mid or late teens, but there is no reason they cannot occur even in earliest childhood. Soul encounters also happen *after* soul initiation; there is always more to learn about our soul powers.

At the time of my first soul encounter, I was given the image of a cocoon. Although the deeper meaning was mysterious to me, I immediately recognized that weaving cocoons would in some way be a central task of my life. I understood a cocoon as a place of extraordinary transformation, but, other than that, I could not have said what the image meant nor how I might go about embodying it. I only knew that creating places for transformation was one of my soul powers. Soul did not tell me to become a vision quest guide, a psychologist, or a writer. It remained for later experiences to flesh out the meaning and also what forms I might employ for living it.

You might glimpse your own soul image only once in a lifetime, or you might observe it, and variations of it, many times. You might encounter somewhat different images on different occasions. Each new encounter elaborates on the previous ones, offering further differentiation, clarification, or extension. The soul image is most commonly experienced visually — we humans are especially sight oriented, both behaviorally and neurologically — but, for many people, the image is auditory, kinesthetic, or emotional. The image might occur as a sensation in your body, a song you hear with every cell, or a powerful feeling coursing through you. You may or may not be able to put words to it. The image might be an inner one (like a dream image or one from your waking imagination) or something you perceive in the outer world. Sometimes it combines both imagination and sensing. Often we simply don't know whether it is inner, outer, or both.

Each person's soul image is as unique and mysterious as his or her destiny. One person I know, for example, carries within her the image of a sacred chalice from which others may drink. Others have discovered that their gift is to journey through darkness bearing light; to stand at the edge of the waters and help those who are ready to cross; to bring the power of healing hands to the world; to shine the light of the north; to sing the song that calls the Divine Beloved; to be for others a glistening web over waters; to mirror the hearts of others; to walk rainbows; to stalk the heart like a wolf; to sing the songs of the soul; to offer the compassion, courage, and wisdom of a strong and nurturing tree; to be the gift of a sparkling heart; or to echo the cry of the earth. Malidoma Somé, the African shaman and teacher from the Dagara tribe, learned, during his initiation, that his gift was to make friends with the stranger or enemy.[3]

In contrast to soul encounter, soul initiation refers to that extraordinary moment in life when we cross over from psychological adolescence to true adulthood, from our first adulthood to our second. At that moment, our everyday life becomes firmly rooted in the purposes of the soul. The embodiment of our soul powers becomes as high a priority in living as any other. But it's not so much that we *choose* at that moment to make soul embodiment a top priority; it's more as if the soul *commands* us to that task and we assent.

In the Western culture, we need to be careful with the word *initiation*. Many people associate it with elitism, secret societies, flaky or nefarious cults, and oppressive, hierarchical organizations. For some people, the word evokes, on the one hand, a sense of their own inadequacy (if they have not undergone an initiatory experience and believe they ought to have) and, on the other, suspicions of arrogance or ego inflation on the part of those who participate in initiatory rites. Due to its considerable charge, it may be best to avoid public declarations of being initiated. Soul initiation is not something to be worn like a badge or status symbol; it is to be quietly embodied through a life of soulful service.

Soul initiation transforms our lives by the power of the truth at the center of our soul image. Embracing that truth results in a radical simplification of our lives. Activities and relationships not supportive of our soul purpose begin to fall away. Our former agendas are discarded, half-completed projects abandoned. Many old problems are not solved but outgrown. Old ways of presenting and defending ourselves become less appealing, and less necessary.

At soul initiation, our lives are changed forever, irreversibly. We have, in effect, understood a certain truth and have made the sort of promise of which David Whyte writes:

> ... By the lake in the wood
> in the shadows
> you can
> whisper that truth
> to the quiet reflection
> you see in the water.
>
> Whatever you hear from
> the water, remember,
>
> it wants you to carry
> the sound of its truth on your lips.
>
> Remember,
> in this place
> no one can hear you
>
> and out of the silence
> you can make a promise
> it will kill you to break,
>
> that way you'll find
> what is real and what is not....[4]

It is possible your soul initiation will occur during a soul encounter, one so profound that it fundamentally changes your sense of what your life is about, and so clear that you see right away how to translate it into action and a life of service. More typically, however, soul initiation occurs at some moment other than a soul encounter. You might wake up one morning and recognize that your old priorities have been superseded by new, soul-centered values, as if a profound but gradual shift within your psyche had been reverberating underground, hidden from your awareness.

What ultimately *confirms* your initiation is neither your experience of an image nor the blessing of a community authority — even an elder — but rather the depth of fulfillment you derive from embodying your soul image and your community's recognition and celebration of that embodiment.

SOULCRAFT TEACHERS

Soulcraft teachers appear when you are ready, when you have sufficiently loosened your attachment to your adolescent identity. The teachers sometimes come in the form of other-than-human beings as well as the more familiar human variety.

I met my first soulcraft teachers in 1980. In the summer of that year, traveling through the Southwest with two friends, I attended a conference on experiential education. The keynote speaker was Dolores LaChapelle, a popular author in the field of deep ecology. A mountaineer, powder skier, ceremonialist, and radical environmentalist, Dolores looked the part — tall, wiry, and fit, with long gray-blonde hair braided to her waist. Her open and attractive face was well weathered by life at high altitude, with inquisitive and skeptical gray-blue eyes, a wry smile, and a voice that simultaneously conveyed shyness, ferocity, a mountaineer's joy in ineffable beauty, a resolute intelligence, an implacable sadness about the world, and a school-marm's sweetness.

I was inspired by Dolores's talk, especially her declaration that protecting sacred lands was one of the finest things one could do in life, and that we could help others wake up to the sacredness of *all* of nature.

A month later, my friends and I sat in Dolores's cabin in Silverton, an old mining town at 9,100 feet in the San Juan Mountains of southwest Colorado. As the cool air of early fall spilled through the open windows, Dolores told us about a thousand-acre ranch in the nearby mountains, one of the most beautiful and sacred places she had ever been. The woman who owned the ranch was willing to sell it far below market value if she could find the right group to protect it and establish there a wilderness education center. Dolores thought my two friends and I might be interested.

She disappeared into her storage room to find a photo of the ranch and emerged with a copy of the very first issue of *Outside* magazine. She explained how the ranch was really more visually striking and energetically moving than any photograph could convey, but the image on the cover would at least give us an idea.

One glance and I fell off my chair, landing hard on the floor. The others looked down at me, amused and perplexed. I looked back, mute, mouth agape, arm pointing. You might say I recognized the place.

Eight years earlier, I had moved from North Carolina to Colorado to begin graduate school. My first week there, in Boulder, I went to the campus store to look for some inexpensive art for my apartment. One poster jumped out like an alluring memory from another life. The scene was breathtakingly beautiful — an exuberant forest of trees in fiery fall colors, yellow, gold, and red; above them a luxurious band of dark-green conifers; and, higher still, a majestic snow-capped peak and azure skies. But the odd thing was how strangely familiar the place felt. I found myself irresistibly drawn into that landscape, tumbling into the golden mountain meadow by the old cabin in the foreground, feeling as much at home there as I had ever felt anywhere despite it being only a photograph and my having no idea where on the planet it might be.

I bought the poster. I told my closest friends, were I to die before them, I wanted my ashes scattered from the summit of that peak — if they could identify its location.

Now, in Dolores's cabin, I was looking at a nearly identical photograph. The Ute people, who have lived on the Colorado Plateau for thousands of years, call her Shandoka, which means "storm maker." Rising 14,017 feet into the southern Colorado sky, her massive shoulders reach several miles east and west of her pyramidal peak, a silver helmet of bare rock jutting twenty-five hundred vertical feet above tree line. Shandoka creates her own weather systems, summer and winter storms alike forming around her summit and clinging there long after surrounding skies have cleared.

Shandoka has been the primary site of the summer vision quests I lead, with base camp high on a bench at tree line. Her slopes hold extraordinary treasures — crystal-clear springs gushing from black shale hillsides, mysterious caves whose dark mouths beckon from high on her sheer ramparts, glaciers of rock flowing down from craggy ridges, stunningly lush meadows of wildflowers, waterfalls cascading through pristine forests of spruce, and alpine basins of astonishing proportions filled with summer snowfields.

The power of Shandoka's presence humbles me each time I visit. High on her upper benches, a summer thunderstorm with furious winds and thrashing hail is an experience not soon forgotten. She has graciously hosted us many times, allowing us to wander her slopes, dance in her basins, sing with her winds, and trade speech with the many creatures that call her home. I have learned many lessons essential to my soul work from Shandoka and prefer not to think what my life might have been if I had never found her. But I did — or perhaps it would be more accurate to say she found me.

Only a couple of weeks before visiting Dolores in Silverton, I had ventured into the wilderness for my first vision fast. During that journey, my beliefs radically shifted about what my life was to be. Following my quest, a series of synchronistic events unfolded that confirmed and further fleshed out the vision I received. Discovering the identity and location of Shandoka was one of those events. The soul does more than call to us once or twice; it sends regular signs that assist us on the path to our destiny. Every once in a while, we actually notice!

Dolores and Shandoka were two of my first soulcraft teachers. With Dolores, I studied earth festivals, ritual, chanting, nature observation, sacred storytelling, nature mysticism and poetry, and, not least, backcountry powder skiing.

During that first year, Dolores introduced me to another teacher, Elizabeth Cogburn, a dancer, ceremonial leader, and shaman from New Mexico. With Elizabeth I studied council work, trance rhythms (with shakers and drums), trance dancing, ceremony, and soulful community building.

In the early eighties, I met Steven Foster, Ph.D., and Meredith Little, the two teachers whose programs, books, and example have been most influential in my wilderness work. For over thirty years, Steven and Meredith have been brilliant and enthusiastic students of nature, of nature-based human traditions, and of everything wild in human nature. They have restored to the Western world the ancient way of the wilderness vision fast and the entire body of passage rites that contains it. Wise elders and wily tricksters, humble teachers and wholehearted friends, they are the founders of the School of Lost Borders in California's eastern Sierras. With them, I studied many arts, including those of the vision fast, the death lodge, nature dialogues, self-designed ceremony, storytelling, and story mirroring.

The second cocoon provides your best opportunity in life to study pathways to soul encounter. The lessons typically come in unpredictable forms through the guidance of teachers who are often eccentric and enigmatic. In the next four chapters, we'll explore more than twenty of the most common pathways you might study.

CHAPTER 7

INNER WORK

And he was the demon of my dreams, the most handsome
of all angels. His victorious eyes
blazed like steel,
and the flames that fell
from his torch like drops
lit up the deep dungeon of the soul.

"Will you go with me?" "No, never! Tombs
and dead bodies frighten me."
But his iron hand
took mine.

"You will go with me."...And in my dream I walked
blinded by his red torch.
In the dungeon I heard the sound of chains
and the stirrings of beasts that were in cages.

— Antonio Machado

D reamwork and deep imagery journeys are the traditional tools of twentieth-century psychology for lighting up "the deep dungeons of the soul," helping us befriend the demons and angels who dwell there. These are *inner* work tools, practices for exploring the intricate and intimate corners of our individual psyches. In contrast are those pathways to soul that we walk in the company of other psyches — our fellow humans and the other, more wild creatures of the planet.

The inner is no less real than the outer, and, although it is part of us, it is not literally inside our skin. We imagine the unconscious or the soul as something private and inside us, like the iron-handed angel-demon and dungeons of Machado's dreams. But the unconscious can equally well be imagined outside our bodies, out in the world, like a dark, wild forest through which we roam. There are equal measures of mystery in dreams and wilderness.

SOULCENTRIC DREAMWORK

Dreamwork reaps transformation, healing, direction, and initiation from the rich landscapes of our nocturnal visions. Cultures from every corner of the planet since the dawn of humanity have consulted dreams for guidance. We should not be surprised, then, to find a hundred ways to approach a dream. Beliefs about dreams in our own society range from the dismissive — that they are the meaningless results of random neuronal firings while we sleep — to the more reverential view that they hold greater reality, meaning, and potency than our waking hours.

Soulcentric dreamwork diverges from other methods in its premise that every dream is an opportunity to develop our relationship to soul, to who we are beneath our surface personalities and routine agendas. Each dream provides a snapshot of the unfolding story and desires of the soul, and a chance for the ego to be further initiated into that underworld story and those underworld desires.

A few years ago, I found myself losing inspiration for guiding wilderness journeys, one of the primary delivery systems for my soul work. During that same period, I was struggling with an alluring but difficult romantic relationship. I awoke one morning with this dream:

> Two women, approximately my age, are having a conflict. They've been close friends or partners or possibly lovers for twenty years. This is their first significant conflict, although it might have been brewing underground for the entire twenty years and has just now breached the surface. The three of us are in the midst of a long journey, equally important to all of us, but the conflict is serious enough to interfere with any forward motion. One woman, Jacquelyn, is dark haired and carries a large red leather notebook or briefcase overstuffed with papers. The other is blonde and carries an identical notebook, equally stuffed, but it is blue. (I don't remember her name.) Jacquelyn/Red appears to be arguing for more warmth or heart or love. (I don't remember what blonde/Blue wants.) I realize it is *my* job to get them to talk — of this I have no doubt. We cannot continue our journey until their conflict is resolved.

This dream got my attention. For the next two days I lived with the images of these women and the unsettling feeling of impasse between them. I felt the disturbance, mystery, and alarm of the standoff. It was *not* comfortable.

On the following day, my girlfriend called and announced, out of nowhere, she was ending our relationship — with virtually no explanation. I was utterly devastated.

Over the next few weeks, in the midst of grief, I did additional work with the dream of the two women. Clearly my relationship with the inner feminine was in trouble. Now my outer relationship was over, too, and I felt altogether incapable of engaging my soul work. Red and Blue were at cross-purposes and the journey of my life had indeed ground to a halt.

In the following pages, I'll share some of the ways I worked with this dream.

Approaches to dreamwork can be divided into three categories: objective, subjective, and archetypal.[1] These approaches differ as to how they see the relationship between the nightworld (i.e., the events, locations, and characters of the dream) and the dayworld (i.e., the waking world). All three approaches can be used with any single dream.

In the objective approach, we imagine the dream as a sort of psychological X ray of our waking lives, revealing previously hidden truths about the dayworld people, places, and relationships portrayed in the dream. In my dream of Red and Blue, the two women did not in fact correspond to people in my dayworld, but if they had, we'd assume the dream had something to say about their relationship to each other and my relationship to them. We might have said the dream exposed an unconscious suspicion or fear in me of a huge conflict about to erupt between them. Or maybe the dream would have revealed that I felt to blame for their conflict or that I should help them resolve it. All these possibilities are *objective* in the sense that the dream would be about two women from my waking life.

In soulcentric dreamwork, we rarely employ the objective perspective because it traffics in surfaces and we are headed for the depths. We want to know about the soul and its desires and about the relationship between the ego and the soul. We're not so interested in better understanding the ego's place in the dayworld.

In the subjective approach, we regard every part of the dream as a part of the dreamer, part of the dreamer's psyche. The elements of the dream are not seen as corresponding to things from the dayworld; rather, we understand the dream components as representing the dreamer's sub-personalities, attitudes, feelings, wounds, rejected qualities, and hidden potentials. The *I* in a dream represents the ego, the way the dreamer thinks about himself. The dream reveals the relationships between the ego and other elements of the psyche. The dream — and the dreamwork on it — afford the opportunity to facilitate integration and wholeness within our psyches.

Red and Blue, for example, would be two aspects of my inner feminine. The dream would be revealing the relationship between my ego and the inner feminine, apparently that it's my ego's job to resolve a conflict between the heart and . . . something feminine and blue so that the inner journey can continue.

The subjective approach helps us integrate our conscious personalities with parts and potentials that have been lost, hidden, rejected, or repressed. This facilitates soul work because soul seeks wholeness.

With the archetypal approach to dreams, we again say every part of the dream is a part of the dreamer, but now we expand our meaning of the dreamer to include the collective (universal) unconscious as well as the personal unconscious embraced in the subjective approach. The archetypal perspective, which subsumes the subjective and goes beyond it (or better, *beneath* it), was developed by James Hillman, the American depth psychologist and founder of Archetypal Psychology. Some parts of the dream are seen as archetypes, the gods and goddesses that act through our psyches, as well as representing our more personal qualities. Perhaps Red is Aphrodite, goddess of love and beauty, and she is in conflict with another feminine archetype, another goddess. A conflict of that magnitude within the psyche could result in the rearrangement of a lot of inner furniture.

A key principle in the archetypal approach is this: the archetypal presences in our dreams — and the dream more generally — may not be the least bit interested to help with the ego's dayworld agenda of personal happiness or adjustment. The agenda itself may be the primary obstacle to soulful growth. Rather, the dream affords the ego an initiation opportunity in the underworld, in Hades, that would bring about not a healing or patching up of the ego but something quite contrary: a death to the ego's current way of being in the world.

From the archetypal view, the dream wants to separate the ego from its surface life, at least temporarily, so it can be introduced to a deeper, richer, larger possibility, a life more in keeping with the desires of the soul. Ultimately, this will render the conscious personality more whole, but not without an intervening death.

The dream ego (i.e., the *I* in the dream) finds itself in the position of Persephone, abducted from her middleworld home by Hades. Persephone becomes Hades's wife, his queen, the goddess of the underworld, thus, ultimately, fulfilling her destiny. Every dream, in this view, perpetrates an abduction of the ego for the sake of its education in relation to soul.

Red and Blue, seen subjectively, might represent two feminine potentials within me that, if I could resolve their conflict, might be integrated into my conscious personality, rendering me more whole and allowing me to continue my journey. On the other hand, Red and Blue might represent two universal feminine archetypes that are there to initiate some intrapsychic change. They may want to shift my ego's beliefs and attitudes that block its greater soulful potential. My dream ego believes, for example, that the conflict between Red and Blue must be resolved, that it is in fact resolvable, that *he* has the job of resolving it, and that his journey, as he has conceived of it, is supposed to continue. "This is just like women," the masculine ego might mutter, "disrupting my journey again!" Maybe, ego thinks, he'll just have to go on without Red and Blue (as if that were possible) and let them resolve their damn conflict on their own. But perhaps ego is confused about what is going on and who holds the greater power. Perhaps the dream events offer an initiation opportunity in relation to the feminine. What then?

In the subjective approach, the dream is seen as information *for* the ego as to how to grow more whole (by resolving the conflict between Red and Blue). In the archetypal approach, the dream is a divine power that can have a direct transformative impact *on* the ego (e.g., ending his stale, twenty-year journey in order to open to a more imaginative possibility).

The specific strategies of archetypal dreamwork (reviewed below) impel the dayworld ego to dwell as long as possible in the world of the dream, *among* those nightworld images, giving them plenty of opportunity to alchemize the ego. This contrasts with strategies that keep the ego in the driver's seat, extracting the dream's images into the dayworld, where the ego, unscathed, can have *its* way with those images. Will the ego allow the civil war between Red and Blue to transform him? If not, the ego might imagine he can heroically descend into the nightworld of the dream as Super Mediator, resolve the inconvenient female squabble, and ascend victoriously to thunderous middleworld applause, allowing its journey to resume as if nothing had ever happened.

Looked at with soulcentric eyes, every dream reveals hidden potentials of our deeper lives and stories and provides the opportunity for the ego to be rooted more firmly in the soils of soul.

Dreams are one of the foremost and universal ways the soul speaks to the ego. But the soul does not merely speak by way of dreams; it can also *do* something *to* us. In addition to capturing our conscious imagination, the dream can capture the ego itself. We are pulled down into a strange realm of confounding events we may or may not understand intellectually but that profoundly impact, through our emotions and imagination, our beliefs about ourselves and the world. The dream can and does transform the ego, especially when we cooperate (surrender) during dreamwork.

Through soulcentric dreamwork, dreams can have the same transformative effect on the ego as a thorough immersion in nature. The inner wilds of dreams and the outer wilds of nature are our most powerful allies, teachers, and guides in our maturation and initiation. To intensify the transformative effect, we can work with our dreams while immersed in the natural world, bringing dreamwork to an exceptionally deep level and opening new doors to the sacred garden of nature.

Dreams arise from the waters of our deepest human nature. And the magic and splendors of the natural world constellate the flowing dream of the earth. The earth, every day, invites us to dive into her dream stream.

Imagine dreams as currents in an underground stream — a soulstream — flowing beneath our surface lives. The rock group the Talking Heads has a song, "Once in a Lifetime," about waking up to that other, more real, meaningful, and wild life waiting and flowing beneath our everyday, overly civilized routines. That deeper life can be recovered and lived. "Under the rocks and stones," they sing, "there is water underground." Beneath the ground of our habit-bound lives, with our beautiful houses, large automobiles, and nine-to-five jobs — "same as it ever was" — there is the constant flow of a deeper, hidden life. We may not get many chances in a lifetime to enter that underground stream, maybe only one. If and when the ground beneath our feet suddenly swells and bursts open, we shall find ourselves aghast at the life we have been living — and the deeper life we have not.

Dream researchers have shown that the neurologically normal person has a dream, remembered or not, every ninety minutes during a regular night's sleep. Every hour and a half, we dip into a stream, a Great Underdream that is always flowing even when we are not having what we normally call "a dream." We might imagine this Underdream as the soul eternally musing about its life, and inviting the ego in ("the water's fine," it murmurs). The Underdream is what the soul wants the ego to embody in the dayworld. The Underdream surges and swells, floods and spouts, night and day. Each night dream represents our brief descent into the Great Underdream, a dipping of our toes into the soulstream, a briefing on one or two points about the deeper life waiting and longing to be lived.

The earliest remembered dreams of our lives, the ones from early childhood, say age three to five, represent especially clear and portentous glimpses of the Underdream. These dreams occur when the ego — a solid sense of "I" — first appears in a stable form. It's as if the soul attends the launching of the ego into the vast ocean of life with a message tacked to the mast. The message outlines the soul's greatest hope for the ego and provides vivid clues to the ego's destiny. These early dreams are especially fertile when worked with soulcentrically. Carl Jung, for example, dreamed, at age three or four, of being out in a meadow and then descending a stone staircase into an underground temple that contained a great golden throne with a "subterranean God" upon it in the form of a fifteen-foot erect phallus.[2] In his memoir, written at age eighty-one, Jung wrote that this dream

> laid the foundation for everything that was to fill the second half of my life with stormiest passion.... Through this childhood dream I was initiated into the secrets of the earth. What happened was a kind of burial in the earth.... Today I know that it happened in order to bring the greatest possible amount of light into the darkness. It was an initiation into the realm of darkness.[3]

And, as we know, Jung spent his life illuminating that underworld realm of darkness and its strange cast of potent gods and goddesses.

Imagine that the soul ceaselessly yearns to dream itself into the world, not just in early childhood. Sometimes the ego cooperates; mostly it doesn't. If it doesn't, it's not likely to inherit the greater life of the soul. The ego tends to think of itself as fully in control. The soul constantly calls the ego to die to its current illusions. To surrender to the underworld is death (to the ego). We long for transformation but don't want it *that* way. As W. H. Auden wrote, "We would rather be ruined than changed."

To respect the power of dreams, the first rule in a soulcentric approach asks you to refrain from interpreting your own dreams too soon and *never* interpret someone else's dream. Rather, permit yourself the sometimes disquieting luxury of hanging out among the rich symbols and events of your dream, wandering slowly though its images and emotions, twisting slowly in the breeze of its seductions and abductions. Whenever you can during the day, let the dream do its tidal work on the ego rather than allowing the ego to do its analyzing work on the dream.

You might approach each dream as if you were entering a vast desert inhabited by sun-scorched canyons, craggy mountain ranges, hidden springs, furtive mammals, blossoming cacti, and inscrutable dangers, a shape-shifting world in which you might choose to dwell for an indefinite span, paying close attention to how things feel there. You might be changed in ways terrifying or liberating, or both.

You might do best to avoid all those so-called dream dictionaries and other books that purport to tell you what a dream symbol means, as if each dream element could be extracted from its dreamworld and have a fixed meaning independent of its relationship with the dreamer and all other elements of the dream. Reserve such texts for party entertainment, but, for the gods' and goddesses' sakes, don't consult such books when you want to enter the interior of your dreams.

There are many techniques for working with dreams without interpreting them right off the bat, or ever. First and foremost, you can gain an enormous amount by simply *telling your dream,* out loud, to one person or more, without any comment. Like a poem (it is a poem, a soul poem), try recounting your dream in the present tense (as if the action is happening as you speak) and talk very slowly, *very* slowly, even slower, like reading a world-class poem, savoring every word. Allow the emotions of the dream to flow through you as you speak. Pause often. Add details you remember as you speak. Let the emotions and images do their work on you. Go slowly. Describe the sensory qualities of the dream in great detail — the sights, scents, sounds, tastes, and textures. Describe the subtleties of the personalities and the emotional nuances of the encounters. Linger.

Tell the dream in this manner at least twice, the second time immediately after the first. Maybe several times. Your goal at this point is to simply *be in the dream,* not to figure it out. You might choose to insert the word "inner" or the phrases "of me" or "in my life" after significant elements of the dream to more fully feel, as you speak, that the dream is making a statement about the larger you, and that it is speaking in metaphor, like poetry: "In my life, I am on a journey with two women of me. The Red of me and the Blue of me are in conflict, and my ego feels the responsibility to resolve this conflict. My inner journey has ground to a halt. . . ."

Several dreamwork methods can help you *merge with the dream elements,* offering the experience of being the woman, for example, or the conflict or the journey. One method is to act out the role of one or more dream characters. You might, for example, walk down the road just the way Red did (or would) and say what she said and do what she does in the way she does. Do that repeatedly, perhaps exaggerating it, in order to sink deeper into that dream character. You might have a friend or a dream guide interview you as if you are Red and ask you how she is feeling emotionally, how her body feels, what she wants, how it feels to be her. Then you can do the same with Blue, or with the journey itself, or the conflict.

Another psychodrama-allied method is to ask the people in a dream group to play the characters and/or things or places in your dream. Be sure to carefully explain to them the qualities, attitudes, styles, and intentions of the dream elements so that the actors remain faithful to your dream and not spin off their own variations or fantasies. You play the part of the dream ego. Act out the whole dream. Do it a few times. Let yourself *feel* the full dream image. Later, you might take a turn at embodying other dream elements.

You might *journey back into the dream through your deep imagination.* (Deep imagery is explored on pages 145–51.) With or without assistance from an imagery guide, first enter a deep state of relaxation. Then, in your imagination, go back into your dream and relive it, lingering as long as you can in that world and experiencing it as fully as possible. Allow that particular dreamworld to take you where it will. While there, you can also interact with the dream characters, getting to know them, not trying to change who or what they are. Or you might ask their permission to merge with them and be them for a while.

You might, as another method, *enter into dialogues between two or more dream characters* (including the character that is you, the dream ego), taking the place of one and then the other. Do this in your imagery, or with your eyes open and body engaged (with or without the help of a dream guide or friend), or in written dialogues in your journal. Stay true to the way the characters are in the dream, their attitudes, desires, feelings, agendas, and personalities. Keep in mind, with a soulcentric approach to dreams, that you never want to rewrite the script, to change the action for ego comfort or to give the dream a "happy ending."

These methods permit you to get inside the dream, to crawl into the skin of different dream characters and discover the conflicts, potentials, and desires — yours — embodied in those beings. You can do this not only with the people in the dream but also with the dream's animals, trees, rivers, mountains, clouds, houses, cars, situations, emotions, sounds, speech, and even qualities such as colors or size.

Another dreamwork method *explores your direct associations* with the elements of your dream, allowing your imagination to reveal the significance of a dream symbol. For each element of the dream, note any word, idea, feeling, person, or memory that spontaneously arises. Write them down and hang out with those associations until one or two click with the dream more strongly than the rest. Then retell the dream (out loud, to yourself or someone else), substituting that association for the original element. Notice how the dream comes more alive, evokes stronger emotions, or triggers additional memories.[4]

With my two-women dream, for example, I explored associations with the colors red and blue, the name Jacquelyn, with blonde and brunette, briefcases, and, more specifically, with briefcases overstuffed with papers. My associations with red, for example, included heat, anger, love, heart, a red dress, romance, and barns. Focusing on the feel of the specific red of the briefcase of this dream, "heart" and "love" and "romance" were the associations that popped out of that list and clicked with the dream. Jacquelyn apparently has a hardworking agenda concerning affairs of the heart, which is in conflict with Blue/blonde's equally earnest agenda.

Another way to explore your dreams is to *journey into deep imagery to meet an animal who will serve as your dream guide.* With a good relationship forged with your animal guide, you can request its help in learning from or being changed by your dreams. You might, for example, enter a recent dream in your deep imagery, meet your dream guide there, and wander together through that dreamworld. Or, while you are working one of your dreams in a dream group, you might ask your animal dream guide to be present in the room (vividly enough so you can virtually see it there), watch its response as you work with the dream, and perhaps ask it for suggestions about interacting with dream characters and situations. You might also consult your dream guide as you help others with *their* dreamwork.

My current dream guide is a cross between a coyote and a bear. Coyote-Bear takes an approach to dreams both coyotelike (humorous, lighthearted, nonattached, and prone to laughing at my ego's tendency to cling or be extreme or unbalanced) as well as bearlike (burrowing into the dark underworld mysteries, unveiling the gods and goddesses operating there, and uncovering the images to be made visible through my soul work).

One last example of a soulcentric dreamwork method is to *enact the dream either literally or symbolically in your waking life*. Within the bounds of ethics and propriety, take the course of action, in your dayworld, that the dream ego or another character does in your dream. This is done *not* with the belief that the dream maker wants you to conduct your dayworld life in the manner of the dream. The purpose, rather, is to submit yourself to the dream's nightworld, to go back into that world, to give the nightworld images another chance (beyond the dream itself) to do their shape-shifting work on you. You hope to discover what the dream does to you independent of what your dayworld logic might predict.

I went for a long canyon walk, for example, with two women friends (a blonde and brunette, in fact) with a long-standing friendship of their own. I kept my inner eye open for a conflict between them that might even halt our journey. One emerged. I encouraged the conversation to stay on the conflict. I resisted my temptation to mediate or make the journey resume. I let the conflict affect *me*. It did.

The soul speaks primarily in images. Dreams are one example. Although we might engage in thought in non-dream sleep, we don't think when we dream; we imagine. The dream is a series of images. Hillman suggests we imagine a dream as a *single* image like a complex painting. When we look at a painting, we start in one place and then move our gaze across the painting until we have seen it all. But despite our sequence of glances, it is still one painting, a single complex image. We might try relating to dreams this way:

the images can be looked at in any order; together they make up a single symbol. This will help us avoid "making sense" of the dream too soon, imposing our everyday logic and perspectives. Give the dream a chance to do its work on you by dwelling in its images and feelings as long as you can before coming out (or up).

Jungian analyst Robert Johnson recommends we avoid understanding our dreams in a way that flatters the ego. The dream maker, the soul, wants to help the ego mature and transform, which, as we have seen, often begins with the ego dying to its current worldview. The dream maker is not interested in congratulating the ego, but rather in suggesting where it might be limited, wrong, confused, mistaken — that is, where it has opportunities for initiation into a larger story, a larger life.

James Hillman takes this point a step further. He says in every dream, the ego is just plain wrong, mistaken about *something* in the dreamworld, and maybe many things. The ego, after all, is a visitor from the dayworld and everything else in the dream is a nightworld citizen, even if some dream characters are disguised in the dayworld appearance of our spouse, parents, or the woman in the red dress at last night's party. The ego gets confused in the nightworld — and misled — when it tries to understand things in dayworld terms and logic.

You might succeed at imposing your dayworld perspective on the dream but that won't help you in the long run. Try, instead, to see how the dream suggests where the ego's perspective might be broadened or deepened. Try on the perspective that whatever the dream ego is most sure about is surely false. How does that shift everything around?

In working with Red and Blue, I came to understand the dream ego as mistaken in a fundamental way.

During imagery sessions guided by a friend, I alternately merged with Red and Blue. Then I allowed the two to talk to each other. I got to know them better, and the nature of their conflict became clearer. I began to see that the Blue of me was all about soul work. She longed for the full inspiration once experienced working in the inner/outer wilderness. She felt the Red of me was interfering with this all-important work; most of my psychological energy, Blue felt, was being invested in the creation of a sustainable romantic bond. Jacquelyn/Red, in contrast, felt *too* much effort was going into work and not enough into (or through) the heart. She wanted to see more heart come through in my work as well as in my relationships.

Red and Blue were in a stalemate. Together they represented my relationship to my soul (which for most men is feminine), Blue directing the soulful qualities of my work, Red the soulful qualities of my loving. Love and work were in conflict and my soul journey was going nowhere. Although the dream ego believed it had the job of resolving the conflict, I (the waking ego) felt incapable of that (and, given my state at that time, that was correct).

After enough time of living with this dream, I came to see, to my horror, that the conflict — which I called, for short, soul work versus soul mate — was unresolvable. No either/or solution was going to work here, nor a compromise between them. The conflict was not going to go away by, for example, adding more soul to my loving or more heart to my work. Rather, the ego would have to surrender attachment to *both* the soul-work story and the soul-mate story. The ego was being asked to change at least as much as the two disputants.

My soul-work and soul-mate stories had been the psycho-spiritual foundations of my life for twenty years, and both now needed to be released. This proved to be one of the most difficult tasks of my life. I began to prepare for a vision quest during which I would ritually sacrifice both stories — so the road could open again.

Archetypal dream struggles are common for people poised for a great spiritual leap. During the weeks before a vision quest, for example, death-rebirth themes regularly appear with motifs such as being in labor or giving birth, often in odd ways such as from the mouth or by the torso being ripped open, or men being pregnant and giving birth; being split in two or torn apart, dismembered, diseased; being on or falling off dangerous edges or ledges; and, of course, diverse images of dying, being dead, being stalked, and murder. Themes of journeys and displacement are common: searching for a new home; moving from one residence to another; embarking on a mysterious, long, or difficult journey; or a journey reaching a sudden impasse. Underworld images are widespread: diving into water or entering subterranean tunnels, sewers, or caves; entering a bizarre room, town, or wilderness; visitations from animals or magical beings; dangerous and exotic ceremonies and rituals.

A large percentage of people preparing for an underworld experience, such as a vision quest, are terrified that they will literally die on the journey. Once one has said yes to the call to adventure, the ego is securely in the grip of the soul, and the soul serves notice that the ego will not emerge unchanged.

On a weeklong soulcraft program in the redrock canyons of southern Utah, a woman named Maya — a forty-year-old single health care professional — chose to work with a disturbing dream:

> I am on an extended visit at a friend's house. My friend has two babies and she has a refugee woman staying with her who also has a baby. I am to sleep in the refugee woman's room. I rearrange things there to make it less cluttered. Later, I overhear my friend saying how inappropriate it was for me to do that, being I am only a guest and the refugee woman gave up her room for me. I feel ashamed. The babies' diapers are being changed and even though I don't want to deal with it, I feel obliged to help. In the process, I get runny baby shit on my hands and on the floor. I also notice animal scat in the living room and under the bed where I had been sleeping. I see people stepping on the shit and distributing it all over the floor and kids decorating the scat piles. I feel disgusted, try to wash the shit off my hands, so I can leave. The refugee woman says, "If you rub it, it just goes in deeper."

The themes of not being at home and not fitting in were common to both Maya's nightworld and dayworld. She harbored shame and anger over her sense of dislocation.

To get inside this dream and wander there awhile, Maya was encouraged to go off alone and find a place in the canyon where she might make an "extended visit." She was to find a place that seemed cluttered and then she was to rearrange the things there, being careful to pick a spot where her rearranging would not harm the environment. Then she was to express in sound and gesture her anger about being mistreated by others and her shame about not fitting in. Finally, she was to find animal scat, get it all over herself, and try to remove it by rubbing it.

Maya accepted this task with some reluctance. She found a place in a side canyon and rearranged some rocks and sticks at the edge of the creek. She asked the canyon for permission to express her rage about not fitting in. Soon she found herself on all fours, screaming and growling with a fierce animal wildness. Then she removed her clothes and, unable to find animal scat, rubbed slimy red mud from the creek all over her body. Her legs looked to her like furry animal limbs, which reminded her of another dream in which she in fact had animal legs and worried about her lover's and friends' reaction to her being part animal.

During her dream task, a transformative process began for Maya. In contrast to the dream ego's disgust over baby shit and animal scat, Maya discovered a wild power derived from the earthiness and carnality of muck. And, in contrast to her dayworld ego's shame about not fitting in, she found a social courage and resilience that grew out of her full-bodied enactment of feral anger.

Her side-canyon experience became a pivotal part of the ceremony Maya performed the next evening in base camp. With the group drumming in a circle around her, she gradually emerged from beneath piled bark and sticks — as the mud-covered, wild animal of herself. Moving around the circle on all fours, she growled and hissed, approached each member of the group, and looked fiercely into their eyes.

Maya began to reclaim her wildness, her otherness. She had previously experienced these qualities as shit, as socially unacceptable features of the wild animal of herself and the unsocialized babies of herself. She had rejected the "cluttered" ways of her inner refugee, the aspect of self displaced from both mainstream society and from her ego, the psyche's mainstream. She came to see that her rejection of the refugee of herself had kept her alienated from the wildness of her soul. This rejection left her feeling socially unfit, without a "room" of her own. Now she knows that to have that room she must embrace her refugee soul powers.

The refugee was correct when she said, "If you rub it, it just goes in deeper." Fortunately, Maya found the courage to rub, and the wildness and earthiness of that mud-dung went in deep enough to be inerasable.

The denied qualities that once caused Maya so much shame and suffering have a positive and essential function in her life — and in society, too. Since her canyon time, she has been retrieving and integrating her wild nature and other "undesirable" qualities. Maya has come to understand her soul powers to be those of a woman who bestows an essential dose of wildness to the village and whose place in the human community is at the edge, on the boundary between the village and the wild.

In our egocentric society, soul-rooted self-discoveries are challenging to integrate into community life. Initiatory journeys can consequently lead to social isolation and depression. When something wild and potent is released but doesn't have a place to go, it can turn on the ego, and the ego may defend itself in self-injuring ways. Maya's success in integrating her soul powers was greatly facilitated by the support she received immediately after her ceremony. The women openheartedly surrounded her, helped her wash off the mud, and spoke warmly to her as she changed into her more socialized self, allowing her wildness and humanness to live side by side.

Dreamwork draws upon many soulcraft themes: altered consciousness (the ordinary ego state is dissolved when we are asleep), metaphor and symbol, imagination, intense emotion, nature (dreams arise from the soul or the unconscious, our most natural dimension), and the arts (dreams provide the primary creative material for many artists; and poetry, painting, music composition, and so on, are often employed in the expression and exploration of dreams).

Dreamwork can interact in complex and synergistic ways with all other pathways to soul. When two or more soulcraft practices are woven together, they form a vehicle for soul discovery more effective than the independent use of one. A dream, for example, might serve as the symbolic basis for a ceremony. Or the dreamworld might suggest the next step to take following a seminal dayworld interaction with an animal in the wilds — an encounter with a bear, lizard, or dragonfly. A dream might indicate when or where we are to enact a vision fast, or it might turn out to be one of the primary gifts received during a fast. We might recount a dream as a way of introducing ourselves during a council.

Dreamwork is an essential tool in the Wanderer's bag of soulcraft tools.

DEEP IMAGERY

As a culture, we downplay the importance of imagination, especially in education, even though the people we acclaim as our greatest artists, writers, leaders, teachers, and scientists are the ones with the most magnificent imaginations. Imagination is our most valuable power on the journey to soul.

Deep imagery refers to inner journeys in which you interact, while awake, with the other-than-ego inhabitants of your psyche. Also known as *active imagination* by Jungians, deep imagery is distinct from guided imagery, in which another person (the guide) invites you to imagine specific scenes suggested *by the guide.* A guided image might be an idyllic beach on a tropical island, suggested to help you relax, or little white-suited men running around inside your leg with trowels and buckets of cement to help heal your broken bone. With deep imagery, in contrast, the images come from the depths of your own unconscious, and the guide (when there is one) doesn't know any more than you what will take place on your journey.

A deep imagery guide is like a wilderness outfitter, someone you hire to take you into a desert, forest, or mountain range. Your guide is familiar with the opportunities and dangers of the inner wilderness and knows how to interact respectfully with the wildlife; but it's your choice where you'll go in that wilderness and how long you'll stay. The guide helps with the logistics of the journey and makes suggestions as to how to handle what arises. Yet, once the journey begins, both of you know that what you encounter rests in *neither* of your hands: the wilderness decides.

There are many methods for cultivating deep imagery, but among the most effective are those that involve *power animals,* inner guides to healing, growth, and soul work. The most soulcraft-resonant work with power animals was developed by the American psychologist Eligio Stephen Gallegos and is known as the Personal Totem Pole.[5]

The human unconscious often represents itself in the shape of animals. Perhaps this is because, as a species, we evolved hand in claw with creatures prowling through the tall savanna grasses, or swinging from limb to jungle limb, parting the air above us, or drifting through the waters. Animals are the Others of the outer wild. Why should we be surprised that the Others of the inner wilds prefer to take similar forms?

Children learn much about the world and themselves by imitating and *becoming* animals as they play, imagine, and feel. Across the planet, the casts of children's stories are drawn from fields, forests, and farms. We understand intuitively that the animals represent the Otherness of the world, the Otherness that both frightens and attracts us. Animal stories help us make peace with not only the Otherness of outer nature but also, more significantly, the Otherness of our own emotions, our own so-human fears, hopes, passions, conflicts, loves, and losses.

Appreciating these things, Gallegos developed a powerful and elegant system of deep imagery work that marries active imagination with the Far East's system of energetic body centers (chakras) and the totem pole traditions of the Native American cultures in the Pacific Northwest. In Gallegos's original Personal Totem Pole work, the inner journeyer is guided to meet an animal for each of the seven chakras, the animals embodying the psychological qualities of the individual's crown, forehead, throat, heart, solar plexus, belly, and pelvis/legs.

The animals we meet in our deep imagery want to communicate with us. Sometimes they simply show us something, about themselves or the place in which they live. Or they may take us on a journey on which we might learn something. Other times, the animals converse with us in ordinary human language. They may have something to tell us or teach us, or we may have a request or a response. Or perhaps a dialogue will unfold through intuitive thought (without words) or through feeling or sensation.

As in soulcentric dreamwork, imagery animals are not meant to be interpreted. The goal is to *interact* with the animals, develop a relationship, and see how things unfold. Gallegos suggests that interpreting an imagery animal would be like responding rudely to someone who knocks at your front door: without saying a word to them, you give them a quick once-over, close the door, and ask yourself, "I wonder what *that* meant?" Such a superficial and discourteous reaction to our own images is not uncommon in the West because many people haven't experienced the potency of imagination. Why not begin a relationship with the beings of your inner world the same way you would with an unexpected guest: invite them in, introduce yourself, make them comfortable, thank them for traveling to your home. Don't interpret, relate.

In Gallegos's approach to deep imagery, you are encouraged to develop a respectful relationship with each animal (and thus with the elements of your own unconscious). Your conscious self accompanies the animal on journeys through the non-ordinary realms of the psyche and the body, receives information, advice, or other gifts, and assists the animal with *its* needs for healing and growing. In later work, you might merge with the animal to perceive its world through its eyes, ears, and nose, move with its wings, paws, or fins, and be embodied within its feathers, fur, or scales. You might embark on journeys in which two or more animals come together to help each other, settle their differences, or join ranks on a common project. From time to time, the animals themselves go through major transformations, including death and rebirth, or shape-shifting from one species to another, such transformations both reflecting and at times initiating psycho-spiritual changes within your psyche.

As a Wanderer, you have a desire and a need to make acquaintance with aspects of your own psyche that have lain dormant like a genie in a bottle, or a festering wound covered with layers of bandages, or the gods and goddesses sleeping within you. Deep imagery is a highly effective means of uncovering soul powers, sacred wounds, and archetypal potentials and thereby promoting psychological wholeness. And your imagery journeys are the most direct method for meeting inner guides, who possess the wisdom and capacities to assist you on your underworld journey.

Julie has developed a wonderfully rich relationship with her imagination. Through imagery journeys over several years, both self-guided and other-guided, she has healed, grown, and been challenged at the deepest levels. The following journey took place after five months of an unfulfilling internship in psychotherapy, a component of her master's work in counseling. She found herself in a challenging institutional setting that offered less supervision than she needed, leaving her drained both physically and emotionally — and with her graduate degree incomplete. Most disheartening to her was her own failure to ask for the help she needed or to leave the internship. She felt she had failed herself and had no fight left to complete her degree — or anything else.

Finally, she went to her animal guides for help. She traveled inward, grateful to find them in the place they usually met. They were happy to see her as well — and concerned, as they immediately recognized her state of depletion. Tiger approached her first:

> Tiger asks me to merge with his body and feel his power. My arms and legs become his limbs and I see through his eyes. Almost immediately, however, exhaustion overcomes me and I'm unable to move my limbs. I collapse onto the ground, legs sprawled in every direction. The other animals come quickly. They help me emerge from Tiger, pick me up, and place me on a soft bed. I am very weak.
>
> The Woman in Black arrives. She wraps me in gossamer cloth, circling round my body like a mummy wrap, like I am being cocooned. She says this is necessary for my protection. She instructs the other animals to carry me and to follow her. They take me through a long dark hallway, up a flight of stairs, and into a room. We seem to be in the castle of the Woman in Black. The room is quite dark except for a few white candles in each corner. The animals lay me on a flat stone slab in the center of the room and then leave. The Woman in Black tells me I must stay here.
>
> I am too weak to resist. The Woman in Black leaves and I am enveloped by complete silence and near darkness. I glimpse a green cocoon hanging from the ceiling and wonder if I am giving up old skin.

The first attempt by Julie's animals to help her — by grounding her in Tiger's solid presence — failed. She needed something more radical. The Woman in Black, a longtime inner guide and teacher, understood. Julie needed to be prepared, through a time of rest, for the kind of transformation that takes place in a cocoon. Five months passed before Julie was ready to journey back to that dark room. This is what happened:

> All the animals are gathered around me on the stone slab. My favorite animal, Owl, is close by my side. Owl is my heart animal and has been my

main inner guide for years. The wrappings around my body begin to fall away.

All of a sudden, out of nowhere, an ax comes down and chops off Owl's head. I scream out "No!!!! This isn't possible! I don't understand!!" Then an eagle appears who takes up Owl in his talons. Eagle tears Owl into pieces and feeds them to the other animals. It is violent and bloody. My heart is broken, ripped into a thousand pieces.

The Woman in Black appears. Tears streaming down my face, I ask her what this means. She says this is the only way for me to go forward. She says Owl so loved me he was willing to sacrifice himself so I might be transformed. There is always a sacrifice of the old before the birth of the new, she says. A part of Owl lives on in each of the animals — and in me. The Woman in Black says I will always be able to feel Owl's presence. I ask who will replace Owl. She says Eagle, who can see in far-reaching ways, is powerful in flight, and will take my heart to places not previously imagined.

This astonishing and painful transformation in her imagery world supported Julie to shift out of her pattern of not acting on her own behalf. She began to surrender her childhood defenses of invisibility and beliefs of unworthiness that led to her passivity in her internship. Soon, Julie found a more supportive environment to complete her internship, one that also challenged her to take greater risks with her heart. She was awarded her degree within a few months.

The sacrifice and communion-like consumption of Owl — who embodied Julie's less mature way of loving — opened the way to profound personal change. The heart shift from Owl to Eagle reflected Julie's recognition and eventual recovery of her dormant soul power: her extraordinary capacity to see into other people's hearts with the shrewd and certain eyes of Eagle.

For many Westerners, use of the imagination is an unfamiliar skill. Some people have great difficulty, at first, accessing their deep images; they may have spent too much of their lives relying on thinking, or perhaps were taught as children that imagination was dangerous, bad, or foolish. Other people, as they begin again to imagine, become concerned they are "just making it up." They ask, "How do I know this is real or valid? Am I doing this right?"

These are real concerns. Keep in mind that uncertainty and tentativeness are common when learning *any* new skill or beginning to use a new faculty. Recall how uncertain you were when you first began to play a musical instrument, draw, write poetry, dance, make love, or any other activity requiring a good imagination.

The best answer to novices is this: be patient. Your imagination may have been largely dormant since childhood, but it is alive and well inside you. On your first several journeys, your imagination may in fact not go very deep. You may not "see" or "hear" or "feel" much. Stick with it. You may even get a black screen at first. Good. Start there. *Explore* that black screen, including its edges and what may be beneath it. If your images are hazy or elusive, remain in relationship with those images. Engage them. Call them back if they disappear. Make fun of them, if you want, for being so tentative (like you). Stay with them.

Gradually, what you experience in the window of imagination will connect in startling and profound ways with: (1) images from other experiences (such as dreams, memories, visions, and previous and future imagery journeys); (2) information from the other three windows of knowing (namely feeling, thinking, and sensing); and (3) your relationships with other people and other-than-human beings. As this begins to happen, the initial questions about validity will have curiously vanished, as if they had been "just your imagination."

Trebbe Johnson regularly consults her inner animals for advice and support in her soul work. Years ago, when she started guiding wilderness journeys, she would invariably wake up on the second day with nausea and a splitting headache. She assumed this was due to the huge responsibilities of the first day as well as the anxiety of beginning a long program with so much to plan, think about, organize, and be fully present for.

> After five or six of these experiences, I had the idea of asking Raven, my guide to leading quests, what he had to say. He showed me an image of a mill wheel churning and churning. He said, "You think you're responsible

for this journey's success. You think it all has to come from you. You're working too hard. This is Spirit's work. All you have to do is open the door on the top of your head, so Spirit can come though, then open the doors on the tips of each of your fingers so Spirit can move through you and out to the questers." I saw Raven himself gently pecking those little outlets in me.

Since then, before beginning each quest, Trebbe has called upon Raven to come and help her open those outlets. She has never again been sick while guiding.

CHAPTER 8

COMMUNING WITH
THE OTHERS

I know that nothing has ever been real
without my beholding it.
All becoming has needed me.
My looking ripens things
and they come toward me, to meet and be met.

— Rainer Maria Rilke

The Wanderer discovers much about what is real and what is not through relationship and communion. In this chapter, we explore pathways to soul encounter rooted in reverential interactions with our fellow humans and with the animals, plants, landforms, waterways, and residents of the sky — in other words, with the Others. From the perspective of soulcraft, all the Others are sacred beings. Our interactions with them reveal us to ourselves and also teach us about them and *their* needs, vulnerabilities, perspectives, gifts, and dreams. By deepening our relationships with the Others, our gratitude for the whole world grows and we become more capable and responsible members of the world community. We also uncover mysteries about our unique way of belonging to this world of Others. Through communion with all of life, we weave a healthier and more balanced world back into being.

COUNCIL WORK

Council is a way of holding a meeting that empowers people to speak from their hearts; it is an ancient practice transforming the experience of contemporary group process, from primary education classrooms to corporate boardrooms, from men's groups to vision quest groups, from couples and families to groups of strangers. Councils enable us to open to the radical otherness of our fellow humans, thereby knitting together the sort of true community that has become rare in the Western world. Councils also support us in accessing and expressing our deepest truths, not only by making it safe to do so but also by creating a social lens that reveals our own unknown depths to ourselves.

The basic format of council, for any gathering of two or more, requires only a suitable place to meet, a ceremonial object (the "talking piece") to pass from one person to the next, a set of four intentions, and a few shared agreements. The best meeting places are those in which the participants can sit in a circle, either on the floor or in chairs with open space in the center.

Ideally, it is a quiet and private place that will not be disturbed by visitors, ringing phones, or other interruptions. Whether indoors or out in nature, each participant should be able to see the face of every other person when all are comfortably seated. When each person can look into the eyes of every other, you have a true circle.

At every moment in the council, each person knows whose turn it is to speak because only the person holding the talking piece is empowered to do so (with three exceptions mentioned below). This way, no one need worry about being interrupted, a common deterrent to speaking our truths. The talking piece can be anything easily passed, but typically it is something regarded as special or sacred by at least the person who convenes the council, and ideally by all present. Often the object takes the form of a small staff or stick, thus the common reference to council circles as "talking-staff councils" or "talking sticks." In groups with a long history, the talking piece may be highly revered, having been passed from hand to hand around hundreds of circles. For new groups, the talking piece may be a simple stick or something chosen in the moment, and perhaps used only once.

Jack Zimmerman and Gigi Coyle have written a fine book on the way of council.[1] They elegantly capture the spirit of this practice by identifying four intentions we practice while in circle. Each intention leads us back to our hearts.

First, our intention is to speak *from* our hearts when we hold the talking piece. We speak only what is true and has heartfelt meaning. We speak by way of our emotions, our imaginations, and our senses, as well as from our thoughts. But always, we speak from our hearts.

Second, when we sit in council, we practice listening *with* our hearts. Our primary goal is to feel what the person is saying, whether or not we understand it with our heads. We hope to experience where the other is sitting in their lives and in relation to the circle without worrying about whether we can quantify it, rationalize it, or explain it.

Third, when it is our turn to speak, we practice brevity or, as Jack and Gigi put it, "being of lean expression." The goal is not to offer an exhaustive account or a defensible explanation of how we got to be where we are, but rather to simply *be* there. If we have some faith that the others are listening with their hearts, then they won't need an elaborate explanation. If we explain too much, we may end up inadvertently encouraging the others to listen with their heads rather than their hearts. Indeed, we might not need to utter a single word. Just sitting there in our truth, with or without tears streaming down our faces, may be more than enough for everyone to heartfully feel where we sit.

Fourth, and often most challenging, we practice spontaneity. It is, of course, tempting and only human to rehearse, especially when we are about to speak in front of more than one person! We want to present ourselves in a good light or at least not misrepresent or make a fool of ourselves. So we are naturally tempted to rehearse. There are two problems, though. It's difficult to listen with our hearts when we're busy rehearsing. And there's no guarantee what we rehearse will be relevant to what we find in our hearts by the time it's our turn; more often than not, it isn't. If we speak what we have rehearsed and not what is in our hearts, those listening with *their* hearts will know it. If, on the other hand, we speak our hearts, the others will be on our side no matter how much we might stumble. So we are called upon to practice a radical faith that, when the talking piece reaches us, we will indeed be able to access our hearts and find a way to express what's there.

Still, most people find themselves rehearsing. As I said, it's only human. Sitting in council, then, can be approached as a meditation practice (an extra benefit). When we notice our attention has strayed from the heart, we simply let go of our rehearsal and gently (with self-love) come back to the heart, both our own listening heart and the heart being expressed by the other.

A council also needs a few shared agreements. You already know the first one: speak only when you hold the talking piece. But, in fact, there are three exceptions: If what someone says really resonates with you, either because it is true of you as well or because you felt its poignancy for the other, you might indicate your resonance with a simple sound. Most common is *ho!* which affirms without interrupting. Letting others know you're with them weaves the council closer and increases the council's depth. The second exception is the converse: if you literally didn't hear what someone said, you might ask them to speak up or repeat themselves. The third concerns the person who convened the council. This person's task, in addition to being a full participant like everyone else, is to help all stay in alignment with the shared agreements and intentions of the council. Although rarely necessary, the council holder can speak out of turn to offer gentle reminders or resolve questions such as the council duration or whether there will be a break.

Other agreements include how the council will commence (with or without ceremony, with or without an invocation or an acknowledgment of the tradition in which the council is convened); how the talking piece is passed from one person to the next (e.g., with eye contact or with a ceremonial phrase or question such as "What's in *your* heart?"); what topics the council might be limited to or especially focused on; how many rounds the talking piece will make; which direction the staff will be passed (this is symbolically significant for some groups) or whether it will be returned to the center after each person speaks to await the next to pick it up; whether or not people can get up to relieve themselves without a general break being called; and so on.

Many people assume the tradition of council originated with Native Americans, but in fact it's found in many cultures and has been traced clear back to the Stone Age in what is now France.[2] I first studied the way of council in 1980 with Elizabeth Cogburn, whom I met at Dolores LaChapelle's Way of the Mountain Center in Silverton, Colorado. Elizabeth's clan of ceremonial dancers adopted the practice of council from the Greeks. During one of their gatherings many years ago, a dispute arose about the conduct of a particular ceremony. To resolve the conflict, Elizabeth's husband, Bob, suggested they sit in council and pass a staff in the manner employed by ancient Greek warriors. They did. It worked, and they have since passed their tradition to many others.

The magic of council arises from field dynamics. When we speak and listen with our hearts for a sustained period, a group field emerges in which everyone's power of empathy (for both self and others) grows exponentially. We come to see that each person holds a piece of the truth. Like a circle of mirrors, each person ends up reflecting a part of everyone else, *and everyone sees that.* The group field grows in this way and transforms everyone in it, and everyone's heart opens more. The rigid boundaries between ourselves and others dissolve or at least become more fluid and dynamic. This is what anthropologist Victor Turner referred to as *communitas* — true communing between souls, the same phenomenon Martin Buber referred to as *I-thou.*

That often rigid boundary between each person's mind and their own heart and soul loosens up as well. And the same with those carefully constructed fences on the border between the self and the world; everything comes into closer contact with everything else. The world comes back together again. Yes, conflicts and disputes can be resolved in council, but the potential goes far beyond that. Council facilitates a deep encounter with self, other, and Other. If this sounds like more than one could hope for from a bunch of people sitting in a circle passing a stick, you probably haven't yet experienced a council.

SACRED SPEECH AND SILENCE

Unlike the heartfelt conversations of council, we spend much of our time talking about trivial matters and practical ones — the weather, plans for the day, routine office events, frivolous gossip, the new movie, canned jokes, the latest shopping acquisition, the next technological miracle, stock-market shifts. Chitchat, the everyday wins and losses. So little of our conversation addresses our passions, loves, emotions, dreams, or our creative insights and soul stirrings.

An effective strategy for tuning our awareness to the frequency of soul is to minimize everyday conversation that separates us from the here and now and from what is truly meaningful. This can be a rather challenging discipline. Sometimes it seems almost everything in our culture conspires to distance us from heart and soul. So many messages are ads, trying to sell us something of questionable usefulness while ruthlessly pandering to our vanity, insecurity, or unhappiness — new toys, fashion, entertainment, or insurance against the inevitabilities of life. Few people ask the bigger questions. For the Wanderer, however, nothing is more important: she seeks the hidden treasure, the spring bubbling in the desert, the song of the world.

Constant superficial conversation keeps us from noticing what's going on with us emotionally or spiritually or in our bodies. Small talk alienates us from ourselves — perhaps a purpose as well as a result.

Surrendering an addiction to nonstop chatter is hard enough. Should we succeed, we then face a greater challenge: the *internal* dialogue. Our minds are in constant motion, fretting about the future and second-guessing the past. This endless cognitive activity keeps us well rehearsed in our current worldview and lifestyle: safe (or so we might think). In order to approach the deeper truths of soul, we must quiet the inner chatter. Meditation practice is one way. Another path to inner peace is the discipline of sacred speech and silence.

Sacred speech is conversation that deepens. It deepens relationship and enhances the fullness of our presence wherever we are and whomever we are with. It is dialogue centered in what exists here and now between us. We speak from the heart and address what truly matters — our feelings, imagery, dreams, life purpose, our relationships, soul stories, our discoveries of how we project aspects of self onto others or learn to withdraw those projections, and our meetings with remarkable humans, animals, plants, and places. There is no requirement that such conversation be solemn or hushed. The sacred is often funny as well. We laugh at our oh-so-human foibles and the jokes life plays on us every day. The more real our conversations become, the more alive we become, the more we want to scream or shout or cry.

Silence with others is, of course, the natural complement to sacred speech. Too often we attempt to fill every social moment with chatter as if we are terrified of the silence between us. Often we are; we're scared of who or what might jump into the conversation, the voices from below or behind. The Wanderer, however, chooses to leap into that void and find out who's lurking there. So we might make it a practice, from time to time, to express our preference for and enjoyment of silence when in the presence of others, especially after we have already spoken of the meaningful things.

A regular diet of sacred speech and silence nourishes the soul and opens the door to soul encounter. Gradually, our everyday consciousness shifts.

TRANCE DRUMMING AND RHYTHMS

The incantation of the drum is one of the oldest and most celebrated methods for entering trance states, opening the door to the otherworld, and unearthing what lies beneath our surface lives. For millennia, shamans everywhere have traveled on the beat of the drum into the underworld in search of healing or transformation for self and others. The drum has been used from the beginning of time by every culture in the world and has a direct, potent effect on human neurophysiology.[3]

Trance drumming requires some skill and practice — and usually some instruction. Not just any thumping of an animal hide stretched over a frame will do. The tempo and cadence are important. Different beats work best for different purposes, some trance beats being quite complex to the novice ear. By learning and practicing the vocabulary of rhythm, you will be able to converse with the otherworld more eloquently and unselfconsciously when drumming.

Once a session of trance drumming begins, however, it is essential to allow the rhythm to develop a life of its own. You allow the beat to go and flow whither it will, without conscious attempts to direct it. Most commonly, a given beat repeats for some time and then, gradually and subtly, it alters. The shape-shifting rhythm is the vehicle upon which you ride, like a galloping horse. The resulting trance ushers you into the mercurial realm of deep imagination.

In most traditions, the drum is joined by shakers (especially gourd rattles), bells, and voice for a more full-bodied ensemble of percussive rhythm. Flutes, recorders, and other instruments may also be added.

Trance drumming in groups can significantly amplify the intensity and value of the experience. Each person (with drum, rattle, bell, or voice) enters the circle with the intention of allowing an unidentified rhythm to claim her. This rhythm will arise from her center without thought or deliberation, yet will mesh with the emerging group rhythm. Indeed, not only does it fit in, it becomes an indispensable component of the richness and roundness of the group beat, helping to drive it forward into its full potential. Group trance drumming is most powerful and captivating when each person surrenders any attempt to figure it out or make it work. Rather, everyone submits to the unique rhythm evoked in them by the particular blending of human souls in that circle. All participants become totally themselves and yet totally with all the others. In this way, group trance drumming becomes a living metaphor of the search for soul: we each seek our individual truth that, when embodied, enriches the song of the world.

Trance drumming pushes us over the edge and we fall into other worlds. During a recent session I had this experience:

> The drums growl and troll in low voices, filling the room with a roar and rumble as the tall gods and goddesses dance among us. The earthen floor and walls reverberate with the pulse. The gourd shakers, filled with tiny pebbles gathered from the base of anthills, trill and rasp, dancing above the groundswell of the drums. The cadence swells and sways, gathering at times into great pulsing waves, soothing at other moments into gentle swings and rolls. Exotic and outlandish voices, human and yet not human, emerge from behind columns of sound, singing in melodious whispers or grunting in muted tones.
>
> Merging with the beat, I am drawn beneath the surface, spiraling down as if beckoned, emerging in a jungle. Wandering through a thousand shades and shapes of green, I follow the trail of a distant pulse. I break through thick brush into a sunlit clearing. Sitting around a small, blue-green lagoon, are the others. Each beats a drum or shakes a rattle. Each chants in

low notes. One spot is open. Taking my place, I gaze into still water mirroring sky and forest canopy. I fall forward and up, riding on rhythm.

Trance drumming is commonly employed to facilitate deep imagery journeys. One person might drum to assist another, or a practiced drummer will accompany her own journey. The drumbeat becomes the vehicle and companion for the journey to the otherworld.

Because it induces non-ordinary states, trance drumming is often employed at the outset of an individual or group ceremony to facilitate the shift from ordinary time and space to that of the sacred. A vision quester may drum during much of his fast to keep the everyday thinking mind at bay and to stay in tune with the dreamtime, the deep imagination, the realm of the tall gods and goddesses.

ECSTATIC TRANCE DANCING

Dance adds a universe of bodily expression and possibility to the drums and other instruments. In trance dancing, we surrender to the images and entities, inside and out, that want to move us, to be danced by us.

Trance dance is not the time to learn or practice new moves, to work on flexibility or range of motion, or to develop the body's expressive repertoire. There are other times for those things. It's also not about impressing others or being ashamed. Trance dance invites us to release our embodied selves into ecstasy — realms beyond our ordinary ego states — to discover what the soul has to say through our body's own improvisations. If traditional movements are employed, they are simple and repetitive. The opportunity that is offered, as with all soulcraft skills, is to slip beneath the ego's everyday shtick, diving into mystery.

Indoors or out, most prefer to trance dance at night, with subdued light from candles or a small fire. Some people dance blindfolded. The drum is always an essential factor enabling the dancers to reach the trance state together. Most trance dancers are accompanied by live, experienced drummers. Some dance alone to recorded music or inner rhythms. Some are able to dance while drumming.

When a person's inner animals want to dance, the ego's job is to get out of the way. The dancer does not try to limit or embellish how the dance unfolds; she surrenders to the rhythms, the grammar of her own body, and the presences, inside and out, that want to take form during the brief but eternal moments of the dance. A story, a myth, a feeling, or a new way of belonging to the world may want to be embodied. Sometimes two or more people, to their astonishment, will meet in the inner circle of a group trance dance and discover something wants to be nudged into existence through the interweaving of their energies.

Regardless of what form the trance dance takes, we find ourselves in an exotic kingdom, an exquisitely creative world brimming with soulful potency.

We may find ourselves invited to dance by beings from a dream, deep imagery experience, or vision. The Wanderer learns to embrace these requests with a wild faith in their necessity, knowing he will learn something essential and be enabled to offer himself more fully to the world. This is a central feature of soulcraft: one encounter with soul points the way to one or more others. It is up to us to follow the thread.

Michael DeMaria, a psychologist at the University of West Florida, is that kind of faithful Wanderer. On a wilderness journey in the San Miguel Mountains of southwest Colorado, Michael felt called to a difficult and unlikely place. Camped at 11,400 feet, a mountain peak loomed three thousand feet above him. Halfway between his camp and the summit, at the top of a steep rock slide, was a dark opening:

> In the San Miguels, in August, I found myself in a cave. I lay down on the moss-covered floor. Before long, visions and dreams danced in my head. The old woman appeared once again. Whispering by the fire, she pulled out a large, old book... ancient paper worn by time, the pages filled with diagrams, writings. She pointed to a spiral of people dancing in a circle. She said, "There... dance... dance for four years... from sunset to sunrise... with the people... for the people... for the earth... for life and healing... dance."

In late December of that year, Michael and friends held their first of eight solstice dances, summer and winter. Their dances were enacted on a south coast beach of pure white sand, bordered by ocean on one side and pine and oak on the other. Dusk to dawn, they danced in the rain, in the heat, in the cold. They danced half-clothed, half-crazed. They danced with mosquitoes, deer, and sand crabs.

> We've danced and we've drummed. And, sometime just before dawn, the old woman can be seen smiling in the shadows of the windswept dunes as the beat of our big drum roars on through the twilight. Toward the end of our most recent dance, some of us heard her whisper:

> This night is every night
> and this dawn
> remains forever.

Two days before the start of his vision fast in the redrock desert canyons, a man once known as John trance danced for the first time. In the midst of the dance, he found himself invited by the spirit of a deer to perform its dance. The deer was crippled and had only one leg to dance upon. The man-deer danced on his one good leg. The next morning, the man wandered into the desert and came upon the intact skeleton of a deer with three broken legs. The deer then gave him his next soul task in preparation for his fast. We'll revisit this man's story in chapter 11.

On the wilderness journeys I guide, we create ceremonial dances to help us ease out of our ordinary, merely human mode of being and perceiving and cross into the sacred, timeless, symbolic world of myth, ritual, and the whole of life. We use simple musical instruments, especially the original ones: drums, shakers (e.g., gourd rattles, maracas, tambourines, or tin cans filled with pebbles or seeds), bells, conches, whistles, flutes, and recorders. The human voice is invited, too, in the form of nonverbal chanting. The form and spirit of our trance dances were created by Elizabeth Cogburn in the 1970s. These dances take place within four concentric circles, each circle a space on the dance ground in which certain movements are invited. The outer circle is occupied by those who are drumming, playing other instruments (including their voices), and/or dancing in place. This outer circle also creates the energetic container for all that happens within it. The next two circles inside are reserved for a specific pair of repetitive trance movements, the first of which moves sunwise and in a masculine way and the second earthwise in a feminine manner. The final circle marks the remaining space at the center, the inner sanctum reserved for the deepest trance dances and interactions.

By helping us cross boundaries into the mysteries of nature and psyche, trance dances serve to deepen our relationship to soul, foster group bonding, and affirm our membership in nature.

On group vision quest journeys, we dance on one of the evenings before the fast to help the quester come into harmony with: (1) the invisible presences inside him; (2) the other humans in the group; and (3) the wild beings of nature who are ritually invited by name, at the outset, to join in our dance.

Sometimes we also enact a trance dance *after* the fast to help the returning questers embody, beyond words, what they received during the underworld days of solitude.

CEREMONIAL SWEATS AND SAUNAS

Another method for altering consciousness, communing with the Others, and ushering us into sacred time and space, ceremonial sweats and saunas have been practiced for millennia in many cultures around the world, including by the indigenous peoples of the Americas, the Turks, Russians, Scandinavians, and Japanese. Sauna is a Finnish tradition more than a thousand years old. Although its origin is lost in prehistory, some say the Finns brought the sauna to northern Europe from their previous home in central Asia.

Most people in the United States familiar with ceremonial sweats think of Native American sweat-lodge ceremonies. These are traditional sacred rites still commonly enacted as integral elements of native people's religious life.

Just as there are numerous methods of trance dance, council, or dreamwork, there are many ceremonial forms for approaching the soul through extreme heat. Whether employing dry or moist heat, these ceremonies purify body, emotions, and mind, support our journeys through the landscapes of the psyche, and facilitate our communion with each other and the other beings of our world. Sweating together in a ceremonial way creates extraordinarily strong bonds of empathy and intimacy. A soul-supportive group field emerges like that of councils.

I have participated in sacred sweat ceremonies for the purposes of purification, prayer, healing, and envisioning. In one format, we heat rocks in a fire pit several feet from the small sweat house, a round, low, tent-sized structure made of tarps placed over a frame of arched willow or alder poles. Once red-hot, the rocks are carried by pitchfork into a pit in the center of the sweat house. In another format, we burn logs in a woodstove inside a small, square, windowless cabin lined inside with wooden benches. A large pile of rocks sit on the woodstove. In both cases, while the rocks are heating, we sit outside in a circle, sometimes with drums and shakers, and ritually speak our intentions for the ceremony — to help us reestablish a good relationship with all beings, our souls, and spirit. This intention setting helps create the sacred space and is itself a prayer and a spiritual form of purification. We enter into the sweat ceremony with humility, as we might enter a church, but, in this case, it's a visceral, intimate, and emotionally animated church. We express and celebrate all elements of our humanness, especially those we often suppress — our losses, longings, vulnerabilities, and contradictions.

Once inside the sweat house or cabin, the door is closed, sealing us in and shutting out all light. Herbs such as sage, frankincense, or juniper needles are placed on the rocks as purifying incense. Then handfuls of water are splashed onto the rocks to make billows of searing steam. I am invariably stunned, at first, by the utter darkness, the incredible intensity of the heat, and the profuse streams of sweat pouring from my body. Sweating opens our pores and purifies and heals us physically.

During the ceremony, the heat and heartfelt prayers melt away the defenses around my deepest emotions. I become aware of many things I had not allowed myself to feel, the griefs and gratitudes, longings and loneliness, fears and faith. I weep openly along with the others and go deeper, until I find renewed hope and love. It is an emotional purification and healing. While in the lodge, we chant both familiar and spontaneous songs, and we pray silently or aloud for what we *really* want for ourselves, our loved ones, and the world. Sometimes the heat, emotions, and prayers are so strong I see images, or visions, that support me on my soul path.

Talking Across the Species Boundaries: Dialogues with Nature

If you have never traded speech with a lizard, a rattlesnake, an elk, a desert juniper, the wind, or a rock, you have a world-shifting treat in store for you. It's as if you just discovered thousands of new relatives, fascinating and wild beings you can now learn from and commune with. The world is suddenly a different place; a kind of isolation you didn't know you suffered has vanished.

Most modern people would feel foolish to sit and talk with a snake or a tower of rock. Most nature-based people, in contrast, would have the sincerest sympathy for anyone who could not do that with ease, or communicate with a bear, or hear the songs of the stars.

The common Western experience of being mute and deaf in nature suggests how much we have become alienated from the world that gives birth to us. The contemporary eco-philosopher David Abram reminds us that for the vast majority of humanity's time on the planet (up until the advent of agriculture and alphabets about ten thousand years ago), these conversations "across the species boundaries" were a universal experience, part of our birthright as members of the more-than-human community.[4]

Although most Westerners seldom use it, the capacity for these conversations still exists within us as a fundamental feature of the perceptual process. Abram explains how we comprehend the "articulate speech of trees or mountains" through a mixing or converging of our sensory modalities. Something we *see*, for example, induces an auditory or kinesthetic experience:

> [T]he animistic discourse of indigenous, oral peoples is an inevitable counterpart of their immediate, synaesthetic engagement with the land that they inhabit. The animistic proclivity to perceive the angular shape of a boulder (while shadows shift across its surface) as a kind of meaningful gesture, or to enter into felt conversations with clouds and owls—all of this could be brushed aside as imaginary distortion or hallucinatory fantasy if such active participation were not the very structure of perception, if the creative interplay of the senses in the things they encounter was not our sole way of linking ourselves to those things and letting the things weave themselves into our experience. Direct, prereflective perception is inherently synaesthetic, participatory, and animistic, disclosing the things and elements that surround us not as inert objects but as expressive subjects, entities, powers, potencies.[5]

For the modern Wanderer, "direct, prereflective perception" can once again become a commonplace of consciousness.

Go wandering outside, anywhere. Bring your journal. Be prepared to offer a gift — a poem, grief, yearning, joy, your eloquence, a song, a dance, a lock of hair, praise, tobacco, water. Early on, cross over a physical threshold (such as a stream, a stick, a large rock, a passageway between two trees) to mark your transition from ordinary time and space to the sacred. While on the sacred side, observe three cross-cultural taboos: do not eat, do not speak with other humans, and do not enter any human-made shelter.

Wander aimlessly until you feel called by something that draws your attention, by way of an attraction, a curiosity, an allurement, a repulsion, a fear. This might take some time. Don't just choose something with your strategic thinking mind; wait until you are called. It may be a bush, a blade of grass, a stone, an anthill, a lizard, maybe a vulture or a rotting cow carcass. Maybe it will be a rainbow or a constellation of stars. Whatever it is, sit and observe it closely for a good length of time. Interact with your senses, offer your full visual and aural attention to the Other. Record in your journal what you observe. Perhaps offer a gift at this time.

Then introduce yourself, out loud — yes, out loud. This is important. Tell this being all about yourself. Be prepared to go on for an indefinite period of time, maybe a half hour or more. First tell it why you have been wandering around waiting to be called. And no, not just because some crazed writer suggested it, but because of the particular things within you with which the idea resonated — enough to motivate you to go out and try it. Tell the truth, your deepest, most intimate truth. In addition to ordinary human language, you might choose to speak with song, poetry, nonverbal sound, images (feel yourself sending those images to the Other), emotion, body language (movement, gesture, dance). Then, using the same speech options, tell that being everything about *it* you have noticed. Describe its features (out loud, if using words, song, or sound) and, respectfully, tell it what interests you about those features and what it tells you about *you* that you find them interesting. Keep communicating no matter what... until it interrupts you.

Then stop and listen. Listen with your ears, eyes, nose, skin, intuition, feeling, and imagination (aural, visual, kinesthetic, and so on). Listening (direct, pre-reflective perception) is different from your own psyche fabricating metaphors (such as a tree "telling" you to stand tall), but the latter is okay, too. It may take hours before you get interrupted. Or days. Or never. Or it may take only the time for a deer's eye to blink.

Keep the conversation going several rounds. In your journal, record and/or draw what happens. Offer the Other your gratitude and a gift if you haven't already. When you are ready, return to the place of your original threshold and cross back over.

The Other might reflect something back to you about yourself, but, more generally, you'll learn something about the Other. Or about both you *and* the Other. Or about the web that contains you both. It's best to enter wild conversations with the intent to become acquainted with one of your nonhuman neighbors, rather than, say, to receive some oracular information about yourself.

Think for a moment of your relationships with your human friends. You usually don't enter conversations to discover more about yourself. You want to get to know *them* and you want to enjoy yourself and deepen your friendships. You've also undoubtedly noticed that there are many authentic versions of you, and which version arrives on the scene depends a lot on whom you're with. You choose your friends largely on the basis of what they switch on in you, who you can be with them. Some of your most intriguing friends are the ones who are least like you, partly because they draw out surprising and enjoyable dimensions of your own humanness.

Now apply this to relationships with nonhuman Others. A relationship, or even a single conversation, with a tree, butterfly, cloud, heron, moose, or trout is going to fire up dimensions of your wildness, of your soul, that might not have been unleashed through association with even the most exotic human. This is why nature-based people experience us Westerners as hardly human at all. Our neighborhoods, our communities, are so insular, circumscribed, and unimaginative. As you widen the realm with which you are in communication, you become more you simply by virtue of whom you are communing with; you become relational with more of the world.

So, enter your conversations with the Others with the intention of learning about them and developing a relationship, but don't be surprised if you thereby discover more about yourself — perhaps by what the Other tells you or shows you, but, just as likely, by what the conversation draws out of you.

A man on a vision quest in the desert canyoncountry of Utah became fascinated that trees could grow in such a hot and dry land. His fasting place was beneath a spectacular old juniper, half dead, its gnarled and twisted limbs spiraling up defiantly like a spirited old crone full of audacity and wisdom. The juniper grew right out of solid sandstone, bare white rock with no visible soil. He kept asking the juniper, politely, how on earth it managed to live there. Days went by. No answer. Finally, on the last day of his fast, exasperated and wild-eyed, he staggered to his feet, looked up at the juniper one more time, shook his fist, and roared at the top of his lungs, "How the *hell* do you survive here?!" Then and only then did the juniper respond. The old woman looked down at him and said, simply and quietly, yet firmly, "Deep roots." Deep roots. The conversation was over. The man reeled and fell over, astonished to get *any* response and struck dumb to receive that particular response. The man immediately knew this was an answer for him, too, that his survival depended upon his ability to grow intrapsychic roots down through the bare rock of his surface life into the fertile soils of soul. He returned with a name. Not Juniper or Deep Roots, but Rock.

Do trees and rocks speak in English? No. In fact, they don't speak in human languages at all. We just sometimes *hear* them that way because the larger psyche (of which our egos are one small part) does the translation to help us understand. The same thing happens in dreams. As often as not, the Others of nature speak to us through action, imagery, or emotion.

Toward the end of a vision fast in the mountains, I strolled from my solo camp down through a meadow to say good-bye to a furry little pika friend with whom I had exchanged whistles and chatters on several occasions. Upon reaching the edge of my friend's rocky village, I perched myself on the flat top of a six-foot-high cube of a boulder and waited for him to appear, which he did soon enough among the small rocks and grasses below. I spoke to him for a long while. He sat very still. I spoke softly and at length of my gratitude for him and his family, including his ancestral relatives who had lived twenty years earlier at a nearby lake and had taught me about spiritual gathering. He listened attentively. Then I asked him if there was anything he wanted to say before I left. Immediately, and for the first time since I began to talk, he moved. He hopped about a foot to his left beneath the roof of a small boulder in a pika-sized, cavelike room. He sat comfortably in that cozy spot, as if he had just arrived home from a long journey. He looked up at me with his big black eyes and smiled. Then he hopped another foot beneath a tiny spruce and chewed on some seeds he found there. He looked up at me again. "Okay," I replied, as tears escaped my eyes, "Thank you, Pika. You be well, too. God bless you and yours." I found his message to be as eloquent and stirring as the lines from a favorite poem by Derek Walcott:

> The time will come
> when, with elation,
> you will greet yourself arriving
> at your own door, in your own mirror,
> and each will smile at the other's welcome,
>
> and say, sit here. Eat.
> You will love again the stranger who was yourself.[6]

Sometimes the conversation takes place not only without words but also without our even knowing it at the time. A vision quester in the parched Inyo Mountains that rise above the Mojave Desert in eastern California chose a solo spot beneath an ancient piñon. This shy woman's relationship with trees had, for many years, been as meaningful to her as her relationships with humans, maybe more so. Late on her first day, she grabbed a branch above her head for aid in standing. The branch broke off and cut her wrist, resulting in a tumble. Later she stood up and cut her scalp on the sharp end of the broken branch, leaving some of her blood on the tree. Characteristic of her, she was more concerned for the tree's well-being than her own. That night, as she lay beneath the tree, sap dripped onto her shirt where it covered her heart. In the morning, she knew she and the tree had traded blood, and accepted this as a type of communion or initiation.

We wonder if we are alone in the universe, the only intelligent creatures among the stars, not realizing we are surrounded right here at home by intelligent Others, not to mention the stars themselves. We must learn to enter again the conversation with the wild world all around us and gather what poet David Wagoner calls our "fair share of the music of the spheres." We may need to be persistent. A man I know sat alone high on a jumble of boulders in a redrock canyon. He told his life story to the canyon and got no response. This took a couple hours. He told it again. Nothing. A third time. Nothing. Remarkably, he persisted. After he finished a fourth time, the canyon responded, to his utter amazement, and engaged him in a conversation of feeling, images, and thoughts that has continued, off and on, for years.

SIGNS AND OMENS IN NATURE

Signs and omens are two different things. Tom Brown, the tracker and vision quest guide from the Pine Barrens of southern New Jersey, thinks of a sign as an event in nature that follows our request for help with a difficult decision. The sign shows us how to proceed, like a consultation with an oracle. The key to something being a sign is that help is first requested or at least we recognize we have a question. An omen, in contrast, is not requested. It is an event both rare and out of keeping with the typical ways of nature. Omens are weird, outlandish, even bizarre. Often they are also wondrous, conspicuous, and astounding. Sometimes they are subtle, shadowy, or vague. Always they are mysterious. One implication of their rarity is that we cannot claim an omen has occurred without being quite familiar with the natural environment in which it takes place. Seeing a moose in the wilds of southern Utah may rightly be considered an omen, but spotting one doing ordinary moose things in Vermont, Wyoming, or Alaska would not be, although it might well be soul stirring, astonishing, or inspiring.

An omen indicates that an ominous, portentous, or prophetic event is about to occur or *is* occurring. It is a rare opportunity of the greatest significance. What it means for us may depend entirely upon what we do right then. Will we act intuitively and impeccably, responding from our core powers? What will we say or do to acknowledge it in that moment? What if it calls for a radical or "crazy" response? Will we open ourselves to its mystery and power, or will we turn our backs?

A vision quester in the redrock desert of Utah asks for a sign as to whether his solo (fasting) spot might be found at the head of the side canyon in which he wanders. Moments later, he looks down and sees an eagle feather on bare rock. Not accustomed to asking for signs, he isn't sure this qualifies. He asks for another feather. Several minutes later near the top of the canyon in a rounded world of petrified sand dunes, he finds another. He still isn't sure, asks again, and soon enough finds another. He feels appropriately humbled and gives thanks to the Great Mystery. He ends up finding *nine* nearly identical black feathers, by which time he is on his knees, crying. He considers these feathers as a sign that something special and mysterious might indeed happen for him in this place. He would probably have felt different if his request for a sign was followed by a void of feeling or by rockfall that chased him away. As he tells me his story, I am doubtful the feathers are from an eagle, since eagles are rare in these canyons. I suspect they are from the much more common raven. Later he shows me the feathers. I'm not sure whether they are from an eagle, but they are long wing feathers, definitely too large to have belonged to anything but a raptor. They are rare feathers to find in these desert canyons.

An omen: In a remote slickrock canyon where bears are rare and avoid contact with humans, a man on a vision fast constructs a circle of stones in a clearing surrounded by a dense forest of scrub oak. At twilight on the fourth day of his fast, the man enters the circle to begin an all-night vigil. Moments later, a black bear lumbers into the clearing, stops, and looks the man in the eye. There is a moment of possibility. The man, terrified, reaches for his knife, turns the blade toward the bear, and shouts at it to leave. The bear walks off.

Why would we say the bear's appearance was an omen? I've guided thousands of vision questers in dozens of wilderness environments, some of which have high bear populations. Only one other time did a bear visit a person's fasting circle. A second clue: Twilight on the fourth day of a vision quest, just as day turns to night, is a potent moment. This is the time when the door between the worlds opens and questers step into their circle of stones, a symbolic way of entering a tomb, surrendering a way of life that no longer serves. What is experienced at that moment holds great significance. For a bear visitation, rare at any time, to occur at that precise moment is uncanny. A third clue: On the day before, the man had left his circle for a few minutes to fetch water at the creek. Upon returning, he found a rattlesnake coiled and rattling at the center of his circle. Again, this is the only time I've heard of a rattlesnake in a faster's circle. The man, afraid of snakes, did not speak to it. The snake went away.

This man lost two precious opportunities to commune with the wild and possibly to receive an invaluable gift. But saying yes to the soul is not an easy task for anyone. This story reflects something true of all of us: we are at times frightened by our own power; as Marianne Williamson writes, "Our deepest fear is not that we are inadequate. Our deepest fear is that we are powerful beyond measure."[7]

Why are so many of us terrified of wild animals despite how rarely they harm humans? Is it simply because we are unfamiliar with their lives and habits? Or might we also be terrified of the *inner* animals, the power of our own wildness, our own darkness?

A sign: A woman on her fast sits writing in her journal, recording her burning desire to discover her soul qualities and her path of integrity in this life. She wonders how she will ever figure it out. A hummingbird zooms in, very loud, hovers, looks her in the eye, drops a feather in the crease of her open journal, flies off.

How do you go about understanding a sign, or even knowing you've received one? First, if the sign is going to be valid, you will have asked about something deeply meaningful to you, a question both significant and difficult for you to answer. A *big* question. Asking for a sign to a trivial or mundane question is a sign of disrespect toward the sacred.

You recognize a sign by the fact that your request is followed by an event that has power for you; it strongly attracts your attention, generates a significant emotional response, gets your imagination rolling. It ratchets up your aliveness.

If you receive a sign, begin by giving thanks in a meaningful way and then by remembering what inspired you to ask for a sign in the first place. Sit with the sign you received with the same emotions and reverence with which you requested it. Take a deep breath and fully take in the sign with your body, senses, emotions, and imagination. Spend a good deal of time with the sign in this way before you begin to think about it. The sacred Other speaks in images and symbols, and thus working with a sign is like working with a dream. What does the sign evoke in you, deeper than your personality and everyday thoughts? How do you find yourself reacting emotionally? On the heels of the sign, what memories, associations, images, or related symbols arise and have an intuitive click for you? Avoid any attempts to figure out the sign with your mind or impose an answer you had merely hoped for. Let the sign work on you even if one of its meanings is apparent right away.

The woman who received the hummingbird feather was asking the biggest questions of her life as she sat with her sense of lack and her deepest longing. The hummingbird, flying in so close, with so much sound and color and power, startled her and immediately shifted her experience of lack and longing to one of total immersion in the magical now. The hummingbird, for her, was a notification from the soul that she will find her answers by paying attention to the miracles present in the moment, *especially to the little things of authentic power.* There she will receive the gift. The gift of the feather got her nose out of her journal and beyond her regrets about the past and hopes for the future. It tuned her entire being to the wild world unfolding all around and in her.

Another sign: A woman reverently constructs a circle of four stones in which she will spend the entire next day praying. She goes to sleep puzzling as to how she should enter the circle in the morning — from which of the four directions — a significant decision for her. In the morning, she discovers mountain lion prints tracking through her camp; the west stone has been moved aside as if a door had been opened.

Another: A woman, while in the Sierra mountains of California for a week, is preoccupied by her questions about what "medicine" or soul power she possesses. As she runs through tall grass, she is bitten on the leg by a rattlesnake. She is frightened but, after an hour, there is still little swelling. The snake drew blood but injected no venom. Grateful, she accepts her apprenticeship to the powers of rattlesnake. She cuts off all her hair and dedicates a year for spiritual wandering and study. At the end of the year, she returns to enact her vision quest. During her fast, she performs a dance in honor of snake.

Yet another: High in the Colorado mountains, a woman hikes many miles through dense forest to a remote lake where she intends to commence her fast in the morning. All night she is terrified by the wildness and foreboding darkness of the forest. She wonders if she should abandon her plans and leave in the morning.

> At dawn, I awake to the crystalline sound of a duck quacking in the still air, its clear voice inviting me to stay. As I open my eyes, the peace and serenity of this wilderness settles around me like a comforting soft woolen cloak — I am home. There are fears inside of me — fears about finding my way out of this place, fears about being absolutely and unequivocally alone, but the duck says, "Please stay," and who can refuse a duck?

One more: On the third afternoon of my fast at tree line in the northern Colorado Rockies, I sit under my tarp, in wind and light rain. I am there in part because of my dream about Red and Blue, which showed me that my spiritual journey with these two inner women had reached an impasse. I was there to make a sacrifice. On the first two days of my fast, I had enacted ceremonies that released my attachment to the agendas of both women — my way of understanding romantic love and my way of understanding my soul work. Now, under my tarp, I notice the wind has slowed and the rain has let up. I hear a loud snort to my east, not far, maybe a hundred feet or so. From my position under the tarp, I can't see in that direction. Another snort. Sounds like a deer trying to get me to identify myself. A third snort, this time with hooves pounding earth. I duck beneath the edge of the tarp and stand up. To the east, a perfect rainbow stretches from one end of the mountain valley to the next. All the colors are there and all are bright. The mountains I see beneath the rainbow's arch are bathed in golden light. Then my attention is claimed by a slight movement directly in front of me, in the center of the scene framed by the rainbow. A buck with a large rack is listening and looking right at me. On each side of the buck is a doe. A male and two females. The buck nods to me and then the three deer resume their journey that I had interrupted, passing in front of me and heading west through the low pass that shortly leads to Love Lake. I bow and give thanks for this sign with a smile and tears.

A sign and maybe an omen: At dusk on the fourth day of his fast, a young man stands in an alpine meadow at the edge of a circle of small stones about eight feet in diameter. Here he will spend the night awake, watching the slow turning of the heavens, crying for a vision. He stands, trembling on weak knees, and waits for a sign. He waits for the exact moment when day turns to night, the moment to step into his tomb. The air is still and cooling, the forest behind him silent. The mountain peaks and sky take on the rosy glow of sunset. It is almost time. At that moment, a huge noise arises, like a squadron of jets flying toward his camp a few feet above the tundra. He actually ducks. But there are no jets. Still, the terrible sound grows in volume. He looks up and in the kaleidoscopic twilight sees a luminous gray cloud forming just beneath the summit of the mountain rising two thousand feet above him. This, alas, is the peak that, on his first day, he had proudly named after himself. The cloud grows rapidly in size at its bottom. Thousands of tons of rocks are sweeping down the mountain in his direction. Surveying his location, as if he had just arrived there, he notices his circle is at the edge of a gentle slope populated here and there with boulders like a huge, tilted chess board. Behind him stretches the dark forest. Suddenly, he realizes how the boulders got there and why the forest extends no closer to the mountain. He runs screaming and wild-eyed into the trees, but *this* avalanche does not reach his circle. Humbled and with his senses, emotions, and imagination enlivened, he returns to commence his vigil.

ANIMAL TRACKING AND OTHER METHODS OF SKILLFUL NATURE OBSERVATION

A man wandering in a sere mountain range of California's Mojave Desert spent some time stalking lizards, just to get close enough to learn something, maybe have a conversation. He spotted one sunning on a rock next to a primitive jeep road. He tried talking, but this lizard had other ideas and scurried under a sage bush. Accustomed to such behavior from lizards, the man began to hum and sing softly, confident the lizard would be curious and come out to talk. The lizard ignored him and disappeared.

Later, he spied a larger lizard on a rock just off the road. Trying a different tactic, the man moved to the far side of the road and sat silently. He watched the lizard stalk a grasshopper — and miss — and then a beetle — and miss again. A large fly buzzed over to the man and took up residence on his skin and clothing. This gave the man an idea. Ever so slowly, he inched across the road.

> Lizard was watching fly intently. Fly was on my hat. I reached my hand up, and she perched on my finger. I slowly lowered my arm and finger to the rock. Lizard was ready. Fly hopped off my finger onto the rock. Lizard immediately leapt and missed. I couldn't believe his ineptitude! And then for some reason, fly decided to give lizard another chance. She crawled up to the top of the rock within four inches of lizard who watched her closely. And what did lizard do? Nothing! He just sat there.
>
> I wondered why he passed up that last easy chance to catch fly. Was it out of respect for a skillful adversary? I became aware of the tremendous patience required of a hunter, a stalker. During the hour I spent with Lizard, he sat motionless for long periods. I am taught to sit this patiently with myself and with others.
>
> But, clearly, even patient waiting doesn't always pay off in the way one expects. Lizard failed three times to catch his prey. And that didn't make him a poor hunter. It's just the nature of things. Sometimes a lot of waiting and work are necessary. And, sometimes, success is measured in having sat quietly, ignoring bodily discomforts, stalking another as I did him and he me.

Nature has much to teach us in her vast classroom. You can acquire an entire education merely by observing carefully. But you must be patient and offer your attention, like a lizard stalking a fly. This takes skill, and practice. What you find in nature is what works. It wouldn't be there if it didn't. Boundless wisdom awaits.

Skillful nature observation requires your willingness to sit motionless for long periods and focus on what is in front and around and inside of you, bringing your attention always back to the present moment. Look with care. Look *into* things, not just at them. Listen to the texture of sound as well as its origin and volume. Track scent as well as color and shifting shade. Become acquainted with the feel of surfaces as well as the touch of wind and stillness, the dance of warmth and chill. Be truly curious. Observe with innocence and delight. In addition to the behavior of animals and insects and the movement of vegetation, there is the lively life of the air and sky, the flow of water and light. Some things you will learn by sitting still. Some by tracking slowly. Some by returning to the same spot time and time again over different seasons and many years, getting to know not just the species there but the individual animals and plants as well.

Whether you track mountain lions through the sands of desert canyons or owls through the night forest, there is much to learn, not only about the animals but also about the land through which you roam, and, most startling, about the one who tracks. In offering your attention generously, you discover astonishing things. Secret gardens. Insect worlds. The shape, feel, and traveling methods of seeds. The way the wind behaves in different spaces. The way moving sunlight plays tricks on the mind. The sound of hoof and paw on rock and on dry leaves. Your own emotions, losses, unexpected identities, and destinies.

In addition to tracking mammals or reptiles, you might also discover species of plants or trees rare in your location, or you might learn to stalk water in the desert. How do you find a rare columbine in redrock canyon-country? Or a flower that blooms only a few minutes each year, at dawn or in the middle of the night? As you wander through the land on your search, you gradually notice your attention wanders less, becomes more present-centered. You arrive.

In spending an hour or more tracking an animal or flower, your consciousness gradually shifts. While focused on an outer, elusive presence, changes happen on the inside. You quiet down. Life becomes simpler. You come to belong more fully to the place you wander, following a track or scent or sound. Eventually, you notice "being on the track" is its own reward, just as life is about the journey, not the destination. You may or may not catch up to the one leaving the prints or other signs. No matter. You begin to notice the one who is tracking now is not the same as the one who began tracking a few hours or days earlier. You wonder, "Who is it that tracks?" And you learn to wonder in new ways. Maybe the question becomes, "What is the quality in me that allows me to track in my unique way?" You need not name that quality, but rather just learn to feel it, imagine it, act it, be it.

You began by stalking a deer but now are captivated by surprises of *any* sort, including shifts in your own consciousness. You might continue with the deer track because that is the path you chose at the start and that is the trail ushering you deeper into the wild world. Yet, in addition to the cloven-hoof prints, the elliptical pellets, the chewed bark on young aspens, and the previous night's bedding place in tall grass, you notice you are incrementally becoming someone who stalks a mystery. Something in you is changing, as if you are growing wild with fur or claws or tail. What is the secret place inside from which you sense the mystery, the place from which you long for the trail as much as the treasure?

CHAPTER 9

BRIDGING INNER AND OUTER

In the very earliest time,
when both people and animals lived on earth,
a person could become an animal if he wanted to
and an animal could become a human being.
Sometimes they were people
and sometimes animals
and there was no difference.
All spoke the same language.
That was the time when words were like magic.
The human mind had mysterious powers.
A word spoken by chance
might have strange consequences.
It would suddenly come alive
and what people wanted to happen could happen—
all you had to do was say it.
Nobody can explain this:
That's the way it was.

— Nalungiaq (Inuit)

In chapter 7, we explored inner work pathways to soul encounter. In chapter 8, we investigated ways to access soul through our interaction with the outer Others. Here we give the lie to the Western notion that the inner and outer are distinct domains — or even truly inner or outer, for that matter. What we call inner is actually what we experience, not through (outer) sensing of things and events in the world but through imagination, emotion, and/or thinking about such things and events. What we call outer, in contrast, always has a sensing component, whether or not it also includes the imaginal, emotional, or cognitive. The inner, then, is the unseen, the non-sensory; outer is the sensory world of form. Both equally pertain to the world in which we live and to the psyche, which is an essential feature of that world. In this chapter, we consider pathways to soul that move back and forth between the sensory and non-sensory and that weave the subtle and unseen forces of the world into form — the true work of what is traditionally called magic.

SELF-DESIGNED CEREMONY

Personal, self-designed ceremony enables us to speak, again, the same language as animals, trees, rivers, and mountains, the same dialect as soul and spirit, the same magical words as the sacred Other.

A two-way exchange, conversation requires us to both hear and speak. We hear the Other through the numinous declarations of dreams, deep imagery, inner voices, sudden insights or revelations, synchronicities, powerful emotion, love, death, the voice of God, and epiphanies of nature. These communications from within (soul) and without (nature) and both/neither (spirit) constitute the Other's way of speaking to us. We make it a conversation by way of ceremony.

Ceremony is especially effective at completing the circle of sacred dialogue because ceremony speaks the same language as the Other: symbols — symbols that come to us, in the first place, *from the Other* in the form of an image, revelation, or epiphany.

I see the dialogue working like this: The Other speaks to us by way of a dream of two women in conflict, to use my example — or by way of a burning bush. We might need to live a while with these symbols before we understand what's being said. Once we do understand (or think we do), if we then desire a conversation, we must first know what we want to say back to the Other. This requires careful feeling and consideration. Then, if we are sincere and gracious conversationalists, we might choose to speak in the Other's language rather than our everyday, middleworld lexicon.

Yes, we could respond with our human language of words and sentences, often called prayer, and this may work well. But at times we might prefer ceremony because of the efficacy or eloquence of the Other's language, because it avoids the common traps of our thinking minds, or just because we prefer the expressive qualities of ceremonial language.

To speak in the Other's language is to symbolically embody in action what we want to say. The enactment expresses our relationship to the symbol originally communicated by the Other.

Each ceremony has a beginning, a middle, and an end. The beginning of the ceremony ushers us from ordinary space and time to sacred space and time. The symbolic statement is the middle component. The ending shifts things back from the sacred to the ordinary.

Once we have spoken via ceremony, we have, in effect, lobbed the ball back into the Other's court. Perhaps this will move the conversation forward.

The Christian mass is a traditional ceremony of this kind. The sipping of the wine and the eating of the wafer are symbolic actions embodying the faithful's willingness to share in Christ's blood and body, his life and love. These symbols (the wine and wafer) derive from the Other — Jesus himself requested these actions at the Last Supper. A Christian responds by way of the ceremony of communion, a means of saying to the Other, "Yes, I share in your life." And the dialogue continues.

The simple acts of entering the church and, after communion, leaving might serve as the beginning and end of the ceremony, demarcating the opening and closing of sacred space and time.

An essential soulcraft skill, the art of self-designed ceremony deepens the conversation between the conscious self and the Other. Being self-designed, some elements of these ceremonies originate with the individual and are not merely the enactment of a tradition. Sometimes the whole ceremony (other than the symbol derived from the Other) is original to the individual. Other times it's only one component of the ceremony, as in the following example.

On the vision quests I lead, on the evening before the four days of solitude begin, we enact a ceremony in which participants sacrifice to fire an object representing the chapter of life that is ending. This is not their good riddance to a dull or painful life, but rather a reluctant and courageous willingness to separate from a life that, regardless of how unfulfilling it might have been, sheltered them as they grew. True sacrifice is a way to make sacred; it is not a release of a burden. The Wanderer will henceforth live without the former safety net and will inherit a new life, challenging in ways not yet imaginable.

Fire sacrifice is a symbolic act with deep roots in the universal human unconscious, and thus the act of fire sacrifice itself derives from the Other. The fire ceremony has essentially the same structure each time, but the objects people bring, what those objects represent, and what it means to them to surrender that way of belonging to the world — all these are unique and personal. Whether it be a piece of wedding dress (used or never used), a psychologist's or lawyer's license, a rosary, a spoonful of cocaine, or a photograph of a loved one, as each object is released into the flames, it is as if the individual has thereby said to the Other, "I have come to the wilderness to say good-bye to a life grown too small. I release my attachment to the security and familiarity of that life, honoring it for what it has taught and given me. In the morning, I shall stride deeper into the wilderness, without food or knowing, and await signs or gifts you might send." The courageous and careful choice of sacrificial object and the symbolic action of surrendering that object to fire say much more than the mere utterance of words.

Personal ceremonies need not be elaborate or complex. Most often the core component is something as plain and spare as a hand releasing a slip of paper into fire. Although simple, the action is profound, perhaps capturing the central mystery of a life — or opening the way to that mystery.

My dream of Red and Blue revealed irreconcilable problems in my relationship to the personal and archetypal feminine. To resume my soul's journey, I had to surrender my attachment to the fantasy of an outer soul mate who would complete my world, rescue me from the doubts and difficulties of life, and unite me forever with the sacred Other. I also needed to surrender my attachment to the image of my soul work, the weaving of cocoons. Both these self-defining stories were depleted as guideposts to my life's journey. After many weeks of preparation, I responded to the dream of the two women by way of ceremony, in fact three ceremonies.

High in the Colorado Rockies of early fall, Annie Bloom and I backpacked several miles over untrailed, boggy tundra and through boreal forests of spruce. Elk were in rut, the bulls bugling and guarding their harems of cows. Red-tailed and sharp-shinned hawks circled and rose on thermals. The tall alpine grasses, in reds and golds, bowed before the cold breezes forecasting winter. Silver peaks pushed into azure sky.

The first ceremony took place the next dawn, near our camp on Rock Lake. Annie and I walked slowly and silently into a sloping meadow at lake's edge, surrounded by magnificent old spruce trees, the very spot where I had met the monk and butterfly twenty years earlier. I was truly astonished that the place actually existed. But it had changed: the monk had recently died, his trunk shattered six feet from ground level, undimmed shards of yellow wood freshly scattered about the lakeshore like a slaughter — or a giveaway. Here in this meadow mythic to me, I would say good-bye to my life-directing and life-sustaining vision. Not that I had been mistaken about my work as a weaver of cocoons, or that I had questions about whether I would continue weaving; it was just that this way of understanding my work had grown too small. It was time to uncover a larger story that held the cocoon as a special case. To find that larger story, I had to release my attachment to my first vision.

Sitting facing the lake, I dug a small hole in the earth, made a pyramid of twigs there, and then told stories, to the lake, the sky, the peaks, the dawn breeze, and Annie, who sat behind me, holding me as I trembled. I recounted the events of my first visit and expressed my gratitude, one last time, for the lessons of the monk and his friend. And I gave thanks for the young man who had embraced his vision with so much intent and faith, and told a story or two of adventures over the previous two decades. Grief-stricken and proud and frightened, I said good-bye forever to that young man, then lit the twigs and burned a small painting of a butterfly — and wept hard over that little grave.

Later that morning, after our final meal, I parted company with Annie, leaving her to enact her own fast at Rock Lake. I backpacked a few steep miles up through thick forest to a higher lake I had not been able to reach twenty years earlier. Love Lake sits so high on the mountain that trees cannot grow to full size in her thin air and severe weather. Dwarfed spruce barely taller than me surround her on three sides.

After making a simple camp a few hundred yards from the fragile ecology of the lake, I performed my second ceremony, once again simple: Overlooking the sparkling waters, I sacrificed to fire a small object representing my adolescent yet earnest soul mate fantasy. Releasing my attachment to a second mythos that meant as much to me as anything for which I had lived, sobs of heartache and despair echoed off the mountain walls.

On the second day of my fast, I performed the third ceremony. Taking the entire day, I very slowly circumnavigated that small slate blue tarn of Love, crossing over expanses of flat-topped boulders, through late summer wildflower meadows and golden carpets of grass, ghosting past the dwarfed and twisted spruce, leaping over snow-fed streams bordered by iridescent green moss. I walked counterclockwise, an earthwise circling to take me down deeper, inward, more receptive, to the change-place.

I stopped and sat many times on my circumnavigation. I spoke out loud to the Lady of the Lake, the goddess of the waters. At each stop, I told the lady the story of my relationship with one significant woman in my life. There were many stories to tell. I began with my mother, and then my sister and grandmothers, and then the others — my friends, teachers, colleagues, and especially my lovers. With each story, I honored the goddess, sometimes naming her Aphrodite, as she manifested through each of these women. I gave thanks for the exceptional feminine qualities each woman embodied, naming those qualities with words of adoration, and for the many things I had learned from each encounter. I sang the praises of each woman, giving thanks for their virtues, both those that confounded me and those that enthralled me.

Bowing to the lake at the end of each story, I apologized to the lady for having unconsciously projected her qualities onto those women, for not having distinguished the woman from the archetypal Woman she embodied. I apologized to the human woman for having attempted to make her carry so much of the feminine, including my own unembodied feminine qualities. Upon finishing one story, I arose and walked a little farther, sat again, and told another. I spent the entire day this way. With each story, I made a gesture of withdrawing the projected feminine (this gesture looked like someone pulling in a rope), and then another (a bow with upturned hands extending outward) to acknowledge the goddess's qualities, not just in that woman but also immanent and evident everywhere in the world, even within me.

These then were the symbolic acts at the center of the third ceremony: walking earthwise around a lake, bowing, and telling love stories to the waters.

Two days later, before I left that place, the Lady of the Lake spoke to me while sporadic gusts rippled her surface and created effervescent rainbows streaming directly to where I stood on her shore. "Look at me," she said, in emotion, wind, and color. "I am constantly filling. Even now in early fall. *And* I am constantly emptying. I am filled with love waters from above and I embrace them for a while, but I do not hold on to them. They all flow through me. Every part of me, every drop that makes me the lake I am, flows through me on the way to the all-receiving ocean. I let everything go. This is what makes me a lake. I am a place on the earth that embraces the waters; I am a place through which the waters flow. I hold the waters of love and life without holding *on* to them."

Since then, I have been inspired to emulate Love Lake, allowing myself to be filled with "love waters from above," to not dam them with attempts at control, to allow them to flow through me.

Annie, meanwhile, also enacted ceremonies during her fast at Rock Lake. Unbeknownst to each other at the time, our ceremonies had some astonishing similarities.

On her first night alone, Annie lay semi-awake beneath her tarp and heard a presence she called "the Lady of the Lake" ask her to tell the stories of the men whom she had loved in her life. In the morning, she went down to the lake's edge and began with the story of her father. She told the lady of his strong, warm, loving presence during her childhood. She recounted the story of the one and only special week she had had alone with him. She was twelve and, among all her siblings, was chosen to accompany Dad on a long road trip from Chicago to Florida. That week shaped her experiences with every man in her life afterward — both her hopes and fears. Whenever she recalled that road trip, her heart would fill with gratitude for that time but also ache with disappointment for never having had another week like it.

All day Annie told her stories. She felt her heart grow full to bursting. She felt the blessing of having loved and been loved by many beautiful, remarkable, and respectful men. The gifts of relationship with the outer masculine had been abundant in her life.

That night, as Annie lay under the stars in the clear mountain air, she felt a profound peace.

At dawn, I walked down to the water where gusting winds whipped the surface into kaleidoscope patterns. I spoke to my dad, telling him he had always been my hero and how proud I was of his life. I expressed my gratitude for all the things he provided me, especially that precious week when I was twelve and learned the warmth of sharing. I told him that my disappointment in not knowing more of him had been like a lead ball in my heart and I was ready to dislodge it and forgive him. I asked in kind for his forgiveness of my resentment and disappointment all these years.

All the while I spoke, the water churned on the lake's surface. The moment I finished, the wind died and the lake became exquisitely calm. I sat and absorbed the serenity and felt how simple and profound forgiveness is.

Then Annie realized what she would do next. During the months prior, she had had a recurring image of herself dancing under the moon and stars in a pure-white dress. She had gone to town, found just the right dress, and brought it with her, as ridiculous as it seemed to stuff into a backpack something special and gorgeous and white.

Now, at the edge of the water, she imagined a sacred marriage she would enact while standing in the middle of the shallow lake. She spent the rest of the day in preparation. Circling the lake, she placed in the four quadrants symbols representing the most important men in her life. Trembling with anticipation and gratitude, she sat in a green glade and wrote her wedding vows.

At dusk, I watched the sun's last radiance illuminate the lake — and felt suspended in time. Gazing softly upon the water, I saw the lady, milky white and effervescent, rise up from the lake. I sighed with rapture at her beauty and told her so. At once, another form arose beside her, this one unmistakably masculine. Gasping, I asked, "Are you the Lord of the Lake?" He chortled mischievously.

In the morning, I awoke to clear skies and went down to the lake's edge, where luminous spindrifts of mist glided lazily from one side of the lake to the other. This was my wedding day! But I felt fear too. What if someone were to appear when I was standing in the middle of the lake in my dress? And what if the lake swallowed me up? And who was my groom?

I offered up all these things churning inside me to the Creator, the Spirit that moves in all things.

Taking a container of water up onto the mosses, I gave myself a goddess bath, invoking the image of mystical union. My masculine radiance poured forth and the deep receptivity of my feminine opened wide to receive.

After my hair dried in the sun, I braided it. The dress emerged wrinkle-free from my backpack and I slid on its filmy softness. I placed a circlet of beads and ribbons on my head and added sparkles to my cheeks. I felt beautiful, and the lake and forest were enchanted. I would not have been surprised if unicorns had appeared.

With solemn dignity, I walked slowly down my runway of mosses and out into the lake. I brought gifts for the lady and lord and, by name, invited the feminine role models in my life to be honored witnesses. I cast a length of cord in the direction of each of the men I had symbolically placed on the lake's perimeter. I drew back the cords as I spoke my vows. "Do you, Annie Christine Bloom, joyfully take unto you each of these men with whom you have shared love, laughter, creativity, the pleasure of bodies uniting, mystery, dance, struggle, and the full range of emotions from tenderness to bitterness — the ecstasies as well as the disappoint-ments? Do you take them back into your body completely, cherishing each as part of who you are? Will you hold steady with your vision of mys-tical union and embrace each moment in its entirety? If you are ready to hold yourself as you have held others, I pronounce you wedded."

The ceremony was simple, serene, and profound. Then I danced and sang for hours and envisioned a sumptuous feast with all my friends and family.

At midday I began to get drowsy and made a nest upon the forest floor, slipping into a perfect, restful sleep. Never had I felt so full of well-being and peace.

TRADITIONAL CEREMONIES, RITUALS, AND NATURE FESTIVALS

Personal ceremonies like Annie's are custom-designed for specific individu-als and purposes, for personal conversations with the sacred Other. Each is unique. Many other ceremonial practices (like the Christian mass, the

Japanese tea ceremony, or the vision quest) are enacted more or less the same way year after year within a given community. Sometimes this is a sign that all life has long departed from these practices, but other times it indicates an exceedingly potent form, honed through the ages. To participate in vital traditional ceremony is to remind ourselves, in the presence of the sacred Other, how we humans stand in relation to universal and eternal truths, truths like birth, death, soul, spirit, love, fertility, wholeness, light, darkness, the Tao, sacrifice, grief, atonement, community, and the mysteries of nature. Traditional ceremonies, rituals, and nature festivals can serve as pathways to soul; they can open the gates to transpersonal experience, alter consciousness, facilitate communion with the Other, and help us see ourselves and the world from a perspective more resonant with soul.

Nature festivals such as those celebrating the solar equinoxes and solstices are good examples. These festivals, which mark the beginning and end of each season, orient us within the great round of terrestrial life. They align our social and psychological lives with the rhythms of growth and decay, light and dark, outward turning and inward turning. By aligning our conscious selves with the rhythms and cycles of outer nature, we invite and support the embodied expressions of our souls, our inner nature.

In the next chapter, we'll take a closer look at the power and elements of ritual, especially in the form of the contemporary vision quest. The resource section at the back of the book lists several books that explore nature-based ceremonies, rituals, and festivals as enacted in a variety of cultures.

SYMBOLIC ARTWORK

We are all artists. The artistic potential lives within each of us, sometimes dormant, sometimes aroused. Some say it's not possible to be fully human and not be an artist. Many nature-based cultures have no word for *art* or *artist* because producing what *we* call art is simply part of being human. True art has nothing to do with impressing or entertaining others with pleasant or stunning creations; it's about carrying what is hidden in the soul as a gift to others. However we embody our souls in the world, that is our art. Soul expression, like true art, is an intrinsic act — we do it simply for the joy it generates. It does not have ulterior motives such as entertainment, wealth, or fame.

In addition to being the expression of soul powers, art can also be a way to discover those powers. There is much to learn about our soul's purpose from the creations that spontaneously flow from us. When guiding underworld journeys, I often use a symbolic art process from the transpersonal psychology school of psychosynthesis. After a relaxation process, participants are invited to shift awareness to a receptive place inside. There they can receive images from the soul in response to a set of four general but evocative questions. Then, with crayons, pastels, or colored pencils, they draw what appeared in their deep imagery. As they draw, the images will further differentiate themselves, the symbols speaking more clearly as they are embodied on paper.

During a symbolic art process of this kind, Nancy, a jeweler/metalsmith in her early thirties, produced an elaborate drawing. Like most people who uncover images in this way, she had no idea where they came from. On the bottom third of the page, she drew a three-colored wave form suggesting water. She imagined herself between this wave and an impassable wall. This part of her drawing was her response to the first question, "Where are you now in your life?" Then, on the top third of the page, in response to "Where are you going, or what is your next step in your life?" she drew a rainbow arching over a black space. Each color of the rainbow represented a step she must take in her spiritual journey. In the middle of the page, in response to the third question, "What stands in your way?" she created an image of herself trapped by a firebreathing, green-scaled dragon with bared teeth and glowing red eyes. The final question was "What quality or resource waiting inside you must emerge so you can move through your obstacle and take your next step?" Just beneath the black space at the top of the page, she drew a large blue and red-brown bird, a raptor, flying upward and to the right. The bird had distinctive outstretched feathers on its wings and tail. Beneath the bird was a moonlike orb connected to the bird by colored strands. The orb was positioned on the horizon, directly beneath the raptor and above the dragon. Nancy understood the orb to represent her essence, her soul, being pulled aloft by the bird.

Several days later, Nancy hiked into a desert canyon for her first vision fast. On her solo, she received a name from the canyon but did not reveal it upon her return to camp because, as she said, the name didn't seem quite right, she wasn't certain she had heard it correctly. Something seemed off about it, as if her conscious mind had not yet been able to hear her name accurately.

A couple weeks after her quest, I received a call from Nancy. She sounded stunned and excited. She had just been in a bookstore, where the cover of a book had caught her eye. On it was a painting identical in many ways to the four-part drawing that had sprung from her deep imagery months earlier. This was particularly startling given the complexity of the image.

The scene on the cover has an inlet in the foreground. In the water is a green, double-headed dragon with bared teeth and glowing red eyes. Above the dragon sits the moon in a star-studded sky. Above the moon, a man with cloud white hair and wearing a sky blue cape flies with his back to the viewer. Painted on the back of the blue cape, in browns and reds, is a raptor, possibly a red-tailed hawk. The hawk, nearly as large as the man, is flying upward and to the right as in Nancy's drawing. It has distinctive outstretched feathers on its wings and tail.

The uncanny resemblance of the cover to her drawing was something like a déjà vu for Nancy, except even more astonishing — it was like walking into a room and meeting her double. After several seconds of disorientation, Nancy looked at the book's title, and suddenly her entire life came into focus. The title of the book was *Dreamspeaker*.[1] Her jaw dropped and her eyes widened. She was immediately certain this was the name the canyon had whispered in her ear: Dreamspeaker. While in the canyon, she had thought it said "Dreamseeker," which is, curiously, how she had understood her life *before* her quest, someone endlessly seeking a dream worth living. In the desert, Nancy had found that dream; she knew it was her soul's desire to manifest through her art the not yet visible stories of soul and nature.

As she stared at the book cover, Nancy understood that Dreamspeaker was, for her, the name of someone who renders the invisible visible for her people. Dreamspeaking was indeed her soul power. The caped man/raptor on the cover is the Dreamspeaker, and Nancy's drawing leaves no doubt that the raptor, the Dreamspeaker, is the one who pulls aloft the moonlike orb of her soul, thereby making the invisible soul visible for her people.

How did Nancy come to draw this image prior to her vision quest? What brought together into a single whirlwind so many numinous elements — the image from her depths, her experience of receiving not quite the right name on her fast, the title of the book, the painting chosen for the book's cover, the actual name the canyon had given her, and the meaning of that name? Some would say Nancy had, in her deep imagery journey, tapped into the collective human unconscious. Others might speak in terms of past lives, extrasensory perception, or a karmic connection between Nancy and the book's author. However we might explain it — or refrain from explanation — the fact remains: symbolic art that springs from our deep imagination has much to teach and show us on our journey to soul.

I introduced Dorothy Mason in chapter 4. We learned how Dorothy's time of wandering had begun upon her enrollment in a dreamwork group. Fifteen years later, at age forty-four, she had her first glimpse of her soul image.

> The image that has called me to most deeply live who I am is the chalice. This symbol came to me, unbidden, through a drawing I was asked to do while preparing for my vision fast in 1987. It was my soul's response to the question, "What is being born in you?" The image that emerged through my hand and onto paper was a stoneware chalice. The stem of the chalice rests in the vast waters of the sea, and the bowl reaches into an infinite carapace of sky. Where the stem and bowl meet, the colors intensify to a deep blue-green. Though my heart in some way recognized this image, I had no words for its meaning. Yet, the symbol of the chalice came to rest inside me as both an invitation and a challenge to which I felt, simultaneously, open and resistant. So resistant, in fact, it would take me another six years to fully open to its implications and the power it held for my life.

Two days after drawing the chalice, Dorothy hiked into a redrock canyon for her fast. She was drawn to a spot between two huge rocks, with an opening down the middle that looked to her like a great canyon goddess with legs spread in childbirth. On the last night of her four-day fast, she sat in vigil, facing the east, and awaited her birth. She called upon the canyon goddess for her teaching, and this is some of what Dorothy heard and felt in reply:

> I will birth you from between my legs. Feel the strength, the sensuality, the earth knowledge, the dark night in my bones as you move through me. You have come to me to remember your soul as Woman. The powers

of birth and knowledge of the shadows are yours. It is time to reclaim them and share them so the feminine in all things can reawaken and heal.

Take the passion of your soul and the poetry in your heart to your people. Let ceremony, symbols, and images emerge from your fertile belly so they may touch the forgotten ancient places so many of your people need to remember.

You are a chalice from which others shall drink of their own living water, from the well of their own souls, their own sacred source. In drinking, they will remember themselves.

You are Chalice Bearer.

JOURNAL WORK

In a soulcraft approach to journal work, you write to connect with your depths. You write as a way of tracking and cultivating a relationship with the sacred, the numinous, the mysterious. You record your memories, dreams, reflections, visions, trances, hopes, emotions, major life transitions, and meetings with remarkable people (including those in the form of animals, birds, plants, trees, rocks, wind, rivers, mountains, and stars). You chronicle your experiences with soulcraft practices. You track the strands and themes of your soul story and, when the time is right, weave them together into a single personal mythology.

Here are some soulcrafting ideas for your journal work:

- If it feels like you are approaching a major life passage or are already in one, write about the stage of life that is ending. Be as specific as you can. Describe what is actually dying, not merely what you *hope* is dying. A true life passage is not an opportunity to happily and easily rid yourself of unwanted or unpleasant traits, roles, or relationships. A recognition of what is really dying should evoke some grief whether or not it also evokes relief. What transition(s) are you going through? How do you feel about these shifts? What in you is getting ready to be born? Make your best guess. Don't worry, it will be different from what you imagine. Project it nonetheless. Imagining what's next will help you cast off from the shore of your past.

- As a Wanderer, there will be times you must take your heart in your hands and, like Mary Oliver, leave the home of your current identity and walk into the wild night, striding "deeper and deeper into the world." At such times, take up your journal and record your impressions and images about why this is, finally, the right time. In what way is it "already late enough"? In what way is this the only thing you could do? What do you know about the life you may be saving? How do you know you are about to strike out into mysterious territory? What is the old story that is now dying? What is the nature of your past, your routines, and your roles from which you now have the opportunity to break? What is your experience of that urgent, passionate call to embark on a spiritual journey? What is the wildness now coursing through your veins? Have demons already appeared to hinder your progress? Have guides, teachers, or allies appeared? What/who are they?

• Record your dreams. If you are having trouble remembering them, do this (it works 95 percent of the time): Have your journal ready at your bedside. On the top of a new page, write the next day's date and the words "Dream Report." Place the pen on that page like a bookmark. Turn the light out and begin a long conversation with yourself concerning the specific reasons you want to recall your dreams. List the reasons in your mind and store each one in a different part of your body. Keep the conversation going until you fall asleep. As soon as you wake up, don't move an inch until you have fully replayed your dream in your imagination. Perhaps give your dream a title, such as "My Journey with Two Women Comes to a Halt." Then reach for your journal.

Transcribe your dreams in the present tense as if you are recording actions and experiences occurring as you write them. Include all emotions. Ask only yourself what they mean, or don't ask at all. Review the section in chapter 7 on soulcentric dreamwork.

• Contemplate and begin to answer the following questions: What do I most deeply seek? In what specific ways am I prepared to surrender to the deepest strivings of my soul, to my unique gifts or powers? Who are my people (not necessarily limited to humans, they are the ones to whom you hope to carry a gift, a giveaway that's as much an act of service on their behalf as an act of self-fulfillment for you)? For what do you pray?

• Compose a personal myth. (See the section on storytelling below.)

• Pay attention to the edge of awareness and record in your journal what you find there. This will include subtle and fleeting thoughts, feelings, images, perceptions, memories, dreams, and daydreams. It will also include imaginary conversations some part of you is carrying on with important people in your life, living or dead. To whom are you talking? About what are you trying to convince them?

THE DISCOVERY, CREATION, AND USE OF SYMBOLS AND SACRED OBJECTS

The path to soul is a road full of images. You encounter mysterious, evocative images whenever you enter the depths, whether in dreams, imagery, romance, nature, underworld rites and ceremonies, or the encounter with death. These images reveal qualities and desires of your soul.

Soul images can be embodied in two- or three-dimensional objects discovered in nature or fashioned by hand. If the latter, the image might be drawn on paper or canvas, formed with leather or cloth, on rock or in sand, with wood or ice, in clay or bronze, with your clothes or jewelry, on your skin or with your hair. Living with these sacred objects can accelerate your descent to soul and provide ways to represent what you discover there. They can serve as regular reminders of those discoveries, a considerable help as you work to manifest soul in your everyday life.

Some people place soul-image symbols on their business cards and letterhead, or on their products or artwork. Kate Errett, a glass artist, received her soul name, Rising Moon, on her vision quest. She places the image of a rising moon on each piece of her glass art to remind her who the artist really is and to project that identity into the world.

Sacred objects can also embody universal, transpersonal qualities, in contrast to personal soul images. Like most people, you probably live with significant objects that evoke qualities from myths or archetypes, or of courage, insight, intuition, imagination, love, and so on, and that stimulate, focus, or amplify your experience of those qualities. These objects might take the form of stones, seeds, jewels, figurines, paintings, weavings, jewelry, sculptures, bones, shells, teeth, claws, photographs, feathers, powders, crystals, liquids, or carvings. They might aid you during moments of fear or confusion or remind you of teachers, allies, or guides and the qualities they possess. The Christian cross, the Jewish Star of David, the American flag, and the universal heart, crescent moon, or setting sun are familiar examples of sacred symbols. Many other symbols and objects have meanings specific to small groups or to single individuals.

The talking piece used in council work is a materially embodied sacred symbol. Some groups might use a courting flute, resonating with the theme of one heart calling another. Others might prefer a beautiful bowl that each fills with his or her truth.

The talking piece we use at Animas Valley Institute is a wooden flute hung with dozens of smaller objects gifted by vision quest and soulcraft participants over the course of twenty years. These include rings, religious medallions, earrings, shells, small carvings, bones, rocks, and beads, all sacred to those who offered them and, soon enough, to all who sit in council. The staff, like a small shrine or a house of prayers, ushers us into a sanctuary where we more easily access our hearts and souls.

Sacred objects, whether of the universal or unique variety, animate and deepen our ceremonies. Wearing a medallion, cloak, or mask, or carrying a staff or wand can enhance ceremonial roles. Symbols evoke transpersonal qualities, universal archetypes, and deeply personal meanings, bringing them into play within the ceremony and our lives.

What is essential to the use of ceremonial symbols and sacred objects is not how they look to others but how you feel when employing them and what qualities they help you access.

Mark, a chemist in the biotechnology industry, entered the underworld during a journey in the Utah canyon lands. Before he left home, a small stone dragonfly was loaned to him by a friend who spoke of the dragonfly as a symbol of transformation. He put it in a leather pouch with other special objects and didn't think much more about it.

One morning in the canyon, the group helped Mark work with the previous night's dream in which he (the dream ego) turns into a large dragonfly with a colorful banner floating behind him. At first, he had no clue what it would mean to be a dragonfly. In submitting himself to his dream, however, Mark discovered how much the unfettered feeling of being a dragonfly contrasted with his habitual fear of changes and his somewhat conventional and controlled life. Indeed, in his dayworld, Mark was in the midst of an unwanted divorce and distressed about how his world was about to shift. The group's guide — who did not yet know about Mark's stone dragonfly — said the dream appeared to be about transformation and that, to transform, he, like everyone, must first surrender his former way of being in the world. At that moment

> a big blue dragonfly flew over my head and into our circle. Everyone noticed and laughed. So I shared the story of the stone dragonfly my friend had loaned me and what she had said about it being a symbol of transformation. Then we each went off wandering alone with the task to dialogue with a being in nature who called to us. I was called by a beautiful, intricately carved sandstone wall. I spoke to the wall and it responded through flowing curves, intricate patterns, and opposing qualities of softness and hardness. Then a gentle breeze blew and a shell of a dragonfly dropped out of nowhere right in front of me! I drew a dragonfly in the sand as an expression of gratitude. I accepted Dragonfly as my name.

Gradually, Mark is learning what it means to *be* Dragonfly. Since returning from the canyon, he has grown bolder and more creative in several ways, exploring art, spiritual disciplines, and new relationships. He fashioned his first sculpture, in copper and stained glass: a dragonfly with a three-foot wingspan. He is exploring what it means to "trans-form," to attune more with soul and spirit than to the merely physical preoccupations of his earlier life. He is discovering that the art emerging from him is "the fire of life, why I move, why I burn, why I feel, why I live."

Upon entering a time of wandering, you might study a craft for creating sacred objects or symbols. You might learn to work with wood, leather, clay, paint, marble, or cloth or with a form of expression such as music, dance, poetry, or performance art.

Or, if you have a teacher in a particular religious or spiritual lineage, you might study a ceremonial tradition that employs sacred objects, such as the construction and use of prayer arrows, the building and walking of labyrinths, or the proper care and use of prayer pipes.

The discovery, creation, and use of symbols and sacred objects help you focus your attention, intentions, and actions as you journey toward and through the realms of soul.

THE USE OF HALLUCINOGENS WITHIN SOULCRAFT CEREMONIES

The ceremonial use of hallucinogens is found in a great number of nature-based societies throughout the world. Many plants and extracts — ingested, inhaled, or otherwise bodily absorbed — can bring about profound changes in consciousness and, when used in a ceremonial context, can usher the journeyer into the underworld of soul. We can enter the mysteries of wild nature by taking wild nature inside.

Each psychotropic plant creates distinct effects on consciousness as a function of its particular biochemical qualities or (as nature-based people would say), its personal traits and intentions. The effects of a hallucinogen also depend enormously on the user's psychological frame of mind and the social and spiritual context — "set and setting."

Nature-based people who employ botanical hallucinogens consider the plant to be a close relative, a nonhuman person, an ally or sacred being with whom it is essential to maintain good relations through the exchange of gifts. There is great blessing and promise in this relationship, as well as obligation and risk. The plant is gathered and prepared in a ceremonial manner. Gifts are offered to the plant at the time of gathering. Gratitude is expressed during its use. The plant ally is not consumed merely for the purpose of altering consciousness but as one element of an otherworld journey undertaken for specific spiritual or healing purposes. The other ceremonial elements may include a guide or shaman, traditional myths and sacred stories, chants and music, drumming, dances specific to both the ceremony and the use of that particular plant, prayers, fasting, ritual purging, offerings, incense, symbols, sacred objects, masks, ceremonial clothing, and other preparatory and concluding ceremonies.

It is the ceremony as a whole, inextricably embedded in the larger web of meaning that supports and informs the worldview or culture, that constitutes a soulcraft practice, not the mere use of a mind-altering substance. Outside the context of such ceremonies, the effects of the same substance may range anywhere from absolutely nothing to entertaining, from ecstatic to lethal, but, in any case, they are not likely to be soul evoking or of lasting spiritual significance.

The use of hallucinogens, whether or not for the purpose of soul encounter, can, of course, be dangerous, especially in our society, where there is so little understanding of or respect for plant allies. There is the possibility of adverse psychological or physical consequences when an unprepared person ingests a hallucinogen without suitable intention, context, and guidance. Besides, with most hallucinogens there are no settings in the United States where such use or guidance is legal, except within the religious practices of some Native American peoples. Outside those indigenous cultures, there are few responsible guides in this country who know how to (1) assess a person's readiness for a plant-assisted soul encounter; (2) properly prepare him; (3) conduct such a ceremony or initiation effectively; and (4) assist him in integrating the experience. But if you manage to find a guide who employs hallucinogens, please be certain that he or she is highly experienced and capable in all four areas.

Being a child of the sixties, I have long been interested in the question of the religious and spiritual use of plant allies. Twenty years ago, I began an informal poll, asking hundreds of people if they have had hallucinogen-assisted soul encounters. Most had used hallucinogens in casual, unguided settings, while some had experienced guided trips or participated in traditional indigenous ceremonies under the guidance of native medicine people. More than half of those who had used plant allies reported spiritual experiences. Most, however, were referring to the upperworld sort of spiritual experience, ecstatic moments of transcendence, bliss, and oneness with creation. Many spoke of experiencing unfamiliar dimensions of reality leading to a radical and permanent shift in how they conceived of the world, life, consciousness, or the self. Some, with specific religious affiliations, reported visions of spiritual beings from their traditions.

About 25 percent reported experiences that sounded like underworld journeys: exotic beings, animals, plants, demons, angels, or rapturous events from the collective or personal past or future, including their own births or deaths. These journeys were invariably intense and emotional, often terrifying but also often ecstatic.

But when I narrowed the focus and asked, "Did you ever learn, from these experiences, something specific about the unique qualities of your deepest self, something about the particular gifts or soul qualities that are yours alone to bring to the world?" the answer was almost always no. Yet there were exceptions. Several people recounted experiences that were undoubtedly soul encounters.

The rarity in the Western world of plant-assisted soul encounters does not imply that these substances are ineffective in evoking such experiences.

Rather, it reflects the loss of the traditions, ceremonies, knowledge, and skills essential to prepare for and create a genuine opportunity for soul encounter. We have lost, in other words, the entire soulcraft context.

Hallucinogens such as LSD and those found in peyote, psychoactive mushrooms, and ayahuasca are not psychologically habit-forming and certainly not physically addictive like alcohol, nicotine, and barbiturates, all of which you can legally consume in the United States, or cocaine, methamphetamine, and heroin, which you cannot. The addictive drugs are consciousness constricting, while the hallucinogens are psychedelic, which means mind opening. Are hallucinogens, then, dangerous drugs that ought to remain outlawed in much of the Western world? Or are they significant soulcraft tools whose use ought to be decriminalized and even venerated?

Decriminalized or not, hallucinogens will not realize their potential spiritual value in the contemporary West until true elders appear again on the scene, elders who know how to employ these substances within sacred ceremonial settings. As long as their use is illegal in this country, this is not likely to happen except in the most secretive settings.

Perhaps one of the underlying reasons for the illegality of psychotropic substances rests in a fear of the underworld journey. Many people in positions of egocentric power and authority are terrified by the prospect of losing their own ego control and the self-confrontation and radical personal shifts that could be evoked. But even more likely they are attempting to suppress the use of substances that might render other people less controllable and less interested in lives of unrestrained consumption and soul-starving jobs. If they could, Western governments might attempt to outlaw *all* soulcraft practices.

Pharmaceutical companies that manufacture narcotics — and the physicians who liberally prescribe them — are not the primary causes of substance addictions. Neither are beer companies and liquor stores, or drug smugglers and pushers. Rather, egocentric societies are, societies that ignore, discourage, or obstruct the individual's soul-level encounter with nature, meaning, and creative self-definition, and instead promote ego aggrandizement, profits, and a shallow sense of self and security as the primary agenda of their citizens. Egocentrism leads to the suppression of individual depth and passion, which in turn leads to a grief too horrible to bear. Many attempt to numb that grief through the use of habit-forming substances like alcohol and other drugs.

Are psychotropic plants necessary for soul encounter? Definitely not.

There are many other, equally effective pathways to soul, as I hope this book conveys. The legal and widespread readoption of psychotropic substances as soulcraft aids will have to wait for changes in our society's attitudes (which may take a long time) and the emergence of a new generation of soulcraft practitioners who understand the subtleties and ceremonies of the spiritual use of these substances. (This has already begun in a small way, but you won't find these practitioners in the Yellow Pages.)

The value of plant allies for soulcraft is considerable. We need to support those explorers and guides who are responsibly developing this knowledge and skill. And we need to support those sociopolitical activists who are speaking up and making clear the difference between soul-numbing drug addiction and the soul-animating use of hallucinogenic substances.

STORIES AND STORYTELLING

Here's a story about stories.

Joyce enacted her vision quest in a deep, red, sheer-walled canyon in the lower Utah desert far from anywhere. She was a young businesswoman — single, attractive, successful, ambitious — but she did not believe in herself. No matter how many friends and lovers she collected who believed in her, it didn't take away, in the end, her lack of self-faith. She was a dark place wrapped in a cloak of light.

For her solo time, Joyce hiked miles into an exceptionally remote side canyon, into a hidden recess halfway up a canyon wall to a place so isolated she felt safe enough to remove her cloak. Dark, nearly dead memories like blackened bones and gray ash tumbled onto the red and beige sandstone. Two days went by. Nothing much happened. Occasionally she wandered over to the pile of bones and kicked them around a bit with the toe of her boot.

On the third day, she sat next to the dark pile and began to examine it, sifting through the ash, fingering the shards of broken dreams. Then, as she watched in horror, the bones assembled themselves into an ugly old woman who began to tell stories from Joyce's life, the true stories of her childhood, of how she had been betrayed by loved ones, stories she had almost managed to forget. She listened and she cried the entire day and the entire night.

The next morning she returned to our group base camp. She did not look good. She had lost her radiance. Later that day, still miserable, she began to tell the story of her fast, of the hag who told her the true stories. She shared some of those terrible stories with the group, and as she did, her body and face changed. She began to look...real. By the time she finished, she was radiant again, but in a different way. A misty luminance burned from her very core. By telling her story, Joyce finally caught up to the truth of her life and was thereby freed to move into a larger story.

I have witnessed many such transformative stories. In our healing and growing, we must, inevitably, make peace with our own stories and then tell them to at least one person. The telling is crucial. We must own our true stories. In doing so, we begin again to belong to the world in the way only we can. The door to soul opens.

Uncloaked, Joyce eventually became an artist — a watercolorist — and a practitioner of the art of organizational transformation, helping soul breathe again in corporate environments.

Story is the very fabric of our lives. Every life begins and ends with a story and, taken as a whole, *is* a story. Every relationship is a story. Every dream. Every experience. Each soul — whether embodied or not in that person's life — is a story longing to be told. The world itself is a story; indeed, it might be more accurate to say the world is made up of stories than to say it is made up of atoms, earth, trees, and other things. The German philosopher Ludwig Wittgenstein insisted the world divides up into facts, not things; I prefer to say *stories,* not facts.

Storytelling has an enormous power over us. It conveys meaning in a way a mere explanation never could. Telling and listening to stories are essential tools in approaching the soul and embodying what we find there.

There are many soulcraft skills and practices that incorporate storytelling. Here are a few of them:

MYTHS AND OTHER SACRED STORIES

Genuine myths are not false stories, as we often think in the Western world. *Myth* is one of many sacred terms our de-souled society has turned on its head (like *ritual, witch, underworld,* or *hoodwinked*). A myth is, in a sense, the very truest of stories, a story that reveals universal qualities of the human condition, of the world, and the deeper meanings and possibilities of our lives.

Each myth carries more richness and meaning than could ever be fully explained or that could be assimilated in a single telling, or even several. Invariably there are layers upon layers of significance, like bands of rock in a canyon wall, each stratum holding and hiding untold treasures and mysteries. We become aware of the different layers only as we develop spiritually. There is always more to learn from time-honored myths, and so we listen to them and tell them, and tell them again.

PERSONAL MYTH WORK

There are a thousand ways to tell the story of a life. How you tell *your* story determines, in part, what story you are in fact living and what it might become: a story, for example, about blind ambition and revenge, or about redemption and love. A soulcraft approach to your own story asks you to see your life in the light of the universal dynamics and archetypes of humanity.

Consider crafting your life story as a personal myth, framing the events of your life in a symbolic perspective. Compose an autobiography told in the third person, a story symbolically authentic to the central themes of your life. Have it take place anywhere and anytime that fits best with your myth. Add or subtract or modify characters from your life if this aids in portraying the thematic truths of your life. Have yourself represented by one character, two, or several (or, if it fits, none). Give yourself a symbolically significant name such as Golden Hair or Night Horse (or use "the hero" or "the heroine"). You might want to begin your myth with "Once upon a time. . ." If you wish, have your myth include the full story of your life (past your present age), all in the past tense, including the way it would likely end as the predominant themes play themselves out. The historical facts don't matter! Think and feel — and write — mythically.

As you write, remember that good myth honors the whole story as essential. Your early woundings and later losses are as necessary to your story as the victories and loves. The story transforms itself through the gift you recover at the center of your sacred wound, and you will find there redemption. (Review the section of chapter 5 on the sacred wound.)

TELLING THE STORIES OF YOUR LIFE

As with Joyce, the woman cloaked in light, there is also great value in simply telling your personal stories, not as myth but directly, just the way they happened. Tell the stories of your griefs, ecstasies, wanderings, and encounters with soul and other remarkable beings. It's important your listeners are people who know how to use the ears of their heart. You must be in a setting (like a council) in which people are *enabled* to listen in that way. And it's important that your story embody your deepest truths, irrespective of the facts.

SENSITIVE LISTENING AND MIRRORING

Just as there is an art to telling a story, there is an art to hearing one. Mirroring is receiving, embracing, and honoring people's stories of journeys into the inner/outer wilderness. In mirroring, you neither project nor interpret, but rather celebrate the enchantment of the story and the gift and giftedness of the one offering the tale. Help the storyteller glean and reap the jewels, both the radiant and dark ones. Draw out additional nuggets from the hidden veins of ore. Practice being as clear a mirror as possible so the teller, too, can taste and embrace the fullness and beauty of the story and be able to hold it as a sacred tale, as a mythos that opens the road again to spiritual adventure. Help the teller burst through barriers that might limit his experience of the fascination and joy of his own story. Learn to witness and endure the pathos and grief of the story without flinching or avoiding. Listen with love and compassion.

One of the most healing and empowering things we can do in this life is to tell our stories, *really* tell our stories! And one of the greatest gifts we can give is to *really* hear and embrace those stories, to resonate right down to our bones like tuning forks and to share that resonance with the storyteller.

SOUL POETRY, MUSIC, CHANTING, AND THE BARDIC TRADITION

Given that the soul prefers to speak in images and symbols, poetry — our own and others — is a natural pathway to soul. Poetry, "soul speech," brings together the linguistic, linear part of the psyche with the imaginal, holistic part, enlisting the thinking mind in the service of soul, image, and feeling. By immersing ourselves in the rich symbols of verse, we enhance the ego's ability to converse with soul.

The subject matter and style of some poets resonate more with the spiritual descent than do others. The poets quoted in these pages — David

Whyte, Rainer Maria Rilke, Mary Oliver, Jelaluddin Rumi, T. S. Eliot, and others — are extraordinarily soulful. The soul is enlivened and emboldened by poetry such as theirs. Not only is the soul content to listen to this poetry, it is also encouraged to speak up, to join in, to sing its own song.

Make a habit of reading the soul poets, alone or with friends. Read each poem aloud, very slowly, at least twice at each sitting. Let your imagination and feeling meander. Memorize some of your favorite soul poems. Recite them aloud in wild settings. Compose your own soul poetry and record your dreams in verse. Wander with and in poems and let your awareness cross boundaries. Make notes, in verse or prose, on what you find beyond the frontier.

Music, with or without lyrics, adds another dimension to verse. Soul-rooted music opens the door to our depths, seduces the gods and goddesses of the underworld as did Orpheus with his golden lyre. As a Wanderer, you may wish to fill your life and home with the mysterious and seductive strains of soul-stirring music, music that evokes other worlds, unfamiliar themes and emotions, and life lived wildly beyond the pale of our surface lives.

Chanting is another universal means of diving beneath the surface. Nature-based chants, especially, reconnect us with our deeper selves, with each other, and with plants, animals, and the land. It is perhaps best to begin with those nature-based chants that have been used for many years, but, once you get the hang of it, you can create your own.[2] But the ego alone cannot create chants useful for soulcraft; the words and melody, as with soul poetry, must have roots in the mysteries of nature and psyche, as gifted by the Other, allowing you to express the astonishing and sometimes dangerous insights beyond your ego's everyday understandings.

The soul poets were once called bards. They employed music and rhythm as well as verse. Dolores LaChapelle tells us that the bard is "the one who puts together the drum, gourd rattle, and chanting of all 'the people' into words and recites it back to his people so that they can continue to build their culture."[3] The bard takes all the individual stories of the people and of the land itself and combines them into a great story, reminding us that nature and humanity are not separate. One of the modern poets most influential in reviving the bardic tradition is Gary Snyder.

Poetry, dreams, nature, and soul weave through one another. Dreams are the poems of our souls. Soul is our deepest human nature, the under-dreamstream of our lives. Wild nature is the ongoing dream of the earth, and our souls are essential components of that dream. Our individual night dreams are strands of the earth's dream, just as our bodies are part of earth's body. Nature offers herself to our senses in images, and poetry conveys those images. Immersion in nature is as effective a way as any to uncover and recover the soul. Soul-resonant poets are visionaries, people who have recovered their soul's desires and strive to make those desires visible to others. Each one of us has this visionary capacity to sing the song of our souls.

BODY PRACTICES FOR ALTERING CONSCIOUSNESS

There are many methods for bridging inner and outer, the seen and unseen. Many, like self-designed ceremony and the use of psychotropic plants, work in part by altering our consciousness. Altered consciousness enables us to perceive actualities and imagine possibilities that we might otherwise miss, thereby assisting us to weave the subtle and unseen forces of the world into form, making the unconscious conscious.

There are several body practices, found in cultures the world over, that alter consciousness by shifting the body's physiological state. These, too, can serve as pathways to soul.

Consciousness-altering breathing techniques — from ancient practices such as yogic *pranayama* to modern disciplines like holotropic breathwork as developed by the transpersonal psychiatrist Stanislav Grof — act literally to inspire us. As we breathe in fully and rapidly, our biochemistry shifts and we take in and join with the essence of the world. By altering the depth and rhythm of our breath, we can alter our relationship to the world and to our selves.

In addition to their use of breathing techniques, the many schools of yoga offer a great variety of physical postures *(asanas)* and movement *(vinyasa)* that not only stretch our bodies but also alter consciousness, thereby providing a doorway to soul. Many yoga practitioners understand the body to be the materialized unconscious and thus an entry to both the underworld and upperworld.

Extreme physical exertion can also lead to non-ordinary states, in part through changes initiated by sustained cardiovascular effort, the full use of the lungs, and the biochemical changes that are thereby induced. Long distance runners and other aerobic athletes know this well. As with breathwork and psychotropic plants, the participant's intent determines the effectiveness of these practices as pathways to soul.

Trance states are often induced through the extended exertions of running, rowing, climbing, or dancing. On some wilderness trips I lead, we backpack miles through rugged country into remote, wild, and spellbinding places. The sustained exertion alone stretches our physical and emotional limits, nudging us a bit sideways psychologically, allowing self-limiting beliefs to loosen. As we arrive more fully in the present moment, we discover more creative and soul-resonant ways of belonging to the world.

Fasting, as part of a vision quest or not, is another ancient and common method for altering consciousness. Literally emptying ourselves, we become a more receptive vessel for the gifts of soul.

There are at least three ways that fasting works its magic on us. First, fasting (with or without water) for three days or more profoundly affects our nervous system and thus our consciousness.[4] Most people report by the third day an astonishing clarity of perception, thought, feeling, and imagination. For many, hunger disappears and a refined physical energy and alertness arise. Second, frequent hunger pangs remind our wandering minds to refocus attention on soulful intent. Third, as we grow weaker physically, our ego defenses weaken as well. It becomes more difficult to maintain those everyday boundaries separating us from the vast mysteries within and without, the mysteries through which the soul might speak.

CHAPTER 10

THE VISION QUEST AND
SOULCENTRIC RITUAL

I am clearing a space—
here, where the trees stand back.
I am making a circle so open
the moon will fall in love
and stroke these grasses with her silver.

I am setting stones in the four directions,
stones that have called my name
from mountaintops and riverbeds, canyons and mesas.
Here I will stand with my hands empty,
mind gaping under the moon.

I know there is another way to live.
When I find it, the angels
will cry out in rapture,
each cell of my body
will be a rose, a star.

If something seized my life tonight,
if a sudden wind swept through me,
changing everything,
I would not resist.
I am ready for whatever comes.

But I think it will be
something small, an animal
padding out from the shadows,
or a word spoken so softly
I hear it inside.

It is dark out here, and cold.
The moon is stone.
I am alone with my longing.
Nothing is happening
but the next breath, and the next...

— Morgan Farley

To enact a vision quest is to *clear a space,* as Morgan Farley does in (and with) her poem. To quest is to honor a fallow time in our spiritual lives, an emptiness into which something utterly new and generative might enter. It is to create an open vessel capable of being filled to overflowing by the sacred Other — perhaps by the moon, whose light is not the light of everyday consciousness. Often on a quest, a circle of stones is constructed as a physical embodiment of such a vessel — one stone in each of the four cardinal directions. It is a place into which mysteries are invited.

A mystery may or may not arrive, but should we be so graced, its form will surely surprise. It is best to be humble and not expect something majestic, for then we would probably miss what *does* arrive. Yet, if our sensing is subtle, such that each bodily cell becomes a star or a rose, we will recognize the mystery when it arrives. Its impact, like an earthquake, might rearrange the very ground of our lives.

If we can remain open to what emerges from the shadows, our new life will begin to arrange itself and unfold with each subsequent breath.

THE VISION QUEST

Soul encounter, as we've seen, can be brought about by many methods. Vision quests (wilderness-based fasting rites) are among the most effective. They interweave many of the soulcraft practices discussed in earlier chapters to form a single extended ceremony of several days' duration.

Since earliest times, people have received profound insight about themselves and their world by means of a vision quest, whose basic, universal elements include:

- a remote wilderness setting
- fasting from food and, sometimes, water
- solitude (no other *human* companions)
- direct exposure to the forms and forces of nature (i.e., only enough clothing and shelter necessary for physical survival and basic comfort,

and no distractions from ceremonial intentions, no items of entertainment, reading materials, et cetera)

- attention-focusing and consciousness-shifting ceremonies, prayers, and practices
- a significant period of time — at least a full day, but usually three or four days and up to as much as several weeks (in which case, small amounts of simple foods are eaten).

Among nature-based peoples, such a rite is enacted by individuals reaching a critical turning point in their lives, such as those making the passage into true adulthood.

There are countless cultural variations on the archetype of a wilderness fasting rite. European anthropologists coined the term *vision quest* to refer to rituals practiced by the indigenous people of North America, but this term could be employed equally well to refer to similar rites found in European, Asian, and Middle Eastern cultures. The wilderness sojourns of Moses, Jesus, and other heroic figures from Judeo-Christianity as well as those of the Hindu, Islamic, Buddhist, and other faiths were vision quests.

As a rite of passage, the vision quest facilitates the transition through a major life crossroads. Crossroads such as puberty, leaving home, marriage, starting or expanding a family, terminating a pregnancy, vocational change, loss of a loved one, divorce, major injury or disability, or a spiritual crisis are often disorienting and emotionally charged, but these times of disruption and profound change are also unavoidable and potentially pivotal, serving as thresholds to deep healing, growth, and self-empowerment.

As a rite of initiation, the quest is a ceremonial descent to find our soul image and derive greater clarity regarding the purpose and meaning of our life. The initiation is not into any social, religious, or spiritual group but into our own soul path and deeper levels of authentic adulthood.

In my wilderness work, I have taken a contemporary, Western approach to the vision quest. Although different from Native American and other indigenous ways, it is very much nature-based and soul-oriented.[1] It is, in its basics, as follows.

During five or six days of group preparation time at a retreat center, campground, or wilderness base camp, we work with dreams, poetry, deep imagery, trance dance, dialogues with nature, council, shadow, the Loyal Soldier and sacred wound themes, and other practices to help participants separate from their surface lives and begin diving toward underground streams. Then the questers go off to spend three or four days and nights alone. Each establishes a remote camp, with only water and basic survival gear. Exposed to the forces of the wild world, questers engage in practices designed to facilitate and intensify the encounter with soul, including the death lodge, dialogues with nature, self-designed ceremonies, trance drumming and chanting, responding to signs and omens, and other forms of nature observation. Like Morgan Farley, the questers may choose to conclude their solo time with an all-night vigil inside a ritually constructed circle of stones. Then they return to base camp to begin the assimilation of their experiences. A total of three days of activities support them in embodying what they have learned during their fasts. Within that time, they recount, in council, the events of their underworld journeys. These stories are celebrated and mirrored back by the guides and other group members. As their egos begin to root themselves in soul, they learn to incorporate their renewed selves — enthusiastic yet unripe — into the social world, first with their quest group and then with the larger community back home. Their guides offer additional one-to-one mentoring during the year following the quest.

In the approach I have taken, the primary goal of the quest is to empower participants to commune with their souls, which, they discover, are reflected back to them from nature as revealed through their senses, emotions, and deep imagination.[2] The ceremonial symbols and practices employed before and during the fast place the questers in the portal to soul. If they have the grace and good fortune to enter the inner sanctum, what they see in the mirror of inner/outer nature will reveal clues to the riddle of their lives.

What makes a particular vision quest design effective at facilitating soul encounter is not simply a matter of specific methods or ceremonies, but rather a context that encourages conversation between the conscious self (in a non-ordinary ego state) and the sacred Other. Through this exchange, the questers move beyond ordinary consciousness to find a new foundation for their lives. They are shape-shifted by the vastness and enchantment of their own psyches.

THE VISIONARY ENCOUNTER: INNER OR OUTER?

What the quester receives on a vision quest may or may not be visual. It's possible it will not be sensory based at all. The conscious encounter with soul occurs as either (1) a non-sensory experience such as a dream, a waking image, a spiritual voice, an energetic shift in the body, and/or a strong emotion; or (2) a sensory-based epiphany appearing, for example, in the form of a flower or snake, a canyon or mountain, the wind or rain.

Given the profound alterations in consciousness evoked during a wilderness fast, the vision is difficult to categorize definitively as of the sensory (outer) world or the non-sensory (inner) world. Indeed, it is often a blending or synergy of *both* psyche and nature. James Hillman maintains "we live in a world that is neither 'inner' nor 'outer.'" For the quester, to be sure, the inner/outer distinction between psyche and nature loses merit.

The individual may meet, for example, an animal who speaks to him intimately, or a corona around the moon that emanates a melody of wisdom, or a gift-bearing ancestor in the form of a desert whirlwind. Are these events inner or outer? Of imagination or sensing? Both? Maybe it would be best to abandon the Western way of separating inner from outer and to say, instead, that these experiences, these visions, reflect a conversation between the human soul and the soul of nature. A visionary encounter is often a moment when the imagination and senses work together synesthetically and amplify each other brilliantly. The conscious self tunes in, as a third party, to the conversation ceaselessly unfolding between psyche and nature, and then perhaps responds with the heartfelt gestures of self-designed ceremony. The communion between self and nature is restored and celebrated.

Maybe you've had the disturbing experience of misplacing your soul. You might have asked, "Is my soul found inside me or is it 'out there' in nature?" The answer surprises: You can learn about your soul by looking "inward" through the windows of imagination and feeling. And you can learn about your soul by looking "outward" to the wild world. But the soul itself is *neither* inside nor outside you. If by *soul* you mean your true self, who you really are, then your soul *is* you, and you/your soul are in nature because *you* are in nature.

The individual human soul is one element of the fabric of nature. You are not in any way separate from nature. The wild world reflects your essence back to you just like a still lake reflects your image. Is that reflection in you or in the lake? Neither. Both you and the lake are in the world, and the lake reflects that fact back to you. In the same way, your soul, your essence, is in the world, and nature mirrors *that* fact back to you.

VISIONARY EXPERIENCE AND PARADOX

Visionary experience is paradoxical as well as liminal. In the midst of a vision, we find ourselves bridging nature and psyche, image and sensation, the old life and the new, the dayworld and the nightworld. We go into the dark and find light, are lost and thereby found, hardly know ourselves and end up finding our deepest truths.

Visionary experience springs from dichotomies that at first seem irreconcilable. There is desire and despair — the desire to commune with the soul, the despair born of soul estrangement. There is attraction and repulsion — attraction to the rich realm of the dark, repulsion from its monsters and demons. There is danger and seduction, the threat of death and the allure of a new life. There is knowing and not knowing. There is hope for a new and joyous way of living, and grief for years passed in emptiness.

If we sink deep enough into these dichotomies, they shift into paradoxes — not either/or but both/and. Soul embraces the poles. We are both light and dark, both knowing and not knowing, both lost and found, both living and dying, filled with both angels and demons. If we can accept the opposing elements and endure their collision in full consciousness, we, too, can embrace the poles. Robert Johnson, following Carl Jung, says that the capacity for paradox — the tolerance of ambiguity — is "the measure of spiritual strength and the surest sign of maturity."[3] Johnson suggests there is a "divine progression" from conflict to paradox to revelation.[4] The revelatory vision arises through the acceptance of paradox — or at least the open-eyed confrontation with it.

This both/and quality of the visionary experience is facilitated by the non-ordinary state commonly known as trance. When entranced, we temporarily cease distinguishing between what is real and unreal, possible and impossible, me and not-me, paradoxical or logical.[5] This allows our relationships to all worlds to shift. The difference between real and not real, after all, is a function of which world, which reality, one is operating in. Something real in one world may not be so in another. When such distinctions are suspended, we can experience paradoxical events otherwise incompatible with our conventional worlds. For example, in trance a contemporary American might have an elaborate conversation with a rock — an unreal occurrence in the everyday Western world but one accepted as commonplace among nature-based peoples. A non-ordinary experience during visionary trance can become the seed for our new story. When the distinction between imagination and perception dissolves, we can roam between worlds and find our lives transformed by the Other.

In "The Song of Wandering Aengus," the great Irish poet William Butler Yeats captured in verse an event that transformed his life in his mid-twenties. He was entranced by an interior fire that perhaps laid waste to his beliefs about the world, by the spell cast by nature in the transitional moment between night and day, and by the visionary influence of hazel trees. Yeats's experience, I believe, was a soul encounter, precisely the sort that occurs during vision quests. As on a quest, Yeats was alone, in nature, and caught between an old story and a new one.

THE SONG OF WANDERING AENGUS

I went out to the hazel wood,
Because a fire was in my head,
And cut and peeled a hazel wand,
And hooked a berry to a thread;
And when white moths were on the wing,
And moth-like stars were flickering out,
I dropped the berry in a stream
And caught a little silver trout.

When I had laid it on the floor
I went to blow the fire aflame,
But something rustled on the floor,
And some one called me by my name:
It had become a glimmering girl
With apple blossom in her hair
Who called me by my name and ran
And faded through the brightening air.

Though I am old with wandering
Through hollow lands and hilly lands,
I will find out where she has gone,
And kiss her lips and take her hands;
And walk among long dappled grass,
And pluck till time and times are done
The silver apples of the moon,
The golden apples of the sun.[6]

While entranced, Yeats caught a fish that then caught him when it shape-shifted into a glimmering girl who spoke his name, utterly altering his life forever. We can bet she did not call him "Mister Yeats" or "William" or even "Billy." She called him, no doubt, by his true name, a name encapsulating his soul powers and the way he would spend the rest of his long life and, through his poetry, all of eternity.

As his poem reveals, Yeats's soul powers blossomed as he wandered in search of the glimmering girl. A common theme woven throughout Yeats's work, from his twenties to his final book, *A Vision*, unites the metaphysical symbols of the apple, the sun, and the moon. We might say that Yeats's soul work, his foremost service to humanity and the source of his deepest fulfillment, was his exploration and literary animation of "the silver apples of the moon, the golden apples of the sun": the feminine and masculine mysteries of the universe. Perhaps, then, the girl with apple blossom in her hair (his anima?) called him "the One Who Plucks Apples," the truth at the center of the image he was born with. Or perhaps she called him "Wandering Aengus," Aengus being the Irish god of love, beauty, and poetry. We might see Yeats's poetry as one of the ways he celebrated his relationship to those apples and his obligation to that way of wandering.

INTERPLAY BETWEEN THE SENSES, EMOTIONS, AND IMAGINATION

Visionary experience blends the senses. When talking across the species boundaries, for example, two or more of the five senses often work together synesthetically. We not only see but also *feel*, in our limbs, the shifting shadows that cross a boulder, experiencing the movement as meaningful gesture. With Yeats, we not only see but *smell* the glimmering girl's apple-scented gesture as she runs from the room. Clearing a space with Morgan Farley, we both see and *feel* the moon stroke the grasses with her silver. Through their seen shapes and felt textures, we *hear* the stones call our name.

During a vision quest, the senses not only blend synesthetically but they also work together with the other functions of consciousness.

Of the four windows of knowing — described by Stephen Gallegos as thinking, sensing, imagination, and feeling — the latter two are invariably active during visionary experiences.[7] A vision quester's imagination and feelings work together with the perceptual senses. For example, something we see or hear or smell or touch in the natural world resonates powerfully with the soul, and the soul responds with an emotion-stirring image from the depths.

This interplay between sensed nature and the intrapsychic realms of feeling and imagination is also found in our experience with dreams. Many dreams are anchored in a dayworld sensory experience that the dream transforms through imagination and feeling. Our waking perceptions constitute the grist for the dream mill; they can do the same for the vision mill.

I may dream, for example, of hiking in a canyon I visited the day before. High above, on the rim of the canyon, I see my friend (from my waking world). She is riding a horse (very much like the one I had seen two days before). She calls my name in a way that evokes an emotion simultaneously containing and transcending sadness and hope.

In this example, the dream has borrowed from sensing (the canyon, friend, and horse) and from imagination (riding a horse on the edge of a precipice) to offer the gift of a profound emotion. We might imagine a similar dynamic when the glimmering girl called Yeats, who always associated apple blossoms with his first meeting with his beloved, Maud Gonne, the Irish nationalist.

An encounter with soul on a vision quest might come as a dream, a waking image, or through a sensory encounter with a being in nature. The image or perception may be visual, kinesthetic, or auditory, or some synesthetic blending of modalities.

Sabina Wyss, a personal coach and holistic health professional, was in her mid-twenties and on a vision fast. Alone in the Yosemite high country, she awoke one night out of a sound sleep. In the moonlight, five inches from her nose, she saw a stationary bear paw. Before her body knew to panic, she looked up and was mesmerized by the magnificent animal towering above her sleeping bag. What a blessing, she thought. She lay perfectly still. Then a wave of fear came, soon followed by a calm willingness to die should this be her time. The bear was so close his body heat and scent engulfed her.

The bear moved a few paces to Sabina's backpack and started pawing. Without conscious intention, Sabina sat up and heard a soft warning sound emerge from her throat that alarmed her as much as it did the bear. The bear dropped into a crouching, attack position. Sabina, her heart now beating wildly, assumed this was her last moment. The two stared into each other's eyes, three feet apart. Then the bear turned on his heels and disappeared into the forest.

Sabina did not go back to sleep. In the morning, she discovered the bear had taken her necklace, a large African masterpiece of silver plates and ebony inlays, a gift from a teacher who had his own opinions of who Sabina ought to be. Although she had brought the necklace to honor her teacher, she didn't wear it because it would have been an attempt to please him in the face of her own deeper knowing. The necklace was now the bear's.

The bear left her with two gifts in exchange: the freedom to claim her own path independent of her teacher's projections and a visceral image-feeling of Bear. When Sabina feels in need of spiritual support, she calls on Bear. He is a palpable presence walking alongside her. "He guides me toward my true, innate power and how to live that power in the world."

Sabina's midnight exchange established the image-feeling of Bear at the center of her soul path. The interplay between the sensory experience of the bear (sight, scent, and sound), the extraordinary emotions (terror, calm, and gratitude), and the numinous image (Bear as spiritual ally) composed the fabric of this encounter with soul.

Whether the soul speaks to the ego through dreams or waking visions, its imaginal and archetypal language must be translated into the linguistic and cultural realm of ego. This translation can occur in part subconsciously and in part consciously. Subconsciously, soul might make things easier for ego by employing images borrowed from dayworld sensing, such as the sight, sound, and scent of an animal. The result of this subconscious translation appears to the conscious self as a visual image, a non-embodied voice, or a bodily sensation or gesture. Because the image is borrowed from a waking sensory experience, the conscious self can more readily grasp its symbolic significance. Once conscious, the image can then be further assimilated by the ego through thinking (e.g., associations, analysis, interpretation), feeling (e.g., encouraging the emotions evoked by the image), or imagination (e.g., deep imagery journeys).

EGO-DESTRUCTURING, LAMENTING, AND WILDERNESS

How do wilderness fasting rites facilitate soul encounter? In order for the conscious self to glimpse and be sustainably impacted by soul, the everyday state of consciousness must be sufficiently disassembled such that the ego cannot easily reshape itself in its old form. This radical shift in awareness — often termed *ego-destructuring* — evokes a non-ordinary state without loss of consciousness. Vision fasts are designed to destructure the ego.

At times of major life transitions, when vision fasts are usually undertaken, our self-definitions no longer fit or provide enough meaning or passion for living. Yet we are stuck in those definitions like an outgrown set of clothes. Our egos, in their current form, have become an impediment to growth and fulfillment instead of the vehicle for soul embodiment they ideally are. You might say management has become an enemy of soul progress.

At times like this, we need to shake up the management team by way of the underworld journey. This is ego-destructuring, experienced by the ego as a dying. As ego-destructuring gets underway, the ego becomes terrified and may try to stop the process — even when the ego itself has chosen it. Signing up for soul encounter can be like getting on a roller coaster and then thinking better of it as you are towed up the initial incline. What's at risk is your entire way of belonging to the world. The ego signs up for such an experience only when it's time to make a sacrifice for the possibility of a greater life. As Rilke put it,

What we choose to fight is so tiny!
What fights with us is so great!
If only we would let ourselves be dominated
as things do by some immense storm,
we would become strong too, and not need names.[8]

At the point in the descent when the ego feels seriously threatened, it may react with desperate attempts to save itself — like jumping off the roller coaster. This is why initiation rites are designed to minimize the ego's ability to escape, to give the soul a chance to prevail over ego. The key is a sustained debilitation of the normal ego state; in other words, an ordeal.

On a vision quest, the principal elements of the ordeal are prolonged isolation, fasting, and exposure to the wild, but for added effect, you can include fire sacrifices, time in the death lodge, a particularly fierce ceremonial sweat, shadow work and other methods of confronting the dark, meditations on death, an all-night vigil or two, and/or lamenting.

Here I want to explore two especially facilitative features of a vision fast ordeal: the practice of lamenting and the effects of exposure to wilderness.

LAMENTING

The anthropologists' term *vision quest* is not an accurate translation of the words originally used by the indigenous people of the Americas to refer to their fasting rites. What they did call it varied from tribe to tribe. Black Elk, a chief of the Lakota people, said that their word, *hanblecheya,* means "lamenting" or "crying."[9] For me, lamenting is in fact a more accurate and fitting term for wilderness fasting rites than vision quest.

Lamenting puts the emphasis in the right place. An individual embarks on a rite of soul encounter when he recognizes the story he has been living has become too small. He will have to sacrifice the old story, provoking the ordeal of a good deal of grief. He longs for a new, larger story but knows he cannot discern it with the limited powers of his thinking mind, which naturally clings to the old story. He has many reasons to lament.

Lamenting is central to the Lakota fasting rite. The Lakota lamenter is expected to cry nearly continuously during his three or four days alone on the mountain. He cries for help and for "mercy," as Black Elk explains, because he is having "difficulties," "a troubled mind." He laments and he cries "most pitifully" because he wishes "to gain knowledge" or "wisdom," to receive a "vision" or a "message" from the Great Mystery, Wakan Tanka, "that my people may live."[10]

An unrestrained lament is a crowbar into the dark depths of the self. The lamenter opens to his deepest and most difficult truths of loss and hope and dares to gaze into the bottom of his unprotected heart. His vision waits in those shadowy realms. He will not gain access without wrestling with demons, with what is unsettled or wrong with his life. Although contemporary nonindigenous lamenters might not lament in the same form or idioms of the Lakota, lamenting is an essential component of a vision fast.

The lament expresses, in essence, that the quester has lost his way, has strayed off his path of heart, or has gone as far as he could with what he knows. Perhaps it admits that the adolescent personality cannot take him further, and that this recognition and loss are difficult and painful, an ordeal. For the modern vision quester, the lament may sound something like this: "Dear God! Help me! I can no longer find my way in the world by figuring it out. My old way doesn't provide enough meaning to go on living! I seek a way to help my people, to offer something good to the world. I see people suffering everywhere around me; the animals, the waters, and the land itself are suffering. I long for a vision, a gift to bring back to my community. I release my former understanding of self and world. I am willing to sacrifice everything — my social position, my belongings, my home; they mean nothing without vision. I lament and go without food. I dwell alone beneath the sky. O, God! Help me!"

Your lament starts with what is most troubling to you, your greatest anguish. Eventually, your lament brings you to your deepest longing. As David Whyte notes, we feel our lack before we feel our longing. Once lament opens to longing, you must give that longing your full attention. As Rumi has said, "It is the longing that does all the work."

Your lament, once begun in earnest, gathers emotional momentum; it opens your eyes wide to the world as it opens your heart to your deepest longing. The longing forges a vessel capable of receiving a vision.

On a vision quest, unless you reach the center of your longing, you will not be able to stay focused during your fast, to pray long and deeply enough, to offer your attention reverently to the animals, signs, images, and dreams that appear. To open the door to vision, you must surrender fully to your deepest yearning.

Lamenting takes you to a level of consciousness far deeper than familiar ego concerns. A tool for ego-destructuring, lamenting introduces your conscious self to your soul.

EXPOSURE TO WILDERNESS

Dwelling in wild nature is another essential element of the vision quest, quite possibly the most important, not merely or primarily because it removes you from the distractions of everyday life. Wilderness contributes toward the goal of ego-destructuring in two other ways — in what it lacks and in what it affords.

First, in the wild world, you find none of the social or physical structures that constellate the ego's everyday commerce. The wilderness does not mirror to your ego its familiar ways of organizing itself or propping itself up. The things you take for granted in your surface life (e.g., clocks and schedules, human relationships, social groupings, jobs, buildings, hobbies, TV, books, computers, automobiles) do not exist in wild solitude. Your ego finds itself adrift in an enormous and unfamiliar sea, without anchor or landmarks. It has few means to maintain or defend itself. After several days without companions, food, anything to read, or conventional entertainment, and (thanks to the fast) without the energy to distract or busy itself in any of the normal ways, the ego loses its grip.

The second way wilderness facilitates ego-destructuring is through its powerful resonance with the depths, thereby supporting soul to speak louder. When the soul's voice thunders, it topples the ego's worldview, shatters its fortress of logic and limited values. In every moment, wilderness offers forms and forces that reverberate with the soul: the plunging canyons and soaring mountains, the cascading creeks and placid lakes, the valley fog at sunrise, the alpenglow on the peaks, the bugling elk and the howling wolf, the iridescence of hummingbird and lizard, the fragrance of pine sap and cliff rose, the leap of rabbit and slither of snake, the desert stillness, the daily journey of the sun, the nightly odyssey of the moon and stars, the caress and whisper of the wind.

The soul responds to the allurements of nature with tidings and yearnings from the psyche: stirrings of deep feeling, memories from this and other worlds, dreams and images, archetypes of the human unconscious — and visions.

With good fortune, your ordinary ego state dissolves, and you discover the outer wilderness reflecting the lost secrets and mysteries of your inner wilderness.

On a vision quest, you suffer an ordeal, becoming empty of your normal ego state in order to be filled with a soul-rooted sense of self. Like Morgan Farley, you must stand with hands empty and mind gaping, and if something comes to take your life, perhaps you shall not resist. Becoming empty is both the purpose and symbolism of fasting. Along with fasting, the solitude and exposure constitute the physical aspect of the ordeal. Your lament and the resulting ego-destructuring make up the psychological ordeal, suffered to make possible a communion with soul.

THE POWER OF SOULCENTRIC RITUAL

Vision quests are grand and complex rituals. Much of their transformative power arises simply from the fact that they are rituals. Several features of rituals support the encounter with soul.

Rituals are bodily enactments in real time and space, engaging us not only verbally, cognitively, imaginatively, and emotionally but also through our bodies, by way of symbolically rich gestures. As ritual participants, we are thoroughly active, not just listening, observing, or imagining but also *living* our deepest questions and truths, *embodying* our sacred symbols and life themes, and *physically interacting* with the archetypal qualities of the earth and the universal human experience. Immersion in the ritual process draws from us more than we anticipate.

The vision quester, for example, is not sitting in a room, feeling, imagining, and thinking. She is out on the land, in the wind, heat, and cold, exposed to the storm and the cries in the night. She is setting stones in the four directions. She is dancing her prayers, singing her heart out, crying to the earth and shouting at the sky for a vision, talking to the trees, the hawks, the moon, and the mountain. She is dressed in sacred robes, tying prayers into cloth bundles, adorning herself with flowers or thorns or mud, all in accord with the counsel of nature and her own soul. She is out on the land and fully embodied there. She is as fully present to her body and the breaking wave of her life as she has ever been.

Most rituals also derive their effectiveness from intimate and vital social support. Even the vision quest, with its central time of solitude, involves other participants — family members, friends, guides or ceremonial leaders, and fellow questers. Family and friends provide physical, psychological, and spiritual support as the quester prepares for her ordeal, and, upon her return home, encouragement to live her vision. And, immediately after her fast, she is enthusiastically welcomed back to base camp and witnessed — and truly seen — by her ritual community.

Rituals are rooted in deeply meaningful symbols and the sacred objects that embody those symbols. The quester is in conversation with the quadrated circle, the wounded heart, images of the butterfly or dragonfly, the broken stick, the prayer arrow or God's eye, the ancestor's blessing, the parent's ashes, the family's coat of arms, the religious icon, the wedding ring, the medicine bag, the mask, the drum, the sacrificial fire. These symbols arouse the deepest desires of her heart, her greatest griefs and fears, the archetypal possibilities of the collective human unconscious, and her religious and spiritual yearnings. Through numinous power absorbed and emanated, they uncover sacred layers of her humanity. And they effectively awaken suppressed feeling, often provoking a profound healing crisis.

In the sacred time and space of group ritual, the intimate sharing of emotions and revelations results in unusually strong interpersonal bonding, rarely experienced in the Western world except in romance and war. Ritual participants enjoy profound connectedness, their hearts breaking open, which, in turn, opens them that much more to the power and poignancy of the ritual itself, of the natural world, and of their own souls.

Perhaps the most significant attribute of ritual is the empowered conversation with the sacred Other. As we have seen, the Other speaks to us through dream images, deep imagination, archetypes, myths, and nature signs and omens. Our ritual enactments are the human half of the conversation.

The vision quest includes many ritual conversations. The four-directions circle — constructed of stones, branches, or other objects from nature — is a good example. The circle is big enough to stand or lie in, big enough to pray in or enact ceremony. Quadrated circles are universal symbols of wholeness, and thus a symbol the Other readily understands. The quester constructs the circle in a ritual manner, aligning each cardinal stone with the corresponding direction of the world. The message the Other hears may be something like, "I am here to align the totality of me with the totality of the world. I'm here to discover my true place, my particular way of belonging to the world." The circle of stones becomes a request to the Other to come visit, a wrestling invitation to an angel, a beacon for the soul.

Another power of ritual lies in the archetypal symbols and ceremonial enactments that usher the participant into the realm of the Great Mystery. Signs of mystery may appear — visions as astonishing as a burning bush. The incomprehensible heart of the cosmos, the Great Mystery reveals both the boundless possibilities and the sacred obligations inherent in the adventure of life. If the ritual participant opens to the Great Mystery, he will be gifted a radically shifted perspective on being alive, a reconciliation between the conscious self and the *mysterium tremendum* of the soul, and a deepened appreciation for the sacred, the unknown, and the unexpected. David Whyte gives us an image of Moses at his very first moment of opening to the Great Mystery and being opened by it:

And we know, when Moses was told,
   in the way he was told,
"Take off your shoes!" He grew pale from that simple

reminder of fire in the dusty earth.
    He never recovered
his complicated way of loving again

and was free to love in the same way
    he felt the fire licking at his heels loved him...[11]

Moses had been standing on holy ground all his life (like all of us) but he didn't know this until he heard God's voice for the first time. Afterward, Moses was a transformed man, forever conscious of the Great Mystery in everything.

Finally, rituals such as the vision quest allow the individual to access and utilize the unique but unusual personal power available during times of major life transition. Typically in our society, we feel weak, empty, and hopeless when confronted by change. But ritual can help us draw upon the power inherent in being neither here nor there, neither this nor that, dead to the old life and not yet born to the new. This is the power of existential freedom, of maximal psycho-spiritual possibilities, of unfettered potential. It is the power of the shape-shifter. Ritual celebrates and enhances this liminal power by allowing the individual to live in the now in relation to truths not easily accessed from conventional awareness. Ritual evokes a time before time began, the "once upon a time," the "time long ago and far away," the trance time or dreamtime existing parallel to and separate from our everyday lives and concerns.

During periods of major change, we are stripped of our old place in the world. Ritual helps us relax into a type of homelessness, a lack of stable ground. Ritual enables us to enjoy the uninventoried possibilities encountered while wandering in the magical desert of our lives.

Times of transition are, in fact, the best opportunities to renew the search for meaning. As our old stories fall away, we begin to see new possibilities. When most empty, we're most able to be filled anew. Our eyes open wide to the vastness of life's horizon. Then, our world having become as spare and clear as the open desert, we can, at long last, behold that one feathered gift settling down softly before us on the untrammeled earth.

PART THREE

THE RETURN

CHAPTER 11

CULTIVATING A SOULFUL RELATIONSHIP TO LIFE

Part 1

HOW TO REGAIN YOUR SOUL

Come down Canyon Creek on a summer
  afternoon
that one place where the valley floor opens out
  You will see
the white butterflies. Because of the way
  shadows
come off those vertical rocks in the west, there
  are
shafts of sunlight hitting the river and a deep
long purple gorge straight ahead. Put down your
  pack.

Above, air sighs the pines. It was this way
when Rome was clanging, when Troy was being
  built,
when campfires lighted caves. The white
  butterflies dance
by the thousands in the still sunshine. Suddenly
  anything
could happen to you. Your soul pulls toward the
canyon
and then shines back through the white wings to
  be you again.

— William Stafford

After learning and employing several pathways to soul encounter —
and thereby beginning to understand her destiny — the Wanderer
turns her attention to cultivating a soulful relationship to the wider world
and to her life as a whole. She discovers ways to regain and celebrate
her soul every day and not just during those hours devoted to the practice
of soulcraft skills. The more she and others in her community learn to live
soulfully, the more her community itself shifts from egocentric to soulcentric. The lifestyle practices explored in this and the next chapter assist
the Wanderer in not only discovering her soul gifts but also in changing the
world.

A soulful relationship to life is cultivated through a set of practices and
disciplines with a larger scope than the mere acquisition of skills or techniques, as was the focus with the specific soul-encounter methods in part 2.
The goal now is a radical, soul-centered shift in the Wanderer's orientation
to life. A similar distinction between technique and lifestyle is found, for
example, in spirit-centered Buddhism, where the practitioner not only learns
specific skills such as meditation but also cultivates an approach to everyday
living, the noble eightfold path, that includes the practices of right speech,
right action, right livelihood, and right thinking.

The lifestyle practices explored in these two chapters have a common
theme: giving one's life over to something *other*, the desires of the soul,
something distinct from the familiar Western, egocentric goal of "getting
ahead."

What cultivates a soulful existence? What follows (in this and the next
chapter) are a dozen answers applicable to women and men from any culture or tradition.

THE ART OF SOLITUDE

Solitude does not come naturally to many of us. Even when not socializing,
most Westerners avoid true solitude through a myriad of distractions —

TV, the Internet, computer games, newspapers, crossword puzzles, solo sports, busywork. Maybe we're afraid of solitude because it threatens us with boredom or an anxiety that can lead to difficult truths, unfinished emotional business, and the shadow side of our human nature.

Although true solitude — alert aloneness without diversions — can be challenging, it is often the necessary gateway to our deepest passions, and the discovery of what we must do to live them. As David Whyte writes,

> ...Sometimes it takes darkness and the sweet
> confinement of your aloneness
> to learn
>
> anything or anyone
> that does not bring you alive
>
> is too small for you.[1]

The Wanderer learns to look deeply into the face of her aloneness and discover what truly brings her alive and what doesn't. She practices the art of solitude. She spends several hours at a time alone, awake, unoccupied, undistracted by everyday routines, letting what comes come. She works her way up to several days alone. She practices true aloneness, not at home or with her dog, her music, or a book; just her, unprotected from the immensity of her psyche and the world.

Through the practice of solitude, you, too, will discover the ways you are alienated from yourself and the world. You will come to grips with one of the most profound and implacable facts of the human condition: that in an essential way you are, in fact, alone. You were born alone and will die alone. In solitude you will learn how to live as a mortal human. You will learn to more deeply comfort yourself. You will learn how to move your attention from one place to another, neither avoiding nor indulging in the painful places.

As a Wanderer, you must develop a relationship with your aloneness that is as profound and sacred as any other relationship in your life. You will come to belong to your aloneness as much as to any place, job, or community.

Solitudo is Latin for nature. In true solitude, you remember yourself as a part of everything, a part of nature. You rediscover ease, inspiration, belonging, and wisdom in your own company.

Sabina Wyss, the woman who traded gifts with a bear on her vision quest, has uncovered many treasures from her solo interludes in nature. She writes of one of her weeklong wilderness journeys:

> As usual, it took several days to shed my thick city skin, to calm the city noise of carousel thoughts. Addicted to accomplishment, my "got-to-do-that" urge kept overriding my inner voice. Stormy feelings oozed out of neglected wounds.
>
> Upon first entering silence and solitude, the same questions throw me for a loop every time: What the heck am I doing out here? Am I nuts to be here alone? If something happens to me, will I ever be found? This is boring — don't I have work to do at home, *real* work?
>
> After a day or two, I dive deeper, beginning with my senses. Flowers look brighter, caves feel darker, scents are stronger. Then old feelings swirl up and flood in, overtaking me. Fear, laughter, bliss, impatience, anger, each wanting to be heard.
>
> Another day or two and it calms down. I grow still inside, more open to the present.
>
> A level deeper. There it is. Vastness so deep I need the safety of solitude to dare lose myself into it. Surrendering control of the everyday mind, there's nothing to hold on to. Letting go, diving, trusting, moving into unmapped terrain.
>
> Most of the gifts received are indescribable, too deep for words. Teachings from my soul.
>
> Sometimes I get very lucky and the most intimate thing happens. The roar of silence — the sound that is color and melody and bliss and expansion, all at once. The tone of a color and the color of a tone merge. Harmony. God's presence. An eternal, internal orchestra plays all the instruments of being, weaving an immense harmony. This is when solitude reveals truth. Alone becomes All-One.

When you first began wandering, you learned to use your solitude to make a break with one world — the world of your adolescence and first adulthood — in preparation for your discovery of another. You learned to turn the second cocoon into a type of withdrawal, a time to prepare, to make sacrifice, to examine self, to heal, to purify.

Now you can learn, in addition, to use the unavoidable fact of your aloneness to fuel your daily longing for soul, the Other to whom you have a unique relationship, not taking away your final aloneness, but still, calling to you and revealing your true relationship to the world.

NATURE AS MIRROR

On a soulcraft journey in the redrock canyons of the Utah desert, our group included a Mexican-American man, Miguel Grunstein, who had studied the Peruvian flute — the *quena* — with an Incan master in Peru. Early each morning, while still in my sleeping bag, I would hear Miguel somewhere near camp, on a ridge or in a hollow, playing the most serene and delicious song to greet the dawn. For several days, it was more or less the same haunting tune. But later in the week, after we had moved camp, the tune changed.

Over breakfast, I asked Miguel about the source of his melodies, suspecting they were traditional Incan songs. But he said he was playing *the songs of the canyon.* Each place has its own song, he said. He followed the canyon walls with his eyes and heart and played what he saw and felt there, as his Peruvian teacher had shown him. When in the high country, Miguel played the songs of the mountain ridges, letting his flute sing the notes flowing up and down the horizon like a musical score, inviting nature to offer itself to his imagination.

Each song that emerges from Miguel's flute reflects a unique facet of his soul that comes alive in the particular wild place he visits. It is an interaction, a conversation between Miguel and the wild. An award-winning documentary filmmaker who captures the eloquent gestures of the human heart and soul, Miguel is himself such a gesture. His elegant *quena* songs are a mirror of nature, both within and without; they are a communion, an exchange of essences.

Our relationship to the wild unfolds through several developmental stages. In a healthy childhood, nature holds great fascination and wonder, the wide arena in which we discover and explore the world of our inheritance. By imitating the animals, birds, and trees, we acquire a vocabulary of gestures that we assemble into our own way of being human.

Then, in adolescence, our relationship with nature changes. The natural world becomes a mirror of our developing adolescent personality, a screen upon which we project our fears and hopes for belonging. But we don't yet know we are projecting. We experience our emotions as if they are qualities of nature rather than our own. We enter the wilderness as a place of danger, self-testing, and self-discovery.

The next stage occurs in the second cocoon as we become conscious of our projections. But now it is not only the personality but also the soul, we discover, that we are projecting. Like the poets, we begin to observe in the patterns of nature the essence of courage, love, sacrifice, desire, faith, belonging — all the possibilities of our own humanness in their primary and most vital forms. In time, we encounter reflections of our deepest individual natures and perhaps hear our true name spoken for the first time. We come to understand that what is reflected by nature is not just who we are now but also who we could become. And so we begin entering nature as a pilgrim in search of his true home, a wanderer with an intimation of communion, a solitary with a suspicion of salvation.

The mirror of nature is not always pleasant or comforting. On a vision quest in the redrock canyons, a psychotherapist named June, whose mother died when she was ten, arrived with a curious history of being tormented by bats. One evening under a full moon, accompanied by drums and rattles, we danced on the compacted sands of a dry creek bed. Several times a bat landed on June, on her shawl or dress, her arm, or in her hair. It never flew into anyone else though there were fifteen of us and we were dancing wildly and weaving among each other in a small forest clearing. On three occasions, the bat became entangled in June's hair or shawl, and another person carefully freed it while June squirmed and the bat squealed. The bat, apparently an abandoned juvenile, was at least as traumatized as June.

During her subsequent days alone and fasting, bats visited her again. June knew the bats had something to communicate, something about *her* but also about *them* and her relationship to them. Finally, she accepted the inevitability of conversing with Bat. At sunset, while two bats flew circles overhead, June introduced herself out loud and spoke openly of her fear of them. She asked what they wanted to tell her. Suddenly she became painfully aware of how she had felt, ever since childhood, like a victim, of other people and circumstances. This awareness was her catalyst to dive into her sacred wound, and dive she did. Alone in the wilds, June relived heartbreaking and sometimes harrowing memories, especially her mother's death. She came to understand that the young bat at the dance was mirroring her own sense of being abandoned, orphaned, and yet emotionally entangled in another (her dead mother). She reached the central core of her lifelong experience of being a victim and vowed to disentangle herself from the ghosts of her past.

June's encounters with nocturnal fliers did more than facilitate her healing, however. The bats, she discovered, were also mirroring her unclaimed soul power of navigating in the dark, her exceptional capacities of intuition and imagination. On her fast, she was able for the first time to experience these powers as awesome — not merely terrifying. By entering her sacred wound, June beheld nature reflecting her soul's gift as well as her childhood traumas. Her encounter with Bat held the potential for profound changes in both her social life and her work as a psychotherapist. Yet only time would tell how adept she might become at navigating in the dark.

Earth so effectively mirrors our soul powers simply because our souls are elements of earth's soul.

Archetypal forms and patterns exist not only in the human psyche but also in the outer world of nature. Wind, water, fire, mountain, rain, rainbow, bird, bat, butterfly, fish, snake, bear: earth archetypes. In the shamanic traditions, the apprentice learns his craft by using the refined powers of his imagination to become the various animals and qualities of nature, by merging with the earth archetypes and "re-membering" as he remembers he has always *been* nature. Moving from one archetypal nature identity to another: this is the genius of the shape-shifter within each of us. By becoming earth, through her forms and forces, we regain our souls.

The earth archetypes illuminate the edges of our understanding. We see the rainbow, and if we allow our imaginations to be generous, we discover the possibility of realizing our fondest dreams, the longing for treasure, the enchantment of the world, the thinness of the shimmering veil that separates us from the sacred, or the bridge to this world for the gods.

We experience earth archetypes as significant, evocative, emotionally captivating, enchanting. Why are different individuals drawn to different elements of nature? Why *those?* Possibly these are the earth archetypes to which our (unconscious) psyches already attribute meaning, that resonate with the deepest possibilities within us.

In its attempt to be made manifest, the soul takes every opportunity to resonate with any element of nature that stirs it. As we offer our attention to the world, we discover the beings to which we are most drawn. Our fascination with a particular facet of nature is how our souls say "Yes!" to an earth archetype that we, as individuals, especially tune to. As we open ourselves to that element of wildness, we discover a quality of our own soul that longs to be embodied in the world, sung to the world, danced, cried, celebrated.

The earth provides us with not only the means to be physically born into this world but also the spiritual means to recognize our deeper identities. Why would she provide one without the other?

Jerry, an accomplished fifty-year old songwriter and recording artist, took a walk high in the summer mountains of Colorado and came upon a small spruce at the edge of tree line. He noticed part of its top had been sheared off, probably by a massive spring snowslide. He sat down beside the tree and spoke to it out loud, something he had never done before.

> The connection between us was extraordinary. I felt such compassion and strength from that tree — about how you must hang in there through the storms of life, about standing firm in your spot. Our connection was so amazing I just sat and wept with love. Yes, I saw myself in the mirror of that tree — a bit ragged at fifty, but still strong and open and willing to bring all of me to the world.

Jerry does indeed bring all of himself to the world, courageously sharing his radiant heart through his soulful music. A year later, Jerry visited the tree a second time. It was still thriving at the edge of the avalanche path. Even from his home on the edge of the avalanche path called Los Angeles, Jerry says he can feel his bond with that tree.

During the most life-changing soul encounters, nature holds up a mirror and shows us the face we have longed to see but been terrified to behold, at once bestowing the greatest of blessings and burdening us with a seemingly impossible charge. In the lightning-strike moment, the soul confronts us with our true name, the one we were not brave enough to say or embrace.

In the midst of a storm in the Mojave Desert, Annie Bloom saw her soul image mirrored by nature, and her life was transformed, profoundly and irreversibly:

> I sat in my circle of stones upon a knoll. I was in the middle of a dry wash in the upper reaches of Death Valley. It was the fourth day of my fast. The day began dark and filled with brooding clouds. I watched big black thunderheads roll over the mountain range in the west and march down the valley toward me. The wind began to howl and gusts raced past me pell-mell like specters for some unknown destination. The intensity of the sky and wind and my feeling of being completely exposed roused me to dance and drum within my circle. I raged with the approaching storm, shouting all the things of which I was sick and tired. I implored God, "What shall I do with my life?!" Finally, utterly spent, I fell exhausted to the ground. Astonishingly, the thunderheads soon passed and the wind died to a whisper. All that intensity and yet no rain — and no thunder or lightning.
>
> This drama of storm and then nothing repeated itself several times through the day. As dusk drew near, I watched yet another thunderhead roll over the mountain range and begin its descent toward me. This was the biggest, darkest one yet, and I thought "Okay, this is it, I'm really going to get slammed now!" I bundled up and sat in my circle hugging my knees. I considered retreating to my tarp, but I felt pinned to that spot. The cloud approached and the tempest roared. The sound of it was deafening. I trembled from head to toe, terrified I was about to die.
>
> The cloud stopped, suspended directly above me, and I looked up into its vast blackness. I saw the image of two hands opened wide within its velvet darkness. I reached out my own hand as if to touch it and heard myself cry out, "Why hands? Why hands?!" a lament torn from a primal place inside. I had been seeing hands in the clouds from the moment I entered my circle on the first day. The hands were always benevolent, always forming gestures of caring. And now a voice came booming from the cloud, saying, "You are Hands to the World. We are honoring the work you do through your hands. This tempest is fierce, but gentle; this is your nature as well."
>
> Seconds later, the thundercloud passed, the wind died down, and I

was left shaken and alone atop my little knoll. Tears of gratitude and fear streamed down my face. In agitation, I ran up and down the knoll, repeating to myself over and over, "Hands to the World. Hands to the World." Then the doubts began: Did I really hear that? What had just happened? For an hour, I fluctuated between wild ecstasy and agonizing self-doubt.

Gradually, the evening unfolded, serene, clear, and crystalline. The stars came out in their abundant radiance. Deep in the night, a lady appeared to me in the stars, with lights shining from the palms of her hands. She sang words of encouragement and I was left with the terrible and awesome task of carrying the gifts of my soul into the world.

Despite her awe and terror, Annie has lived as Hands to the World ever since that day. She uses her spiritual and physical hands in her daily work as a soul-oriented massage therapist, a "hands-on body-soul worker," as she says. She listens to her clients' body-souls through her hands, which she experiences as extensions of her heart, and responds with healing touch.

Annie also extends Hands to the World through her work as a wilderness, ceremonial, and soulcraft guide. She has committed her spiritual hands to breaking open people's wild hearts and tending the raw, shimmering vulnerability that arises in that breaking.

WANDERING IN NATURE

The Wanderer seeks the hidden, the mysterious, the wild. She knows the changes she goes through while searching are as important as finding what she seeks. She is not in a hurry. Wandering is as valuable as anything else she might do.

Where shall she wander? "Through hollow lands and hilly lands," says Yeats in "The Song of Wandering Aengus." She shall wander through both psyche and nature until she can no longer tell them apart. She shall adopt a meandering style as her way of life.

A man named John came to southern Utah to enact his vision quest. He hadn't known it before, but he had a knack for rambling deeply into nature. While wandering, he learned new things, remembered old things, and returned to a precious innocence he, like most of us, had lost when he was a child.

On our first day, John bravely introduced himself to the group, saying that, truth be told, he didn't *really* know who he was. He had always been called John, he said, but the one thing he knew for sure was that he was *not* John. My guide partner, Steve, deftly responded, "Welcome, Not-John!" and the name stuck. A few days later, the night before we hiked into redrock country, Not-John had a vivid dream. In it, he was called by his real name:

> A lovely buxom nurse comes to me and asks, "Has Windy Marrow played yet?" I say to myself, "What's that? A movie?" I turn to the other people who had been there a moment before, but now I see I'm all alone — all alone with my name, Windy Marrow.

And Windy Marrow, who did not yet understand the meaning of his name, was now ready to play.

One morning in base camp before the start of his fast, Windy Marrow got up early to wander. He was drawn to a pair of red sandstone towers he had spotted up a side canyon. He started from one direction but couldn't find a way up. Backtracking, he tried from another. Finally, he reached the base of the two immense rock columns and walked between them.

> There in front of me, suspended four feet off the ground between the massive boulders, is the entire skeleton of an eight-point buck. *The entire skeleton.* This has a huge impact on me. I fall to my knees. The night before, in our trance dance, I had danced the dance of a dying buck, or it might be more accurate to say he danced me. In my dance, and now in this skeleton before me, the buck has only one unbroken leg. He is hanging in the air, his shoulders and hips wedged in the narrow spot where the boulders come closest together. He must have fallen during winter from high above. He has been picked clean of meat and fur but is still in one piece.

The next thing Windy Marrow knew, the buck was asking him to take the antlered skull and run the deer trails, and return the skull afterward. The buck wanted to wander his favorite trails one last time.

> Off I go running the deer trails. I am not myself, but I am. My head is a rush of energy I can't translate or understand. What is happening to me? I run the deer trails bare-chested and know this is what I'm supposed to do.

Upon his return to camp, Windy Marrow told the group what had happened.

I tell my story, but I see some of their looks. I can't help it, people! We're out here on a hunt! Or am I the one who is hunted? I'm at a crossroads. I can't live the so-called sane life my father chose to live. But is this *in*sane? This is no ordinary time. I am in another world and it's totally me. I don't know the language or the culture, but I will learn it. I have to. There's meaning in this. Something is going on in my being. I've entered a magical time. I once had that magic when I was little and I wrapped it up and put it away because it wasn't at all accepted in my family.

On his fast during the following four days, Windy Marrow began to understand the meaning, mysteries, and gifts contained in his name and how he might carry those gifts to others. But it is not for me to reveal the mysteries of another's name, which sometimes is best kept secret. Windy Marrow also met a spirit guide on his fast who is still very much with him today, twelve years later. He has learned to live both in the everyday world and the other, sacred world and how to journey back and forth between them. He teaches others how to do this. Much of his soul power is rooted in this ability.

The Wanderer explores the interweavings between psyche and nature, how a dream or a myth, for example, suggests a place in nature in which to wander or a *way* in which to wander or an image to seek in his wanderings. Or he might ramble in the wild and run smack into a repeating dreamscape from childhood, his eyes wide and mouth agape. *Now* what will he do? Inner and outer wanderings support, extend, and enrich one another — a key feature of soulcraft.

The Wanderer allows plenty of time to roam in wild nature, and roam alone. Maybe he will start out on a trail, but if the landscape allows, it won't be long before he wanders off the beaten track. Because he is stalking a surprise, he attends to the world of hunches and feelings and images as much as he does to the landscape. He tunes in to calls to go right or left, upstream or down, sunwise or earthwise, to sit or stand, or to lean against a boulder. Like the poet Theodore Roethke, he "learns by going where to go."[2] Sometimes he will be called to crawl into a low cave, to dance on top of a knoll, to swim to the center of a lake, to roll in the tall spring grasses, to rub against a tree, or to fall asleep by a bubbling spring. Sometimes he will spot an animal track and follow it — or not. Sometimes he will gurgle back to a brook or trade music with a songbird. Often he will sit with beings he meets — a flower, lizard, rock, pika, wind, or the moon — and begin a conversation.

Sometimes he will wander into the wilds with the expectation of finding one thing, one thing in particular, material or not, that calls him most strongly. Other times he will go out without an intention to find anything at all.

He will wander often, and often for an entire day, sometimes for several days with his home upon his back. He will get good at wandering, good at allowing his initial agenda to fall away as he picks up new tracks, scents, and possibilities. He will smile softly to himself over the months and years of his wanderings as he notices how he has changed, how he has slowed down inside.

Through his wanderings, he cultivates a sensibility of wonder and surprise, rekindling the innocence that got buried in his adolescent rush to become somebody in particular. Now he seeks to become nobody for a while, to disappear into the woods so that the person he really is might find him.

Wandering in nature is perhaps the most essential soulcraft practice for contemporary Westerners who have wandered so far from nature. The earth speaks to us in a manner and muscle with which nothing in town compares. What nature has to say is the necessary complement to what we hear all day long from news, ads, and social chatter. To save our souls, we need *nature's* news.

Wandering in nature can serve as the hub from which all other soulcraft practices radiate. For example, nature wandering is one of the ways to practice the art of solitude, self-reliance, or, as we shall see, of being lost, the practice of befriending the dark, or the art of shadow work. And obviously, natural landscapes are the best places to practice tracking, nature observation, attending to nature signs and omens, and talking across the species boundaries. Our wanderings might provide the seeds for dreams, deep imagery work, self-designed ceremony, storytelling, sacred wound work, symbolic artwork, council processes, or soul poetry — any one of which will eventually lead us back into nature.

Ann DeBaldo is a professor in the Department of Environmental and Occupational Health at the University of South Florida, the director of USF's Center for Positive Health, and a guide of spiritual pilgrimages in Asia and South America. She bumped into the deepest truth of her life by crossing into the mysteries of nature and psyche on her first vision quest.

Ann rode with me up the long, dusty mountain road through a forest of scrub oak and ponderosa pine. At last we rounded a bend and there, below us, was the deep sandstone gorge into which we would descend by foot. The canyon's two-thousand-foot red walls, towers, and luxurious pines always astonish. But Ann gasped and cried out because somehow she recognized this place; this was the canyon she had visited in her imagery several year's earlier.

In the midst of a massage, years before she even knew what a vision quest was, Ann had fallen into a profound reverie.

> I saw a huge teepee perched on a rocky shelf at the edge of a great canyon. Out of curiosity, I peeked into the lodge and stiffened with surprise at the sight of my dead body lying on the ground, wrapped in blankets, and surrounded by six ancient wise women. I felt no fear or regret, simply acceptance and calm as I gazed at the Indian crones with their lined and weathered faces, their dark slitlike eyes cast down toward my body, and beautiful blankets draped over their heads for warmth. Each blanket was distinctive and finely woven with intricate, colorful, earthy patterns like an ancient forgotten language.
>
> Suddenly, out of the breast of my dead body, arose a beautiful bird, a huge raven of many colors with an eagle's beak and fierce eyes. My consciousness merged with the raven and I soared over the redrock canyons and pine forests, feeling the warmth of the sun on my wings and the hot desert wind on my face. The scent of sage filled my lungs with pleasure. The delight of perfect freedom was mine. There was no limit to my vision. The mouse sleeping beneath the blooming cactus and the snake in the tumbled rocks were not hidden from my sight as I soared up and up into the azure sky.

Seeing the canyon now in her dayworld, Ann wished to soar again in the body of that raven.

Four days later, she sat in a circle of stones on a beautiful flat rock in the depths of the canyons.

> Becoming progressively weaker from the fast, the border blurred between me and the hot and fragrant land. A hollowed-out lair became my place

for dream-filled afternoon naps. At night, I sat in vigils as the constellations slowly circled.

In the middle of the third night, before moonrise, the six ancient crones came to my circle of stones accompanied by a great host of people apparent only by the sound of their murmurs and the barking and shuffling of dogs.

To say the crones and I "spoke" would be inadequate to the depth of the conversation that ensued. It was more like a literal meeting of minds. This is what I learned:

> I have sat in this circle many times before. The crones are reminding me. I feel very loved and at home, brought here by a deep longing of which I had been unaware.
>
> The crones tell me I must weave my own blanket like the beautiful ones in which they are wrapped. When my blanket is complete, I will take my place among them.
>
> This lifetime is not about what I had previously believed. I have been pulled back into this circle to continue The Work.
>
> The Work is so much larger than me and my role. I am awakening and the blanket is the warm, protective, grandmotherly aspect of the wisdom required for that awakening. The designs on the blanket are an ancient yet vibrant and alive language, like a beautiful web woven by spiders.
>
> The blanket is a vehicle, a tool, a symbol. It is a robe worn by what we would call, in our culture, a nun or priestess.
>
> My true name is Web Spinner.

It was not long before the sun rose and warmed Ann's chilled face. In her hands, she found a beautiful stone with weblike designs in many colors, the design for her blanket.

After her quest, Ann bought a loom and learned how to weave. She understood the weaving of her visible blanket could progress only as fast as the weaving of an invisible blanket of grandmotherly wisdom.

But progress on both blankets eventually stalled. In the midst of her busy university life, Ann gradually lost touch with her vision.

A few years later, Ann was guiding a pilgrimage to sacred sites in Tibet.

Climbing Mount Chimpu one morning, the thin air took my breath away and reminded me of the difficult climb out of the canyon at the end of my vision quest. As the sun rose over thousands of prayer flags, we reached the caves where the lotus-born guru Padma Sambhava and his consort Yeshe Tsogyal had spent years in profound meditation many centuries before. The cave was warm and welcoming as I stepped inside. Yak-butter lamps lit the dim interior. A tiny woman, an ancient nun silently slipping mala beads between bent fingers, sat in meditation. The honeylike peace warmed the coldest caverns in my body and soul. Suddenly the old nun looked up and her eyes, like shining diamonds, pierced my heart and for a brief moment, we became one. I gazed upon her face with the shock of recognition — in that moment there was no boundary between the nun, the ancient wise women of both my quest and my earlier vision, and the very essence of me. In my eyes, her robes transformed into a beautiful blanket of many colors, weblike figures telling ancient stories in the colors of the earth.

In that moment, Ann understood more fully the meaning of her soul name. The images of a beautiful blanket, a web expressing ancient truths, and Grandmother Spider all merged and Ann saw she must prepare for the role of nun-priestess.

Ever since age five or six, I have *known,* on a visceral level, my role in this life is to be what I would now call a nun-priestess, although there is no exact equivalent to this role in our culture. This role remains to be created — or remembered. I had always known, in this role, I would wander the world, have no family or true home of my own, and use my personal power for the good of others. This knowledge used to be a source of confusion for me because it seemed in direct contradiction to what was expected of me at any given stage in life. Until now, I had not been able to understand where I belonged in the world, the nature of my personal power, or what I was supposed to do in this life. I had always felt uncomfortable with this sense of a nun-priestess, but at another level, it is the best possible description of me.

The weaving of Ann's beautiful blankets resumed. They are works in progress. She understands that the invisible blanket, the one deep in her psyche where the ancient and vibrant language lives, is the true blanket.

THE ART OF BEING LOST

What does it mean, exactly, to be "lost"? Perhaps this: we don't know how to get from where we are to where we want to be. It's not the same as being stranded (when we *do* know how to get where we want to go) or abandoned. Being lost is not a simple problem of immobility or imprisonment.

Neither is it the same as not knowing where we are. I may find myself in an unfamiliar room in a city with no idea whose home or office it is, but if I recognize landmarks out the window or am in the company of a trusted guide, I'm not lost; I know how to get from where I am to where I want to go. Or, conversely, I may know where I am physically but be lost because I have no idea what I want to do next in my life or where I want to go.

We can also be lost intellectually, emotionally, or spiritually. It's not unusual to feel lost in the middle of our lives while sitting in our own living room, and it's possible to remain lost for months, years, or permanently. Lost souls.

We might even be lost without knowing it. That's how the seventeenth-century Spanish missionaries thought of the indigenous people they encountered in the southwest corner of what is now known as Colorado. The missionaries named the river that runs through that country the River of Souls Lost in Purgatory (El Río de las Ánimas Perdidas en Purgatorio), believing the natives were necessarily lost because they were living without the benefits of the missionaries' religion. Who do you suppose was really lost without knowing it, the missionaries or the indigenous people? Like the missionaries, it is possible to be looking for a kind of paradise without knowing you are already there. That is one way to be lost.

But being lost is not at all a bad thing — if you know you're lost and you know how to benefit from it spiritually. Most of us consider being lost a bummer, highly undesirable or even terrifying. We all have important things to do, there's not enough time in the day as it is, thank you, and getting lost is a major fly in the ointment of success, a monkey wrench in the gearbox of progress. In the Western world, where "progress is our most important product," we are encouraged from our earliest years to know exactly where we are at all times and precisely where we are going. Yes, such knowledge is often desirable if not necessary, but not knowing is of equal benefit.

When wandering, there is immense value in "finding ourselves lost" because we *can* find something when we are lost, we can find our selves. Indeed, the deepest form of wandering *requires* that we be lost.

Imagine yourself lost in your career or marriage, or in the middle of your life. You have goals, a place you want to be, but you don't know how to reach that place. Maybe you don't know exactly what you want, you just have a vague desire for a better place. Although it may not seem like it, you are on the threshold of a great opportunity. Begin to trust that place of not knowing. Surrender to it. You're lost. There will be grief. A cherished outcome appears to be unobtainable or undefinable. In order to make the shift from being lost to being present, admit to yourself that your goal may never be reached. Though perhaps difficult, doing so will create entirely new possibilities for fulfillment.

Surrendering fully to being lost — and this is where the art comes in — you will discover that, in addition to not knowing how to get where you had wanted to go, you are no longer so sure of the ultimate rightness of that goal. By trusting your unknowing, your old standards of progress dissolve and you become eligible to be chosen by new, larger standards, those that come not from your mind or old story or other people, but from the depths of your soul. You become attentive to an utterly new guidance system.

The art of being lost is not a matter of merely getting lost, but rather being lost and enthusiastically surrendering to the unlimited potential of it. In fact, using it to your advantage. The shift from being lost to being found (in a new, unpredictable way) is a gradual and indirect one. The way to encourage that shift is to first accept that you don't know how to get to the place you want to be and then opening fully to the place you are until the old goals fall away and you discover more soulful goals emerging. Then you are no longer lost, but you have benefited immensely from having been so. This kind of being lost and then found is one form of ego death and rebirth, one form of entering the tomb-womb of the cocoon.

Being lost and then found in this way ushers you more fully into the now. We are often so busy trying to get into an imagined future that we've lost the present moment. We've lost the self — the soul — that lives and breathes only in the here and now.

Consider for example being lost in the woods, something few people can imagine enjoying. All of a sudden, the world has shrunk; here you are, sitting beside a stream in a forest. You don't know which way is home. You call out. No one answers; or, only the stream, the wind, and the ravens answer. Maybe you panic, maybe you don't. It sinks in that you are really lost. Gradually, you become aware that everything you can count on now is right here, more or less within reach, and there's no guarantee there will ever again be anything else. You could have spent your entire life on a meditation cushion to get to this radical place of present-centeredness, and now you are here courtesy of dislocation! Like a shipwrecked sailor on a tropical island, this is your world. What will you do with it? You've lost nearly every-thing you thought was important; the old goals are irrelevant, and yet, here you are. *Now* what?

This is precisely where you must eventually arrive, psycho-spiritually, for the purpose of soul initiation: you must be willing to release your pre-vious agendas and embrace the soul's passion as you find it here and now.

By arriving more fully in the present, through being lost *and* accepting it, your life suddenly suffers a radical simplification. Old agendas, beliefs and desires fall away. You quiet down inside and it becomes easier to hear the voice of the soul.

This is why the Wanderer seeks to get lost.

The Wanderer learns there are four necessary components to the art of being lost. First, he must in fact be lost. Second, he must *know* he is lost and accept it. Third, he must have adequate survival knowledge, skills, and physical or spiritual tools. Fourth, and most important, he must practice nonattachment to any particular result of being lost, such as being found by a certain time, or at all. In other words, he must accept his condition, relax into it, and arrive fully where he is.

Whether he is physically, emotionally, soulfully, or spiritually lost, get-ting to know the experience of "lost" in the most intimate terms is his only true way out.

Upon entering the second cocoon, for example, we notice that the ado-lescent life, a life in which social and economic advancement are our primary goals, is no longer so alluring, but we do not yet have an appealing alterna-tive. We're lost. Rather than merely changing jobs, life partners, social groups, or places of residence, we must accept that we are lost and can't extract our-selves by continuing to play by the old rules. What are the relevant survival knowledge, skills, and tools for this kind of being lost? To spiritually survive the second cocoon, you need to know about the relationship between ego, soul, and spirit. You need to know about the call to adventure, ego death, and wandering. You need the skills of self-reliance and of leaving home. You need tools in the form of pathways to soul encounter. And you need to cultivate the art of being lost. Then you must settle into the fact that, as of yet, you do not know what your soul desires for the life you've been blessed with.

Another way the Wanderer might cultivate the art of being soulfully lost is to physically get lost in wilderness.[3] She might wander in the wilds until she is not certain how to get "out." Then she will sit and practice presence, accepting what is, because here and now are all she's got. Obviously it helps if she has previously acquired some survival skills, including ways to find water and shelter and, if she'll be there several days, food. She'll also be glad to have her physical survival tools with her — her pocketknife and a way to make fire and shelter, for example. That's why the Wanderer studied the arts of backcountry living when acquiring the skills of self-reliance. She also studied the art of orienteering, so she knows she eventually can find her way out in good shape. She just doesn't know when that will be, and, truth be told, the lost Wanderer is not in a great hurry. Here's an opportunity to practice solitude, wandering in nature, tracking signs and omens, talking across the species boundaries, and other soulcraft arts. Here's her chance to trust the path that begins at her feet, to be fully in the moment as it unfolds. If she can do this while lost in the wilds, she's more likely to be able to do it when spiritually lost, like Dante, in the middle of her life.

When I find myself lost in the wild, fear starts in my groin and works its way up to my belly and down to my knees. My heart races. My throat wants to shout for help. My whole body begins to tremble and my head whirls. My breath grows shallow and rapid. My heart beats quicker and quirkier. But if I don't panic (or after I'm through panicking), I notice my body actually *likes* being lost! Not the mind, but the body. My skin begins to tingle, as if with delight. I become very awake. My senses grow sharp and clear. The sounds, colors, textures, and edges of things become distinct and radiant. I can't help but notice an enjoyment arising through being so present, so much in this body. Here. Now. Thought slows down and becomes crystalline. What will I do, I wonder. I hear a weird voice say, "Let's enjoy being here before we get in too much of a hurry to be somewhere else. If we can make a life here, after all, we can make a life anywhere."

Perchance you think you do not have the skills or interest (or time!) to get lost in wilderness and then attempt to find your self. Few people do, but few people get serious about *any* kind of wandering. On the other hand, I've known many people who were not the least bit interested in getting lost but had the misfortune — or fortune — of doing so anyway, and learned wondrous things from the experience (other than to never leave home again).

On a vision fast when I was a trainee, there was a woman quester who (like many people) could successfully get lost inside a large paper bag. She got lost in the dry summer mountains of the California desert. She lost her bearings in the middle of a warm blue-sky day while on her way back to her camp after a short walk. She had no camping gear or warm clothes with her. She had just visited the location near base camp where we had arranged for her to leave a stone each day as a signal to us she was all right (without having to interrupt her time of solitude). She left the stone and then became disoriented while attempting to return to her fasting circle. Later that afternoon, I checked to be sure she had left the stone.

The next day, there was no new stone. The quest guide and I hiked to her camp. Nobody there, but her sleeping bag was — a more alarming discovery. We spent the next several hours looking and shouting. No success. We tried to track her, but the desert pavement in that land rarely registers conspicuous prints. Finally, we found her track in the dust of an old dirt road. She was headed away from both base camp and her camp. No telling how far she had gone. Plus we suspected she had already spent a night out, alone without warmth or shelter. We were about to contact the county search and rescue squad when we spotted, through binoculars, about a half mile down the road, a white bra hanging from a lone juniper. We ran down the road. We found her under the tree, out of the midday sun, quite comfortable and enjoying her day, confident we'd show up sooner or later. Despite her lack of wilderness experience, she had managed to make a warm enough bed out of juniper boughs. She was a lot more centered and calm than we were. She wasn't really lost, after all, she told us; she knew right where she was — here, under this juniper.

The lost quester had learned much from her experience. She learned she could comfort herself in difficult circumstances. She learned she could survive a night alone in the (warm) wilds without equipment. She learned how to gather her resourcefulness and to arrive in the full presence of the moment.

Practicing the art of being lost doesn't require external wilderness. You might, for example, spend an extended period of time in a social or ethnic group with strange (to you) customs or styles, in an unfamiliar city or foreign country, with an unusual religious practice or community, or *without* your familiar religious or spiritual practice if you have been employing one regularly for many years — or with people much younger or older than you. Or simply wait for a day your life no longer makes sense, or when someone or something or a role you've depended upon has suddenly disappeared. Remember to apply all four components of being lost to these other unknowns.

The first time I was seriously lost *and accepted it* began at that moment of dazzling light and shadow on Cascade Peak, the story with which this book commences. Suddenly I knew, without doubt, my life was not about academia and laboratory research. I was lost but in an opposite way to being lost in wilderness. At that moment, my geographical position in the Adirondack wilderness was the *only* way I could locate myself in life. I found myself at the beginning of an indefinite period of knowing neither my career, nor with whom I would go through life (if anyone), nor even what my life was about. I was lost, knew it, possessed a few rudimentary skills and knowledge to help me stay lost, and chose to relax into being lost as best I could, by not pretending any longer to be a research scientist and by setting off alone, wandering into the west.

BEFRIENDING THE DARK

During my first few years of backcountry wandering, I carried a large hunting knife, at least seven inches long. I never showed it to anyone, but at night it lived with me inside my sleeping bag. I was panicked by what I imagined might come out of the night to eat me. Every night, upon first getting into my bag, I would repeatedly practice unzipping it as fast as humanly possible, grabbing my knife, and unsheathing it — all in one motion. Just in case. I didn't sleep well.

Gradually, through years of wilderness immersion, I learned to befriend the dark and to uncover (sometimes) the personal demons I projected onto the outer shadows. Now I can say there is no place that feels more like home than my sleeping bag beneath a roof of stars. And I haven't seen that knife for years.

Michael, a fellow psychologist and wilderness guide, has also wrestled with his fear of the wild dark — on the first night of his first vision quest, for example.

> It was past midnight, moonless black, when I prepared my altar. Questions and anxieties began to fill my mind. What if I got really sick? No emergency room up here. What if I became hypothermic or dehydrated, or got stomach cramps? Then I imagined grizzlies, mountain lions, and bobcats. I began working myself into a full-blown panic.
>
> I heard a rustling of leaves in the woods, not ten yards away. My heart jumped. I tried to make out an image. Ever so slowly, the noise moved through the darkness toward me. It must be an animal of some kind. Friend or foe? A grizzly or some psychotic killer hiding out in the backcountry? I froze. A dark shape approached, seeming to show no fear. I sensed a gentleness, an openness. I closed my eyes and tried opening my heart. The sound made its way through the dark. I opened my eyes. Something passed in front of me and mysteriously continued into the woods. A doe! Her beauty and grace deeply touched me. My eyes welled with tears. Such gentleness in the midst of my fears!
>
> On the last day, I began to have anxieties about how to incorporate what I had experienced; how to stay true to myself and not let demands of my home and work life overtake me. I prayed to see the doe a second time. I knelt down, kissed the grass, gave thanks to the earth, trees, air, and the Creator for providing safe passage. I looked up — and there she was. My body shook with elation. I wept.
>
> I knew then that, come what may, life would flow on, as fierce and gentle as the river and the wind. My task was to let go and let myself be carried, each day closer to home.

For me, the key element in Michael's story is this: in the midst of his fear, he closed his eyes, voluntarily going *deeper* into the dark, and opened his heart.

The darkness is as obvious a symbol and site for the soul as any. The dark is the unknown, the mystery, the medium that holds the unpredictable — the possible. It is the best blank screen upon which to project all that is unsolved and unloved in our hearts. We are afraid of the dark simply because we can't see what's there and we naturally assume the worst. When it comes to the dark, "better safe than sorry" turns out to mean "better paranoid and vigilant than murdered." Most children — and the children inside us — are terrified of the dark, especially the dark *beneath* things, and thus afraid of what might be in the basement or under the bed — or in the subway.

The Wanderer knows she's not likely to run across her soul in the broad daylight of the village. If it had been waiting there, she probably would have found it long ago. The dayworld of family and culture is the setting within which her ego has acquired its particular qualities, both its vulnerabilities and strengths, and so her ego has already embraced most of the possibilities that exist there. Now she must look elsewhere. She must sink into deeper, more fertile, darker soil in order to tap her greatest and wildest possibilities.

One practice you might adopt is spending extended periods of time in true physical darkness, outdoors on moonless nights or in caves, with the goal of discovering and retrieving some treasures from the symbolic dark, your personal wilderness. Wendell Berry knows the dark:

To go in the dark with a light is to know light.
To know the dark, go dark. Go without sight,
And find that the dark, too, blooms and sings,
And is traveled by dark feet and dark wings.[4]

In befriending the dark, offer your careful attention to everything you hear and feel and smell there, knowing much of what you experience will be "just" your imagination projecting unassimilated elements of your own psyche. You will learn much from what you project. But what you encounter in the dark will also include flesh and blood entities of the night — owls, bats, deer, raccoons, spiders, mice — that may be curious about you and even drawn to you. (People of some nature-based cultures say if you regularly encounter raccoons, for example, you might have "raccoon medicine"; on the other hand, you may just have a habit of sitting on raccoon trails in the middle of the night without knowing it.)

The greatest gift of the dark, however, will not be what you find there, but how the dark changes you. Offer your self to the dark and ask it to initiate you in whatever ways it will, making yourself a gift to the dark as opposed to merely hoping for a gift *from* the dark.

Going into the literal dark serves as a mutually synergistic companion to several other strategies you might employ concurrently for entering the symbolic dark — dreamwork, for example, or deep imagery journeys, work with your sacred wound, with your shadow and projections, or confronting the inevitability of your own death. Each is a way to stretch your limits and become acquainted with yourself on a deeper level, each practice reinforcing and extending what is learned and set in motion by the others.

Rilke, too, learned to appreciate and love the dark:

> You darkness from which I come,
> I love you more than all the fires
> that fence out the world,
> for the fire makes a circle
> for everyone
> so that no one sees you anymore.
>
> But darkness holds it all:
> the shape and the flame,
> the animal and myself,
> how it holds them,
> all powers, all sight—
>
> and it is possible: its great strength
> is breaking into my body.
>
> I have faith in the night.[5]

Rilke understood that our very origin is the darkness. We emerge from the darkness of the womb and, simultaneously, from the darkness of spirit, the Great Mystery. When Rilke writes that the fire fences out the world, I hear "world" as that greater portion of the universe we know little or nothing about. The darkness holds it all and so the Wanderer bravely enters that darkness to discover what is there and what is drawn to him. And the Wanderer, like Rilke, hopes not just to find something but to be changed, to be broken into, bodily. We must learn, like the poet, to have faith in the night.

Annie Bloom had long suffered a debilitating fear of the night. Sometimes, after dusk, she would find herself huddled in a corner of her house, hyperventilating and terrified someone would break in and murder her.

The first time she went to the wilderness to spend three days and nights alone, she hoped to confront this terror, find its source, and put it to rest. As the time approached to go, her fears increased. Upon entering the desert, there were two things she had to do in order to feel safe.

The first was to embrace the wilds. After setting up my tarp and getting myself settled, I walked around the perimeter of my camp and spoke aloud to the unseen critters, telling them I was not there to harm them. I told them I respected their home and would not interfere in their lives, that I was going to be quiet and unobtrusive. I was surprised at my own words. I noticed I was not saying, "Please don't hurt me." This calmed me. I felt if the animals knew I wouldn't bother them, that's all that was needed.

The second thing was to ceremonially set a time to look my fears in the face. At twilight the first day, I sat in the center of a beautiful spiral I had assembled from rocks and symbolic objects I had brought to give me strength. I spoke aloud to my fears and told them I wanted to look at them during the second night of my solo — at exactly two hours before dawn. It was important to me to set my own parameters. (Several months later, I understood I was empowering myself to take control of my fears.)

The second night came and I got into my sleeping bag thinking, "You know, I really don't think I have to look at my fears anymore. I've been feeling quite comfortable and safe out here, and I think I've been lucky and have just gotten over it." Ha! Do you think I got off that easy? Two hours before dawn, I awoke to rustling in the oaks. The hair on my neck stood on end and I bolted out of my bag, shaking. I thought I would die of a heart attack. I grabbed my rattle and ran into the center of the spiral. I had a small ax in my left hand, raised, and I rattled furiously with my right. I spoke aloud about my old fears and asked whatever was in the oaks to reveal itself. I kept whirling around to check behind me. Then I asked the trees and rocks if they would guard my back and let me know if I was in danger. I "heard" a gentle affirmation and felt the presence of many beings come in close to hold me. I relaxed and stopped rattling.

In the silence that followed, I was flooded with memories of being sexually assaulted when very young, before words. In the space of minutes, I remembered so much. So many incidents that had made me feel crazy suddenly all fell into place in one resounding crash.

This was the beginning of Annie's healing time with her sacred wound. She went through months of grief and trauma work. She gradually pieced together how she had been molested at the age of two and how the two boys had threatened her if she were to tell anyone. In time, she found and confronted her abusers. She reassembled herself. She rendered her wound sacred as she healed and came to understand the gift within it, a gift that has become a key element of her soul work.

> One of the things I do as a bodyworker is contain and hold people when they go through an emotional maelstrom. I have the capacity to remain calm and present in the midst of turmoil and pain. My intuition about what people hold in their bodies is keen. I believe this capacity comes from my experience of holding a long-repressed memory in my own body, and unwinding the story step-by-step, reliving and assimilating it through understanding and expression. I see this experience as key to my ability to walk people to the edge of the underworld and calmly say, "Go ahead. It is your death and your life and you will survive it if you have the courage to cross this threshold." The day I was molested was cataclysmic; my world was shattered. When I faced the demon head-on that night in the wilderness, I changed forever my pattern of running and hiding. Not only can I now be completely at ease in the darkness, but I cherish its comforting shadows. With this new relationship to the dark, I lead other people into their black despairs, bottomless griefs, chasms of disillusionment, voids of self-worth, and yawning cavities of fear. It is where we meet power.

Like Annie, the American poet Lyn Dalebout has learned there are great treasures to be found in the dark:

> It is the universal statement of a star,
> the message Orion
> has carried
> in winter
> through the ages:
>
> It is the dark
> which illuminates.[6]

LIVING THE QUESTIONS OF SOUL

In 1903, Rainer Maria Rilke famously recommended in a letter to a young friend to *live* the questions of soul. Rilke counseled his friend that no one could answer his deepest questions for him, and that he would have to wait before he could answer them for himself. Rilke also recommended that his friend spend time in nature, offering his careful and loving attention to "the simple in Nature, to the little things that hardly anyone sees, and that can so unexpectedly become big and beyond measuring."[7] Rilke's primary advice for those seeking their true way in the world was "to go into yourself and test the deeps in which your life takes rise."[8] The essence of this time of life, he wrote, is in the questions:

> I want to beg you, as much as I can, dear sir, to be patient toward all that is unsolved in your heart and try to love the *questions themselves* like locked rooms and like books that are written in a very foreign tongue. Do not now seek the answers, which cannot be given you because you would not be able to live them. And the point is, to live everything. *Live* the questions now. Perhaps you will then gradually, without noticing it, live along some distant day into the answer.[9]

In the popular European myth of the Holy Grail, the young man, Parsifal, goes out into the world to seek life's deeper meaning — his soul (which is what the Grail ultimately symbolizes). His travels take him to the castle of the sick Grail King (who, as in most myths, symbolizes the old story, the ego's old and fortressed way of being in the world). The only cure for the king is for an unknown knight (a Wanderer) to come along and ask the king two specific questions. But Parsifal's mother had taught him that questions were foolish or rude, and so Parsifal does not ask. Consequently the castle (and the vision of the Grail) vanishes, and Parsifal finds himself in a great wilderness through which he must wander for many years, until he has learned enough, through the trials and losses of life, to be ready to ask the right questions.

The first question is, "Lord, what ails thee?" By asking ourselves (our egos) that question — and living it — we, like Parsifal, develop understanding and empathy for how we cocreate many of our ailments and how those difficulties teach us what we need to learn. We begin to uncover our sacred wounds. We develop compassion for ourselves, learning to appreciate our mistakes, failures, and wounds as much as our talents and successes.

The second question is, "Whom does the Grail serve?" By asking, "Whom does *my soul* serve?" we learn to turn our attention to the deeper purposes of what we do. We enlarge our vision of what's possible and gradually learn to root our actions in soul. Eventually we learn who and what to serve. The answer will have two parts to it, like two sides of a coin: we serve the specific purposes of our souls and we serve our people, and we do one by doing the other. By living the question, "Whom does the Grail serve?" we come to know our true destiny and the identity of our people. By staying attuned to the question of meaning, we learn to sanctify life.

One of the key features of the Grail myth is that, in order to heal the king, and thereby the land, Parsifal need only ask the questions. He doesn't need to answer them himself (nor does the king). The Jungian analyst Robert Johnson writes, "To ask well is virtually to answer." When an answer does arrive, it does so not by way of the ego but by way of the soul.

Johnson reminds us that we do not achieve happiness by striving for it. Rather, we achieve happiness by doing the work of our souls:

> If you ask the grail for happiness, that demand precludes happiness. But if you serve the grail properly, you will find that what happens and happiness are the same thing.[10]

Whom does the Grail serve? This, alas, is the question the Wanderer, like Parsifal, hopes to carry throughout his days, constantly deepening the question as he lives it.

CHAPTER 12

CULTIVATING A SOULFUL RELATIONSHIP TO LIFE

Part 2

When it's over, I want to say: all my life
I was a bride married to amazement.
I was the bridegroom, taking the world into my arms.

When it's over, I don't want to wonder
if I have made of my life something particular, and real.
I don't want to find myself sighing and frightened,
or full of argument.

I don't want to end up simply having visited this world.

— Mary Oliver

I n this chapter, we turn, at last, to what I call the "None Others" — none other than death, shadow, romance, consciousness, and spirit — arguably the most profound mysteries of human life.

Wrestling with the None Others — as one might with an angel — is essential for cultivating a soulful relationship to life. In order to live your soul into the world, you must continuously loosen your beliefs about who you are. The realities of death will help with that loosening. Shadow work will help as well; in the process of reclaiming your wholeness, you will find many fragments of soul in the shadow, where the Loyal Soldier hid them to keep you from accidentally stumbling upon dangerous secrets. Romance, too, if you take it deep enough, will surely shatter the restrictive yet fragile shell of the ego. Discovering the mysterious core of your consciousness will do the same. And certainly spirit has some things to say about your true identity.

When it's over, you'll want to be confident you made your life something particular, and real, as Mary Oliver says. You'll want to know you did not shrink from an intimate conversation with the great existential givens of life. You will, therefore, look Death in the face before He comes calling for you. You will reach your trembling hand into the dark shadow behind you. You will say yes to the dying that is as much a part of romance as its joys. You will discover what remains of consciousness after the mind is quieted. And you will forge your own intimate relationship with the Divine.

CONFRONTING YOUR OWN DEATH

The courageous encounter with the unalterable fact of mortality supplements and extends the activities of the death lodge discussed in chapter 5. In the death lodge, you made peace with your past and prepared to leave behind an old way of belonging to the world; you prepared for a "small death." Now you have the opportunity to prepare for your inevitable and final death, look your mortality in the eye, and make peace with the brutal fact that, ultimately, you will have to loosen your grip on all of life, not just a life *stage*.

On September 11, 2001, Ann DeBaldo was leading a journey in a remote corner of Tibet, unaware of the events unfolding in the United States. But like most Americans that day, Ann had the opportunity to become more intimately acquainted with death. At fourteen thousand feet in the Himalayas, Ann witnessed the extraordinary Buddhist ceremony of sky burial while, elsewhere in the world, people witnessed another kind of sky burial in the air over New York City.

> We were camped near Drigung Til Monastery. The evening before the sky burial, we attended the *powa* practice. A specially trained lama sat in front of the four corpses, each of which was folded into a small bundle and wrapped with blankets tied with ropes. Offerings to the monks — bags of flour and other staples — were taken off the horses by family members who had carried the bodies here, a journey of many days, perhaps weeks. The lama went into a profound meditation and at regular intervals made a loud sound — *phat!* — to open the crown chakras of the corpses, allowing any remaining life force to depart. We sat in silence as the offerings were casually divided among the monks and the lama performed his task.
>
> Very early the next morning, we walked silently and slowly up to the hilltop where the sky burial would take place. I walked with an elderly man whom I had earlier tried to discourage from coming to Drigung Til. He was ill-prepared to handle either the altitude or the primitive camping, yet in Lhasa it became clear to me that attending the sky burial was what his journey was all about. The group moved ahead and we took the less steep pathway, his labored breathing increasing with each step. As we reached the top, a monk gently untied the ropes on one of the bundles and removed the blankets revealing a very old woman with limbs lying at impossible angles to her torso. A great calm came over me. The old man gasped and almost fell. To prepare the food for the vultures, the monk flayed the meat and then crushed the bones into grain on a great round stone. We were so close that bits of flesh landed on our clothes. The old man was unable to stand and so we moved even closer to lean upon the stone wall next to the monk. I felt a warm strength as I supported my

companion's weight, understanding how close he was to his time of departing this life. I could feel his heart beating and his heavy breathing as the huge golden vultures edged nearer to their breakfast.

Each corpse was similarly handled. Wave after wave of vultures descended upon the meat and grain until abruptly, there was nothing left. I watched, filled with a strange joy as the great birds lumbered down the hill before jumping into the sky and soared away over the valley toward the snow peaks in the distance. Oh, to fly freely — man becoming bird! What is death but an opening of a door?

We walked in silence down the steep hill toward the monastery where the monks began parading and chanting to the sounds of their great long horns and drums. As I sat in the hot sun, I shivered so hard I almost fell off the wall, my mind reeling. It was difficult to think and perhaps consciousness was briefly lost. Then, in my belly, I felt the presence for the first time of a great mountain of peace and silence — a feeling of solidity and calm strength, quite new to me. We left the monastery, each of us affected in our individual ways, but certainly forever changed by our visit to the burial grounds.

Confronting your own mortality, intimately and bravely, imagined or vicariously witnessed in graphic detail, is a powerful soulcraft practice, possibly an essential one. The embodiment of soul that you seek is not going to go far if you are living as if your ego is immortal. Put more positively, your soul initiation will be rich to the extent you can ground yourself in the sober but liberating awareness of limited time. This very moment may be your last.

The confrontation with death is an unrivaled perspective enhancer. In the company of death, most desires of adolescence and the first adulthood fall away. What are the deepest longings that remain? What are the surviving intentions with which you might enter your second adulthood? The confrontation with death will empty you of everything but that kernel of love in your heart and your sincerest questions. It is in such a state of emptiness and openness that we hope to approach the central mysteries of our life.

As a Wanderer, it is a good practice to look Death in the eye. Contemplate your unavoidable aging and inevitable demise, "the bitter unwanted passion of your sure defeat," as David Whyte puts it.[1] You might, for example, look carefully at photographs of decaying bodies, of human and other skeletons, of people dying of horrible and wasting diseases or starvation, of autopsied cadavers and funeral pyres.

You might make it a practice to imagine your own aged, diseased, or mortally wounded body. Remind yourself regularly that you, too, like all flesh, will one day leave behind your body and all else, and that it will happen on a day very much like this one, maybe in a place, if you are fortunate, like the place where you are this very moment, with or without the presence of the other people who are with you now. Visualize your own earth burial, sky burial, fire burial, and/or water burial.

During your wandering time, you might visit cemeteries, mortuaries, crematoriums, or charnels and sit there for hours or days and *really* look and listen and feel and breathe the thick air in those places. You might learn the traditional and sacred practices of those who prepare a body for burial or cremation.

Perhaps you will volunteer for hospice and spend hours gazing into the eyes of those who lie at death's door, your heart stretching ever wider, both your eyes and your companion's peering over the edge of life's cliff. In hospice, you will witness the dying process, life ebbing away, and the moment of death itself. You will see people die well and not so well. You will see how families deal with death or refuse to deal with it. You will see some people embrace their deaths and celebrate their lives, and others die bitter and angry, never having acknowledged they were dying.

Discuss death with your teachers and fellow Wanderers. Sit in councils specifically dedicated to talk of death. While alone, wonder about death, wander with it, wrestle with it. Feel its presence, both emotionally and physically. Ask yourself and others questions about death and share your feelings and speculations. Along with Mary Oliver, rhetorically ask, "Doesn't everything die at last, and too soon?"[2]

Should you suffer the loss of a loved one, permit the force of that death to transform you with its weight, fully feeling and expressing the immense grief, allowing it to irrevocably alter the world and your place in it. And should your people suffer an unthinkable loss at the hands of others (as on September 11, 2001), surrender to your anger and grief, but also look for the enemy of life within, the elements of self not in alignment with life. Find where death lives inside.

When you progress from one stage of life to another, celebrate the promises and possibilities of the new, but do not shirk from grieving the little deaths inevitably accompanying these shifts — the death of youth, unrealized dreams, cherished hopes, bedrock illusions.

Gradually, you will come to live in the light of death, not morbidly but with an increasingly joyful appreciation for this moment, and your presence in it. You will cling less and less to who you are and how you are and become more attuned to your destiny, with allegiance to neither your social past nor the current accommodations of your personality.

As Carlos Castaneda was taught by his teacher, the Yaqui sorcerer don Juan, ask death to be your ally, to remind you, especially at times of difficult choices, what is important in the face of your mortality. Imagine death as ever present, accompanying you everywhere just out of sight behind your left shoulder.

In these ways, make peace with your mortality. One day you will find you are not so attached to your life being just one certain way. Then you will be better prepared to converse with soul and its outrageous requests for radical change.

With any soulcraft practice, the Wanderer seeks to put his ego in a double bind, a checkmate that makes it impossible to continue the old story. Confronting the inevitability and ever presence of his death loosens his grip on his routines, dislodges his old way of obtaining his bearings, ushers him to the threshold beyond which lies the unknown. Horrified, he discovers he must give up everything in order to get what he really wants, with no guarantee of success or even of surviving his quest.

He is like a dog playing fetch when someone suddenly throws the stick into a bonfire. Stunned, the dog stares into the flames with big eyes. The soul wants the Wanderer to jump into that fire. The Wanderer's deepest instinct for survival is counterbalanced by his passion for the quest. What will he do?

By confronting the truths held by death, the Wanderer gradually relinquishes his illusion of immortality and finds himself with a new hope for the world. He sees all things must change to evolve. He sees that death and impermanence provide hope for an evolving universe.

THE ART OF SHADOW WORK

The soul lives contented
by listening,
if it wants to change
into the beauty of
terrifying shapes
it tries to speak.

That's why
you will not sing,
afraid as you are
of who might join with you.[3]
— David Whyte

The candidate for initiation knows the underworld portal is guarded by demons and there are monsters even more fierce beyond the threshold. She has come to understand, at least intellectually, that some — perhaps all — of these demons and monsters reflect unconscious elements of her own psyche. The ego has rejected them and labeled them "not me," "evil," or "bad." Carl Jung referred to these unknown or unrecognized aspects of self as composing the archetype he called "the shadow." Beginning in the second cocoon, the Wanderer has the opportunity to ferret out and reclaim these terrifying shapes. They are essential components of her wholeness, and wholeness is what she is after.

Most elements of self in your shadow — your wildness, say, or your carnality or selfishness — were disowned and repressed during your childhood and adolescence in the process of your attempts (successful or not) to win acceptance from your family and peers. Far from being a mistake, this self-rejection was necessary in order to form a socially adaptive ego and personality, your first identity. Now, to be initiated into your soul identity, you must descend into those dark realms to retrieve lost pieces. Therein lie key elements of your destiny.

Although the shadow cast by the ego contains perverse and socially unacceptable qualities, it also contains what would be considered positive traits, such as generosity, or creative urges like spontaneous public singing. The shadow is always the converse of the ego, and the ego includes some destructive and antisocial attitudes. We might have been abandoned or punished as children, for example, if we had embodied healthy qualities our parents considered inappropriate to their social standing or that made them uncomfortable or envious. The shadow contains all aspects of the psyche inconsistent with the position of the ego, both good and bad.

To proceed toward wholeness and manifest the promise only you can bring to the world, you must investigate your shadow. It contains values and perspectives needed to round out your conscious personality. It contains personal powers you'll need when you befriend or wrestle with the inner and outer dragons and angels encountered on your soul journey.

In the encounter with shadow, your conscious personality will sometimes be overwhelmed or shattered. Your ego might experience a death, but it will thereby be enabled to later rise from the ashes like a phoenix endowed with new powers.

The American poet Robert Bly says our first twenty years are spent stuffing 90 percent of our wholeness into "the long black bag we drag behind us" and the rest of our life attempting to retrieve those items.[4] The bag is long because it's so full; it's black because we can't see or understand its contents; and we drag it behind us, like our literal shadow, because we tend to walk toward the light and because there is no alternative; it is, after all, a part of us despite our reluctance to acknowledge it.

Our Loyal Soldier, of course, is the sub-personality who shoveled all those aspects of self into the long bag in the first place. Think of the Loyal Soldier as a sort of psychic bouncer who throws out any part of self not deemed respectable by the management. The boss, in this case, is the child's immediate family and cultural setting. When the boss spots an undesirable, the Loyal Soldier starts shoveling.

As men and women in our first adulthood, we rarely "sing," as Whyte puts it. We rarely express our full, natural, spontaneous exuberance — for fear of who might join with us, those shadow shapes we've locked in dungeons. We suspect the song would be terrifying, to us and perhaps to others. The truth is, it might be, despite its astonishing otherworldly beauty.

Before being reclaimed, the *negative* elements of the shadow appear to the ego as disagreeable and frightening. They show up as scary dreamworld characters and as dayworld people onto whom we project our own negative qualities, such as greediness, cowardice, rage, weakness, arrogance, or cruelty. We project our negative shadow onto nature, too: hairy beasts, dark forests, swamps, tornadoes, bats, snakes, and volcanoes.

Yet the negative shadow possesses beneficial attributes we need in order to mature. Without these qualities, our personalities remain unbalanced, fragmented, or otherwise incomplete. Unwittingly following the Loyal Soldier's lead, we placed a negative value on these shadow elements to protect ourselves. But as we develop a relationship with these elements and begin to consciously integrate them, we experience their strength, resourcefulness, unique perspectives, and sensitivities.

The *positive* qualities of our shadow — qualities we would consider virtuous, elevated, or otherwise exemplary — are also projected onto others.

These are the exemplary traits we see in others but can hardly imagine for ourselves.

Often we discover our shadow holds something sacred: our deepest passion. This may be a longing to dance, to create magic, to sing in public, or to love with abandon. Donna Medeiros, a teacher at an alternative high school, says that when we are young, *we name our passion something else* — so we can suppress it. We name it foolish, selfish, odd, crazy, or evil. This misnaming protects us from social injury, from being rejected or marginalized by our family or peers. Donna knows this not only from her own story but also from her daily classroom experience with teenagers whom she guides through the process of self-reclamation. When awareness of their passion begins to return, they don't recognize it at first because it had been mislabeled.

A few years ago, I found myself with the opportunity to reclaim a piece of my shadow. For many years, I had been dreaming of thugs, shadow figures to be sure. These were inner-city street people of color. They ripped me off, mugged me, or stole my car. They treated me like a wealthy, unhip, middle American — not worth giving the time of day and certainly not someone to sit down and be real with. I (the dream ego) felt victimized and saw them, in turn, as mean-spirited trash.

This series of dreams culminated in April one year when I had a thug dream every night for several days running. This got my attention. At the time, I was leading a group of men and women on an eight-day underworld journey through the redrock canyons of southern Utah. One warm evening in base camp, beneath a cottonwood by a desert spring, I asked my companions to help me explore the thug of me. I asked if one or two of them would be willing to role-play the thugs while I took the part of the victimized and frightened dream ego. Two of them, a man and a woman, stood up immediately, with mischievous "Sure, I'll help" gleams in their eyes. Swallowing hard, I gave them the basic scripts and attitudes and asked them to improvise within the framework of my dreams. Meanwhile I took the role of my dream ego, who was rather less assertive and confident than I think of my dayworld self as.

The two thugs did a remarkably good job (the creeps)! They messed with me, pushing me around with their loud questions and comments and, sometimes, their arms. They got in my face, questioned my authenticity, my values, my realness. They didn't give a damn about my precious car or possessions. The other group members, sitting in a circle around us, called out additional invectives for the thugs. The thugs invited them to join in. Before long, there were eleven thugs and me and no one left sitting. Things were getting uncomfortable, and uncomfortably real. I began to panic. Tears of sadness and shame spilled from my eyes. And, astonishingly, an admiration for the thugs.

Through the probing, relentless "assistance" of the role-playing thugs, I realized the thugs of me possessed some qualities I actually admired: a fierce, no-holds-barred genuineness and the ability to look the other guy in the eye and speak the plain truth, regardless of whether it might hurt; their words were from the heart. The thugs possessed an authenticity, courage, chutz-pah, and tough love my ego lacked. This came as a humbling shock: where I had earlier felt self-righteously victimized, I now felt chagrin for my blindness to the rich world of these "poor" people of my nightworld. I could see that in my dayworld I exhibited a constraint, a timidity, a social distance that restricted the range and power in my work as a guide as well as in my personal relationships.

I vowed to free the slaves of thuggery within me. I adopted the practice of embodying the thug of me, to look people in the eye and speak the plain truth to the best of my ability and with as much love as I could muster. My job was to *become* that loving thug, to assimilate him. This required emulation of the *heart warrior* about whom I had spoken for years but had not embodied as much as I might have. I found when I did it skillfully, it worked; people felt seen, honored, deeply met. With few exceptions, they didn't go away feeling mugged, but loved. Imagine.

So after years of being accosted by nightworld thugs, the dreams ended that spring. I have not had another since — except one, that is, a few months later. But in that one, I (the dream ego) was the thug!

Carl, a software engineer from the urban East Coast, was in his mid-thirties when he enacted his vision fast. He had just left his job to seek greater opportunities for creative expression. He hoped to discover some direction and resources during his quest. A man with a warm manner and positive outlook, Carl expected his vision fast to be all love and light. But he did admit to an immense fear of wilderness camping, and especially of the possibility of menacing animals. Like everyone, he projected his shadow outward.

On the morning of our second day together as a group, Carl awoke with a dream about menacing animals. In the dream, he is outside the urban apartment complex he lived in during his childhood. A ram is running in his direction. Carl makes a mad dash for the building and runs down into the basement. The ram follows. Carl tears down a hallway, in the center of which lies a sleeping black bull. He jumps past the bull, waking it, and runs up another staircase to an exit door. After a while, Carl peeks out the door and sees the bull pulling the ram out of the building through another doorway.

Carl recognized he had the opportunity on his fast to become acquainted with the ram and the bull and what they represented. Why was the black bull asleep in the basement (underworld) of Carl's childhood? Had the bull of himself been banished to the basement and subdued when Carl was young? What aspect of Carl's shadow might be represented by the dark, powerful bull, and how was it a danger to him (and others) when he was young? Why, just before his vision quest, is he inadvertently waking the bull? What shadow potentials are held by the ram, and why does the bull want the ram out? Might these shadows within him — hardly the figures of love and light he expected — provide resources for the creative expression he longed for?

Going into his fast, Carl wisely chose to live these questions. He asked to be called Sleeping Bull to be reminded of his dormant shadow power. In deep imagery, he began a conscious relationship with the bull and ram, and, through self-designed ceremony, he invited them to accompany him on his fast. When he entered the darkness of his solo time, these questions and the powers of Bull and Ram walked beside him.

Familiarity with the art of shadow work is of immeasurable value to the initiate during the second cocoon and after. When the Wanderer enters the dark cave of initiation, he wants to be better equipped for shadow encounters than Luke Skywalker in the *Star Wars* film, when his teacher, the elder-sage-fool, Yoda, gave him the task of entering a particularly ominous zone of the fearsome forest. Yoda encourages Luke to go in without his weapon, a light-saber, because, as Yoda tells him, he would not find any monsters there that he did not bring in with him. Luke finds this idea to be neither comforting nor entirely believable. Not having trained in shadow work, Luke chooses to take his saber when he enters the gloom. Soon he encounters a demon guarding the threshold — it is his sacred wound in the form of his father-tyrant Darth Vader. But Luke does not yet understand psychological projection, so he reacts as if it is literally his enemy, brandishes his saber, and cuts off the demon's head. As the severed head falls to the forest floor, Luke watches in horror as it transforms into his own visage. He has failed his first test and lost an opportunity to come to terms with this aspect of his wholeness, to reclaim a piece of his own soul. He'll get another chance, but it will be even more difficult the next time.

If Luke had acquired sufficient skills of shadow work before this point, he might have known that the apparition of his father-tyrant was an opportunity to assimilate, or "eat," some of his shadow. He might have known, for example, how to develop a relationship with that demon, to attempt to discover what lesson, opportunity, or gift it possessed for him, to inquire of it what it *really* wanted of him.

What the demon wants is always something different from what we first suspect or fear. My thugs, for example, didn't really want my car. That was just their way of getting my attention. (It worked.) What they really wanted was for me to embody more of my authentic heart power.

As a Wanderer, it would be good to adopt the regular practice of identifying and engaging the shadow. Take careful note, for example, when you find yourself with a strong charge — positive or negative — around another person, especially someone you don't know well. Ask yourself what qualities of the other you like or dislike. Look for these same qualities in yourself, perhaps expressed in subtle or unexpected ways, or only occasionally but with a vengeance or a flare. Begin to wonder about the other qualities of that person, the ones you didn't notice at first. Let yourself imagine how it might change you if you were to embrace that person as an ally, and what would happen if you assimilated the qualities of the other. Whether the other is from the dayworld or the nightworld, dialogue with this shadow figure. In your imagination, allow yourself to merge with the figure and give it the opportunity to express itself through drawing, painting, writing, movement, music, or dance.

James Hillman encourages us to learn to love the negative shadow wherever we find it, to care for it, laugh with the paradox of our own folly (which is everyone's), embrace the rejected and the inferior, find ways to live it. Hillman advises both laughing acceptance of the negative shadow and harsh judgment of it (until you are no longer tempted to act it out in destructive ways).

Loving the positive shadow can be equally challenging because the Loyal Soldier will try to keep you from acknowledging your own magnificence.

Many soulcraft skills will help you engage the shadow. For example, through soulcentric dreamwork, you can learn how to identify shadow figures that appear in your nightworld (e.g., Jung said they tend to be of the same gender as the dreamer and that they often frighten or threaten the dream ego). You could learn how to use deep imagery to dialogue with and develop a relationship with these shades. So, too, you can learn how you project your shadow onto others in your waking life, and through council work you might practice the skills of owning back those projections. As another example, you might learn how to look for the shadow when it appears during trance dancing with others, how to spot the shadow as you project it onto another dancer... and then dance with it.

WITHDRAWING PROJECTIONS

Through her shadow work, the Wanderer inevitably discovers that she often projects her repressed and disowned qualities onto nature — animals, mountains, the ocean, the wind, the earth itself — as well as people in her community or from different nations or ethnic groups. She discovers, too, the many ways she unconsciously projects her unfinished relationships onto others, treating them as if they are some hero, god, goddess, savior, tyrant, or villain from her past. She learns that (1) by becoming conscious of her disowned experiences and projected qualities and accepting them as part of her, she is less likely to act them out; (2) some keys to her soul powers are buried in that repressed material; and (3) many of the capacities and resources she needs to live her soul qualities are also buried there. The Wanderer, then, has plenty of motivation to learn to withdraw her projections, to gradually learn, that is, to own back and reassimilate those parts of her self.

Why do we project our repressed parts? Why can't or don't those parts just remain peacefully buried — or asleep in the basement — and let us go on undisturbed with our "normal" lives? One possibility is that projection increases the psychological distance between ourselves and the projected qualities, thereby defending ourselves from the possibility that *we* possess those qualities. Projection is one of the Loyal Soldier's foremost survival strategies.

But there is another possibility. As the mythologies of all time — and the depth psychologists of the twentieth century — have been telling us, there is this irrepressible urge within each of us toward wholeness. Some would say this is why we have incarnated, to become more fully who we are in our deepest essence. The long black bag we drag behind us is an all-inclusive, custom-made storehouse of everything we need in our quest to become whole. The soul is not going to be happy if we try to sleep away our lives, although we may succeed at it nonetheless. The soul can't *make* us wake up, but it can and does see to it that we project. That way we are likely to run smack into the wall of our own unlived potential. If we can recognize our projections, then we can embrace the painful opportunity to both heal and whole ourselves.

So we project. Apparently there is no way to avoid it even while there are limitless ways to ignore or deny it.

Robert Bly agrees that projection is a fortunate thing indeed. Without it, he notes, we might never have the opportunity to own back those hidden, not-yet-embodied parts. Thank god, then, for the screens upon which we project: our friends, family, the famous, the infamous, foreigners, infidels, and the forms and forces of nature. Without those screens, our projections would simply sail into outer space like errant radio waves, and we would never get to see our hidden aspects.

There are actually *two* ways in which we project onto others. The first is when we project our own unrecognized personal qualities. The second is when we project the qualities of someone from our past onto people in our present.

Psychologists refer to the latter as *transference* — unfinished emotional business from our past is transferred onto our current relationships. Most commonly what is unfinished is our relationships with our parents (or other childhood caregivers). Our souls want us to revisit those central, often traumatic, and incomplete relationships so that we can heal and learn. The soul does this by arranging for us to experience people from our current life — our lovers, friends, friends' spouses, colleagues, bosses, teachers, psychotherapists, gurus — as if they were the same sort of people as those major players from our childhood. That way we can find ourselves forming current relationships that resemble those from our past.

Consciously, we don't want that. But our souls recognize an opportunity. If we can re-create the same kinds of relationship problems we were unable to solve in childhood, we have another chance to get it right, to act and relate in ways that don't limit us. Transference gives us the opportunity to discover how we have unwittingly created many of the dysfunctional qualities of our relationships (both old and new) in our attempts to protect ourselves from abandonment or emotional annihilation as children. In other words, our Loyal Soldiers understand that dysfunctional relationships are a better choice than those horrible alternatives. Now, in adulthood, we have the opportunity to remove those barriers to self-expression and individuation and heal the wounds exposed when we do. But we aren't likely to do that work until we can *see* those barriers. How are we going to see them? Through the transference of old feelings onto current relationships.

The Jungian analyst James Hollis summarizes five stages in projecting and re-owning the abandoned parts of ourselves.[5] In the first stage, we are convinced that what we are unconsciously projecting is true of the other. When we fall in love, for example, we are certain the other (about whom we almost never really know anything) is the most extraordinary being on the face of the planet. We are projecting the desirable and desired qualities of the inner Other (the soul) and/or the desirable qualities of someone from our past. In stage two, we become increasingly and shockingly aware of the discrepancy between who we thought the other was (and was *supposed* to be) and who they are turning out to be. We become certain there must be something wrong with the other and we attempt to control them, change them, fix them. Now we are projecting onto the other the negative qualities of the inner Other and/or the person from our past. The third stage requires us, for the first time, to *really* look at the other, to see more clearly who they are, and to begin to ask what is actually going on in our relationship. In stage four, we withdraw the projections by recognizing that we were in fact projecting, that what we thought was the outer Other was actually, in part, the inner and/or the person from our past. And, finally, in stage five, through our inner work, we come to see exactly what it was in us we were projecting in the first place, and why.

The withdrawal of projections obliges us to consciously suffer the discrepancy between what we had hoped for and what we have. This takes much courage, heart, honesty, and a great desire to grow and become whole, a desire that must be stronger than the wish to be saved by an omnipotent other or to remain comfortable and secure.

How do we know when we are projecting versus being in genuine conversation with another? No guaranteed signs. But projection is likely to be a significant part of the mix when we fall in love, when we have strong feelings — positive or negative — about people we know little about, when we have a strong somatic reaction (e.g., queasiness, butterflies, lightheadedness) to someone, and/or when we notice our emotional reaction seems to be much greater than the circumstances warrant. We are surely projecting when we see another person (or nation) as evil or, conversely, when we feel someone is going to make everything all right for us.

In order to begin to withdraw your projections, you must first become aware that you are projecting. (There is little or no chance you will catch yourself *before* you do it. You must first suffer the discrepancy and recognize it as the source of your suffering.) Then you can ask yourself: What exactly is the quality I like or don't like in the other? What emotions are evoked by those qualities? How have I acted on those emotions? Where do I find these same qualities in myself? What have I done to disown them and why? In what ways might my experience of this person be similar to how I experienced someone from my family of origin?

Then you might identify the parts of your self that you have disowned and give them names. Using deep imagery work (having a trained imagery guide is recommended), you can develop a relationship with those disowned parts. Dialogue with those parts, either in your imagery or by using empty chairs and imagining those parts in those chairs. You might also choose to sit in the empty chairs and take the place of the other parts and respond to the ego. Or you might carry out the dialogue in your journal.

You might also notice that your disowned parts are showing up in your dreams. These dream characters can serve to enrich the mix of both your journal work and deep imagery with your disowned parts.

What I call the *heart warrior council* is a soulcraft approach to shadow dynamics, a way to help us own back our projections, explicitly, courageously, and respectfully. This council format provides a safe-enough container that allows us to express to one another, face-to-face, our projections and transferences. Before the council, exercises are conducted that help us uncover and own back those projections. Then, in council, we are invited to express our projections directly to our "screens" but *only* if we have already done the inner work to see what qualities of our selves — or what unfinished relationships from our past — are being projected.[6]

In the heart warrior council, we must be willing to open our hearts wide enough to encompass not only the Other but also our own shadows and our Loyal Soldiers and their childhood survival strategies. Heart opening is one of the essential keys to soulcrafting; the less defended we are with others, the less defended we can be with our own souls. The support of the heart warrior council allows us to admit our projections directly to the Other in a sacred circle that serves as a loving and effective container for such risky and potentially humiliating revelations. We can stop tiptoeing around the emotional subtexts of our interactions once we bring them into the light. This frees us up not only in those interactions but also in our relationship to ourselves. The glitches in our outer relationships, after all, are reflections of our inner glitches (that's why we were projecting in the first place).

As the council proceeds, the feeling grows that here, in this circle, the universe is getting to know itself better, and that we are the instruments, the vehicles, for that revelation. Heart warrior councils open our hearts a few additional but very significant notches by making our humanness (e.g., our propensity to project and our vulnerability to being screens) okay, and admissible. Our humanness becomes less of a barrier to relating to one another. Projections that remain unconscious impede authentic relationships. Projections that are recognized, withdrawn, and re-owned are a royal road to the deepening of our relationships to others and to soul. As projections are withdrawn, there is an opening of the heart that feels so big as to be limitless.

In a heart warrior council, Bob, a physician in his forties, worked with an irritation he had with a woman in the group. He felt she talked too much. It seemed to him she was constantly chatting about one inane thing or another on an endless flight from what was real and grounded, on and on about the most superficial topics imaginable. Who knows whether this perception was unfair or not. (Just because we are projecting does not necessarily mean we are wrong.) The evidence that he was in the grip of projection and/or transference included the facts that he was *so* incredibly annoyed by her that he didn't have any compassion whatsoever for her — he merely wanted to kill her — that he had *always* been irritated by women like her, and that he was completely undone by her incessant talking.

In preparation for the heart warrior council, Bob began to explore the form and feeling of this projection and soon found transference: His mother was very extroverted and had minimal capacity for psychological understanding of herself or others. As a child and adolescent, he felt unseen by her. He had harbored the fantasy that if he waited patiently, she would one day really notice him. Projecting this relationship and this hope onto other women, Bob continued to passively wait, often feeling that women were oblivious to his emotional reality. Of course, he was fully complicit through his self-protective style of revealing very little. Although being seen was what he most wanted, the prospect also terrified him. Harboring the conviction that there was nothing he could do to change his relationships with women, he felt helpless. Helplessness bred anger and despair.

As he prepared for the council, he saw that he was not in fact helpless. He had the opportunity to shift the conversation himself, or at least to express his feelings and ask for what he wanted.

But before the council began, Bob had another insight. He saw how he was projecting onto the chatty woman his own suppressed capacity. Bob was an extreme introvert: the world of the psyche held much more fascination for him than the outer world of everyday affairs. His introversion had been, in part, a way of protecting himself from too much intercourse with a social world he perceived as dangerous. He developed an arrogant attitude that everyday chatter about mundane things was always an avoidance of what really matters. He had undermined his capacity to be in a good relationship with the mundane. Developing his neglected extroversion was an essential task in his path to wholeness.

During the council, when it was his turn to speak, he told the chatty woman about his projection onto her *and owned it back,* revealing his recent insights. This served three additional purposes beyond what he had already achieved through his private inner work: (1) Owning all this openly in the council, he could feel more of the projection and its deep roots in his psyche. Public admission freed up blocked emotional energy; (2) By speaking the unspeakable to the Other, the tension between them, which had blocked their connection and subtly undermined the entire group, vanished. Now he had the opportunity to get to know her as the truly Other she was (as opposed to his projection), and the group was freed to move in new ways; and (3) He was freed to cultivate a deeper appreciation for his extroverted mother.

Working with projections is essential to the process of soul initiation. We must own back and then embody the full magnificence, genius, and force of our individual soul powers.

THE ART OF SOULFUL ROMANCE

Soulfully entered, romance — that delightfully alluring, mad dance that transports and destroys us — can be a powerful soul-deepening adventure and one of the finest opportunities for carrying the soul's gift of love into the world. Through human loving, we become acquainted with spiritual love and the longing for sacred union. And yet romance is also the realm where we unleash our grandest and most delusional projections, where the shadow is sure to emerge in all its dark glory.

Love affairs are propelled by powerful currents — desire, fascination, sensuality, sexual ecstasy, attachment, devotion, communion, union. Affairs of the heart evoke the strongest emotions, from ardent passions to poisonous hatreds and jealousies, and can result in the most stunning betrayals. Through its extreme currents and emotions, romance destabilizes the ego and opens a door to soul.

Romance can be engaged soulfully and consciously, or it can be engaged egocentrically. When approached egocentrically, we unknowingly project aspects of our selves and our parents onto our beloved and thus have a limited understanding of the real person with whom we are partnered. Most of us go through an egocentric phase, sometimes lasting an entire lifetime, in which we fervently believe an intimate engagement with a lover is the thing that will save us, complete us, or make our world right. We believe, in other words, that a romantic relationship will somehow accomplish for us the task of our soulwork.

In Western society, romance is usually entered with the belief — usually unarticulated and often hidden even from ourselves — that we are each half persons. The covert agenda is to find our other half, our one and only soul mate. We innocently trust that once we find him or her, we will become whole by simple virtue of being together.

This longing for wholeness is as strong a pull as any in life. Yet we are terrified of the *actual* journey to wholeness that romance can set in motion. In egocentric romances, we are more likely to subvert the underworld journey than to embark upon it. We act as if the difficulties and uncertainties of soul encounter will be magically avoided simply by meeting him or her. This is the widespread fantasy of the Magical Other, brilliantly described by Jungian analyst James Hollis.

The Magical Other approach to romance, which is adolescent and egocentric, contrasts with an adult and soulcentric approach that opens the door to romance as a soulcraft art.

The easiest way to tell if we are approaching romance egocentrically is to take a radically honest look at our romantic fantasies. In egocentric romance, we have a particular image of the desired relationship even before we fall in love, before we have so much as met our beloved. We enter the love affair as if playing the Dating Game, with a preexisting image of how the other person looks, sounds, what she wears, what his IQ is, what sort of work she does, what his age, race, and religion are — perhaps even how many children we'll have and where we'll live! After we meet and begin a relationship, our primary agenda, whether we admit it or not, is to mold the other to that preexisting fantasy. Truly and deeply getting to know the other is secondary or, in the most egocentric forms of romance, of no interest at all.

Adolescent love affairs begin with a period of ecstasy in which everything is heavenly. All too soon, however, comes the letdown, the mutual perception that the other is not perfect after all. Then we try to shoehorn our lover into our fantasy of how he or she was "supposed" to be. But that flesh-and-blood person is never entirely moldable to that fantasy.

Yet, as egocentric lovers, we feel entitled to our dream. We attempt, in every creative and desperate way imaginable, to make it real. Naturally, it doesn't work. We become angry, hurt, and disillusioned. Soon enough, we convince ourselves we were terribly mistaken in whom we picked. We reject the other as flawed, not good enough. Sometimes we reject *ourselves* in those terms. But, alas, we do not reject the project itself, the Magical Other fantasy. We cling firmly to that egocentric dream and steady ourselves to do a better job next time, resolved to cast the right person into the romantic drama living inside our adolescent heart. What Hollis calls the "Eden project" — attempting through romance to return to the wholeness and perfection of the womb or the original garden — lives on intact.

Egocentric romance is so common and compelling in the initiation-deprived Western world because the uninitiated ego approaches romance from the perspective of its own experience, which is one of deficiency and incompleteness. The ego is in fact a "partial person" within the greater whole of the psyche. Before soul initiation, the ego feels a genuine and inconsolable loneliness and longing. It really does need to be completed by *something*. The problem is that that completion will never take place through a romantic relationship with another. It is only the soul, the divine lover, that fully completes the ego and allows it to feel fittingly partnered.

The uninitiated ego, without knowledge of the soul's world, has little choice but to project all of its longing onto an outer human beloved. Its loneliness continuously fuels the desire for love affairs. Until it discovers an alternative, it will keep seeking completion in that way — and failing.

In contrast, the Wanderer knows that the Other lives inside, or, alternatively, that the Other exists as the divine. Both the candidate for initiation and the initiated adult understand that human romance can deepen the sacred marriage between ego and soul, but it is not a substitute for it. As Rumi reminds us,

> The minute I heard my first love story
> I started looking for you, not knowing
> how blind that was.
> Lovers don't finally meet somewhere.
> They're in each other all along.[7]

Egocentric love is what makes the egocentric world go round. It is one of the central fantasies upon which our egocentric culture is built. The adolescent dream of romance is celebrated in myriad ways — in pop music, mainstream cinema, advertising, "true romance" novels, in prince and princess fantasies. This is all good fun as far as it goes. A youthful approach to love is not itself the problem; the problem is the rarity of what comes next developmentally: a more mature way of engaging a lover that has a deeper, more spiritual, sustainable, and, yes, even sexier set of possibilities, an approach to romance that encourages and supports soulful development.

The Magical Other fantasy, so deeply rooted in our Western psyches, does not die easily. Surrendering that fantasy can evoke a grief and experience of cosmic betrayal greater than the loss of any lover.

Like many, I used to suffer great anxiety at the outset of romantic relationships. If she was indeed the one and only Magical Other, then my salvation, I imagined, depended upon her wanting to be with me forever. A single misstep by me was potentially fatal to all future happiness, and so I was debilitated by a painful self-consciousness.

After my sacrificial ceremonies at Love Lake, however, I no longer sought a lover as a means to personal salvation. Having grieved the loss of the Magical Other fantasy, I began to experience myself as whole already, fully eligible to be in love with the world either alone or partnered. Having experienced the Feminine as immanent in the world, I was less prone to project Her exclusively on a lover. This is the rearranging power of ceremony. I became more capable of embracing romance as a dance, an engaging way of being in the world in the present moment, an end in its own right, as well as a doorway to a spiritual union with the beloved of the soul.

Part of our longing for a human lover arises from our accurate recognition, at some level, that we can come to know ourselves more deeply through romantic union. In the mystery of love, as we learn to love another truly, we meet the beloved of our own soul through the eyes of the human Other. Our personal destiny is to incarnate that beloved. Ultimately, we become the inner Other we first saw in the outer Other.

Through egocentric loving in adolescence and the first adulthood, the Wanderer acquired basic skills of sexual relating and social bonding. This was foundational and necessary. Then, during the second cocoon, the Wanderer learns that when she falls in love, she will project not only the most noble qualities of her own soul but also, eventually, her most negative shadow qualities.[8] She knows it will be a while before she sees her shadow in her lover's face, but, when she does, it will be disheartening, frightening, possibly repulsive. Knowing this is inevitable, she'll say yes to love anyway. She understands that unveiling the shadow is as valuable a result of romance as any other.

The Wanderer knows her love affair has the potential to reveal mysteries, lessons both joyous and painful. Intense feelings and non-ordinary states of consciousness will threaten to alter forever her understanding of what life is, and who *she* is. She hopes for this as much as she fears it. If, like all young lovers, she should feel like her true self for the first time in her life, she will know that her partner is only a catalyst and that if she does not learn how to own it, the experience will fade and she will blame her lover for the loss as much as she had once given him or her the credit.

In soulcentric romance, rather than attempting to make the other fit their preexisting fantasies, the lovers revel in endlessly exploring the mysterious nature of the Other in the here and now. The only relationship the lovers presume is the one they have earned through their unfolding conversation. They anticipate no potential relationship result (e.g., monogamy, polygamy, cohabitation, marriage, children, economic or professional advancement) as being preferable to any other. Any such intent would interfere with the deepening experience of true contact. Neither tries to unilaterally make the relationship more comfortable for himself or herself, because doing so would interfere with their being present to the magic of true conversation.

Soulful romance is held like a fragile flame in the unflinching gaze and steady embrace of the lover as he is revealed to himself and to his beloved in each moment of the dance. As in the unfolding of any sacred mystery, there is no telling what might happen next but there is a faith that whatever it is it will unfold with authenticity and integrity, and whatever happens will deepen the journey of both parties.

James Hollis suggests that both the value and process of soulful romance rest in what he calls *radical conversation,* in which one intends, continuously, to discover more and ever more about oneself and the other. Through such an exchange between two mysteries, one draws nearer to the central mystery of life. Hollis lists three components to such a soul-to-soul encounter:

1) The partners must assume responsibility for their own psychological well-being.

2) They must commit to sharing the world of their own experience without reproaching the Other for past wounds or future expectations. Similarly, they are to endeavor to hear, without feeling defensive, the experience of the Other.

3) They must commit to sustaining such a dialogue over time.... Only radical conversation, the full sharing of what it is like to be me while hearing what it is really like to be you, can fulfill the promise of an intimate relationship. One can only engage in radical conversation if one has taken responsibility for oneself, has some self-awareness, and has the tensile strength to withstand a genuine encounter with the truly Other.

Loving the otherness of the partner is a transcendent event, for one enters the true mystery of relationship in which one is taken to the third place—not you plus me, but we who are more than ourselves with each other.[9]

Radical conversation has emotional, imaginal, sexual, and spiritual dimensions as well as verbal ones. And the conversation is approached not only with skill and intent but also with innocence and wonder. Neither the other nor the self is a fixed thing. The bottom is never reached. One hopes to be forever surprised.

But of course it's not all delight and ease. Far from it. We are constantly discovering how we project our shadow — both its light and dark aspects — onto the other. The dance of soulful romance always includes owning back those projections and transferences. Our relationship will expose all the places we are emotionally blocked, blinded, wounded, caged, protected, or otherwise limited.

Invariably, upon first bumping — or crashing! — into those constricted places, we'll feel fear, anger, hurt, shame, or guilt. Eventually, we learn to recognize these emotions as opportunities to learn about ourselves and sometimes the other. Rather than avoiding these emotions, we dive into them, thereby discovering the holes in our personalities, the places that need attention if we are going to move toward wholeness.

These holes are the wounds we refused to feel earlier and that we avoided by means of our Loyal Soldier's survival strategies. In our romantic relationships, we keep running into these holes because they are the relationship's growing edge. We have the choice either to write off our partner or ourselves or to examine our holes. Healing another layer of our sacred wounds reclaims the promise of our lives.

The candidate for soul initiation learns that soulful romance keeps her in direct communication with the unknown, that it uncovers her sacred wound, that it reveals her shadow, and that it opens the door to ecstasy and union with the beloved of the soul. She learns that sexual love is a spiritual experience as well as a carnal one. She learns to look into her lover's eyes and see not just her friend and sexual partner but also a reflection of her own animus (i.e., the inner man who serves as her guide to soul) and also, perhaps, a reflection of the divine lover.

Our relationship with our deeper selves is the foundation upon which we achieve any notable communion with others. Several people I know have ceremonially married *themselves* or their anima/animus, either before a marriage or a new relationship to another or simply to deepen their relationship to soul. Vows are taken, prayers are offered, rings or other symbols are consecrated, and gifts are given and received. Human witnesses are present or not. The relationship between ego and soul is honored as having a primary position in the individual's life.

The inner marriage is often foretold or enacted in the dreamworld. After many years of inner work, Peter, a psychologist in his fifties, received a dream that has become the most important of his life:

> I am at a social gathering. I don't know anyone. In the dining room, someone hands me a platter of food, saying I should eat. But I don't have a plate. Through a swinging door, the hostess comes in, a very gregarious black woman. She is beautiful, tall, and imposing. She hands me a plate, looks me full in the eye, and asks with enthusiasm, "Do you know a man named Fakir?" I answer no. Continuing to look at me intently, she says, "My psychic told me I was going to meet and marry a man named Fakir."

Peter understood his ego was being asked by his anima to find and recognize the authentic adult man within and to own that man's soul power. His initial association to "Fakir," the name of that authentic man, was a

Hindu ascetic or wonder worker, one who plays a flute and charms the deadly cobra that dances to his music.

> In one sense the fakir is a faker, because he seems to be doing something dangerous when he really isn't. What he does is safe because he knows the nature of the snake and the snake knows his. The snake and the fakir are separate and yet the same, and they dance together. If a fakir did not know his own nature and that of the snake, it would indeed be a deadly game.
>
> The snake is also interchangeable with the black woman of myself. They both represent the feminine energy, the archetypal goddess as well as my anima. She asks to be married to my adult masculine self.
>
> I was not yet ready for the marriage. I had received a proposal but suspected it would be a long engagement. I accepted the name she gave me, Fakir. I committed to discovering her in all of her aspects and to becoming more fully my adult male Fakir self. I knew that unless I came to her with my authentic masculine self, she, like the cobra, would eat me alive.

Several months later, Peter was wandering alone in a Death Valley canyon. He felt called by a distinctive red boulder that emanated a grandfatherly wisdom. The boulder gave him a small heart-shaped stone fired in the depths of the earth and asked him to return that evening. He spent the entire night there, awake, asking for guidance. Before dawn, Grandfather Boulder gave Peter his soul name, Heart Mirror.

Heart mirroring is one of Fakir's powers. Peter has been learning to open his heart to others in a way that creates a mirror in which the other can see the extraordinary beauty of his or her own heart.

After a fourteen-month engagement, Peter, who began his work life as a Roman Catholic priest, created a ceremony of self-ordination that was also a marriage of Fakir and Black Woman. During the ceremony, Black Woman offered Peter food for his soul, Grandfather Boulder gifted him with his heart-mirror rock, and Fakir gave him the necklace he now wears as a reminder of his commitment to his authentic adult male self.

Peter's inner marriage has manifested in his life in a variety of ways. As a psychologist, he is more empathic with his clients while, at the same time, courageously challenging them to encounter their disowned parts. As a vision quest guide, Peter has learned to be more tender and compassionate, like Black Woman, as well as more fierce in his guidance toward the deeper mysteries, like Fakir.

In soulcentric romance there is an essential relationship between our sexual nature and nature in general. The Wanderer explores how the full expression of her sexuality — her full-bodied, uninhibited, healthy sexuality, experienced either alone or with a partner — deepens her membership in the natural world. The more she surrenders to the wild, passionate currents flowing through the world and allows them to move through her, the more the ego-imposed barriers between her and the rest of creation dissolve. Through her sexuality, she comes to experience herself as a force of nature as well as something acted on *by* nature.

In addition to arousal, coitus, and orgasm, sexual desire can guide us to something more: soul. Our sexual nature is the human expression of nature's inherent desire to make ensouled life. If sexuality is understood as that electric longing to physically, emotionally, and spiritually merge with an Other and, through that union, to create something new, then our sexual desire is an agent of soul, which desires to embody in the world a never-before-seen treasure.

Our sexuality, when fully honored, stirs our most creative juices and urges us to cross into the mysteries of nature and psyche. The aroused heart of the lover has inspired many of the most visionary and artistic achievements of humanity. And our sexual desire can nudge us toward unions that further our soul's journey, even when those unions undermine our social or economic standing. When approached soulfully, we ask of our romantic partnerships: How does this relationship provide an opportunity to embody my soul's gift in the world?

When surrendered to, the sexual current carries us beyond the limitations of our everyday ego's view of our selves, our partner, and the world, opening our awareness to the very core of our beings and making possible a soul-to-soul communion. Sexual ecstasy can transport us into union with the sacred Other, whether soul, God, human beloved, or nature. Uninhibited sexual opening powerfully alters consciousness. We are released from the commonplace and pulled down toward soul and the heart of the earth, enhancing our capacity to live our deepest truths.

Our soul's passions are precisely what the earth wants us to embody in the world. And our sexuality, experienced fully, propels those passions as an inherent part of greater nature. In his novels, poems, and essays, D. H. Lawrence explored the sex-nature relationship. He showed how surrender to our deepest sexual nature opens our awareness to the greater whole of nature. Our sexuality is one current in the great streaming of nature. Surrendering to either the streaming of nature or our sexuality lands us in the middle of the other. A soulcentric approach to romance reveres sex as a celebration of the nature both within us and without. The deep ecologist Dolores LaChapelle, in her study of Lawrence's work, concludes that a healthy culture "preserve[s] the sacredness and unity of sex within the whole of nature."[10]

What makes something sacred is its embeddedness in the transpersonal, that which is either soulful or divine. Our sexuality is embedded in nature, which is both soulful and divine. Even when we think of our sexuality in a specific genital sense, we might note that it resides in the part of the body we call the sacrum. Sex is sacred and natural.

Western society, however, isolates sexuality from the whole of nature. Consciously opening to the original sacredness of sex can be challenging, especially in our soul-suppressing, sex-superficializing culture, but nature can show us how.

The contemporary American poet Morgan Farley has lived, as did Lawrence, in northern New Mexico, where she has found herself enraptured by nature.

> she ravishes, this woman
> whose body is the world
> she pierces to the quick
> when you least expect it
>
>   two elk
> move across the road
> in the dusk of a day so rich
> in wonders, you couldn't take
> one more —
>
> the sight of them
> rushes up your limbs like flame
> stirs the roots of your hair —

those angular haunches
that dreamlike ungainly motion
is her signature, final flourish
to the love letter she has been writing on your cells[11]

Cultivating such a sensual engagement with the mysteries of the natural world can open us more fully to the sexual current at our core.

Kerry spent twenty-four hours alone fasting in the depths of a desert canyon with the intention to access the source of her passion and to break her pattern of seeking aliveness and meaning through outer relationships, whether with lovers, mentors, or professional projects. She wandered between the redrock walls of a dry wash. She was overtaken by grief over her lifelong alienation from vitality and joy. The land itself felt dull and distant to her.

Through the long day, her despair alternated with a sense of angry entitlement to her passion. Shouting her longing to the canyon, despair slowly gave way to possibility. Gradually the canyon became luminous.

Then an iridescent hummingbird zoomed into the wash and commenced an astonishing dance of arcs and dives. The bird's ecstatic flight raised Kerry's hope that she, too, might recover her passionate dance.

As hope gathered, she began to see how her alienation from joy, although painful, had provided the necessary safety when she was younger, a protection from embodying her passion in a world that feared and failed to respect a woman's power.

The next day, while wandering again, Kerry was stunned by the beauty of a sculpted sandstone wall.

> I felt its power and the centuries of winds and waters that had carved it. Although solid, the wall held constant flow within it. I was overcome by its mystery and great age, its intricate weathered patterns and the stories they held. Struck by how the wall had been worn by raging waters, I asked it to share with me its essence. I felt the wall answer:
>
> *In the force of the water's surge, I feel both fear and the desire to be entered and overcome, each thrust penetrating more deeply. I surrender to a power that knows how to enter and caress secret chambers. Every impulse to fight is*

overtaken by an exquisite longing to be penetrated to my core, frenzied by the surges that pull me further. What once was terrifying is now my desire. With each surge, I am stripped of my former curves. I feel the wonder at the edge of existence, to be stripped and worn this way, to feel the aliveness of sweet surrender. O waters, overtake me, penetrate me, mold me! Wear me down so I may live in rapture.

Kerry walked away from that place a changed woman. The sensuous wall had awakened her to the passion at her center and her completeness within herself, out of which she knew anything could happen.

Our capacity for soulcentric romance can be deepened through a cultivated relationship to nature. In some villages of the Huichol Indians of Mexico, before a young man or woman is considered ready for marriage, they "wed" a tree for four years. This initiatory rite, undertaken at about age fifteen, rests on the understanding that the chosen tree represents the initiate's own perfect partner, what the Huichols think of as the opposite hidden within. The initiate regularly visits their tree and pours out their longing for "the perfect love." The young woman or man talks to their tree when happy or sad, when scared, angry, or confused; they confide their losses and successes.

Through this relationship with their tree partner, young Huichols enter the depths of their own psyches, with the tree acting as the screen for projected hopes and fears associated with joining with another person. They cultivate this relationship for four years, an appropriate duration for a beginning marriage with the self.

Western people who have visited the Huichols have been astonished to observe the balance and strong presence exhibited by both men and women, whose relational maturity at age twenty would be considered extraordinary by our standards. Their tree-partner practice undoubtedly engenders much of the equanimity observed among the Huichol people. Of course they employ many other spiritual practices, most significantly their age-old peyote ceremonies, which are at the heart of their religious and cosmological universe and continue to inform all of Huichol life.[12]

Soul-oriented counselors in the Western world appreciate the necessity of inner work as a foundation for romance and recommend to their clients practices kindred to the Huichols' tree partner. Coral Cadman, an astrological and spiritual counselor, suggests six-month internal courtships and full-moon love letters to the self as a prerequisite for couples who plan to marry. Coral reminds us that the *coniunctio* — the union of psychic opposites — of which the depth psychologists and alchemists write, has an inner reconciliation at the heart of the alchemical notion of "making gold" from base material. One pair of psychic opposites is the ego and the complementary gender representative within the self — the male ego with the anima or the female ego with the animus. Their union *(coniunctio)* constitutes the inner sacred marriage.

Coral is representative of the therapists, counselors, ceremonialists, and cultural change agents who have developed rituals and other processes to facilitate the withdrawal of romantic projections. The undoing of these projections is a lifelong process.

The art of soulful romance eventually requires us to confront death — in the form of the ego's defeat. The ego imagines its job as keeping things familiar and predictable, and it has a specific wish list for its romantic alliances. Whatever it desires independent of soul, however, is too small to be sustainably engaging. Romance will ask for something different, something greater, something the ego *could* choose to surrender to. There is more joy waiting in that surrender, that death, than the ego alone could ever generate.

Sometimes, by way of betrayal, romance defeats the ego and thereby helps us grow. When a lover betrays us, as unspeakably awful and agonizing as that is, the resulting trauma cracks open the fragile but restrictive shell of the ego, providing the opportunity to embrace greater and more soulful possibilities. We can only be betrayed romantically, moreover, when we have been blind to something about our lover. That blindness not only set us up for betrayal but also blocked the larger story that we must embrace to inherit our destiny.

Each stage of ego growth contains the seeds of its own betrayal. The soul tricks us into setting up the conditions for that betrayal, which forces a deeper self-reflection that might lead to soul encounter and the next stage of growth. The betrayal by a lover can trigger an ego death followed by the birth of a more soul-rooted self and the discovery of the larger story in which we play a soulful part.

But if we are going to redeem our romantic betrayals, we must ultimately practice forgiveness. We must eventually recognize the betrayer as the instrument of the sacred, the person who was capable of wounding us in just the right way necessary for our further initiation.

Romance places us face-to-face with death in one additional way. The deeper the heart-to-heart connection, the keener the awareness of its inevitable loss, whether through death or other forms of parting. We feel death lingering around the edges of our most intimate conversations. We know we will sooner or later be separated. Therefore, rather than pushing it away or stoically accepting it, we might boldly ask death to become a third party to the romance. Death will then walk with us, bringing us into the presence of every moment. When death whispers that this may be our last chance to touch, the fullness of the now expands and offers the possibility of soul-to-soul contact. Death coaches us in love.

As we surrender soulfully to romance, we may find ourselves experiencing the cosmos as suffused with love, as a gigantic love story. Mystics say love is the evolutionary engine of the universe. Even scientists and philosophers are catching on. The alluring attraction between things, the tendency to merge and create new forms, appears to be the nature of the dance in which the universe unfolds.

Psychologist Jean Houston has reviewed some of the great philosophic contributions to this understanding, highlighting the twentieth-century French philosopher and paleontologist Pierre Teilhard de Chardin:

> Consider the prodigious physical and evolutionary studies of Teilhard de Chardin, which conclude that love is the underlying movement and pattern behind the universe: atoms calling each other in search of union so that they begin to constellate and form molecules; molecules in resonance yearning for the Beloved of the next stage so that they can form more complex systems; these systems yearning to form bodies; bodies attuning until they find their partner and produce more bodies with more

complexities. We yearn for the gods and the gods yearn for us, so that as we are becoming enspirited, godded beings, the gods are becoming human. Likewise, earth and nature long for spirit, and spirit longs for nature; out of this longing emerges a deeply physicalized spirituality and a deeply spiritual embodiment. . . . [13]

Consider, too, process philosopher Alfred North Whitehead's philosophy of God as the loving lure of becoming the Divine Lover calling the world into becoming, as any great and true lover does with any beloved.[14]

Mathematical cosmologist Brian Swimme and cultural historian Thomas Berry write of a cosmic allurement that is the bond of all matter and what we humans experience as love.[15] It is this lure between things that drives evolution. Love is what evokes in us the desire to make our own next evolutionary leap as a species.

The longing to find and join with the beloved of the soul is the allurement that pulls us toward becoming fully human. As our relationship to soul develops, our ability to love the world and all its creatures — through caring, appreciation, gratitude, and service — grows accordingly.

Many soulcraft themes are encompassed in the art of romance: sensuality, death, nonduality, ecstasy, soul, and nature. The great ecstatic mystic poet of thirteenth-century Persia, Jelaluddin Rumi, united all of them in a single embrace.

> I would love to kiss you.
> *The price of kissing is your life.*
> Now my loving is running toward my life shouting,
> *What a bargain! Let's buy it.*[16]

> Love is a madman,
> working his wild schemes.
> tearing off his clothes,
> running through the
> mountains, drinking poison,
> and now quietly choosing annihilation.

There are love stories,
and there is obliteration into love.[17]

❦

Out beyond ideas of wrongdoing and rightdoing,
there is a field. I'll meet you there.

When the soul lies down in that grass,
the world is too full to talk about.
Ideas, language, even the phrase *each other*
doesn't make any sense.[18]

❦

The minute I heard my first love story
I started looking for you, not knowing
how blind that was.

Lovers don't finally meet somewhere.
They're in each other all along.[19]

MINDFULNESS PRACTICE

The final two topics of this chapter, mindfulness and our relationship with spirit, are central elements of the upward-reaching, transcendent half of spirituality. Although predominantly ascent-oriented, these two practices are essential to soulcraft in that our individual relationships to consciousness and spirit are core elements of our souls. Taoists remind us there is some yin in anything yang and vice versa. There is spirit in soulcraft and soulfulness in Self-realization.

Mindfulness is calm presence with what is, whether joy or pain, ease or difficulty, boredom or ecstasy, life or death. It is the cultivation of conscious presence in the eternal now, clinging to neither the past nor the future. Mindfulness practice assists us in becoming fully available to life, to other beings, and to all worlds as they exist right now, right here. It is both a specific skill and an all-embracing approach to life, and it is most commonly developed through the meditation disciplines discussed in chapter 5. The great spiritual disciplines of the East — Buddhism, Taoism, and the Yogas of Hinduism — have, for millennia, honed meditation practices for the cultivation of mindfulness. Many traditions of Western prayer and contemplation have done so as well.

How is mindfulness practice relevant to the soulcraft practitioner? First, she must learn to manage attention and cultivate presence. She knows that as she approaches the soul there will be physical, emotional, and spiritual challenges. She will encounter personal demons. There will be beauty so stunning it hurts. In the midst of ecstatic ordeals, she may weaken and find it difficult to stay awake or present. The mind will try to slip away. A vital presence during such intensity may be difficult to sustain, though this is when it's most valuable. Mindfulness practice gradually cultivates courage, wholeheartedness, and the capacity to remain present with all experiences.

For the Wanderer to succeed in her quest to know her soul, she will need to return, continually, to where soul waits for her — in this very moment, in the image emerging from her depths, in the emotion moving through her like liquid heat, in the truth she is making with her own body, in the glistening drop of water caught in the spider's web spun between the blue-green needles of *this* spruce in *this* snowy meadow.

Second, through mindfulness practice, the Wanderer will gain the mental control that helps her stay faithful to her deepest intentions. As she uncovers her soul's desires, she will be more able to remain centered on her intention to embody those desires.

Patti Rieser is a Buddhist meditation teacher and soulcraft practitioner. She understands how challenging it can be to cultivate the presence needed to hear and respond to the soul as it whispers to us. One summer dawn, high in the mountains of Colorado, Patti slipped out of the retreat house to watch the sun rise and to meditate. She found a seat on a boulder at the edge of a meadow. Within moments, she heard a sound behind her and turned to see three deer startlingly close.

> The buck bolts and disappears down the slope into a dark grove of aspens. The two does stand still, looking straight at (or is it through?) me.
> *"Follow us."*
> Thinking symbolically, I take this as an invitation to enter the darkness, my shadow. I remind myself of the necessity to explore what is hidden within. The does take a few steps, then turn to look at me again.
> *"No, really follow us. Get off your butt and follow us."*

But, but...it's wet and muddy in there! I have on my last pair of clean white socks and I'm wearing only sandals. These are the pants I've been trying to keep dry all week.

The deer run down the slope into the aspens.

I follow. Past wildflowers. Over a fence. My socks get wet.

I reach the edge of the slope, much steeper than suspected. How did they get down there? A faint path appears at my feet. I follow, slipping on mud and tripping over tree roots, down toward the stream.

I catch glimpses of the deer by the water. I relax and become more present. A hawk soars above. Scores of birds in the trees. My perspective has changed completely. From here, I see the grove from the roots up. I linger, enjoying the sounds of water and wind.

Patti found delight in the unexpected outcome of her morning meditation. She gathered some insights, too. She writes,

Meditation practice is important. It's where we learn to watch the mind, develop concentration, and open our hearts with wisdom and compassion. We explore the shadows and the light within. However, the skills we develop while sitting on the cushion are valuable only as we can apply them in the rest of our lives. Sometimes meditation can become an escape from life rather than a catalyst for living it more fully. The deer reminded me that it's sometimes important to get off my cushion, to get my socks dirty, and to walk the path that becomes clear only as I look beneath my moving feet. We are here to engage in life, not to merely watch it from where we sit.

Mindfulness practice is essential to the Wanderer in a third way. In quieting the mind, she learns to temporarily withdraw support from the everyday agendas of the personality, all the hopes, worries, desires, fears, dreams, and plans, even the personality's desire to act as agent for soul. Eventually, she experiences what remains of consciousness after the mind comes to rest. She recognizes the Observer or the Witness, that empty, crystalline point of awareness that awaits after the everyday self has fallen away in the fire of consciousness. She experiences her personal filament of consciousness as unified with the consciousness that pervades and constitutes all of creation.

As she opens to the mysterious nature of consciousness, she comes closer to knowing spirit, and so too her soul.

DEVELOPING A PERSONAL RELATIONSHIP WITH SPIRIT

As we explored in chapter 2, the Transcendent Other — what has been called God, Tao, Buddha, Allah, Yahweh, Goddess, Holy Spirit, Wakan Tanka, the Great Mystery — has been understood in as many ways as there are cultural, religious, and spiritual traditions. Each tradition forges its own relationship to spirit. Each individual, in fact, has a unique approach to divinity. As we mature into soulful adulthood, we each discover our particular way to spirit, within or outside the framework of existing traditions. We each come to our own way of praying — or of rejecting prayer — and to our own way of being in conversation with the All That Is.

The Wanderer, as she relinquishes attachment to her adolescent ego, finds herself asking many questions concerning spirit: If I am not simply my body or my ego, then what am I? If I am a spark of consciousness in the universe, what is the larger consciousness of which I am a part? How am I to be in relationship with this greater consciousness?

The Wanderer's goal is to begin a personal conversation with spirit, something more than just listening. What means shall she employ to speak back? What things are acceptable to express? What not? Is it conceivable that spirit can make mistakes? Is it okay to argue with spirit? Is spirit wrathful? All loving? Both? Is spirit male? Female? Both? Neither? Does spirit prefer we refer to it in capitalized words, Spirit, Him, Her, It, God? Or is "goddess" okay with Him? Does spirit have a sense of humor? Does spirit personally need or want something from *us?* Does spirit itself grow, evolve, or transform?

In developing a personal relationship with spirit, perhaps these questions are best answered through conversation *with spirit* as opposed to asking others for their opinion.

Rilke serves as a clear example of one who developed his own relationship with spirit. The poet recognized he had something to offer God, beyond his poetry. He spoke with God in an intimate way, revealing his most vulnerable truths. In the poem below, he is speaking to God at a time of utter confusion as to his deeper identity, and thus full of grief, which was all he had in that moment to offer God:

> I don't have much knowledge yet in grief—
> so this massive darkness makes me feel small.
> *You* be the master: make yourself fierce, break in:
> then your great transforming will happen to me,
> and my great grief cry will happen to you.[20]

Rilke offers God the darkest emotions in his heart. The poet appears to know that despite the unimaginable pain of fully opening to that grief, doing so is the right thing, and may even be healing. He also seems to understand two other things: he may not be able to open deeply to his grief without God's help, and any success would be a gift *to* God. The poet asks God to be fierce and break in despite his suspicion that he will undergo a great transformation. Rilke embodies extraordinary courage in both his request and his offering.

Rilke also wrote of God as being in conversation with us from the very beginning of our existence and as wanting, perhaps needing, certain things from us:

God speaks to each of us as he makes us,
then walks with us silently out of the night.

These are the words we dimly hear:

You, sent out beyond your recall,
go to the limits of your longing.
Embody me.

Flare up like flame
and make big shadows I can move in.

Let everything happen to you: beauty and terror.
Just keep going. No feeling is final.
Don't let yourself lose me.[21]

Rilke believed that God wants to learn and to *know himself*, and that he wants to do so in a way that depends upon us humans. Addressing us, Rilke writes:

Take your practiced powers and stretch them out
until they span the chasm between two
contradictions...for the god
wants to know himself in you.[22]

Rilke seems to be saying that God acquires self-understanding through the *coniunctio*, the reuniting of pairs of psychic opposites, such as light and dark, good and evil, male and female. Spanning such a chasm is a human achievement gained through practice, Rilke suggests. It is not a matter of luck, magic, or grace.

Our relationship with spirit may be limited, at first, by our preexisting fears, desires, and beliefs about God, but if we remain open, we might uncover new possibilities. As the ego grows, dies, grows, and matures, our conception of spirit dies and grows as well.

We must be willing to engage the conversation. How shall we do it? With what ceremonies, metaphors, symbols, religious objects, or texts? Through prayer or song? Which language? Alone or in community? In relation to earth as well as heaven, or only one or the other — or neither? How will the body be involved, if at all? The emotions? Is it okay to dance our prayers? Are we willing to question religious or spiritual authority as to how it is "supposed" to be done? Are we willing to trust our own experience? Are we eligible for a direct relationship with spirit without the intercessory services of priests or priestesses?

Annie Bloom (Hands to the World) has forged a personal relationship with spirit. These are some of the questions she lives:

> What is Spirit? How do I know when I am connected in Spirit, anointed by Spirit, supported by Spirit, ravished by Spirit, challenged by Spirit, directed through Spirit?

Annie conducts her conversation with spirit in part through gratitude for all feelings:

> When I awake in the morning and am aroused by feelings — sorrow over a loss, excitement for what lies ahead, anxiety over life's many trials, disappointment in my lover's response, joy over my child's recent accomplishment — I can become mired in those feelings or I can offer up a prayer of gratitude for them. In doing the latter, I am transported out of myself and become plugged in to something bigger, vaster, all inclusive, something magnanimous and encompassing beyond words. In my moment of prayer, I feel ears listening, a presence of immense magnitude. I arrive at a full recognition of the feeling that is stirring, the realization that is dawning, the sensation that has captured me in that moment.
>
> I have found prayer to be a paradox. I come into intimate contact with my thoughts, feelings, and desires, while at the same time transported beyond myself into something bigger.

As a body-soul therapist, Annie regularly hears stories of anguish and pain, deceit and betrayal, deaths and births, joys and loves found and lost. She has the gift of hearing the song of people's souls and guiding them to pick up the disconnected threads. With love and encouragement, she supports whatever unfolds in the moment. This is her soul's work.

> When I first understood my work, a door opened wide and I became transparent to Spirit. The more I offer myself to my soul's work, the more I feel touched by Spirit. The portal is open to both the descending and ascending spiritualities. The descent uncovers the mysterious, ineffable essence of my being that has been yearning for expression all my life. The ascent is the glory of being held in invisible compassionate arms as I give this gift — my heart — to the world.

What does Spirit want? Annie has learned this:

> Spirit is thirsty for the expansive heart, for a roaring river of love to flood the dry parched plains of human hubris and the strangling constrictions of fear. I can bear my heart being broken and rebroken in order that it might stretch and encompass the holy waters of compassion.
>
> For me, Spirit and Love are one and the same. I live my life listening for Spirit's Love Directives, which demand a spontaneously shifting mix of gentleness, righteous anger, abiding patience, wild vigilance, disciplined freedom, and utter presence. The veil between the sacred and mundane dissolves when I place my hands on another's body-soul, nurturing the intimate connection with self, Other, and Spirit. In doing this work, I feel ignited. The fire consumes my uninspired and confining aspects. Standing in the center of that fire, I merge with the Love that permeates the cosmos.

Are we willing to forge a personal relationship with spirit?

However understood and embodied, a personal relationship to spirit cultivates humility, a sense of meaning and love in the universe, a bone-deep knowing that one is an integral member of an evolving world. We are empowered to create a life founded upon a sense of interconnectedness and interdependence with all.

CHAPTER 13

LIVING AS IF YOUR PLACE IN THE WORLD MATTERED

Everyone has his own specific vocation or mission in life; everyone must carry out a concrete assignment that demands fulfillment. Therein he cannot be replaced, nor can his life be repeated, thus, everyone's task is unique as his specific opportunity to implement it.

— Viktor Frankl

A person's life purpose is nothing more than to rediscover, through the detours of art, or love, or passionate work, those one or two images in the presence of which his heart first opened.

— Albert Camus

If at the soul's core we are images, then we must define life as the actualization over time . . . of that originating seed image, what Michelangelo called the imagine del cuor, *or the image in the heart, and that image—not the time that actualized it—is the primary determinant of your life.*

— James Hillman

What is the point of searching for personal meaning? Discovering what Michelangelo called the "image in the heart" enables us to participate in the unfolding story of creation, to live as if our place in the world matters. And our place in the world does matter. The gift we receive on the underworld journey becomes the gift we offer, in return, to life. The offering of that gift is our contribution to the ongoing evolution of the human species, whose collective awakening is essential for the continued inhabitation, by all species, of Earth.

SOUL INITIATION: EMBRACING YOUR ONE WILD AND PRECIOUS LIFE

"Tell me, what is it you plan to do with your one wild and precious life?" the poet Mary Oliver asks.[1] Soul initiation is the moment an answer wholly claims you. In that moment, you fully accept, deep in your bones, what Viktor Frankl calls your "own specific mission in life." The answer takes the form of an image, an image burned into your soul before birth, an image in the presence of which your heart first opened, as Albert Camus put it. This image, this symbol, is the gods' way of sending you off to life with a destiny and a task, with a template of how to *be* in this lifetime.

This image identifies the essence of your soul powers — your core abilities, knowledge, or values. It shows you the nature of the gift you were born to bring into the world. Before becoming conscious of this image, you might have an inchoate sense of your soul powers, but this will not support you in embodying your soul as effectively as the conscious recovery and embrace of your soul image.

Once you have identified your soul powers, you must learn how to embody those powers within your specific culture, time, and place. Determining an effective form of embodiment and learning the necessary skills are more the ego's tasks than the soul's. The form of embodiment is the *delivery system* for your soul powers. The delivery system may be art, architecture, raising children, psychotherapy, gardening, teaching, politics, healing, poetry, or dance. The soul, however, is not deeply concerned with the nature of the delivery system, it just wants to know its true gift is being embodied beautifully and delivered effectively.

Soul images, in other words, do not correspond to modern job titles. They do not tell you to become an accountant or a chiropractor, an author or a rock star, a psychologist or a wilderness guide. Indeed, there's no requirement that you embody your soul through a job at all. It may be easier and more effective if you don't. And if you do have a conventional job within Western society, your job description probably makes no reference to your soul powers. Think of your job as merely a setting for soul embodiment. Two people may have the same job and embody very different soul qualities. Perhaps they are both psychotherapists, but one has the soul power of recovering buried treasure, while the other's power is to celebrate inner gardens or to help people open their hearts like blossoming flowers.

The soul image might be a single image but, if so, it is a highly symbolic and extraordinarily rich image, like a dream or a painting or a landscape. "One picture is worth ten thousand words," the Chinese say. Resting in that single image is enough inspiration for a lifetime. Unfolding the multiple layers takes time. It is a treasure of great sacredness and value, emanating a type of noetic antiquity and sanctity, your personal Dead Sea Scrolls.

Before soul initiation, the relationship between your ego and soul is like a child and his guardian angel. The soul is present but in the background, and it's doing its best to guide you. You may sense a benevolent being watching over you. But your awareness of that angel tends to be sporadic at best, and you do not yet understand that it is your job, your destiny, to carry out the angel's desires, or even what those desires might be. Soul *encounters* are conscious experiences, by way of images, of that angel and its desires, of the soul as a living entity at your core. Soul *initiation* is the moment you commit yourself to embodying the specific desires of your soul as revealed in one or more soul encounters. Following soul initiation, the relationship between ego and soul is like a prime minister to a king, a handmaiden to a queen, or a worker bee to a queen bee. You accept your true place as the soul's agent.

After your initiation, life cannot and never will be the same. Now you have made "a promise it will kill you to break," as David Whyte puts it. This is both a joyous obligation and a terrible one, for now there is a sacred responsibility to fulfill. No excuses. Following initiation, Whyte writes, it is . . .

...As if your place in the world mattered
 and the world could
neither speak nor hear the fullness of

its own bitter and beautiful cry
 without the deep well
of your body resonating in the echo.

Knowing that it takes only
 that one, terrible
word to make the circle complete,

revelation must be terrible
 knowing you can
never hide your voice again.[2]

Nature-based peoples throughout the world have cultural practices that assist every individual in the village to experience soul encounter. Soul initiation is a developmental milestone that must be passed before one can be said to be fully human, a truly adult member of the culture. A person who does not have a conscious relationship with his or her soul remains forever a child (or what in the West we would call an adolescent).

Malidoma Somé tells us what the Dagara elders say to the boys at the beginning of their ordeals of initiation. His phrases "where you come from," "why you came here," and "who you really are" correspond to that psychic realm, unique to each individual, that I call soul:

> He who does not know where he came from cannot know why he came here and what he came to this place to do. There is no reason to live if you forget what you're here for.... You chose to be born within a particular family because that made your purpose easier to fulfill.... When you do not know who you are, you follow the knowledge of the wind.
> There are details about your identity that you alone will have to discover, and that's why you have come to initiation to go and find out.[3]
> ...a person who lives in denial of who he really is must have a hard time living, because he would have to invent meaning and purpose from the ground up. No one can tell us who we are or how we must live. That knowledge can be found only within.[4]

We humans evolved within the rich tapestry of nature. Every one of us has something unique to contribute to that tapestry. "That knowledge can be found only within." It awaits like buried treasure, a soulful seed of quiescent potential. Some may be here to bring light into the world; others to retrieve the infinite treasures of darkness. Some may celebrate the miracle of existence by inspiring us through song, others through dance, or through the visual arts, or science. Some may be here to give form to a certain range of ideas, or cultural practices, or stories. Others are here to heal people, to understand, to nurture. The answer is waiting in the part of the human psyche that nature herself gave birth to: the human soul.

As we have seen, soul initiation rarely occurs during our first glimpse of soul. Rather, it takes place at the moment our primary life orientation shifts from security and socioeconomic standing to a sacred commitment to soul embodiment. This usually occurs after many soul encounters. Soul initiation celebrates the turning point when our soul's purpose has moved to the central place in our hearts.

After soul initiation, when we awake most mornings our first inspiration for the day, even before we get out of bed, carries us toward our central life purpose. What stirs us most is embodying our souls in the world. This value is far greater than career advancement, or buying a new home, or a tropical vacation. Now the initiated one says, "I know why I took birth this time, what quality is mine to bring into the world, and there's nothing more joyous or fulfilling."

A SENSUOUS CONNECTION WITH MYSTERIOUS IMAGES

The seed of our destiny waits for us in the form of an image. Images are the most direct window into our psyches. But they are not just windows. Psyche *is* image, according to Carl Jung. James Hillman elaborates:

> Man is primarily an imagemaker and our psychic substance consists of images; our being is imaginal being, an existence in imagination. We are indeed such stuff as dreams are made on.
>
> . . . we live in a world that is neither "inner" nor "outer." Rather the psychic world is an imaginal world, just as image is psyche. Paradoxically, at the same time, these images are in us and we live in the midst of them. The psychic world is experienced as inside us and yet it encompasses us with images. I dream and experience my dreams as inside me and yet at the same time I walk around in my dreams and am inside them.

Because our psychic stuff is images, image-making is . . . a royal road to soul-making. The making of soul-stuff calls for dreaming, fantasying, imagining. To live psychologically means to imagine things; to be in touch with soul means to live in sensuous connection with fantasy. To be in soul is to experience the fantasy in all realities and the basic reality of fantasy.[5]

In that the psyche consists of images, that core aspect of psyche, soul, consists of images as well. Images are not only the language of the soul but also the substance of soul. When we behold an image from a dream or a vision or a revelation, we are in direct communion with soul.

The soul has a choice as to how decipherable it will be when it communicates with the ego, but it never means to bewilder. When the soul speaks most powerfully and directly, it speaks metaphorically, in symbolically rich images, because these are what it is made of. These images are mysterious and cryptic to the dayworld personality. "Cryptic" means enigmatic, hidden, occult, but it also refers to an underground chamber. The soul wishes to pull us down into such a chamber.

The soul might say, for example, we are here to carry a sacred chalice, to help others cross the waters, or to weave cocoons. Such images carry immense significance and richness, but are, at first, confounding to the ego. This is as it should be. An image rich enough for a lifetime will not be decoded in a day.

The soul can also speak to us more directly, less cryptically, in ways the ego understands right away. The soul might speak to us in everyday language or in images with easily understood cultural meanings. Maybe the soul will suggest we become a psychotherapist or a poet or a parent, that we build a house with an innovative design and unusual materials, that we study Taoism or sailing, or that we move to the ocean or to Arizona. These more clear-cut communications suggest either a delivery system for our soul powers or a geographical location or a soul-quickening endeavor. Although simpler to understand, these messages don't go nearly as deep, hold as much meaning, or help us grasp the essence of our soul work. Yet they are certainly better than no soul direction at all, and by following their leads, we get the opportunity to go deeper.

If the soul suggests the work of a psychotherapist, for example, it's only because this would be a *setting* for the soul's real work. The soul's interest is not psychotherapy itself. Rather, it might be carrying a sacred chalice, in one case, or weaving cocoons, in another. That's what the soul desires. It might settle for the ego believing its destiny is the practice of psychotherapy per se only if it can't get the ego to understand something deeper, something wilder. The soul will let the ego choose psychotherapy until the ego can understand the soul's desire more directly. (The soul's desire is the same as the ego's destiny). Like a wildcat waiting in the shadows, when the soul spies an opening in the ego's armor that "protects" it from its own destiny, it will pounce.

Learning to understand the soul in its own language is only the first step in deciphering the soul's desires. No matter how deeply the ego manages to go, there's always more; it's bottomless. There's always more to a soul image, and there's another image below that one that embraces more mystery.

You would do well, then, to become familiar with the soul's imagery language so to understand it more directly and accurately.

The underworld journey to soul is like descending into an unfathomably deep, sheer-walled canyon — Soul Canyon — consisting of layer upon layer of rock bands. The layers near the top, closest to the middleworld, tell you things like "become a psychotherapist." Below that are layers more mysterious, with messages like "move to the Four Corners" or "fall in love with the woman in the snakeskin boots" or "build your house *here*." The yet deeper and older layers say those cryptic things like "help others cross the waters."

The deeper you go, the more puzzling the soul's meaning, but the more useful and transforming the message once you do understand it. Psychologist Peter G. Ossorio says it this way: "The harder the data, the less the significance." The more mystifying the soul image, the more profound and encompassing the meaning. The more concrete the soul message, the further you are from the roots of soul, but the more immediately and easily applicable it is. So there are advantages — different kinds — in both enigmatic and concrete conversations with soul.

When you encounter the soul's more mysterious images, you must live with them for weeks, months, or years (maybe lifetimes!) before you can reach a full understanding. To live with these soul images means to say yes to them, to draw them, paint them, puzzle with them, converse with friends about them, create ceremonies around them, sing them, compose poems from them and for them. And, most of all, it means to make real life decisions, big and small, based on those images, as if they are sacred to you.

(They are.) You must ask yourself as often as possible, "What would I do in this situation right now, in the middle of this day, were I to act as the person with this numinous image alive in my soul, at the center of my heart?"

The way you confirm the truth of a soul image is not by having it blessed by an authority but only by living it. You receive affirmations or disconfirmations as the world responds to your embodiment of the image. If you deeply understand the image, you will receive a giant Yes!

By living the image, not only is its sacredness confirmed but also its full meaning is gradually revealed through the conversation that unfolds between you and the world. Most people learn about their soul image one clue at a time. The important thing is to say yes to each clue and thereby wend your way to the next clue until a pattern emerges, a picture, until you come to grasp the meaning of your soul image.

The reason the soul, at its deeper levels, doesn't tell you how to embody or live its images is simply because it is wild. A wild thing — a mountain lion, a tornado, an undammed river, a soul — doesn't want you to treat it like something from your everyday village world. Wild things prefer to remain wild. To honor a wild thing, converse with it on its terms, in its language, on its territory. Its gift might be to make you wilder.

Imagine that the soul doesn't really know how you ought best live it. After all, how you manifest soul in your everyday life will depend in large measure upon your historical epoch and culture, where you live and what materials are available to you, and what human language you speak. Forms of embodiment, language, and cultural knowledge are the ego's domain, not the soul's. The soul reveals to the ego the deep nature of its gift, but it is the ego's task to fashion ways to give it.

The healthy ego's initiatory task is to journey into the wild, allow itself to be transformed by the wild, and bring its shape-shifted self back to the village as a gift to others. The ego's soul gift to society is also a gift to the entire more-than-human world because it supports the human community in maintaining a balanced relationship with the rest of nature. Such a society coevolves with terrestrial nature rather than threatening the very fabric of the world, as our egocentric societies currently do. When we live as if nature and soul really matter, the wild is constantly gifting the village (with food, shelter, medicine, rain, flowers, children, sunsets, an inspirational diversity of species, hope, mystery, and death) and the village is constantly gifting the wild (with embodied human souls, ceremony, song, gratitude, grief, prayer, praise, tears, love, love-making, children, celebration). This is what healthy cultural life is like: sacred reciprocity with nature, with the wild.

WRAPPED IN SACRED CLOTH

In the midst of a soul encounter, the image you behold may or may not be visual. It may be felt like a caress, heard like the voice of a goddess, tasted like ambrosia, or caught like perfume on a wisp of scented breeze. It may be embodied in an exquisite gesture of your own that astonishes you, or captured in an action that, you realize in the moment of making it, encapsulates the mystery of your life.

Soul images are a far cry from everyday images such as those that occur in daydreams or reveries. But how exactly do you make the distinction?

First, soul images are often first perceived during states of non-ordinary consciousness — in dreams, deep imagery, trance, fasting, sexual ecstasy, illness, coma, or drug-induced states. Non-ordinary states allow the conscious self to perceive what is ordinarily foreign and perhaps threatening to the everyday mind. You know an image is a soul image by how deeply it moves you, by feeling that it resides in the center of your heart or soul, that you are here in this lifetime to faithfully embody that image. The image is uncanny, eerie, or mysterious. It shakes your whole world to its foundations. A soul image is numinous, as if wrapped in sacred cloth, as if God were near.

Synchronicities often accompany soul images. You hear the mysterious voice and the rainbow appears in the same moment. The revelatory and life-shifting symbol appears in a dream and then, in the next moment, the thunderclap, waking you and burning the symbol into your consciousness forever. The butterfly touches your face and says your name in the same moment. The trout becomes a glimmering girl and calls you by your true name.

A soul image evokes powerful emotions of hope, desire, gratitude, and joy. There is often also grief — for the years you lived without awareness of that image, and for the poignancy and preciousness of the world's yearning that gave birth to you and that image. And there is always fear, due to the immensity of what you have been called to do.

When it's a soul image, there's a boundless desire to embody it and an equal terror to do so, knowing how utterly altered your life will be. You feel both blessed by the glimmering gift and burdened by the daunting task of living it. A soul image is experienced as a violation, a ravishment by the sacred that trounces all your prior beliefs about who you are and why you are here. Yet this image gives you faith to risk extending yourself into the world, to go out on a limb, to be radical and wild, to live for something greater than your individual life.

Another distinguishing feature is that although received by individual people soul images ultimately serve a whole community — and you sense this when you first encounter the image. You know that you will carry to others the gift that springs from this image.

Most often there is great joy during soul encounter. In an instant, you know beyond doubt that your life can be aligned with the life of the planet. You know you can contribute to the unfolding of the human drama, to the evolution of human consciousness. You feel aligned with a great story, one that will go on long after the ego has departed.

The encounter with a soul image is ecstatic, beyond reason and the ego's control. It is rapturous, filled with overpowering emotion. You feel lifted out of yourself. There is numinosity, a sense of being in the presence of the sacred or holy. You become receptive to that sacredness not through the thinking mind but by some amalgamation of image, feeling, and sensing. You recognize that you are in the presence of a greater being, but one with whom you have a unique relationship. It is more you than your everyday self.

Finally, you know an image derives from the soul by the relationship between the image and numinous events preceding the soul encounter, as well as those that occur after. A soul image permits extraordinary moments from your past to at last fall into place and shine with a never before suspected meaning. And there will be events following your soul encounter that confirm and amplify its meanings.

Ultimately, a soul image is confirmed as such by the joy of living it.

Pablo Neruda describes an encounter with his soul, the moment he became a poet, possibly the moment of soul initiation:

> ... And something ignited in my soul,
> fever or unremembered wings,
> and I went my own way,
> deciphering
> that burning fire

and I wrote the first bare line,
bare, without substance, pure
foolishness,
pure wisdom
of one who knows nothing,
and suddenly I saw
the heavens
unfastened
and open.[6]

Those mysterious wings and that burning fire changed Neruda's life. He embodied those images in his first lines of poetry, and the world responded with glory.

Soul encounter is rare and difficult to bring about. We might wonder: If soul is the most integral and vital part of the psyche, why weren't its images obvious to us when we were young? Why does the soul at first appear so foreign to the conscious mind? Why is it difficult and dangerous, even in the healthiest of environments, to be initiated into the life of the soul? Why is it, in our society, that few people encounter soul without a life-threatening condition? Why is it, in Malidoma Somé's tribe, some boys do not physically survive the initiatory ordeals?

THE MYSTERY AND DIFFICULTIES OF COMING TO KNOW THE SOUL

Unlike other sentient beings, our human psyches are divided into two components: a conscious self (the ego) and a personal unconscious, the latter being much more extensive. This division is the source of the difficulty of coming to know our souls.

Our conscious understanding of self, especially when we are young, is limited. Self-understanding grows and develops as our bodies do, gradually. At birth, there's no consciousness of a self at all. The ego acquires its initial shape during the first four years. As it matures, the ego is capable of understanding more of the total psyche of which it is one small part.

The soul is one aspect of the psyche rarely grasped by young people, no matter how healthy the individual and the cultural environment. It takes a rather mature ego to do this. The young ego, primarily a product of culture and language, is mystified by soul, which is precultural and nonlinguistic.

Furthermore, our soul qualities are usually not honored or encouraged by our families, partly because they can't see those qualities or are afraid of them, and partly because of their own ideas of who we ought to be. Parents and siblings may in fact actively suppress our soul qualities.

In our youth, our self-image is constrained by the traits or roles favored by friends, teachers, and parents, and we attempt to fit ourselves into an acceptable role — a tough guy or a sweetheart, a leader or a follower, a thinker or an athlete.

Our parents have the most influence on our self-concept, and often family traditions and desires are at odds with the direction of the soul. My parents may want me to be a scholar, a priest, or a comedian, but my destiny is not likely reducible to *any* cultural categories.

Even the healthiest families, those that create a safe and loving environment of self-discovery, unconsciously communicate to the child a host of (mostly positive) messages as to who he is and even some (mostly loving) expectations as to who he should become. This is as it must be; we treat others as having a complementary place in the ongoing drama of our own lives. The unhealthy family actively suppresses and discourages any personal characteristics outside a narrowly defined and codependent range. In either case, the child's plight is like that of the cygnet in the fairy tale. Raised by ducks, he thinks he is one. He just can't understand why he's so ugly. It will be awhile before he discovers his true essence, his beauty and destiny as a swan.

In essence, before entering the second cocoon, we tend to become the people others treat us as being. We become human, first, by apprenticing to our family and culture, and only later do we apprentice to our souls.

A second reason soul qualities are not obvious to the young is that the soul speaks a different language. The child's society may speak English or French or Swahili, but the soul, as we have seen, speaks in emotionally-laden, dreamlike images. The young ego is not equipped to translate the soul's language into its own. Indeed, this is challenging for a mature adult, even one who is poetically minded and versed in the language of symbols.

A third reason is that the young ego is too busy with other important things. It has the full-time, critical job of figuring out how to create a good place for itself in the very context into which it was born — its culture and language. This is a central task of childhood and adolescence.

Our human form of self-consciousness is the greatest obstacle to soul encounter, even though it may be our most defining and significant human attribute. What distinguishes us as humans is that we know that we know — *Homo sapiens sapiens,* "twice wise" primates. Without egos, we would not have the capacity to be self-reflexively conscious of anything (a capacity, for example, an infant lacks), but we *would* be living the lives of our souls as fully and beautifully as do unself-conscious beings, like infants, deer, or blossoms. Not having egos, there is nothing to get in the way of their embodiment of soul. Our form of consciousness is both our greatest blessing and our greatest curse. It may render soul discovery and embodiment difficult, but then, without it, we wouldn't be able to consciously appreciate and celebrate the miracle and mysteries of existence.

A STORM IS COMING: UNAVOIDABLE TRAUMA ON THE WAY TO SOUL INITIATION

In an egocentric environment, soul encounter is exceedingly rare, regardless of the maturity of mind or body. Even in a soulcentric setting, the initial encounter with soul requires extraordinary circumstances. This is not just any sort of ecstatic or transpersonal experience; many non-ordinary states are not soul encounters. We're not talking about a mere glimpse of depth or sacredness in everyday life. A soul encounter is a profound restructuring of self-concept, of who and what we experience ourselves and the world to be. Such a radical shift doesn't happen through everyday learning, working, playing, and loving. It's not likely to happen in a weekend workshop. It is rare even in extended and intensive psychotherapy.

The ego fears an initial encounter with soul, and understandably so: on the way to soul initiation, it will have to surrender everything it has come to believe about itself. Initiation is a process "costing not less than everything," to use T. S. Eliot's phrase.[7] Our ego's job, after all, is to draw the line between what is possible for us personally and what isn't. To undergo a radical change in self-concept, there must be a shift in our understanding of what is possible. This can occur only when we encounter what previously had been literally unthinkable. Such an encounter requires a non-ordinary state of awareness.

Even when we *want* to alter our self-concept, it is exceedingly difficult because we must disengage from something — our very identity — that is the bedrock of everyday functioning. It's like trying to pull the rug from beneath ourselves. Even if depressed and unfulfilled, at least we know where we stand and how to operate. We're likely to wonder: If I surrender my familiar identity, where is the guarantee that I'll find something that works better, or as well, or even at all? What if the deeper identity I discover requires me to quit my (well-paying) job? Or leave my family? Or give up familiar comforts?

The world-rattling nature of soul encounter provokes such an extreme ego crisis that the encounter can hardly occur except during a profound trauma. In fact, this is exactly what we find: soul encounters, especially our first, occur during extraordinary upheavals, all of which involve psychological stress. There are only a few varieties of such upheavals[8]:

- Highly traumatic personal crises, including
  — major physical trauma (injury or illness), often involving a near-death experience
  — loss of a well-established primary relationship (through death or separation)
  — an extreme life event that impels us to reexamine everything (these are often considered calamitous, such as losing a job or the house burning down, but they can also be ostensibly propitious events such as winning the lottery or falling in love)
  — spiritual crisis (including spiritual rebirth)
  — a dark night of the soul
  — world-shattering paranormal experiences that significantly and irrevocably change our understanding of what the world is and how it works (for example, an apparition, an out-of-body experience, a powerfully prophetic dream, or a first or unexpected experience of telepathy or psychokinesis)
- Genuine and extended wanderings or pilgrimages in which we sever contact with and journey far from home in both the physical and psychological senses (e.g., a year in the desert or in a truly foreign culture)
- Rites of soul encounter: ceremonial processes specifically designed to temporarily displace our ego-bound identity to allow for the encounter with soul.

Notice that the first set of six possibilities, the personal traumas, are almost always accidental and unwanted. In an egocentric society — in which soul has been ignored, suppressed, or patronized — these trials and adversities may be the only available opportunities for profound soul encounter.

The last two possibilities, wanderings and rites of soul encounter, are experiences a soulcentric community faithfully provides its young people when they are ready. And they are what modern Western communities could begin again to offer people ready to leave their first adulthood.

All eight possibilities are traumatic, but none, except for the first, are necessarily injurious or physically painful. The required trauma is to the adolescent-ego consciousness, not necessarily to the body. Indeed, once the ego surrenders, the experience can be rapturous, even when there is some physical discomfort.

Although the trauma triggering a soul encounter always has a psychological dimension (the shock to the ego), it may originate in a variety of ways — in a physical event (such as an injury or the ingestion of a mind-altering substance), in a psychological event (such as a paranormal experience, a spiritual crisis, or the loss of a loved one), or in a combination of the two (such as a rite that involves fasting, prolonged wakefulness, and other mind-altering practices).

The induction of soul encounter, through whatever route, is unpredictable in its results, potentially dangerous, and daunting, as well as necessary for entry into authentic adulthood. Rilke reminds us in "The Man Watching" that in order to grow spiritually there are times we must allow ourselves to be defeated by something greater, by something "extraordinary and eternal."

What we choose to fight is so tiny!
What fights with us is so great!
If only we would let ourselves be dominated
as things do by some immense storm,
we would become strong too, and not need names.

When we win it's with small things,
and the triumph itself makes us small.
What is extraordinary and eternal
does not want to be bent by us.
I mean the Angel who appeared
to the wrestlers of the Old Testament:
when the wrestlers' sinews
grew long like metal strings,

he felt them under his fingers
like chords of deep music.

Whoever was beaten by this Angel
(who often simply declined the fight)
went away proud and strengthened
and great from that harsh hand,
that kneaded him as if to change his shape.
Winning does not tempt that man.
This is how he grows: by being defeated, decisively,
by constantly greater beings.[9]

The necessity of trauma and ego defeat to trigger soul encounter is often overlooked. A life of soul is not likely to be initiated in the routine course of an everyday American life. More often than not, entry into the life of the soul demands a steep price.

Lauren was a forty-year-old journalist and soccer mom from suburban Maryland when she experienced her first soul encounter. Triggered by trauma, her encounter took place six years after her first vision quest, at a moment when she least expected it, and through previously unthinkable circumstances.

She was hiking alone in a sandstone canyon in southwestern Colorado during a weeklong soulcraft intensive. Kiva Canyon was home to the ancestral Pueblo people until the middle of the thirteenth century, when they inexplicably abandoned their cliff dwellings and kivas (underground religious chambers). Lauren was expecting a casual stroll through scenic country. Her mood was light, almost giddy.

An hour into her hike, Lauren began to have a physical-emotional feeling she could not identify, a feeling that grew quickly and pulled her into an uneasy, disoriented state. Frightened, she found a place to sit by the deteriorating adobe walls of a cliff dwelling surrounded by sculpted red sandstone cliffs. The rocks seemed to emit an outlandish light that amplified Lauren's fear and bewilderment. She looked up at the ancient dwelling and sensed a tumultuous wave of sorrow surging and thundering toward her. The wave slammed into her and almost bowled her over. She began wailing. She thought her heart would burst from an unknown grief.

And then, sitting amidst eerily glowing rocks, Lauren had a vision of the ancestral people of that canyon suffering an unimaginable loss of life and home. She felt the presence of children in anguish and heard the cries of mothers. She wept for what seemed like hours.

In the midst of her tears, she heard a voice call her by a name that stunned her with both disbelief and recognition. In that moment, she did not know — could not know — all her name implied, but she knew it to be a doorway to her soul work.

In early evening, Lauren emerged from Kiva Canyon shaken, exhausted, disheveled, and no longer able to define herself as merely a journalist and mother. Her world was radically shifting, and simplifying.

On her flight home, she wondered how she could explain or even describe her experience to her husband and children. She pondered, as do all who have had soul encounters, how she would live up to it. On the one hand, she felt unworthy, and on the other, she feared the eventual sacrifices.

Over the next few weeks, as her canyon experience worked its way through her, Lauren came to understand that her destiny was to grieve, to grieve for the living and those long departed, and to help people enter their own grief directly, lamenting what had been locked in their hearts. These tasks felt overwhelming to her, especially in the Western world with hundreds of generations of unfelt and ungrieved losses.

Lauren had experienced what previously had been unthinkable, a terrifying vision of human suffering and a grief greater than she could have imagined. And all this seemingly out of nowhere. Why did this happen when it did? What triggered this psychological trauma? She was neither fasting nor enacting a ceremony nor hoping for a revelation.

The chimerical atmosphere, technicolor geology, and human history of Kiva Canyon are likely to have been significant factors. Also, her vision quest and subsequent years of soulcraft practice had loosened Lauren's grip on her old story. But the primary factor, I believe, was Lauren's vulnerability to the deep, soul-rooted grief waiting inside her. The eruption of that emotion was not itself the soul encounter but served as the trauma that shifted her awareness, opening her to the vision and the voice uttering her name.

Three months later, following a period of psychological preparation, Lauren enacted a self-designed naming ceremony, witnessed by a circle of twenty people. She claimed her spiritual name, assented to her destiny, and forged a pact with soul.

A ceremony like this reinforces and quickens a person's soul path. There is no turning back, the stakes get bigger, the fulfillment deeper, and the opportunities for soulful growth more frequent and significant.

During Lauren's ceremony, Annie Bloom, in her role as elder, addressed the group:

> The name Lauren received from the canyon is her inner name, her secret name, and is mysterious — to her as well as to us.
>
> There is no way Lauren can fully know what her name asks of her. In listening to her story, we could hear how she is sewing together the clues and signs and all the elements of her history, which collectively give meaning to her name. When Lauren emerged from the canyon that day, she was visibly shaken, and still is. An initiatory experience shakes us to the core because intuitively we know we have crossed over. Our whole inner orientation shifts. Before initiation, our life questions have the flavor of, "What does this situation or relationship have in it for me?" Following initiation, the question becomes, "How can I best give of myself in this place, to these people, in this time?" Everything you do and encounter is seen with the eyes of someone looking to give to the world.
>
> When I listened to Lauren's story, I thought to myself, "Oh my god, what a burden to grieve for others!" But I also know the deep joy this has for Lauren. I hear the heart point of longing — her soul expressing the gift of tears in a song that transmutes and liberates the grief trapped inside us both now and from long ago.
>
> When this shift happens — from an ego-motivated orientation to a soul-motivated one — it is both burden and joy. The burden is the "promise that will kill us to break"[10] and the joy arises from expressing again and again the gift that is ours alone to give.

Once we make a commitment to our soul path, the soul assists us in following through, sometimes with additional trauma. Following her ceremony, Lauren knew that major life changes were needed to inherit her destiny, but she procrastinated. Five months later, she returned to the Kiva Canyon area for a training program. On the second afternoon, when she had the opportunity to return to the canyon to take the next step with her underworld work, she chose instead to take a break. She rented a horse and rode into the backcountry.

Lauren had ridden many times before, and that day she rode one of the tamest horses on the ranch. But, several miles into the ride, Lauren's horse spooked for no apparent reason and sent Lauren flying. She landed badly and shattered her right leg. Max, her riding companion, galloped for help. It was getting late, it was November, and soon it would be dark and cold.

Through shock, blood loss, and hypothermia, Lauren came close to death. But, as she lay on the rocks for hours, her fear and panic gradually subsided and she felt an unaccountable peace and stillness. She knew her accident was no accident. A profound acceptance came over her and she gave up the illusion of control for the first time in her life.

Finally, well after dark, help arrived.

This second trauma catalyzed Lauren's transformation. She phased out her journalism work and, with her family, left the suburbs and moved to a wilder place more resonant with the rhythms of the heart and nature.

She devised several ways to embody her soul power. She learned to help people explore and feel the source of their deepest sorrow. People who are in grief — often ancestral grief — find her through word of mouth or chance encounter. Her grief radar, enabling her to sense wounds in people, places, animals, gets stronger every day. Lauren travels to wounded places on the earth to grieve what has been lost there. She guides vision quests that open hearts to people's deepest laments. And she is creating a program to help others take personal grief to the next level: a doorway to soul encounter and spiritual growth.

Lauren's story illustrates how soul encounter and soul initiation can be triggered by psychological trauma such as a paranormal experience and by physical trauma such as a broken bone. These two events sent Lauren into a spiritual crisis resolvable only by a profound restructuring of self-concept and lifestyle and by saying yes to her soul through embodied action. She began to live as if her place in the world mattered.

DEMONS AND GUIDES

The gateway to the underworld of soul is guarded by demons, aspects of your own psyche whose purpose is to keep you from losing social acceptance at too tender an age. These are your Loyal Soldiers, often projected onto outer others. They attempt to protect you from the journey by means of forebodings and threats of disaster if you were to cross the underworld threshold: fear of death or insanity, anxiety over the loss of friends or social standing, terror of losing a marriage or career. Or they might get you to project your fears onto a teacher, guide, fellow journeyer, spouse, neighbor, snakes, or bears so you can find an excuse to stay home. Or you might get sick or obsessed with a minor ailment, or generate a business calamity, a sudden depression, a series of lurid nightmares, or some other "need" for psychotherapy in lieu of the underworld journey. Our demons take many everyday forms.

If you are fortunate, you'll have human guides to help you outwit or win over these demons, but, in a fundamental sense, you journey alone. No one can protect you on the underworld journey. You must undergo your ordeals by your own wits, feeling, and imagination.

Yet you might find help from within. The inner guide is your companion on the journey to soul and will assist you in your encounters with demons and obstacles at the threshold and beyond. Jung spoke of the anima and animus as inner guides. But the inner guide appears in diverse cultural images, everything from faerie princesses to jinns, from good witches to bad, from hairy beasts to slithering serpents, from Hermes to Yoda. Sometimes the inner guide takes a corporeal form in the material world, like a butterfly, a Zen monk, or a snake.

You may at first fail to recognize the guide because it emerges from the underworld of the psyche and may seem fearful or abhorrent to your ego. But this dark one serves as both the herald of the adventure and your guide on the journey. Joseph Campbell explained that in the manifold myths of the world the guide appears in unexpected forms. The frog, for example, is a popular motif:

> The frog, the little dragon, is the nursery counterpart of the underworld serpent whose head supports the earth and who represents the life-progenitive, demiurgic powers of the abyss.... The serpent, the rejected one, is the representative of that unconscious deep...wherein are hoarded all of the rejected, unadmitted, unrecognized, unknown, or undeveloped factors, laws, and elements of existence.[11]

In preparing for soul initiation, you would do well to cultivate a relationship with at least one guide to the underworld. Most often these guides are accessed through the window of imagination — during deep imagery journeys — and commonly take the form of animal totems.[12] Other times, you will meet your guide in a dream; or in the flesh in nature; or during those waking dreamtime experiences that lie somewhere between the everyday middleworld and the imaginal underworld, a world neither inner nor outer.

YOUR JOURNEY INTO THE WILD

With or without guides, it is natural to be frightened by the soul and its desires. In addition to the prospect of losing everything, you might question your ability to succeed at the soul's agenda. It seems overwhelming, and too wild, too removed from conventional life. And so you resist the soul and tremble in the face of its hungers.

Sometimes you forget that the one life you can call your own is *not* primarily the personality's.

But the personality must be well prepared for both the underworld journey and the path of soul work that follows it. You must prepare as you would for a wilderness expedition and remember that the challenges of the journey are part of its draw. The inherent fear and danger afford increased aliveness, the exhilaration of dwelling on the edge where you make discoveries that galvanize and ignite. This is the soul's path, a journey into the wild with the promise of renewal as well as the possibility of decisive defeat. *Both* will grow you.

On my own soul journey, it feels as if I — the ego — am not in control. This is correct. I know I'm in good hands, but it can be terrifying nonetheless. Here is a recent dream:

> I am on a sailboat on the ocean with two other men. I am neither the skipper nor the first mate. I'm the "third," barely more than a passenger. A big wind comes up, filling our sails. We pick up speed and the boat leans heavily to the left. I begin to move right to keep the boat from leaning too far. The skipper yells No, not yet! I'm scared. Soon we have taken on so much speed that we lift off the water. We are flying, sailing in the air. I am gaining confidence in the captain's ability but am still frightened. We are several hundred feet up and crossing over land, an island. It looks like we are going to land in water, just off the beach. We are approaching through a gap in a line of palms. The wind carries us.

The soul is capable of things the personality at one time couldn't even dream of. Sometimes the personality is barely more than a passenger on the soul journey of your life. The soul will reveal what to do at each step. You might never feel completely prepared, but you must consent to the journey when ready enough.

The journey is into the wilderness of your greater life. That wilderness is your soul. To merge with your destiny, you must locate, liberate, and live what is truly wild.

The soul is here to live its joy. The uninitiated ego is here to keep things familiar, safe, and predictable. Which path will you choose?

THE CONVERSATION: LIVING YOUR SOUL GIFTS

If you choose soul, remember that your first soul encounter provides only your opening sentence of a new conversation between you and the world. You must now speak your vision into the world, not knowing how the world will respond. But the world *will* respond. And, no matter how it does, the conversation is off and running.

If you plan on waiting until you more completely understand your soul's desire before you actively engage the conversation, you won't discover much. The conversation itself is the process through which the soul's desire is further revealed.

It may turn out that the conversation has been taking place for a while outside your awareness. Or maybe it has been like barely heard fragments of speech in a half-understood language. But after your first soul encounter, you find yourself sitting face-to-face with soul, gazing into each other's eyes, speaking the same language.

Now you must learn to act on what soul has revealed to you. Speaking your half of the conversation doesn't mean merely telling someone about your vision or your soul image. That might even be a bad idea. You're likely to be misunderstood and very few people — maybe no one — will be able to grasp the luminous vitality the vision holds for you. Talking about your experience may or may not be like casting pearls before swine, but it is often a way of dishonoring what you received. To talk about your vision before you have solidly enacted it may undermine your resolve to make it real. Others might respond with derision or envy. That's bad enough; worse is being killed politely by a half smile, a "how nice," or a change in topic.

You might also trick yourself into believing that recounting your vision is enough and that you can now close that chapter, safely lay that vision to rest in the attic or allow it to gather dust on an altar. A part of you is insecure about how this vision thing is going to shake down, and that part wants the mere telling to be enough.

Later, after you have walked some miles in the shoes of your vision, it might serve you and your vision to speak of it to others. Or maybe not.

The greatest need now is for you to perform your vision in the world so that your people witness you carrying your gift, even though they probably won't know where or how you got it. Through that enactment, you will be in conversation not only with your community but also with both your own soul and the wider world.

Integrating the experience of soul is a huge challenge. Despite their love for you, your friends and family are likely to resist your life alterations because your changes will force unwanted changes on *them*. It doesn't matter how sure you are that these shifts are best for everyone. Even if you are right, you'll probably be resisted. Stay on your soul path no matter what while doing your best to honor your loved ones' emotions and genuine needs. Let them know, in general terms, why you are making the choices you are.

Sometime after your return from the underworld, you may fall into a dark period of spiritual uncertainty and social confusion. You might doubt the value or validity of your soul image. What's more, you might re-encounter the life patterns you thought you had stepped beyond, the addictions or self-defeating behaviors. The details may look different, but familiar themes appear. This is an opportunity to remember your encounter with soul and to recommit yourself to living that promise. If you ignore the soul's call to embody your gift, you might suffer more than you did before your encounter. Draw on your inner resources and on outer guides and allies. Deepen your conversation with soul.

If your old story with its familiar demon reappears, treat it as an ally that has come at just the right time to remind you of the vows you made, the larger story you were shown, the name you were called, or the voice you recognized as your own. By taking *any* action grounded in these experiences, no matter how small, you begin to live your new story into the world.

Remind yourself that the underworld journey was not supposed to fix the life you were living beforehand. It is actually designed to disrupt that life, to ruin it. The path of soul requires you to root yourself in your unique and authentic life. Your old life was not big enough to encompass the magnitude or the subtlety of the soul's desires.

Catch yourself when your Loyal Soldier advises social acceptance over soulful authenticity. Regularly ask yourself, "What did my soul image reveal about my deeper identity? Who did I discover myself to be? What gift was given me to carry to others? What soul name did I claim — or claimed me?" Once you are clear again, ask yourself the following key questions, and ask often: "What would that person — the person I discovered myself to be — do in my current circumstances? What decision would he/she make right now, what action would he/she take?" After soul encounter, make as many of your choices as possible from that place. These actions alone will sink your roots into the rich soils of soul.

At first it might be difficult to identify appropriate actions to take in the middleworld. Stay with it. Call on your deepest creativity. Use your emotions, intuition, dreams, and deep imagery. Identify soul-rooted actions through soulcraft practices such as dialoguing with nature, council, ceremony, befriending the dark, the art of being lost, journal work, signs and omens, and your own poetry. You may at first feel tentative about the ideas that arise, but as you begin to take action on them, you will become clearer. When you take one step toward soul, soul takes several toward you.

Clinging to the memory of soul encounter or trying to recapture the feeling of that moment or merely praying for help — anything not action-based — will fail to help you embody what you received. Before long, even the living memories will fade. You must create ways to act on what you received. A vision without a task is just a dream.

Create projects, practices, one-step actions, and ceremonies rooted in what the soul has revealed. *Projects* are usually most powerful. A project is a course of action with many steps, each step being different from the last. Building a house, creating a work of art, founding an organization, composing a symphony, or learning the art of underworld guiding are examples of projects. But what makes a project a soul project is that it is a way to manifest what the soul has revealed as your gift. *Soul projects are delivery systems for soul powers.*

Most soul projects take a long time to complete, at least a year. The best ones take a lifetime or more. If you've identified one or more of your soul powers, then your foremost soul project is the work of manifesting those powers. All your other soul projects will be special cases of that one. It is best to have two or more specific projects at any given time.

A *practice* is something you do more or less the same way every time. Like a meditation or yoga practice. Or weekly wanderings in a favorite wilderness place. Or regular conversations with other-than-human beings. Or introducing yourself to people in terms of your soul work. Or full-moon rituals. Or telling your children every day that you love them. But remember that a practice is a soul practice only if it is a way to live what you received during a soul encounter. Even though they might not embody soul as effectively as projects, practices are of great value in helping you remain firmly on your soul path.

One-step actions are activities completed in one fell swoop. Examples of potentially soul-rooted one-step actions are forgiving an old offense or asking for forgiveness, quitting a soul-stifling job or saying yes to one that may be risky (physically, socially, or economically) but allows your soul to sing, proposing marriage or declaring a divorce, forgiving a debt or paying one.

Finally, *ceremonies* can effectively empower your soul path, specifically self-designed ceremonies for the purpose of saying yes to your soul, employing the symbols the soul itself has used. If it feels appropriate, you can include other people as participants or witnesses. These ceremonies facilitate your soul path by directly engaging your conversation with soul.

Whatever combination of methods you use to say yes, remember that your soul image lives as a fiery and vital energy within you and it longs for expression. If you do not live it, it may turn inward and manifest as depression, anger, lethargy, or other psychological or physical symptoms. Your soul will not be satisfied with mere thoughts and prayers. Soul is your essential life energy and you must move with it.

You must become willing to risk your ego significance for something greater. This is a lifelong journey, calling for the courage and faith to continually act on what you received during your encounters with soul.

HAZARDOUS JOURNEYS: POLAR EXPEDITIONS, WAR, AND SOUL INITIATION

Ernest Shackleton's heroic journey to the South Pole in 1914 is documented in the film *Endurance.* His ship became trapped in sea ice, preventing him and his men from reaching the Pole, but, remarkably, they survived an entire winter without losing a single man.

To assemble his crew, Shackleton had placed an ad in a London newspaper:

> Men wanted for hazardous journey. Small wages, bitter cold, long months of complete darkness, constant danger, safe return doubtful. Honour and recognition in case of success.
>
> — Ernest Shackleton

Five hundred men applied for twenty-eight crew positions despite the promised ordeals and the phrase "safe return doubtful." Maybe this proves how foolhardy men can be; or maybe it indicates a depressed London economy. But more likely it reflects how deeply men — and women — long for heroic adventure, and shows to what extremes they will go to find it.

It has been said that in the last several thousand years the most compelling adventure available to men of the "civilized" world has been war. Horrendous as war is, battle experiences often provide an uninitiated man's strongest memories because that's when he feels most alive, most engaged, most uniquely himself, and more bonded (to his fellow soldiers) than he has ever felt with any other humans. His experiences are sharpened and his perceptions heightened far more than in his everyday peacetime life. His fundamental human need for non-ordinary states of consciousness is satisfied. No wonder old soldiers love to recount war stories.

War, although hideous, is engaging to most boys and uninitiated men (as well as to many girls and uninitiated women). If psychologically adolescent men don't have war to wage, they might opt for a violence-maximizing or conquest version of, say, hockey, hunting, car racing, mountain climbing ("peak bagging"), polar expeditions, real estate "development," stock market trading and other forms of gambling, corporate raiding, mining, logging, oil drilling, slave trading, or sexual seduction. In the contemporary world, there is an epidemic attraction, even addiction, to socially sanctioned forms of violence: economic aggression against other people, environmental exploitation, species eradication, dehumanization of women, and self-hatred. As Derrick Jensen documents in *A Language Older Than Words* and *The Culture of Make Believe,* we are members of the most destructive culture ever to exist. What can we do? What are the alternatives to war that far more deeply and effectively satisfy the longing to leap into the perilous abyss?

If we are to survive, we must reinvent cultural practices that satisfy our deep-rooted need for non-ordinary states, interpersonal bonding, and the intensification of both our individuality and our tribal belonging. We must create contemporary forms of sacred pursuits that are at least as engaging, enlivening, and complex as war, and which, more importantly, engender life, thriving communities, healthy natural environments, genuine education, joyful service, soulful maturity, cultural evolution, and love. We need a better game than war.

The traditions of nature-based peoples make it abundantly clear that the original, primary, and most sacred pursuit is the underworld journey of initiation and subsequent soul embodiment. In twenty years of guiding contemporary vision quests and soulcraft programs, I have seen that this is still true. I have witnessed thousands of men and women enact underworld journeys that include arduous ordeals — arduous at least spiritually and emotionally, and often physically as well — filled with mystery and intrigue, risk and danger. They return with an always-astonishing radiance in their eyes and treasures for their people. Soul initiation results in mature men and women who are capable of peacefully resolving conflicts and who are fully enlivened by a multitude of creative, life-enhancing projects. Whether intending it or not, initiated people become agents for positive cultural change.

An initiated adult knows in her bones the nature of the gift she was born to bring to her community. She apprentices to an existing craft, career, art form, or discipline that enables her to embody that gift. Later, she develops never-before-seen forms for carrying that gift to others. Eventually, with good fortune, she joins a council of elders who care for the soul of their community — by preparing its youth for initiation, mentoring the initiated adults in their soul work, and ensuring that the village maintains a balanced relationship with the more-than-human community.

Shackleton's ad did not shy away from the dangers and hardships of his hazardous journey, and it promised nothing more than "honour and recognition," even while acknowledging they were hardly a sure thing.

As I watched *Endurance,* I imagined advertising a vision quest — one version of the hazardous underworld journey — in a way that borrowed something from Shackleton's ad:

> Men and women wanted for hazardous journey. Bitter cold and intense heat, long hours of complete darkness, boredom, no food, constant danger, encounters with the unknown, return in same condition doubtful. Vision and more hardships await in case of success.
>
> — Animas Valley Institute

SOUL STORY, WORLD STORY

The underworld journey does not promise you a rose garden. It doesn't even promise to fix what was wrong with the life you had been living. Indeed, the journey of descent often *ruins* the old life, making it less tempting to reconsider. It was too small for you anyway. That's why you abandoned it. Finding and learning how to live the new, larger story is a hazardous and complex challenge. "More hardships await in case of success." *That's* the nature of a soul path.

The good news is that if you commit yourself to uncovering and living your soul image, to living as if your place in the world mattered, you will embark on the most engaging, mysterious, and fulfilling journey of your life, a journey of enchantment, pathos, joy, life, and death. If you dare to sing your true song, you shall inherit the beauty and terror of your deeper life. On your deathbed, you will not be filled with regret for a life unlived. And, following soul initiation, you will experience the unparalleled rewards of contributing your unique gifts to a world in need, more in need now than ever. Doing so allows your deepest human nature to once again join greater nature.

After some years of conversing with soul and embodying your soul gifts, you will become aware of the grand story you are living. This is your soul story, your personal mythology that ties together the themes and symbols of your encounters with soul. It tells the tale of emergence into consciousness — and then into manifestation — of your life purpose and work. It weaves together dream images, visions, ecstasies, dominant life themes, traumas, loves, obsessions, numinous experiences, and encounters with remarkable people and places.

Carl Jung's autobiography, *Memories, Dreams, Reflections,* which he wrote in his eighties, is a soul story. He referred to it as his "personal myth" or "fable" — not what we normally think of as autobiography. He clearly distinguishes his soul story from a historical accounting of victories and misfortunes.

> I can only make direct statements, only "tell stories." Whether or not the stories are "true" is not the problem. The only question is whether what I tell is *my* fable, *my* truth....
>
> In the end the only events in my life worth telling are those when the imperishable world irrupted into this transitory one. That is why I speak chiefly of inner experiences, amongst which I include my dreams and visions....
>
> All other memories of travels, people and my surroundings have paled beside these interior happenings....
>
> Outward circumstances are no substitute for inner experience.... I can understand myself only in the light of inner happenings. It is these that make up the singularity of my life, and with these my autobiography deals.[13]

While the soul story presents the "singularity" of your life, the *world story* is the mythos of the universe as understood by you and your community —

your cosmology, your understanding of what the world is, how it came to be, where it is headed, and your people's place in the grand scheme of things.

If, over time, you patiently hold your soul story within the context of your world story, at some point they will merge like a puzzle piece fitting into a greater mystery. Then you'll experience more fully the unique role you play in the life of your community and, by extension, how your life is an essential part of the grandest story of all, the natural unfolding of a universe whose existence predates yours by an eternity and will outlast yours by an equal span.

When a sufficient number of contemporary people have reentered nature's soulstream and become conscious contributors to the unfolding story of the world, industrialized nations might mature into sustainable, ecocentric, and soulcentric communities, inhabited by people who are wildly creative, imaginative, adventurous, tolerant, generous, joyous, and cooperative members of the more-than-human world.

This is my prayer.

NOTES

EPIGRAPH

Jelaluddin Rumi, from *Open Secret: Versions of Rumi,* trans. John Moyne and Coleman Barks (Boston: Shambhala Publications, 1999), quatrain 91.

PROLOGUE. WEAVING A COCOON

1. Please note that this can be dangerous without an experienced guide or substantial training in backcountry travel and wilderness survival.
2. David Whyte, from "The Soul Lives Contented," in *Fire in the Earth* (Langley, Wash.: Many Rivers Press, 1992), p. 31.

CHAPTER 1. CARRYING WHAT IS HIDDEN AS A GIFT TO OTHERS

Epigraph: David Whyte, from "What to Remember When Waking," in *The House of Belonging* (Langley, Wash.: Many Rivers Press, 1997), p. 27.

1. Rainer Maria Rilke, from *Rilke's Book of Hours: Love Poems to God,* trans. Anita Barrows and Joanna Macy (New York: Riverhead Books, 1996), pp. 116–17.
2. Joseph Campbell, *The Hero with a Thousand Faces* (New York: Pantheon Books, 1949), pp. 245–46.
3. "Belonging," interview of Thomas Berry, *Parabola* 24, no. 1 (February 1999), p. 26.
4. Joseph Campbell, *The Hero with a Thousand Faces,* pp. 55, 58. *Pale* in this context refers to an area or the limits within which a person is protected.
5. James Hollis, *The Middle Passage: From Misery to Meaning in Midlife* (Toronto: Inner City Books, 1993), pp. 22–27.
6. Rilke, from *Rilke's Book of Hours,* p. 61.

CHAPTER 2. GROUNDWORK

Epigraph: David Whyte, "Self-Portrait," in *Fire in the Earth* (Langley, Wash.: Many Rivers Press, 1992), p. 10.

1. Quotations are from David Whyte, *The House of Belonging* (Langley, Wash.: Many Rivers Press, 1997), pp. 24, 28, 37.
2. James Hillman offers an explicit, cogent distinction between soul and spirit in "Peaks and Vales: The Soul/Spirit Distinction as Basis for the Differences between Psychotherapy and Spiritual Discipline," in *Puer Papers* (Dallas: Spring Publications, 1979), pp. 54–74.
3. My understanding of the concept of personal power derives from Descriptive Psychology as developed by Dr. Peter G. Ossorio. See, for example, Mary McDermott Shideler, *Persons, Behavior, and the World: The Descriptive Psychology Approach* (Lanham, Md.: University Press of America, 1988).
4. I am not using the word *soul* to refer to a material or nonmaterial entity that exists independent of the body, that might leave the body after death, and that might be reincarnated at a later time. This is not to imply that I believe such events don't occur; I'm just not using the word that way.
5. Thomas Berry, *The Dream of the Earth* (San Francisco: Sierra Club Books, 1988), p. 208.
6. See, for example, Franklin Merrel-Wolff, *Pathways Through to Space: A Personal Record of Transformation in Consciousness* (New York: Julian Press, 1973).

7. The ascent and descent I write about in this book both begin in the everyday middleworld. There is a different sort of descent that begins in the upperworld and goes to the middleworld. The ontological process by which upperworld spirit manifests itself in the phenomenal middleworld is sometimes described as a descent, but this is not at all the same descent as discussed in these pages. Likewise, a return from the underworld to the middleworld is a type of ascent not to be confused with the journey from the middleworld into the upperworld.

8. James Hillman, *The Dream and the Underworld* (New York: HarperCollins, 1979), p. 76. Hillman is quoting the eighteenth-century English poet Samuel Taylor Coleridge.

9. James Hillman, "The Soul of the Matter" (an interview with Wes Nisker), *Inquiring Mind* 1, no. 2 (1995).

10. See Franklin Merrel-Wolff, *The Philosophy of Consciousness Without an Object: Reflections on the Nature of Transcendental Consciousness* (New York: Julian Press, 1973).

11. See Marion Woodman and Elinor Dickson, *Dancing in the Flames: The Dark Goddess in the Transformation of Consciousness* (Boston: Shambhala Publications, 1997). I like the *feel* of the word *soulmaking*, but I'd say the soul is not what is made: the soul is already there and whole and waiting for us; I'd say what is made is a more intimate relationship between the ego and soul; the ego roots itself in soul.

12. Rainer Maria Rilke, from *Rilke's Book of Hours: Love Poems to God*, trans. Anita Barrows and Joanna Macy (New York: Riverhead Books, 1996), pp. 116.

13. Rainer Maria Rilke, translated by David Whyte, in his *Fire in the Earth* (Langley, Wash.: Many Rivers Press, 1992), p. 27.

14. Rilke, from *Rilke's Book of Hours*, p. 61.

15. Some psychotherapists, especially those with a depth orientation, embrace both goals. Soulcraft and therapy need not be divided into separate professional practices, but I believe it would serve practitioners and clients alike if the two realms were clearly distinguished.

16. See Malidoma Somé, *Of Water and the Spirit* (New York: Arkana, 1994).

17. See Ken Wilber, *The Marriage of Sense and Soul: Integrating Science and Religion* (New York: Broadway Books, 1999). Despite soul appearing in the title of the book, the primary entry under "soul" in the index reads simply "see spirit."

18. See John Tarrant, *The Light Inside the Dark: Zen, Soul, and the Spiritual Life* (New York: Perennial, 1999); the Kornfield quotes are from the back cover of his *A Path with Heart: A Guide through the Perils and Promises of Spiritual Life* (New York: Bantam, 1993).

19. I use the terms *personality* and *everyday conscious self* as more or less synonymous with ego.

20. Frederick Buechner, *Wishful Thinking: A Theological ABC* (San Francisco: Harper, 1993).

21. Abraham Maslow, *The Farther Reaches of Human Nature* (New York: Viking, 1971), pp. 43–44.

22. Rabindranath Tagore, in *Rabindranath Tagore: An Anthology*, ed. Krishna Dutta (New York: Griffin, 1999).

23. Ruth Benedict, quoted in Dolores LaChapelle, *Sacred Land, Sacred Sex: Rapture of the Deep* (Silverton, Colo.: Finn Hill Arts, 1988), p. 86.

24. Mary Oliver, from "Wild Geese," in *Dream Work* (New York: Atlantic Monthly Press, 1986), p. 14.

25. See Gregory Bateson, *Steps to an Ecology of Mind: Collected Essays in Anthropology, Psychiatry, Evolution, and Epistemology* (Chicago: University of Chicago Press, 2000) and *Mind and Nature: A Necessary Unity* (New York: Bantam, 1980).

26. Brian Swimme and Thomas Berry, *The Universe Story: From the Primordial Flaring Forth to the Ecozoic Era—A Celebration of the Unfolding of the Cosmos* (New York: HarperCollins, 1992), p. 40.

CHAPTER 3. SINKING BACK INTO THE SOURCE OF EVERYTHING

Epigraph: Rainer Maria Rilke, from *Rilke's Book of Hours: Love Poems to God,* trans. Anita Barrows and Joanna Macy (New York: Riverhead Books, 1996), pp. 95–96.

1. Joseph Campbell, *The Hero with a Thousand Faces* (New York: Pantheon Books, 1949), pp. 55, 58.
2. Mary Oliver, from "Wild Geese," in *Dream Work* (New York: Atlantic Monthly Press, 1986), p. 14.
3. David Whyte, from "Sweet Darkness," in *The House of Belonging* (Langley, Wash.: Many Rivers Press, 1997), p. 23.
4. Natalie Goldberg, *Long Quiet Highway: Waking Up in America* (New York: Bantam, 1993), p. 55.
5. Ibid., pp. 58–59.
6. Ibid., p. 69.
7. Adrienne Rich, "Prospective Immigrants Please Note," in *The Fact of a Doorframe: Poems 1950–2001* (New York: Norton, 2002), pp. 24–25.

CHAPTER 4. THE WANDERER AND THE SECOND COCOON

Epigraphs: J. R. R. Tolkien, from *The Fellowship of the Ring* (Boston: Houghton Mifflin, 1999); Mark Twain, from *The Quotable Mark Twain: His Essential Aphorisms, Witticisms & Concise Opinions,* ed. Kent Rasmussen (New York: McGraw-Hill, 1998); Lao Tzu, from *Tao te Ching.*

1. These are the four modalities of consciousness described by Eligio Stephen Gallegos in his *Animals of the Four Windows: Integrating Thinking, Sensing, Feeling, and Imagery* (Santa Fe: Moon Bear Press, 1991).
2. Mary Oliver, from "The Journey," in *Dream Work* (New York: Atlantic Monthly Press, 1986), pp. 38–39.
3. Joseph Campbell, *The Hero with a Thousand Faces* (New York: Pantheon Books, 1949), p. 385.

CHAPTER 5. THE DARKNESS SHALL BE THE LIGHT

Epigraph: T. S. Eliot, from "East Coker," in *Four Quartets* (New York: Harcourt Brace & Co., 1977), p. 28.

1. I am currently completing a book in which I propose psycho-spiritual tasks for eight soul-based stages of life. The second cocoon is the fourth stage. The tasks of stage one are ego formation and (for the parents) the care of innocence. For the second stage (middle-late childhood), the tasks are discovering the enchantment of the natural world and learning the social practices, values, and stories of one's culture. The tasks of stage three (early adolescence) are creating a secure and authentic social identity (one that generates adequate amounts of both social acceptance and self-approval).
2. In the Western world, alcohol and marijuana have been among the most commonly abused substances. When used addictively they create a barrier between our egos and our core selves, including our emotions, in somewhat opposite but equally consequential ways. Alcohol, a central nervous system depressant, disinhibits us in small to moderate doses. If used to excess, it simply numbs us, and we become zombies unable to access our selves to any depth. Marijuana, on the other hand, provides something like experiential binoculars: wherever we turn our attention, we experience more of the details of what's there; we're drawn in. When used compulsively, however, these binoculars can turn into blinders, concealing those painful emotional areas so much in need of our attention.
3. Chellis Glendinning, *My Name Is Chellis and I'm in Recovery from Western Civilization* (Boston: Shambhala, 1994).
4. For an original and stunningly personal exploration of the cultural waters of the West, see Derrick

Jensen's *A Language Older Than Words* (New York: Context Books, 2000) and *The Culture of Make Believe* (New York: Context Books, 2002).

5. I was introduced to the image of the Loyal Soldier by psychosynthesists Morgan Farley and Molly Brown. See Molly Young Brown, *Growing Whole: Self-Realization on an Endangered Planet* (Center City, Minn.: Hazelden, 1993).

6. Jean Houston, *The Search for the Beloved: Journeys in Mythology and Sacred Psychology* (New York: Tarcher/Putnam, 1987), p. 104.

7. Ibid., p. 105.

8. Ibid., p. 106.

9. Jelaluddin Rumi, quoted by Annemarie Schimmel, in *Mystical Dimensions of Islam* (Chapel Hill: University of North Carolina Press, 1985), p. 191.

10. Steven Foster and Meredith Little introduced me to the death lodge as a practice in preparing for a vision quest. See their *Roaring of the Sacred River: The Wilderness Quest for Vision and Self-Healing* (Big Pine, Calif.: Lost Borders Press, 1997), p. 34.

11. David Whyte, "The Well of Grief," in *Where Many Rivers Meet* (Langley, Wash.: Many Rivers Press, 1990), p. 35.

12. From the CD *Don't Go Back to Sleep,* by Jan Garrett, 1992. Words and music by Jan Garrett. Lyrics inspired by Jelaluddin Rumi. Available from www.jangarrett.com.

CHAPTER 6. RECOVERING THE IMAGE YOU WERE BORN WITH

Epigraph: David Whyte, from "All the True Vows," in *The House of Belonging* (Langley, Wash.: Many Rivers Press, 1997), p. 24.

1. Mircea Eliade, *Shamanism: Archaic Techniques of Ecstasy* (Princeton University Press, 1972).

2. *Liminal* refers to transitional states in which we are no longer who we were and not yet who we will be (like being in a cocoon).

3. Malidoma Somé, *Of Water and the Spirit: Ritual, Magic, and Initiation in the Life of an African Shaman* (New York: Penguin/Arkana, 1994), p. 1.

4. David Whyte, from "All the True Vows," in *The House of Belonging* (Langley, Wash.: Many Rivers Press, 1997), pp. 24–25.

CHAPTER 7. INNER WORK

Epigraph: Antonio Machado, from *Times Alone: Selected Poems of Antonio Machado,* trans. Robert Bly (Middletown, Conn.: Wesleyan University Press, 1983).

1. I am following the approach of James Hillman in his *The Dream and the Underworld* (New York: HarperCollins, 1979).

2. C. G. Jung, *Memories, Dreams, Reflections* (New York: Vintage Books, 1965), pp. 11–15.

3. Ibid., p. 15.

4. Robert A. Johnson masterfully outlines this method in an easy-to-learn four-step process. See his *Inner Work: Using Dreams and Active Imagination for Personal Growth* (HarperSanFrancisco, 1986).

5. Eligio Stephen Gallegos, *The Personal Totem Pole: Animal Imagery, the Chakras, and Psychotherapy* (Santa Fe: Moon Bear Press, 1990).

CHAPTER 8. COMMUNING WITH THE OTHERS

Epigraph: Rainer Maria Rilke, from *Rilke's Book of Hours: Love Poems to God,* trans. Anita Barrows and Joanna Macy (New York: Riverhead Books, 1996), p. 47.

1. Jack Zimmerman and Virginia Coyle, *The Way of Council* (Las Vegas: Bramble Books, 1996).

2. See Dolores LaChapelle, *Sacred Land, Sacred Sex: Rapture of the Deep* (Silverton, Colo.: Finn Hill Arts, 1988), pp. 290–98.

3. Ibid., pp. 282–87. LaChapelle concludes that trance drumming "links us directly with our real human nature in all its deep aspects and therefore can link us once again to our land."

4. "Talking across the species boundaries" is Gary Snyder's wonderfully lyrical phrase for interspecies communication from his *The Practice of the Wild* (San Francisco: North Point Press, 1990), p. 180.

5. David Abram, *The Spell of the Sensuous: Perception and Language in a More-Than-Human World* (New York: Vintage Books, 1996), p. 130.

6. Derek Walcott, from "Love after Love," in *Collected Poems 1948–1987* (New York: Farrar, Straus and Giroux, 1987), p. 328.

7. Marianne Williamson, *A Return To Love: Reflections on the Principles of* A Course in Miracles (New York: HarperCollins, 1992). Famously quoted by Nelson Mandela in his 1994 inauguration speech.

CHAPTER 9. BRIDGING INNER AND OUTER

Epigraph: "Magic Words," in Edward Field, trans., *Songs and Stories of the Netsilik Eskimos* (Cambridge, Mass.: Education Development Center, Inc., 1967).

1. Cam Hubert, *Dreamspeaker* (New York: Avon Books, 1978).

2. See Dolores LaChapelle, *Sacred Land, Sacred Sex: Rapture of the Deep* (Silverton, Colo.: Finn Hill Arts, 1988), pp. 275–82, for a discussion of "the way of chant," including the words and music to several nature-based chants and suggestions for discovering your own.

3. Ibid., p. 271.

4. Fasting without water for more than a day can be dangerous and should be attempted only by those properly prepared and supported by a guide familiar with this practice.

CHAPTER 10. THE VISION QUEST AND SOULCENTRIC RITUAL

Epigraph: Morgan Farley, "Clearing," in *The Practice of Peace*, ed. Judith Rafaela and Nancy Fay (Santa Fe: Sherman Asher Publishing, 1998), p. 164.

1. I have been neither trained nor authorized to offer a Native American version of the vision quest. Nor is that my desire. My goal has been to create a ritual structure that works best for contemporary Westerners. Given that soul encounter is about authenticity if it is about anything, it is best not to imitate another people or era on the path to soul. It is also disrespectful, I believe, to employ without permission the ceremonial forms of another culture — disrespectful to both the other culture and oneself.

2. In other approaches to the modern vision quest, the primary goal(s) might be to heal emotional wounds, to experience full membership in the natural world, to merge with the divine or experience universal spiritual qualities, to formally mark or celebrate a passage from one life stage to another, to open the heart, to prepare for a major life undertaking such as marriage or parenthood or religious vows, or to prepare for death. No two of these intentions are incompatible. Regardless of expectations of guides or participants, any one or more of these outcomes may occur.

3. Robert A. Johnson, *Owning Your Own Shadow: Understanding the Dark Side of the Psyche* (New York: HarperCollins, 1991), p. 78.

4. Ibid., p. 91.

5. See William B. Plotkin and Wynn Schwartz, "A Conceptualization of the Hypnotic State," in *Advances in Descriptive Psychology*, ed. K. E. Davis and T. O. Mitchell (Greenwich, Conn.: JAI Press, 1982), pp. 139–99.

6. William Butler Yeats, "The Song of Wandering Aengus," in *The Collected Poems of W. B. Yeats*, ed. Richard J. Finneran (New York: Scribner, 1996), p. 59.

7. Eligio Stephen Gallegos, *Animals of the Four Windows: Integrating Thinking, Sensing, Feeling, and Imagery* (Santa Fe: Moon Bear Press, 1991).

8. Rainer Maria Rilke, from "The Man Watching," in *Selected Poems of Rainer Maria Rilke*, trans. Robert Bly (New York: Harper & Row, 1981), p. 105.

9. Joseph Epes Brown, ed., *The Sacred Pipe: Black Elk's Account of the Seven Rites of the Oglala Sioux* (Baltimore: Penguin, 1971), p. 44. I've been told that Charlotte Black Elk, the medicine man's granddaughter, has explained that while *hanblecheya* means "to lament" in informal Lakota usage, the same word means "to experience the voice of the sacred" in its formal use. Notice that "to experience the voice of the sacred" is still not the same as seeing visions, and that it places the emphasis upon sacredness as opposed to visual anomalies.

10. Ibid., pp. 44–66.

11. David Whyte, from "Fire in the Earth," in *Fire in the Earth* (Langley, Wash.: Many Rivers Press, 1992), p. 8.

CHAPTER 11. CULTIVATING A SOULFUL RELATIONSHIP TO LIFE: PART 1

Epigraph: William Stafford, "How to Regain Your Soul," from *The Darkness Around Us Is Deep: Selected Poems of William Stafford*, ed. Robert Bly (New York: HarperPerennial, 1994).

1. David Whyte, from "Sweet Darkness," in *The House of Belonging* (Langley, Wash.: Many Rivers Press, 1997), p. 23.

2. Theodore Roethke, from "The Waking," in *The Collected Poems of Theodore Roethke* (New York: Doubleday, 1953).

3. My lawyer wishes me to state emphatically that I am *not* recommending the reader try this. It can be a life-threatening practice without highly developed survival skills specific to the wilderness environment in question.

4. Wendell Berry, from "To Know the Dark," in *Farming: A Handbook* (New York: Harcourt Brace Jovanovich, 1967).

5. Rainer Maria Rilke, translated by David Whyte, in his *Fire in the Earth* (Langley, Wash.: Many Rivers Press, 1992), p. 27.

6. Lyn Dalebout, "Obsidian I," in *Out of the Flames* (Moose, Wyo.: Blue Bison Press, 1996), p. 21.

7. Rainer Maria Rilke, *Letters to a Young Poet* (New York: Norton, 1934; rev. 1954), p. 34.

8. Ibid., p. 20.

9. Ibid., p. 35.

10. Robert Johnson, *He: Understanding Masculine Psychology* (New York: Harper & Row, 1977), p. 80.

CHAPTER 12. CULTIVATING A SOULFUL RELATIONSHIP TO LIFE: PART 2

Epigraph: Mary Oliver, from "When Death Comes," in *New and Selected Poems* (Boston: Beacon Press, 1992), pp. 10–11.

1. David Whyte, from "Self-Portrait," in *Fire in the Earth* (Langley, Wash.: Many Rivers Press, 1992) p. 10.

2. Mary Oliver, from "The Summer Day," in *New and Selected Poems* (Boston: Beacon Press, 1992), p. 94.

3. David Whyte, from "The Soul Lives Contented," in *Fire in the Earth* (Langley, Wash.: Many Rivers Press, 1992), p. 31.

4. Robert Bly, *A Little Book on the Human Shadow* (New York: Harper & Row, 1988).

5. James Hollis, *The Eden Project: In Search of the Magical Other* (Toronto: Inner City Books, 1998),

pp. 51–59. Hollis bases his discussion of projection on the work of Jung's colleague, Marie-Louise von Franz.

6. I employ the heart warrior council only with groups that meet regularly or have had at least three intimate days together. It takes at least that long for the projections to form and reach the threshold of consciousness *as* projections, and it takes a while to create the sort of group bonding that renders the terrifying work with projection and shadow both feasible and rewarding. The specific format of the council is elaborate and requires training in its use.

7. Jelaluddin Rumi, in *Open Secret: Versions of Rumi,* trans. John Moyne and Coleman Barks (Boston: Shambhala Publications, 1999), quatrain 1246.

8. Harville Hendrix, author of *Getting the Love You Want* (New York: Owl Books, 2001) and originator of the Imago approach to relationships, suggests we always and inevitably fall in love with someone who combines what to us are *both* the best and worst traits of *both* our parents. The "good" traits draw us in and account for our attraction; the "bad" ones allow for the transference and projection that create the unrivaled opportunities for personality growth and, eventually, soul encounter. We meet on similarities and grow on differences.

9. James Hollis, *The Middle Passage: From Misery to Meaning in Midlife* (Toronto: Inner City Books, 1993), p. 61.

10. Dolores LaChapelle, *D. H. Lawrence: Future Primitive* (Denton: University of North Texas Press, 1996), p. 78.

11. Morgan Farley, "Returning the Back Way," unpublished, 1990.

12. See Tom Pinkson's fine book on Huichol shamanism and spirituality, *Flowers of Wiricuta: A Gringo's Journey to Shamanic Power* (Mill Valley, Calif.: Wakan Press, 1995).

13. Jean Houston, *The Search for the Beloved: Journeys in Mythology and Sacred Psychology* (New York: Tarcher/Putnam, 1987), p. 137.

14. Ibid., p. 137.

15. Brian Swimme, *The Universe Is a Green Dragon: A Cosmic Creation Story* (Santa Fe: Bear & Co., 1985); Brian Swimme and Thomas Berry, *The Universe Story: From the Primordial Flaring Forth to the Ecozoic Era—A Celebration of the Unfolding of the Cosmos* (San Francisco: Harper, 1992).

16. Jelaluddin Rumi, from *Open Secret: Versions of Rumi,* trans. John Moyne and Coleman Barks (Boston: Shambhala Publications, 1999), quatrain 388.

17. Jelaluddin Rumi, *The Illuminated Rumi,* trans. Coleman Barks (New York: Broadway Books, 1997), p. 68.

18. Rumi, *Open Secret,* quatrain 158.

19. Ibid., quatrain 1246.

20. Rainer Maria Rilke, from *Selected Poems of Rainer Maria Rilke,* trans. Robert Bly (New York: Harper & Row, 1981), p. 55.

21. Rainer Maria Rilke, from *Rilke's Book of Hours: Love Poems to God,* trans. Anita Barrows and Joanna Macy (New York: Riverhead Books, 1996), p. 88.

22. Rainer Maria Rilke, from *The Selected Poetry of Rainer Maria Rilke,* trans. Stephen Mitchell (New York: Vintage, 1980), p. 261.

CHAPTER 13. LIVING AS IF YOUR PLACE IN THE WORLD MATTERED

Epigraphs: Viktor Frankl, from *Man's Search for Meaning* (New York: Washington Square Press, 1997); Albert Camus, *Lyrical and Critical Essays,* ed. Philip Thody, trans. Ellen Conroy Kennedy (New York: Random House, 1970), pp. 16–17; James Hillman and Michael Ventura, *We've Had a Hundred Years of Psychotherapy — And the World's Getting Worse* (San Francisco: Harper, 1992), p. 63.

1. Mary Oliver, from "The Summer Day," in *New and Selectted Poems* (Boston: Beacon Press, 1992), p. 94.
2. David Whyte, from "Revelation Must Be Terrible," in *Fire in the Earth* (Langley, Wash.: Many Rivers Press, 1992), p. 33.
3. Malidoma Somé, *Of Water and the Spirit: Ritual, Magic, and Initiation in the Life of an African Shaman* (New York: Penguin/Arkana, 1994), pp. 252–53.
4. Ibid., p. 297.
5. James Hillman, *Re-Visioning Psychology* (New York: Harper & Row, 1975), p. 23.
6. Pablo Neruda, from "La Poesia," translated by David Whyte, in his *Fire in the Earth* (Langley, Wash.: Many Rivers Press, 1992), epigraph.
7. T. S. Eliot, from "Little Gidding," in *Four Quartets* (New York: Harcourt Brace & Company, 1943), p. 59.
8. Here, I am following the formulation on self-concept change offered by Peter G. Ossorio in "Being Me, Being Myself OR I Am the Person Who ... OR The Forgotten Parameter" (presentation to the meeting of the Society for Descriptive Psychology, Breckenridge, Colo., 1 October 1993).
9. Rainer Maria Rilke, from *Selected Poems of Rainer Maria Rilke,* trans. Robert Bly (New York: Harper & Row, 1981), pp. 105–7.
10. David Whyte, from "All the True Vows," in *The House of Belonging* (Langley, Wash.: Many Rivers Press, 1997), p. 25.
11. Joseph Campbell, *The Hero with a Thousand Faces* (New York: Pantheon Books, 1949), pp. 52–53.
12. See the section on deep imagery in chapter 7.
13. C. G. Jung, *Memories, Dreams, Reflections* (New York: Vintage, 1965), pp. 3–5.

RESOURCES FOR FURTHER EXPLORATION

Our foremost resource on the descent to soul is our own unprotected experience of the sometimes terrifying, often ecstatic terrain of the underworld. In second place are our guides, teachers, and allies, whether visible or invisible, human or otherwise, who might help us approach the edge, encourage us to leap, and perhaps be available for consultation as we proceed. A third category consists of books (like this one) that might provide advice, information, or inspiration to leap. What follows are some resources of this third kind, divided according to this book's chapters. Complete references for the books mentioned here are listed in the bibliography.

CHAPTER 5. THE DARKNESS SHALL BE THE LIGHT
COMPLETING UNFINISHED BUSINESS FROM EARLIER LIFE STAGES
This personal growth work embraces the entire agenda of psychotherapy. There are thousands of self-help books on the topic, but if you know you need to attend to some significant unfinished business before embarking on the underworld journey, then a talented, experienced, depth-oriented psychotherapist is likely to be your best resource. Your personal work in psychotherapy might turn out, in fact, to be your threshold to the underworld.

GIVING UP ADDICTIONS
John de Graaf, David Wann, and Thomas H. Naylor, *Affluenza: The All-Consuming Epidemic.*
Chellis Glendinning, *My Name Is Chellis and I'm in Recovery from Western Civilization.*
Derrick Jensen, *A Language Older Than Words.*

WELCOMING HOME THE LOYAL SOLDIER
Molly Young Brown, *Growing Whole: Self-Realization on an Endangered Planet.*
Donald Kalsched, *The Inner World of Trauma: Archetypal Defenses of the Personal Spirit.*
Hal Stone and Sidra L. Stone, *Embracing Ourselves: The Voice Dialogue Manual.*

HEALING WORK WITH THE SACRED WOUND
Michael DeMaria, *Ever Flowing On: On Being and Becoming Oneself.*
John Firman and Ann Gila, *The Primal Wound: A Transpersonal View of Trauma, Addiction, and Growth.*
Beth Hedva, *Betrayal, Trust, and Forgiveness: A Guide to Emotional Healing and Self-Renewal.*
Jean Houston, *The Search for the Beloved: Journeys in Mythology and Sacred Psychology.*

LEARNING TO CHOOSE AUTHENTICITY OVER SOCIAL ACCEPTANCE
Greg Levoy, Callings: *Finding and Following an Authentic Life.*
David Whyte, *Crossing the Unknown Sea: Work as a Pilgrimage of Identity.*

MAKING PEACE WITH THE PAST: THE DEATH LODGE

Steven Foster and Meredith Little, *The Roaring of the Sacred River: The Wilderness Quest for Vision and Self-Healing.*

Stephen Levine, *A Year to Live: How to Live This Year As If It Were Your Last.*

LEARNING THE ART OF DISIDENTIFICATION THROUGH MEDITATION

I recommend enrollment in a course of instruction by a qualified teacher; helpful books include the following.

Jack Kornfield, *A Path with Heart: A Guide through the Perils and Promises of Spiritual Life.*

Stephen Levine, *A Gradual Awakening.*

Eckhart Tolle, *The Power of Now.*

    (Also, see the references in the section on Mindfulness Practice on p. 348.)

CHAPTER 7. INNER WORK

SOULCENTRIC DREAMWORK

There is a vast number of books and tapes on dreamwork. For those looking to launch a specifically soulcentric approach to dreams, my recommendations are as follows.

Stephen Aizenstat, *Dream Tending: Techniques for Uncovering the Hidden Intelligence of Your Dreams* (audiotapes).

James Hillman, *The Dream and the Underworld,* and, with paintings by Margot McLean, *Dream Animals.*

Robert Johnson, *Inner Work: Using Dreams and Active Imagination for Personal Growth.*

Jill Mellick, *The Art of Dreaming: A Creativity Toolbox for Dreamwork.*

Jean Benedict Raffa, *Dream Theatres of the Soul: Empowering the Feminine through Jungian Dream Work.*

Marion Woodman, *Dreams: Language of the Soul* (audiotape).

DEEP IMAGERY

To find a professional deep imagery guide or to train as a guide, contact Stephen Gallegos's International Institute for Visualization Research. Their Web site has lists of practitioners worldwide (www.animalimagery.org; tel./fax: [505] 638-9131).

Eligio Stephen Gallegos, *Animals of the Four Windows: Integrating Thinking, Sensing, Feeling, and Imagery,* and *The Personal Totem Pole: Animal Imagery, the Chakras, and Psychotherapy (2d ed.).*

Barbara Hannah, *Encounters with the Soul: Active Imagination as Developed by C. G. Jung.*

Robert Johnson, *Inner Work: Using Dreams and Active Imagination for Personal Growth.*

CHAPTER 8. COMMUNING WITH THE OTHERS

COUNCIL WORK

Christina Baldwin, *Calling the Circle: The First and Future Culture.*

Charles Garfield, Cindy Spring, and Sedonia Cahill, *Wisdom Circles: A Guide to Self-Discovery and Community Building in Small Groups.*

Dolores LaChapelle, *Sacred Land, Sacred Sex: Rapture of the Deep*, pp. 290-298.
Jack Zimmerman and Virginia Coyle, *The Way of Council.*

SACRED SPEECH AND SILENCE
Joan Halifax, *The Fruitful Darkness: Reconnecting with the Body of the Earth;* see her chapters
"The Way of Silence" and "The Way of Language."

TRANCE DRUMMING AND RHYTHMS
John Chernoff, *African Rhythm and African Sensibility.*
Reinhard Flatischler, *The Forgotten Power of Rhythm: Ta Ke Ti Na.*
Micky Hart, *Drumming at the Edge of Magic: A Journey into the Spirit of Percussion.*
Dolores LaChapelle, *Sacred Land, Sacred Sex: Rapture of the Deep*, pp. 282-287.

ECSTATIC TRANCE DANCING
The work of Elizabeth Cogburn and her students is described in Cedar Barstow's chapter
"The Earth Song Ceremonial Dance Form," in Ruth-Inge Heinze's *The Nature and Function
of Rituals: Fire from Heaven;* also available from the author at cedarb@aol.com.
Michael DeMaria, *Ever Flowing On: On Being and Becoming Oneself.*
Dolores LaChapelle, *Sacred Land, Sacred Sex: Rapture of the Deep*, pp. 287-290.
Gabrielle Roth, *Maps to Ecstasy: A Healing Journey for the Untamed Spirit,* and *Sweat Your
Prayers: Movement as Spiritual Practice.*

CEREMONIAL SWEATS AND SAUNAS
Many native people are understandably offended by the unauthorized use of their specific ceremonial forms. Those who wish to participate in an authentic Native American sweat lodge
are encouraged to do so with native medicine people or those who have been trained and
authorized by native people to conduct these rites.

Many guides, however, have developed their own non-native approaches to ceremonial
sweats and saunas or revived traditions from their own ancestry; ask around and you might
be able to find some of them.

Mikkel Aaland, *Sweat: The Illustrated History and Description of the Finnish Sauna, Russian
Bania, Islamic Hammam, Japanese Mushi-Buro, Mexican Temescal, and American Indian
& Eskimo Sweat Lodge.*
Joseph Bruchac, *The Native American Sweat Lodge: History and Legend.*
Nikki Rajala, *Some Like It Hot: The Sauna, Its Lore & Stories.*

TALKING ACROSS THE SPECIES BOUNDARIES: DIALOGUES WITH NATURE
David Abram, *The Spell of the Sensuous: Perception and Language in a More-Than-Human World.*
J. Allen Boone, *Kinship with All Life.*
Linda Hogan, Deena Metzger, and Brenda Peterson (eds.), *Intimate Nature: The Bond
between Women and Animals.*

Derrick Jensen, *A Language Older Than Words.*

Stephanie Kaza, *The Attentive Heart: Conversations with Trees.*

Michael J. Roads, *Talking with Nature: Sharing the Energies and Spirit of Trees, Plants, Birds, and Earth.*

John Seed, Joanna Macy, Pat Flemming, and Arne Naess, *Thinking Like a Mountain: Toward a Council of All Beings.*

Marta Williams, *Learning Their Language: Intuitve Communication with Animals and Nature*

SIGNS AND OMENS IN NATURE

Tom Brown Jr., *The Vision.*

ANIMAL TRACKING AND OTHER METHODS OF SKILLFUL NATURE OBSERVATION

Diane Ackerman, *A Natural History of the Senses.*

Tom Brown Jr., *Tom Brown's Field Guide to Nature Observation and Tracking.*

Paul Rezendes, *Tracking and the Art of Seeing: How to Read Animal Tracks & Signs,* and *The Wild Within: Adventures in Nature and Animal Teachings.*

CHAPTER 9. BRIDGING INNER AND OUTER

SELF-DESIGNED CEREMONY

I wish I could direct the reader to a good book on a soulcraft-resonant approach to self-designed ceremony, but I do not know one. I have written a longer article on the topic, entitled "Ritual and Ceremony: Completing the Dialogue with the Unconscious," which appears in *Circles on the Mountain,* 1991. To access this article, contact the Wilderness Guides Council at www.wildernessguidescouncil.org.

TRADITIONAL CEREMONIES, RITUALS, AND NATURE FESTIVALS

Contemporary Nature Festivals:

Dolores LaChapelle, *Earth Festivals: Seasonal Celebrations for Everyone Young and Old; Earth Wisdom;* and *Sacred Land, Sacred Sex: Rapture of the Deep.*

Native American Ceremonies:

Ed McGaa, *Mother Earth Spirituality: Native American Paths to Healing Ourselves and Our World.*

Celtic Ceremonies:

Frank MacEowen, *The Mist-Filled Path: Celtic Wisdom for Exiles, Wanderers, and Seekers.*

Mayan Ceremonies:

Martín Prechtel, *Long Life, Honey in the Heart* and *Secrets of the Talking Jaguar.*

African Ceremonies:

Malidoma Patrice Somé, *The Healing Wisdom of Africa: Finding Life Purpose through Nature, Ritual, and Community* and *Ritual: Power, Healing, and Community.*

Wiccan Ceremonies:

Starhawk, *The Spiral Dance: A Rebirth of the Ancient Religion of the Great Goddess.*

ESOURCES FOR FURTHER EXPLORATION

SYMBOLIC ARTWORK

Michelle Cassou and Stewart Cubley, *Life, Paint, and Passion: Reclaiming the Magic of Spontaneous Self-Expression.*
Aviva Gold, *Painting from the Source: Awakening the Artist's Soul in Everyone.*
Shaun McNiff, *Art as Medicine: Creating a Therapy of the Imagination.*
Jane B. Seaton, *Artlife: Creative Practices for Making Your Everyday Life Sacred* (audiotapes).

JOURNAL WORK

Christina Baldwin, *Life's Companion: Journal Writing as a Spiritual Quest.*
Deena Metzger, *Writing for Your Life: A Guide and Companion to the Inner Worlds.*

THE DISCOVERY, CREATION, AND USE OF SYMBOLS AND SACRED OBJECTS

Raymond Buckland, *Signs, Symbols & Omens: An Illustrated Guide to Magical & Spiritual Symbolism.*
Shaun McNiff, *Earth Angels: Engaging the Sacred in Everyday Things.*

THE USE OF HALLUCINOGENS WITHIN SOULCRAFT CEREMONIES

Although I've looked for books that explore the use of plant allies specifically as a contemporary Western method for soul encounter, I have not found any. There are, however, some that embrace a more general and psycho-spiritually respectful relationship with psychotropic plants:
Jim Dekorne, *Psychedelic Shamanism: The Cultivation, Preparation and Shamanic Use of Psychotropic Plants.*
Ralph Metzner (ed.), *Ayahuasca: Human Consciousness and the Spirits of Nature.*
Richard Evans Schultes, Albert Hofmann, and Christian Ratsch, *Plants of the Gods: Their Sacred, Healing and Hallucinogenic Powers.*

STORIES AND STORYTELLING

Myths and Other Sacred Stories:
The following provide a sampling of world mythology; see also the periodical *Parabola: Myth, Tradition, and the Search for Meaning.*
Joseph Campbell, *The Hero with a Thousand Faces* and *The Masks of God: Creative Mythology.*
Clarissa Pinkola Estes, *Women Who Run with the Wolves: Myths and Stories of the Wild Woman Archetype.*
Susan Hazen-Hammond, *Spider Woman's Web: Traditional Native American Tales about Women's Power.*
Carl Jung, *Man and His Symbols.*
Ralph Metzner, *The Well of Remembrance: Rediscovering the Earth Wisdom Myths of Northern Europe.*
Martín Prechtel, *The Disobedience of the Daughter of the Sun.* (This extraordinary Mayan tale about the love affair between the ego and the soul is one of the finest tellings in print of a traditional sacred story.)
David Suzuki and Peter Knudtson, *Wisdom of the Elders: Sacred Native Stories of Nature.*

Personal Myth Work:
David Feinstein and Stanley Krippner, *The Mythic Path: Discovering the Guiding Stories of Your Past.*
James Hollis, *Creating a Life: Finding Your Individual Path.*
Jean Houston, *The Search for the Beloved: Journeys in Mythology and Sacred Psychology.*
Sam Keen and Anne Valley-Fox, *Your Mythic Journey.*
Stephen Larsen, *The Mythic Imagination: The Quest for Meaning through Personal Mythology.*

The Art of Mirroring
See the references in the section on council work on p. 342. There is a complex art to mirroring a story without interpretation or projection. If you wish to apprentice to that art, consider courses on mirroring offered by Animas Valley Institute, the School of Lost Borders, or the Ojai Foundation.

SOUL POETRY, MUSIC, CHANTING, AND THE BARDIC TRADITION
Read (out loud) the poems of the poets found in this book. And see:
Dolores LaChapelle, *Sacred Land, Sacred Sex: Rapture of the Deep*, pp. 275-282 (on chanting) and pp. 298–300 (on the bard).
Gary Snyder, *The Old Ways, Turtle Island,* and *The Practice of the Wild.*
Also, listen to Jan Garrett's music (www.jangarrett.com) and J. D. Martin's (www.jdmartin.com).

CHAPTER 10. THE VISION QUEST
For an in-depth account of the contemporary vision quest, see the work of Steven Foster and Meredith Little, the two people most responsible for reintroducing rites of passage to the Western world over the past thirty years: *The Book of the Vision Quest: Personal Transformation in the Wilderness* and *The Roaring of the Sacred River: The Wilderness Quest for Vision and Self-Healing.*

For a full listing of contemporary vision quest guides in the U.S. and internationally, log on to: www.wildernessguidescouncil.org.

CHAPTER 11. CULTIVATING A SOULFUL RELATIONSHIP TO LIFE, PART 1
THE ART OF SOLITUDE
Joan Anderson, *A Year by the Sea: Thoughts of an Unfinished Woman.*
Jean Giono, *The Man Who Planted Trees.* (A stunning video was created from this story.)
Dale Salwak, *The Wonders of Solitude.*
Barbara J. Scot, *The Stations of Still Creek.*

NATURE AS MIRROR
Kathleen Dean Moore, *Holdfast: At Home in the Natural World.*
See also the books listed above, on pages 343–44, under "Talking across the Species Boundaries."

WANDERING IN NATURE

Craig Childs, *The Secret Knowledge of Water: Discovering the Essence of the American Desert* and *Soul of Nowhere*.

Annie Dillard, *Pilgrim at Tinker Creek*.

Kathleen Dean Moore, *Riverwalking: Reflections on Moving Water*.

W. L. Rusho, *Everett Ruess: A Vagabond for Beauty*.

BEFRIENDING THE DARK

Spend time in the dark, preferably outdoors, and preferably in the wilds. See also the books referred to in "The Art of Shadow Work" below.

LIVING THE QUESTIONS OF SOUL

James Hollis, *On This Journey We Call Our Life: Living the Questions*.

Robert A. Johnson, *He: Understanding Masculine Psychology*. (The Parsifal story.)

Rainer Maria Rilke, *Letters to a Young Poet*.

CHAPTER 12. CULTIVATING A SOULFUL RELATIONSHIP TO LIFE, PART 2

CONFRONTING YOUR OWN DEATH

Stephen and Ondrea Levine, *Who Dies? An Investigation of Conscious Living and Conscious Dying*.

Sogyal Rinpoche, *The Tibetan Book of Living and Dying*.

THE ART OF SHADOW WORK

Robert Bly, *A Little Book on the Human Shadow*.

Debbie Ford, *The Dark Side of the Light Chasers: Reclaiming Your Power, Creativity, Brilliance, and Dreams*.

James Hollis, *Swamplands of the Soul: New Life in Dismal Places*.

Robert A. Johnson, *Owning Your Own Shadow: Understanding the Dark Side of the Psyche*.

David Richo, *Shadow Dance: Liberating the Power and Creativity of Your Dark Side*.

Connie Zweig and Jeremiah Abrams (eds.), *Meeting the Shadow: The Hidden Power of the Dark Side of Human Nature*.

WITHDRAWING PROJECTIONS

See the books referred to in the "Art of Shadow Work" section above and the following section on romance.

THE ART OF SOULFUL ROMANCE

James Hollis, *The Eden Project: In Search of the Magical Other* and *The Middle Passage: From Misery to Meaning in Midlife*.

Robert A. Johnson, *We: Understanding the Psychology of Romantic Love*.

Jelaluddin Rumi, *Open Secret: Versions of Rumi*, trans. John Moyne and Coleman Barks.

Jett Psaris and Marlena Lyons, *Undefended Love: The Way That You Felt about Yourself When You First Fell in Love Is the Way That You Can Feel All the Time*.

John Welwood, *Journey of the Heart: The Path of Conscious Love.*

Sacred Sexuality
Margo Anand, *The Art of Sexual Ecstasy: The Path of Sacred Sexuality for Western Lovers.*
Jalaja Bonheim, *Aphrodite's Daughters: Women's Sexual Stories and the Journey of the Soul.*
Nancy Qualls-Corbett, *The Sacred Prostitute: Eternal Aspect of the Feminine.*

MINDFULNESS PRACTICE
Joseph Goldstein, *The Experience of Insight: A Simple and Direct Guide to Buddhist Meditation.*
Jon Kabat-Zinn, *Wherever You Go, There You Are: Mindfulness Meditation in Everyday Life.*
Thich Nhat Hanh, *The Miracle of Mindfulness.*
    (See also the references under "Learning the Art of Disidentification through Meditation" on p. 342.)

DEVELOPING A PERSONAL RELATIONSHIP WITH SPIRIT
Michael DeMaria, *Ever Flowing On: On Being and Becoming Oneself.*
Belden C. Lane, *The Solace of Fierce Landscapes: Exploring Desert and Mountain Spirituality.*
Brian Swimme, *The Hidden Heart of the Cosmos: Humanity and the New Story* and *The Universe Is a Green Dragon: A Cosmic Creation Story;* also, with Thomas Berry, *The Universe Story: From the Primordial Flaring Forth to the Ecozoic Era.*
John Welwood (ed.), *Ordinary Magic: Everyday Life as Spiritual Path.*

BIBLIOGRAPHY

Aaland, Mikkel. *Sweat: The Illustrated History and Description of the Finnish Sauna, Russian Bania, Islamic Hammam, Japanese Mushi-Buro, Mexican Temescal, and American Indian & Eskimo Sweat Lodge.* Santa Barbara: Capra Press, 1978.

Abram, David. *The Spell of the Sensuous: Perception and Language in a More-Than-Human World.* New York: Vintage Books, 1996.

Ackerman, Diane. *A Natural History of the Senses.* New York: Vintage Books, 1991.

Aizenstat, Stephen. *Dream Tending: Techniques for Uncovering the Hidden Intelligence of Your Dreams* (audiotapes). Louisville, Colo.: Sounds True, 2002.

Anand, Margo. *The Art of Sexual Ecstasy: The Path of Sacred Sexuality for Western Lovers.* New York: Tarcher, 1991.

Anderson, Joan. *A Year by the Sea: Thoughts of an Unfinished Woman.* New York: Bantam Doubleday, 2000.

Baldwin, Christina. *Calling the Circle: The First and Future Culture.* New York: Bantam, 1998.

Baldwin, Christina. *Life's Companion: Journal Writing as a Spiritual Quest.* New York: Bantam, 1991.

Bateson, Gregory. *Mind and Nature: A Necessary Unity.* New York: Bantam, 1980.

Bateson, Gregory. *Steps to an Ecology of Mind: Collected Essays in Anthropology, Psychiatry, Evolution, and Epistemology.* Chicago: University of Chicago Press, 2000.

Berry, Thomas. *The Dream of the Earth.* San Francisco: Sierra Club Books, 1988.

Bly, Robert. *A Little Book on the Human Shadow.* San Francisco: Harper & Row, 1988.

Bonheim, Jalaja. *Aphrodite's Daughters: Women's Sexual Stories and the Journey of the Soul.* New York: Fireside, 1997.

Boone, J. Allen. *Kinship with All Life.* San Francisco: HarperSanFrancisco, 1976.

Brown, Molly Young. *Growing Whole: Self-Realization on an Endangered Planet.* Center City, Minn.: Hazelden, 1993.

Brown, Tom, Jr. *Tom Brown's Field Guide to Nature Observation and Tracking.* New York: Berkley, 1983.

Brown, Tom, Jr. *The Vision.* New York: Berkley, 1991.

Bruchac, Joseph. *The Native American Sweat Lodge: History and Legend.* Freedom, Calif.: Crossing Press, 1993.

Buckland, Raymond. *Signs, Symbols & Omens: An Illustrated Guide to Magical & Spiritual Symbolism.* St. Paul, Minn.: Llewellyn, 2003.

Cahill, Sedonia, and Joshua Halpern. *Ceremonial Circle: Practice, Ritual, and Renewal for Personal and Community Healing.* New York: HarperCollins, 1992.

Campbell, Joseph. *The Hero with a Thousand Faces.* New York: Pantheon Books, 1949.

Campbell, Joseph. *The Masks of God: Creative Mythology.* New York: Arkana, 1995.

Cassou, Michelle, and Stewart Cubley. *Life, Paint, and Passion: Reclaiming the Magic of Spontaneous Self Expression.* New York: Tarcher, 1996.

Chernoff, John. *African Rhythm and African Sensibility.* Chicago: University of Chicago Press, 1981.

Childs, Craig. *The Secret Knowledge of Water: Discovering the Essence of the American Desert.* Seattle: Sasquatch Books, 2001.

Childs, Craig. *Soul of Nowhere*. Seattle: Sasquatch Books, 2002.

de Graaf, John, David Wann, and Thomas H. Naylor. *Affluenza: The All-Consuming Epidemic*. San Francisco: Berrett-Koehler Publications, 2001.

Dekorne, Jim. *Psychedelic Shamanism: The Cultivation, Preparation and Shamanic Use of Psychotropic Plants*. Port Townsend, Wash.: Breakout Productions, 1998.

DeMaria, Michael. *Ever Flowing On: On Being and Becoming Oneself*. Pensacola, Fla.: Terra Nova, 2001.

Dillard, Annie. *Pilgrim at Tinker Creek*. New York: Harper & Row, 1974.

Eliot, T. S. *Four Quartets*. New York: Harcourt Brace & Co., 1977.

Estes, Clarissa Pinkola. *Women Who Run with the Wolves: Myths and Stories of the Wild Woman Archetype*. New York: Ballantine Books, 1997.

Feinstein, David, and Stanley Krippner. *The Mythic Path: Discovering the Guiding Stories of Your Past — Creating a Vision for Your Future*. New York: Tarcher, 1997.

Firman, John, and Ann Gila. *The Primal Wound: A Transpersonal View of Trauma, Addiction, and Growth*. Albany, N.Y.: State University of New York Press, 1997.

Flatischler, Reinhard. *The Forgotten Power of Rhythm: Ta Ke Ti Na*. Mendocino, Calif.: LifeRhythm, 1992.

Ford, Debbie. *The Dark Side of the Light Chasers: Reclaiming Your Power, Creativity, Brilliance, and Dreams*. New York: Riverhead Books, 1999.

Foster, Steven, and Meredith Little. *The Book of the Vision Quest: Personal Transformation in the Wilderness*. New York: Prentice Hall, 1988.

Foster, Steven, and Meredith Little. *Roaring of the Sacred River: The Wilderness Quest for Vision and Self-Healing*. Big Pine, Calif.: Lost Borders Press, 1997.

Gallegos, Eligio Stephen. *Animals of the Four Windows: Integrating Thinking, Sensing, Feeling, and Imagery*. Santa Fe: Moon Bear Press, 1991.

Gallegos, Eligio Stephen. *The Personal Totem Pole: Animal Imagery, the Chakras, and Psychotherapy*. Santa Fe: Moon Bear Press, 1990.

Garfield, Charles, Cindy Spring, and Sedonia Cahill. *Wisdom Circles: A Guide to Self-Discovery and Community Building in Small Groups*. New York: Hyperion, 1999.

Giono, Jean. *The Man Who Planted Trees*. White River Junction, Vt.: Chelsea Green, 1995.

Glendinning, Chellis. *My Name Is Chellis and I'm in Recovery from Western Civilization*. Boston: Shambhala Publications, 1994.

Gold, Aviva. *Painting from the Source: Awakening the Artist's Soul in Everyone*. New York: Harper Perennial Library, 1998.

Goldstein, Joseph. *The Experience of Insight: A Simple and Direct Guide to Buddhist Meditation*. Boston: Shambhala Publications, 1987.

Halifax, Joan. *The Fruitful Darkness: Reconnecting with the Body of the Earth*. New York: HarperCollins, 1993.

Hanh, Thich Nhat. *The Miracle of Mindfulness*. New York: Beacon Press, 1999.

Hannah, Barbara. *Encounters with the Soul: Active Imagination As Developed by C. G. Jung*. New York: Chiron Publications, 2001.

Hart, Micky. *Drumming at the Edge of Magic: A Journey into the Spirit of Percussion*. San Francisco: HarperSanFrancisco, 1990.

Hazen-Hammond, Susan. *Spider Woman's Web: Traditional Native American Tales about Women's Power*. New York: Perigee Books, 1999.

Hedva, Beth. *Betrayal, Trust, and Forgiveness: A Guide to Emotional Healing and Self-Renewal*. Berkeley, Calif.: Celestial Arts, 2001.

Heinze, Ruth-Inge. *The Nature and Function of Rituals: Fire from Heaven.* Westport, Conn.: Bergin and Garvey, 1999.

Hendrix, Harville. *Getting the Love You Want.* New York: Owl Books, 2001.

Hillman, James. *The Dream and the Underworld.* New York: Harper & Row, 1979.

Hillman, James. *Re-Visioning Psychology.* New York: Harper & Row, 1975.

Hillman, James (text), and Margot McLean (paintings), *Dream Animals.* San Francisco: Chronicle Books, 1997.

Hillman, James, and Michael Ventura. *We've Had a Hundred Years of Psychotherapy — And the World's Getting Worse.* San Francisco: HarperSanFrancisco, 1992.

Hogan, Linda, Deena Metzger, and Brenda Peterson (eds.). *Intimate Nature: The Bond Between Women and Animals.* New York: Fawcett Books, 1999.

Hollis, James. *Creating a Life: Finding Your Individual Path.* Toronto: Inner City Books, 2000.

Hollis, James. *The Eden Project: In Search of the Magical Other.* Toronto: Inner City Books, 1998.

Hollis, James. *The Middle Passage: From Misery to Meaning in Midlife.* Toronto: Inner City Books, 1993.

Hollis, James. *On this Journey We Call Our Life: Living the Questions.* Toronto: Inner City Books, 2002.

Hollis, James. *Swamplands of the Soul: New Life in Dismal Places.* Toronto: Inner City Books, 1996.

Houston, Jean. *The Search for the Beloved: Journeys in Mythology and Sacred Psychology.* Los Angeles: Tarcher, 1987.

Jensen, Derrick. *The Culture of Make Believe.* New York: Context Books, 2002.

Jensen, Derrick. *A Language Older Than Words.* New York: Context Books, 2000.

Johnson, Robert A. *He: Understanding Masculine Psychology.* New York: Harper & Row, 1977.

Johnson, Robert A. *Inner Work: Using Dreams and Active Imagination for Personal Growth.* San Francisco: HarperSanFrancisco, 1986.

Johnson, Robert A. *Owning Your Own Shadow: Understanding the Dark Side of the Psyche.* San Francisco: HarperSanFrancisco, 1991.

Johnson, Robert A. *We: Understanding the Psychology of Romantic Love.* San Francisco: HarperSanFrancisco, 1985.

Jung, Carl G. *Man and His Symbols.* New York: Doubleday, 1964.

Jung, Carl G. *Memories, Dreams, Reflections.* New York: Vintage Books, 1965.

Kabat-Zinn, Jon. *Wherever You Go, There You Are: Mindfulness Meditation in Everyday Life.* New York: Hyperion 1994.

Kalsched, Donald. *Inner World of Trauma: Archetypal Defenses of the Personal Spirit.* New York: Routledge, 1997.

Kaza, Stephanie *The Attentive Heart: Conversations with Trees.* New York: Fawcett Books, 1993.

Keen, Sam, and Anne Valley-Fox. *Your Mythic Journey.* New York: Tarcher, 1989.

Kornfield, Jack. *A Path with Heart: A Guide through the Perils and Promises of Spiritual Life.* New York: Bantam, 1993.

LaChapelle, Dolores. *D. H. Lawrence: Future Primitive.* Denton, Tex.: University of North Texas Press, 1996.

LaChapelle, Dolores. *Earth Festivals: Seasonal Celebrations for Everyone Young and Old.* Silverton, Colo.: Finn Hill Arts, 1974.

LaChapelle, Dolores. *Earth Wisdom.* Los Angeles: The Guild of Tutors Press, 1978.

LaChapelle, Dolores. *Sacred Land, Sacred Sex: Rapture of the Deep.* Silverton, Colo.: Finn Hill Arts, 1988.

Lane, Belden C. *The Solace of Fierce Landscapes: Exploring Desert and Mountain Spirituality.* Oxford University Press, 1998.

Larsen, Stephen. *The Mythic Imagination: The Quest for Meaning Through Personal Mythology.* Rochester, Vt.: Inner Traditions, 1996.

Levine, Stephen. *A Gradual Awakening.* New York: Anchor, 1989.

Levine, Stephen. *A Year To Live: How to Live This Year As If It Were Your Last.* New York: Three Rivers Press, 1998.

Levine, Stephen, and Ondrea Levine. *Who Dies?: An Investigation of Conscious Living and Conscious Dying.* New York: Anchor, 1989.

Levoy, Greg. *Callings: Finding and Following an Authentic Life.* New York: Three Rivers Press, 1997.

MacEowen, Frank. *The Mist-Filled Path: Celtic Wisdom for Exiles, Wanderers, and Seekers.* Novato, Calif.: New World Library, 2002.

McGaa, Ed. *Mother Earth Spirituality: Native American Paths to Healing Ourselves and Our World.* San Francisco: HarperSanFrancisco, 1990.

McNiff, Shaun. *Art as Medicine: Creating a Therapy of the Imagination.* Boston: Shambhala Publications, 1992.

McNiff, Shaun. *Earth Angels: Engaging the Sacred in Everyday Things.* Boston: Shambhala Publications, 1995.

Mellick, Jill. *The Art of Dreaming: A Creativity Toolbox for Dreamwork.* Berkeley, Calif.: Conari Press, 2001.

Metzger, Deena. *Writing for Your Life: A Guide and Companion to the Inner Worlds.* San Francisco: HarperSanFrancisco, 1992.

Metzner, Ralph (ed.). *Ayahuasca: Human Consciousness and the Spirits of Nature.* New York: Thunder's Mouth Press, 1999.

Metzner, Ralph. *The Well of Remembrance: Rediscovering the Earth Wisdom Myths of Northern Europe.* Boston: Shambhala Publications, 2001.

Moore, Kathleen Dean. *Holdfast: At Home in the Natural World.* Guilford, Conn.: The Lyons Press, 1999.

Moore, Kathleen Dean. *Riverwalking: Reflections on Moving Water.* San Diego: Harvest Books, 1996.

Moyne, John, and Coleman Barks (translators). *Open Secret: Versions of Rumi.* Boston: Shambhala Publications, 1999.

Pinkson, Tom. *Flowers of Wiricuta: A Gringo's Journey to Shamanic Power.* Mill Valley, Calif.: Wakan Press, 1995.

Prechtel, Martín. *The Disobedience of the Daughter of the Sun.* Cambridge, Mass.: Yellow Moon Press, 2001.

Prechtel, Martín. *Long Life, Honey in the Heart: A Story of Initiation and Eloquence from the Shores of a Mayan Lake.* New York: Tarcher, 1999.

Prechtel, Martín. *The Secrets of the Talking Jaguar.* New York: Tarcher, 1999.

Psaris, Jett, and Marlena Lyons. *Undefended Love: The Way That You Felt About Yourself When You First Fell in Love Is the Way That You Can Feel All the Time.* Oakland, Calif.: New Harbinger, 2000.

Qualls-Corbett, Nancy. *The Sacred Prostitute: Eternal Aspect of the Feminine.* Toronto: Inner City Books, 1988.

Raffa, Jean Benedict. *Dream Theatres of the Soul: Empowering the Feminine through Jungian Dream Work.* Philadelphia: Innisfree Press, 1994.

Rajala, Nikki. *Some Like It Hot: The Sauna, Its Lore & Stories.* St. Cloud, Minn.: North Star Press, 2000.

Rezendes, Paul. *Tracking and the Art of Seeing: How to Read Animal Tracks & Signs.* Charlotte, Vt.: Camden House, 1992.

Rezendes, Paul. *The Wild Within: Adventures in Nature and Animal Teachings.* New York: Tarcher, 1999.

Richo, David. *Shadow Dance: Liberating the Power and Creativity of Your Dark Side.* Boston: Shambhala Publications, 1999.

Rilke, Rainer Maria. *Letters to a Young Poet.* New York: Norton, 1934; rev. 1954.

Roads, Michael J. *Talking With Nature: Sharing the Energies and Spirit of Trees, Plants, Birds, and Earth.* Tiburon, Calif.: H J Kramer, 1987.

Roth, Gabrielle. *Maps to Ecstasy: A Healing Journey for the Untamed Spirit.* Novato, Calif.: New World Library, 1998.

Roth, Gabrielle. *Sweat Your Prayers: Movement As Spiritual Practice.* New York: Penguin, 1998.

Rusho, W. L. *Everett Ruess: A Vagabond for Beauty.* Layton, Utah: Gibbs Smith, 1985.

Salwak, Dale. *The Wonders of Solitude.* Novato, Calif.: New World Library, 1998.

Schultes, Richard Evans, Albert Hofmann, and Christian Ratsch. *Plants of the Gods: Their Sacred, Healing and Hallucinogenic Powers.* Rochester, Vt.: Healing Arts Press, 2002.

Scot, Barbara J. *The Stations of Still Creek.* San Francisco: Sierra Club Books, 2001.

Seaton, Jane B. *Artlife: Creative Practices for Making Your Everyday Life Sacred* (audiotapes). Louisville, Colo.: Sounds True, 2001.

Seed, John, Joanna Macy, Pat Flemming, and Arne Naess. *Thinking Like a Mountain: Toward a Council of All Beings.* Gabriola Island, B.C.: New Society Publishers, 1988.

Sewall, Laura. *Sight and Sensibility: The Ecopsychology of Perception.* New York: Tarcher-Putnam, 1999.

Shideler, Mary McDermott. *Persons, Behavior, and the World: The Descriptive Psychology Approach.* Lanham, Md.: University Press of America, 1988.

Snyder, Gary. *The Old Ways.* San Francisco: City Lights, 1977.

Snyder, Gary. *The Practice of the Wild.* San Francisco: North Point Press, 1990.

Snyder, Gary. *Turtle Island.* New York: New Directions, 1974.

Sogyal Rinpoche. *The Tibetan Book of Living and Dying.* San Francisco: HarperSanFrancisco, 1994.

Somé, Malidoma Patrice. *The Healing Wisdom of Africa: Finding Life Purpose Through Nature, Ritual, and Community.* New York: Tarcher, 1999.

Somé, Malidoma Patrice. *Of Water and the Spirit: Ritual, Magic, and Initiation in the Life of an African Shaman.* New York: Arkana, 1994.

Somé, Malidoma Patrice. *Ritual: Power, Healing, and Community.* New York: Penguin, 1997.

Starhawk. *The Spiral Dance: A Rebirth of the Ancient Religion of the Great Goddess.* San Francisco: HarperSanFrancisco, 1999.

Stone, Hal, and Sidra L. Stone. *Embracing Ourselves: The Voice Dialogue Manual.* Novato, Calif.: New World Library, 1993.

Suzuki, David, and Peter Knudtson, *Wisdom of the Elders: Sacred Native Stories of Nature.* New York: Bantam, 1992.

Swimme, Brian. *The Hidden Heart of the Cosmos: Humanity and the New Story.* Orbis Books, 1999.

Swimme, Brian. *The Universe Is a Green Dragon: A Cosmic Creation Story.* Santa Fe: Bear & Co., 1985.

Swimme, Brian, and Thomas Berry. *The Universe Story: From the Primordial Flaring Forth to the Ecozoic Era — A Celebration of the Unfolding of the Cosmos.* New York: HarperCollins, 1992.

Tolle, Eckhart. *The Power of Now.* Novato, Calif.: New World Library, 1999.

Welwood, John. *Journey of the Heart: The Path of Conscious Love.* New York: Perennial, 1996.

Welwood, John (ed.). *Ordinary Magic: Everyday Life As Spiritual Path.* Boston: Shambhala Publications, 1992.

Whyte, David. *Crossing the Unknown Sea: Work as a Pilgrimage of Identity.* New York: Riverhead Books, 2001.

Wilber, Ken. *The Marriage of Sense and Soul: Integrating Science and Religion.* New York: Broadway Books, 1999.

Williams, Marta. *Learning Their Language: Intuitive Communication with Animals and Nature.* Novato, Calif.: New World Library, 2003.

Woodman, Marion. *Dreams: Language of the Soul* (audiotape). Louisville, Colo.: Sounds True, 1992.

Woodman, Marion and Elinor Dickson. *Dancing in the Flames: The Dark Goddess in the Transformation of Consciousness.* Boston: Shambhala Publications, 1997.

Zimmerman, Jack, and Virginia Coyle. *The Way of Council.* Las Vegas, Nev.: Bramble Books, 1996.

Zweig, Connie, and Jeremiah Abrams (eds.). *Meeting the Shadow: The Hidden Power of the Dark Side of Human Nature.* New York: Tarcher, 1991.

ACKNOWLEDGMENTS OF PERMISSIONS

Grateful acknowledgment is given to the following for permission to reprint previously published material:

EPIGRAPH

From *Open Secret: Versions of Rumi,* by John Moyne and Coleman Barks. © 1999 by John Moyne and Coleman Barks. Reprinted by arrangement with Shambhala Publications, Inc., Boston, www.shambhala.com

PROLOGUE. WEAVING A COCOON

From "The Soul Lives Contented," in *Fire in the Earth* by David Whyte. © 1992 by David Whyte. Reprinted by permission of Many Rivers Press, Langley, Washington, 360-221-1324.

CHAPTER 1. CARRYING WHAT IS HIDDEN AS A GIFT TO OTHERS

From "What to Remember When Waking," in *The House of Belonging* by David Whyte. © 1997 by David Whyte. Reprinted by permission of Many Rivers Press, Langley, Washington, 360-221-1324.

"Wenn etwas mir vom Fenster fallt.../How surely gravity's law...," and excerpt from "Du siehst, ich will viel.../You see, I want a...," in *Rilke's Book of Hours: Love Poems to God* by Rainer Maria Rilke, translated by Anita Barrows and Joanna Macy. © 1996 by Anita Barrows and Joanna Macy. Reprinted by permission of Riverhead Books, an imprint of Penguin Group (USA) Inc.

CHAPTER 2. GROUNDWORK

"Self-Portrait," in *Fire in the Earth* by David Whyte. © 1992 by David Whyte. Reprinted by permission of Many Rivers Press, Langley, Washington, 360-221-1324.

From "The Soul of the Matter" (an interview with Wes Nisker), by James Hillman. Reprinted by permission of *Inquiring Mind: A Semiannual Journal of the Vipassana Community.* © 1995 by Inquiring Mind, P.O. Box 9999, Berkeley, CA 94709.

From "Wenn etwas mir vom Fenster fallt.../How surely gravity's law," and "Du siehst, ich will viel.../You see, I want a...," in *Rilke's Book of Hours: Love Poems to God* by Rainer Maria Rilke, translated by Anita Barrows and Joanna Macy. © 1996 by Anita Barrows and Joanna Macy. Reprinted by permission of Riverhead Books, an imprint of Penguin Group (USA) Inc.

From "You Darkness," by Rainer Maria Rilke, translated by David Whyte, in *Fire in the Earth* by David Whyte. © 1992 by David Whyte. Reprinted by permission of Many Rivers Press, Langley, Washington, 360-221-1324.

From "Wild Geese," in *Dream Work* by Mary Oliver. © 1986 by Mary Oliver. Reprinted by permission of Grove/Atlantic, Inc.

From *The Universe Story* by Brian Swimme and Thomas Berry. © 1992 by Brian Swimme. Reprinted by permission of HarperCollins Publishers, Inc.

CHAPTER 3. SINKING BACK INTO THE SOURCE OF EVERYTHING

"Dich wundert nicht.../You are not surprised...," in *Rilke's Book of Hours: Love Poems to God* by Rainer Maria Rilke, translated by Anita Barrows and Joanna Macy. © 1996 by Anita Barrows and Joanna Macy. Reprinted by permission of Riverhead Books, an imprint of Penguin Group (USA) Inc.

From *The Hero with A Thousand Faces,* by Joseph Campbell. © 1949 by Bollingen Foundation Inc., New York, NY. Reprinted by permission of Princeton University Press.

From "Wild Geese," in *Dream Work* by Mary Oliver. © 1986 by Mary Oliver. Reprinted by permission of Grove/Atlantic, Inc.

From "Sweet Darkness," in *The House of Belonging* by David Whyte. © 1997 by David Whyte. Reprinted by permission of Many Rivers Press, Langley, Washington, 360-221-1324.

"Prospective Immigrants Please Note," in *The Fact of a Doorframe: Selected Poems 1950–2001* by Adrienne Rich. © 2002, 1967, 1963 by Adrienne Rich. Reprinted by permission of the author and W. W. Norton & Company, Inc.

CHAPTER 4. THE WANDERER AND THE SECOND COCOON

"The Journey," in *Dream Work* by Mary Oliver. © 1986 by Mary Oliver. Reprinted by permission of Grove/Atlantic, Inc.

From *The Hero with A Thousand Faces,* by Joseph Campbell. © 1949 by Bollingen Foundation Inc., New York, NY. Reprinted by permission of Princeton University Press.

CHAPTER 5. THE DARKNESS SHALL BE THE LIGHT

From "East Coker," in *Four Quartets* by T. S. Eliot. © 1940 by T. S. Eliot; renewed in 1968 by Esme Valerie Eliot. Reprinted by permission of Harcourt, Inc.

From *The Search for the Beloved,* by Jean Houston. © 1987 by Jean Houston. Reprinted by permission of Jeremy P. Tarcher, an imprint of Penguin Group (USA) Inc.

"The Well of Grief," in *Where Many Rivers Meet* by David Whyte. © 1990 by David Whyte. Reprinted by permission of Many Rivers Press, Langley, Washington, 360-221-1324.

From "Don't Go Back to Sleep," words and music by Jan Garrett. © 1992. Reprinted by permission.

CHAPTER 6. RECOVERING THE IMAGE YOU WERE BORN WITH

From "All the True Vows," in *The House of Belonging* by David Whyte. © 1997 by David Whyte. Reprinted by permission of Many Rivers Press, Langley, Washington, 360-221-1324.

CHAPTER 7. INNER WORK

"And he was the demon of my dreams, the most handsome," by Antonio Machado, in *Times Alone: Selected Poems of Antonio Machado,* translated by Robert Bly. © 1983 by Robert Bly. Reprinted by permission of Wesleyan University Press.

From *Memories, Dreams, Reflections,* by C. G. Jung, edited by Aniela Jaffe, translated by Richard and Clara Winston. © 1961, 1962, 1963; renewed 1989, 1990, 1991 by Random House, Inc. Reprinted by permission of Pantheon Books, a division of Random House, Inc.

CHAPTER 8. COMMUNING WITH THE OTHERS

"Da neigt sich die Stunde.../The hour is striking...," from *Rilke's Book of Hours: Love Poems to God* by Rainer Maria Rilke, translated by Anita Barrows and Joanna Macy. © 1996 by Anita Barrows and Joanna Macy. Reprinted by permission of Riverhead Books, an imprint of Penguin Group (USA) Inc.

From *The Spell of the Sensuous,* by David Abram. © 1996 by David Abram. Reprinted by permission of Pantheon Books, a division of Random House, Inc.

From "Love After Love," in *Collected Poems 1948–1984* by Derek Walcott. © 1986 by Derek Walcott. Reprinted by permission of Farrar, Straus & Giroux, LLC.

CHAPTER 10. THE VISION QUEST AND SOULCENTRIC RITUAL
"Clearing," by Morgan Farley. © 1998 by Morgan Farley. Reprinted by permission of Morgan Farley.
From "The Man Watching," by Rainer Maria Rilke in *Selected Poems of Rainer Maria Rilke: Edited and Translated by Robert Bly.* © 1981 by Robert Bly. Reprinted by permission of HarperCollins Publishers, Inc.
From "Fire in the Earth," in *Fire in the Earth* by David Whyte. © 1992 by David Whyte. Reprinted by permission of Many Rivers Press, Langley, Washington, 360-221-1324.

CHAPTER 11. CULTIVATING A SOULFUL RELATIONSHIP TO LIFE, PART 1
"How to Regain Your Soul," in *Listening Deep* by William Stafford (Penmean Press). © 1984 by William Stafford. Reprinted by permission of the Estate of William Stafford.
From "Sweet Darkness," in *The House of Belonging* by David Whyte. © 1997 by David Whyte. Reprinted by permission of Many Rivers Press, Langley, Washington, 360-221-1324.
From "You Darkness," by Rainer Maria Rilke, translated by David Whyte in *Fire in the Earth* by David Whyte. © 1992 by David Whyte. Reprinted by permission of Many Rivers Press, Langley, Washington, 360-221-1324.
"Obsidian I," in *Out of the Flames* by Lyn Dalebout. © 1996 by Lyn Dalebout. Reprinted by permission of Lyn Dalebout.

CHAPTER 12. CULTIVATING A SOULFUL RELATIONSHIP TO LIFE: PART 2
From "When Death Comes," in *New and Selected Poems by Mary Oliver.* © 1992 by Mary Oliver. Reprinted by permission of Beacon Press, Boston.
From "The Soul Lives Contented," in *Fire in the Earth* by David Whyte. © 1992 by David Whyte. Reprinted by permission of Many Rivers Press, Langley, Washington, 360-221-1324.
From *The Middle Passage,* by James Hollis. © 1993 by James Hollis. Reprinted by permission of Inner City Books.
From "Returning the Back Way," by Morgan Farley. © 1998 by Morgan Farley. Reprinted by permission of Morgan Farley.
From *The Search for the Beloved,* by Jean Houston. © 1987 by Jean Houston. Reprinted by permission of Jeremy P. Tarcher, an imprint of Penguin Group (USA) Inc.
From *Open Secret: Versions of Rumi,* by John Moyne and Coleman Barks. © 1999 by John Moyne and Coleman Barks. Reprinted by arrangement with Shambhala Publications, Inc., Boston, www.shambhala.com
From *The Illuminated Rumi,* by Coleman Barks and Michael Green. © 1997 by Coleman Barks and Michael Green. Reprinted by permission of Broadway Books, a division of Random House, Inc.
From *Selected Poems of Rainer Maria Rilke: Edited and Translated by Robert Bly.* © 1981 by Robert Bly. Reprinted by permission of HarperCollins Publishers, Inc.
"Gott spricht zu jedem.../God speaks to each of us...," in *Rilke's Book of Hours: Love Poems to God* by Rainer Maria Rilke, translated by Anita Barrows and Joanna Macy. © 1996 by Anita Barrows and Joanna Macy. Reprinted by permission of Riverhead Books, an imprint of Penguin Group (USA) Inc.
From *The Selected Poetry of Rainer Maria Rilke,* by Rainer Maria Rilke, translated by Stephen Mitchell. © 1982 by Stephen Mitchell. Reprinted by permission of Random House, Inc.

CHAPTER 13. LIVING AS IF YOUR PLACE IN THE WORLD MATTERED
From *We've Had a Hundred Years of Psychotherapy — And the World's Getting Worse* by James Hillman. © 1992 by James Hillman and Michael Ventura. Reprinted by permission of HarperCollins Publishers, Inc.

INDEX

ABOUT THE AUTHOR

B ill Plotkin, Ph.D., is a depth psychologist, wilderness guide, and one of the leaders in the field of contemporary, nature-based personal development and initiation programs. He holds a doctorate in psychology from the University of Colorado at Boulder and was previously on the teaching and research faculty at the State University of New York, where he studied dreams and non-ordinary states achieved through meditation, biofeedback, and hypnosis.

Bill is the founding director of Animas Valley Institute (AVI) in southwest Colorado, a nonprofit organization with twenty guides that has been leading nature-based soul-initiation programs since 1980. Each year, AVI's staff guide hundreds of people — professionals, artists, therapists, parents, teachers, and high school and college students — on soulcraft journeys into the inner/outer wilderness. Bill also conducts five-day soulcraft seminars at retreat centers throughout the United States, as well as a training and apprenticeship program for soulcraft guides.

Bill has written many articles and book chapters on psychotherapy, consciousness, and wilderness rites. He is currently completing a book on soulcentric human development wherein he proposes tasks and archetypes for the eight stages of life when we allow soul and nature to guide us in our growth.

ANIMAS VALLEY INSTITUTE

Since 1980, Animas Valley Institute (AVI) has been offering nature-based programs supporting the recovery and embodiment of the life of the soul — the unique truth, passion, and wisdom we each were born with. Our thirty-five programs include eleven-day wilderness Vision Quests; five-day retreat center–based Soulcraft Seminars; and Intensives on soulcentric dreamwork, shadow work, conversations with nature and the Sacred Other, council work, deep imagery journeys, and others. Our comprehensive Soulcraft Apprenticeship and Initiation Program is designed for educators, psychotherapists, health professionals, and wilderness guides, as well as those ready to initiate and empower the life of their own souls. AVI Director, Bill Plotkin, and the other Animas guides have created and shaped over forty contemporary practices that assist people of Western cultures in their quests for more meaningful and fulfilling lives aligned with both nature and soul.

In addition to our English language programs, AVI also offers programs directed in German in both the United States and Europe.

For our full catalog of courses,
visit our website: www.animas.org,
email us: soulcraft@animas.org,
call: 800-451-6327,

or write:

Animas Valley Institute
PO Box 1020
Durango, CO 81302